MOUNTAIN VIEW
PUBLIC LIBRARY
Mountain View,

S0-AUH-881

I'm Having a Baby!

Well-Rounded Perspectives

Christine Traxler, MD
Elizabeth Heller

Expert Consultants
Susan Loeb-Zeitlin, MD, OB-GYN
Jennifer Y. Levy-Peck, PhD
Patricia Wynne, PhD, MBA

www.lessonladder.com
21 Orient Street, Melrose, MA 02176

XAMonline, Inc., Melrose, MA 02176
© 2013 Sharon A. Wynne (Text and illustrations)

All rights reserved. No part of the material protected by this copyright may be reproduced or utilized in any form or by any means, electronic or mechanical, including photocopying, recording or by any information storage and retrieval system, without written permission from the copyright holder.

To obtain permission(s) to use the material from this work for any purpose, including workshops or seminars, please submit a written request to:

Lesson Ladder: an imprint of XAMonline, Inc.
21 Orient Street, Melrose, MA 02176
Toll Free 1-800-301-4647
Fax: 1-617-583-5552
Email: customerservice@lessonladder.com
Web: www.lessonladder.com

Text: **Christine Traxler, MD**

Contributing author: Elizabeth Heller

Medical Consultants:
Jennifer Y. Levy-Peck, PhD
Susan E. Loeb-Zeitlin, MD
Patricia Wynne, PhD, MBA

Illustrations: Rachel Enos, Moira Gillis Gray, Angela Montoya and Carol Swift
Cover photos: 121356523/iStockphoto/ThinkStock
101922862/Hemera/ThinkStock
Book design: iiCREATIVE
Production: nSight, Inc.

Library of Congress Catalog Card Number: (pending)
Traxler, Christine, Dr.

I'm Having a Baby! Well-Rounded Perspectives
A: Well-Rounded Perspectives / Christine Traxler, MD, Elizabeth Heller. 432pp., ill. Includes index.

1. Title 2. Pregnancy—Handbooks, manuals, etc. 3. Obstetrics—Popular works. 4. Prenatal care. 5. Childbirth.

This book is intended to educate and provide general information about pregnancy. This book should not, however, be construed to dispense medical services or be used to diagnose or treat any medical condition. All questions and decisions about your pregnancy and medical care should be addressed directly with your own qualified healthcare professional, including your physician and obstetrician. Accordingly, you are encouraged to consult your personal healthcare provider before adopting any of the suggestions in this book or drawing inferences from it.

While the author, editor, and publisher have endeavored to prepare an accurate and helpful book, they make no representations or warranties, express or implied, with respect to the accuracy or completeness of its contents and specifically disclaim any warranties of merchantability or fitness for a particular purpose. The author, editor, and publisher do not assume and hereby disclaim any liability to any party for any loss, damage, or injury caused, directly or indirectly, by any error, omission or information provided in this book.

The names, conditions and identifying details of people associated with the events and advice described in this book have been changed to protect their privacy. Any similarities to actual individuals are merely coincidental.

RG525 T7395 2012   618.2 T699 2012
ISBN: 978-0984865-734

Dedication

I dedicate this work to my two beautiful daughters and my granddaughter.—C.T.

With love for my son Jared Heller who inspires me every day
to feed my dreams and starve my fears.—E.H.

Acknowledgements

The authors and publisher would like to thank the many individuals who helped to conceive and give birth to this important project: Kesel Wilson, Anna Wong, Kristin Kroha, Beth Kaufman, Nini Bloch, Lise Creurer, Charles Peck, Dave and Judy Kroha, Scott Hochfelder, and the entire book team at nSight. We would especially like to thank the many moms and dads who bravely offered their insights and experiences throughout the pages of this book—in particular, Lysander Wright, Richard Smith, and Phil Cowen.

About the Authors

Christine Traxler, MD, is a family practice physician who cared for hundreds of mothers and newborn babies in her clinic and hospital in Minnesota for more than a decade. She successfully counseled many mothers with high-risk pregnancies who then went on to deliver healthy babies. Dr. Traxler received her medical training at the University of Minnesota Medical School and currently lives in Minneapolis, Minnesota, with her daughter and her new infant granddaughter. She credits some of her ability to write this text to the excellent care her daughter recently received during her pregnancy. Dr. Traxler has two grown daughters.

Elizabeth Heller is a mother and the author of seven books about children and parenting. She has more than twenty years experience as a writer, journalist, and children's radio show host and producer. Her previous books include *The Potty Training Survival Guide, A Parent's Little Book of Wisdom, The Kid's Book of Prayers About All Sorts of Things, Little Lessons of Love, The Best Christmas Presents are Wrapped in Heaven*, and *Grandparents are Made for Hugging*. She lives in Brookline, Massachusetts, with her son Jared.

About the Expert Consultants

Susan Loeb-Zeitlin, MD, is an obstetrician-gynecologist who treats women of all ages, from adolescence through menopause. Her goal is to provide complete, personalized women's healthcare that encompasses all the special health issues women face, including family planning, balancing work and personal life, and the challenges of aging. A *cum laude* graduate of Brandeis University, Dr. Loeb-Zeitlin received her medical degree from the University of Medicine and Dentistry New Jersey-New Jersey Medical School, where she was in the Alpha Omega Alpha Honor Medical Society. She completed her residency at Cornell University Medical College and accepted a faculty appointment at Weill Cornell Medical College in 1998.

Jennifer Y. Levy-Peck, PhD, is a clinical psychologist with more than 30 years of experience working with individuals, couples, and families. She has served as director of a family counseling center and a university counseling center. Her professional interests include women's psychological and physical health issues as well as trauma recovery. As a psychologist, a mother of adult daughters, and a grandmother, Dr. Levy-Peck is an advocate for the empowerment of women to become educated consumers of healthcare services. She is an author and editor and has presented training workshops at the state, regional, and national levels.

Patricia Wynne, PhD, MBA, obtained her doctorate degree in Neuroscience from the University of Massachusetts Medical School. Her diverse passions include researching the molecular underpinnings of alcoholism, business development in the biotechnology sector, intellectual property law, and teaching. As a result of her multifaceted interests, Dr. Wynne also earned her Master's in Business Administration from the University of Massachusetts, Isenberg School of Management, and is a registered patent agent with the United States Patent and Trademark Office. She has been published in journals such as *Neuron, The Journal of Neuroscience,* and *The Journal of Pharmacology and Experimental Therapeutics*. She is also the mother of two young children.

Contents

Chapter 2: Pregnant! Now What? Ensuring a Healthy Pregnancy

Part 2: Your Pregnancy Month by Month

Chapter 3: Month One—Weeks 1 through 4

Chapter 4: Month Two—Weeks 5 through 8

Chapter 5: Month Three—Weeks 9 through 12

Chapter 6: Month Four—Weeks 13 through 16

Chapter 7: Month Five—Weeks 17 through 20

Chapter 8: Month Six—Weeks 21 through 24

Chapter 9: Month Seven—Weeks 25 through 28

Chapter 10: Month Eight—Weeks 29 through 32

Chapter 11: Month Nine—Weeks 33 through 36

Chapter 12: Month Ten—Weeks 37 through 40

Chapter 13: Labor and Delivery

Part 3: You and Your New Baby

Chapter 14: Caring for Your Newborn—A Quick Guide

Chapter 15: Postpartum Issues

Chapter 16: Beginning Your Journey as New Parents —Embracing Change

Recommended Web Resources   374

PREFACE

Why You'll Love This Book

Welcome! You are embarking on an experience that every woman who becomes pregnant finds unique. No two pregnancies are the same, and each offers different joys and different challenges. There usually aren't "one-size-fits-all" solutions to the problems that you may encounter on your pregnancy journey. That's why we wrote *I'm Having a Baby! Well-Rounded Perspectives*—to offer you the collective wisdom of respected authors, doctors, experienced consultants, and successful parents. Whether you read this book from cover to cover or dive straight into information on a topic that concerns you, you'll find all the most trusted and effective answers for your pregnancy and postpartum period. We want to help you quickly find the answers that are most helpful to you, written in language that's easy to understand, to ensure a healthier and smoother pregnancy for you and your baby!

Your Trusted Companion

I'm Having a Baby! is for all kinds of expectant parents. It is for you if you have a loving partner and want to be sure you share the experiences of pregnancy and parenthood together. It is for you if you are approaching single parenthood, by choice or by circumstance. It is for you no matter whom you love, no matter how old you are, no matter where you live. It will be your trusted companion on the journey: a source of knowledge, inspiration, practical advice, and encouragement. You will learn what to expect and how to cope. It will help you understand what is happening inside your body, how to take the best possible care of yourself and your baby, how to prepare for the transition to parenthood, and what to do when your baby arrives.

Respect: The First Principle

Above all, this book treats you with respect. As an intelligent woman who cares enough to learn about your pregnancy, you can make good decisions with good information. Women have more options than ever before in pregnancy care and birth. Would a doula (a specially trained pregnancy and birth-support person) be helpful to you? Would you prefer to deliver at a birthing center rather than in a traditional hospital setting? *I'm Having a Baby!* outlines the pros and cons of each decision you face about prenatal care, childbirth, and your baby's early weeks.

Have a Doctor "in the House"

Our book team is led by Dr. Christine Traxler—a seasoned physician who has helped hundreds of women through pregnancy, birth, and the care of their babies. That means that all the information in this book is based on valid, up-to-date medical research and principles, thus offering you the most accurate knowledge to make the many decisions that lie ahead. What medications are safe to take during pregnancy? Should you have an amniocentesis or other prenatal testing? Are you exercising too much or too little? How will you know if your baby is healthy and developing normally, both before and after birth? You will learn the general principles for having a healthy pregnancy, including what to eat, how to stay active, and what physical changes to expect, but a successful pregnancy is more than that.

You Need Balance; We Offer It

Some pregnancy books give a sugarcoated view of this stage of life, while others make it seem as though disaster is looming at every step. We take a more balanced approach. We know that not every woman is thrilled with the news that she is pregnant and that not every relationship is 100 percent positive and supportive. We know that you want to do the best you possibly can to ensure the health and well-being of your baby. We focus on wellness, not illness, and on helping you feel as good as you possibly can while making sure you can find appropriate help if you do need it.

You are doing something amazing, and you deserve to treat yourself kindly. We offer encouragement, assist you in sorting the important stuff from the trivia, and use other parents' stories to help you laugh as you face the challenges that any major life change creates.

You Need a Consumer Guide

While you are pregnant, you will probably have more contact with the medical profession than you have ever had before. This book will help you become an informed consumer of healthcare services and an advocate for your own—and your baby's—care. But pregnancy and birth are not simply medical conditions, not by a long shot—they are life experiences that have a profound effect on your identity, your everyday activities, and your relationships.

You'll Learn from the Experiences of Others

Becoming a mother is both a natural event and a stunning transformation. When you lie awake at night thinking about having a baby, you may wonder, "What will it really be like to be pregnant, to give birth, and to have a newborn?" Throughout this book, you will find the words of parents themselves, sharing a variety of experiences to address those questions. These parents' experiences are illuminating—some are hilarious as well—and they all help you feel you are not alone during your pregnancy.

Your Feelings Count, and We Address Them

Thoroughly reviewed and edited by a clinical psychologist, our book offers insights and in-depth consideration of the powerful feelings that may surface when having a baby. *I'm Having a Baby!* examines how past experiences may affect your feelings during pregnancy and the postpartum period and guides you in sorting out whether your feelings are a normal part of pregnancy and parenthood or something that requires professional attention. This book promotes a positive mental attitude while recognizing that some pregnant and newly parenting women may have mental health concerns that should be addressed. Most new mothers find it reassuring to learn coping techniques for the normal but intense feelings during pregnancy, and your partner will gain greater understanding as well.

The Fun Part of Pregnancy

Pregnancy and parenthood are serious subjects, but they should be fun as well. In addition to talking about medical care and other more weighty topics, we help you plan an attractive nursery (even if it is in a corner of your bedroom!), decide what you really need for your baby, enjoy sex with your partner, treat yourself well, and keep your sense of humor. You are going to need it!

This Book Is for Your Partner, Too

If you have a partner, he may be the baby's father (welcome, Dad!), but we don't assume this is so. *I'm Having a Baby!* uses gender-inclusive language in talking about partners, so it will apply to all kinds of couples. Your partner will learn how to support you through pregnancy and birth, and you can educate yourselves together to prepare for the decisions you will face. This book offers tips as well on keeping your relationship healthy and vital.

If You're Single, You're Not Alone

Sometimes single moms feel ignored by pregnancy books. This one celebrates your strength and offers you resources instead, whether you are married, living with a partner, or on your own. Throughout the book, we consider your relationships with friends, parents, and coworkers and address your personal needs. Because having a baby affects all sorts of relationships, you will find out how to connect with people who can best support you during and after your pregnancy. It does indeed take a village to raise a child, and you will want to choose your village early and wisely!

How This Book Is Organized

You can read this book from cover to cover or dive straight into the chapter that has the information you need at a given moment. For convenience, we address each of the four-week periods of pregnancy as a month (for a total of ten months rather than the traditional nine), to give you the precise month-by-month knowledge you need. You will learn how your baby is developing each week of your pregnancy. Each month, you will find out about common concerns, changes in your body, and how you may be feeling, both physically and emotionally.

Chapters also include the following features:

Pregnancy Vignettes
First-person stories about all aspects of pregnancy and what moms learned from it

Parent/Partner Points of View
Stories told by real parents (including dads and partners) about their experiences

For Dads and Partners
Tips to help dads and partners fully participate in the pregnancy and childbirth experience

Prenatal Testing
Clear explanations of what to expect at your prenatal medical visits each month and any decisions you may need to make about your care

Knowledge Is Comfort

In the face of the exciting but overwhelming experience of pregnancy, many women scramble to get every scrap of information they can find; it gives them a sense of control. Sometimes, however, the sheer quantity of available information can be daunting. *I'm Having a Baby!* calls out critical issues and highlights must-know topics so, at a glance, you can identify what you really need to know.

Most of all, however, we celebrate you and your baby. Your experiences are unique, and nobody can or should tell you what to do. You can find out what your options are, and then you can make your own decisions. It is our hope that you will find your own strength and wisdom as a parent and that this book will support you in your journey.

Things to Think About
Smart considerations for parents-to-be at every step along the way

Exercise Ideas
Up-to-date information about staying active safely as your body changes

Nutritional Tips
Suggestions about what to eat to keep you healthy and support your baby's development without gaining excess weight

What Now?
Critical information, like logically organized reminders for developing a birth plan, setting up your baby's room, and so on

I'm Having a Baby!

Part 1

Beginning Your Pregnancy Journey

Mention to anyone that you're thinking about having a baby, and be prepared for a landslide of advice. And here's mine: Listen to yourself, listen to your partner, and know that what you two think is all that matters. The rest is a magical, unpredictable journey that no one is ever truly prepared for!

—*Angela, 29, mother of twins*

Chapter 1

Preparing for Pregnancy—
Let the Journey Begin!

For every parent, birth is a personal miracle. The path there is exhilarating, exhausting, fascinating, incredible, scary, and funny. Though you won't be able to feel the baby in your womb for months, you are growing another being inside you, one with a new spirit, a unique mind, and a heart that beats stronger each day. There are a host of realities and considerations when it comes to becoming parents. You'll feel more confident and comfortable embarking on life's greatest adventure armed with knowledge and faith in the process. To help you on your way, this chapter explores answers to the following questions:

- How can I best prepare for my pregnancy?
- How do I know if I am truly ready—both physically and emotionally—to have a baby?
- What if this baby is a surprise?
- What specific health issues should I be concerned about before conceiving?
- What things will I need to avoid while trying to conceive?
- What if I have a chronic illness?
- What challenges will I face if I am older than the typical mom?
- How long will it actually take to become pregnant? And what if we have trouble?

My husband and I went back and forth for ten years about whether or not to have a child. It never seemed like the timing was right. We had so many excuses for not doing it: Work was too interesting or too busy; I was ready, he wasn't; I thought we didn't have the financial resources even though my husband said we did. I admit that I had body issues, too. I always worked out and ate healthy foods, so sometimes the idea of a bulging stomach and stretch marks from pregnancy was too much to bear. We just kept putting off the decision. It wasn't until I was in my thirties and had to have an ovary removed due to a benign cyst that we got serious. "It's now or never," I remember telling my husband, "We don't know what will happen to my other ovary." We finally agreed it was time, but it took almost a year to get pregnant. My advice is this: If you're thinking about having a baby, don't wait for the perfect time. There's no perfect time. Take good care of yourself, get informed, and don't make excuses—make a decision instead! —*Bridgette, 40*

Preparation Begins with Knowledge

Congratulations! If you are reading this book, you are probably seriously considering having a baby, or you may already be pregnant. Welcome to one of the most exciting experiences that life has to offer. For some, the excitement starts when that magical "plus" sign shows up on a pregnancy test. For others, the anticipation of being pregnant has been going on for many months or even years before the pregnancy test becomes positive. Whether you have been planning a pregnancy for a long time or suddenly discover that a baby is in your future, it does not take long to realize that having a baby takes physical and emotional preparation, planning, and acquisition of as much knowledge as possible. You are off on the right foot by choosing the perfect book to guide you from pre-pregnancy through childbirth to those first few months as a new parent. But when thinking about acquiring information, where do you begin? What does it mean to "prepare" for pregnancy?

Read This Book!

This pregnancy guide is filled with up-to-the-minute information on the emotional and physical changes that you will experience during pregnancy, as well as what is happening inside your uterus as your fetus develops. You will find valuable guidance on everything from healthy eating to choosing your healthcare provider to deciding on a hospital or home birth. The hope is you will feel completely supported and informed as your pregnancy journey progresses.

Talk to Your Healthcare Provider

It's a great idea to talk to your primary care physician, nurse practitioner, obstetrician, or nurse-midwife about pregnancy in general and about what pregnancy might mean for you emotionally and physically. You can also talk to your healthcare provider about the most likely ways to get pregnant. Many couples have no idea when a woman is most fertile during her menstrual cycle, and your provider can help you understand how to plan your best days to conceive and increase your chances of becoming pregnant.

Talk to Other Women —Especially New Moms

Talking to other women who have been pregnant is another fantastic way to get first-hand knowledge about pregnancy. Although every pregnancy is different, everyone who has been pregnant has her own wisdom to share. Many women are very open and willing to talk about their difficulties in getting pregnant, their first trimester symptoms, the labor and delivery process, and the trials and tribulations of parenthood. Such women can be a valuable resource for you as you sort through your feelings about getting pregnant or already being pregnant.

If you are close with your mother or have another important older woman in your life, she can also be a great source of information and support throughout your pregnancy. Through memories and stories, these women can offer a personal view of what it was like to be pregnant and what pregnancy and delivery were like in the past.

Know How Much Information You Can Handle

Remember that you know yourself best. Many women experience "information overload" or become overly anxious when armed with too many details. Everyone has a different pregnancy experience, and just because one woman had a difficult time does not mean that you will too. Be selective when choosing people to consult for advice. If you find people who are overly negative or fear-inducing, thank them politely for their input and then move on to more supportive friends or family.

Know that the information and parental advice offered within this guide is all meant to be supportive and positive. Although you will read about health-related issues that can happen during pregnancy, know that this information is meant to educate and not to frighten you! Pace yourself. If you are not ready to read a particular section, feel free to come back to it when you are prepared. In the overall scheme of life, you are only pregnant for a very brief time. Stay relaxed and enjoy the journey!

Are You Truly Ready for Pregnancy?

How does pregnancy typically unfold for most women? In a committed relationship—married or common law, heterosexual or same-sex—the couple usually shares in the decision to have a baby. Some women make the decision entirely on their own, perhaps choosing artificial insemination and single parenthood. Because there are many excellent birth control options available today,

Pregnancy Preparedness Checklist **What NOW?**

There are some common issues that women and their partners might want to consider before getting pregnant. If you are already pregnant, thinking through these important issues is still a beneficial exercise. Have you considered the following?

- Timing
- Emotional readiness
- Your sense of self
- Your overall state of mind
- The strength of your relationship
- The safety of your relationship
- Your partner's readiness to be a parent
- Making time for yourself and your partner
- The impact on your romantic relationship
- Other family considerations
- Balancing family and work
- Job flexibility

the decision to have a baby can usually wait until the woman or the couple is completely ready. Of course, this doesn't always happen (see page 8 about handling unintended pregnancies).

Things to Consider before Becoming Pregnant

Though it may be difficult to understand now, everything changes when a child enters your life. Everything! Before conceiving, women and couples usually spend time processing the idea of having a baby.

Are you prepared to make some sacrifices in your current lifestyle? That slick two-seater car that you have been eyeing—are you willing to give that up if you have to? How will you organize time with your partner, your baby, your friends, your job, your extended family, and still find time for yourself? What was once simply running to the gym, to the grocery store, or out for coffee will become a feat of organization. Can you be flexible? Can your partner?

In considering how to prepare for pregnancy, it is important to acknowledge the diversity of relationships in which women conceive children. Some women are approaching parenthood completely on their own, whether by choice or by circumstance. In fact, the U.S. government reports that 41 percent of all births are to unmarried women. Some women are in relationships with varying degrees of commitment and involvement on the part of a partner. Your partner may be the father of your child or not. This book strives to fully include those partners who wish to be active parents, while recognizing that many women seek support from friends and other family members rather than a husband or other partner.

Timing: Is it the right time in your life? Actually, there is absolutely no perfect time to have a baby. There are, however, times that are better than others. You and your partner can sit down together, look over your life circumstances, and decide what makes sense for both of you. If you are always finding reasons not to have a child, you may want to discuss whether you are fearful of parenthood. You may even need to face the reality that being parents is not something you really want to do. Remember that it can take up to a year from the time you decide to conceive until you actually achieve the pregnancy, so do not put off making a decision.

Emotional readiness: Some women do not feel that sense of readiness to have a baby until *after* they conceive a child. Worry about the ability to love and care for a completely dependent human being may get in the way. In some cases, total fear about becoming a parent does not go away until several weeks after the baby is born. Are these kinds of fears keeping you from becoming pregnant?

Your sense of self: What will the impact of having a baby be on your self-esteem? If you have spent years putting your heart and soul into your job, what will happen when you have to juggle motherhood and your work life? What would it be like if you stayed home with your child? If you feel that having a baby will negatively affect your self-esteem because it will take focus and energy away from your job, you need to make sure that having a baby is the right thing for you. Talk to a counselor if you feel you have strong concerns about having a baby as a working mother.

Your overall state of mind: If you suffer from depression or another mental health problem, it is a good idea to talk to your therapist or psychiatrist before conceiving. Some medications cannot be taken during pregnancy, so you will have to decide together if you can tolerate nine months without a crucial drug. Your healthcare provider will work with you to weigh the risks and benefits of taking any medication during pregnancy. There are only a small number of medications that pregnant women are strongly discouraged from taking. You may need to change medications or increase the frequency of therapy sessions to maintain your mental health during pregnancy. Some women feel better psychologically during pregnancy, while others encounter mental health challenges they have not experienced before. With careful supervision and increased support, you can have a successful pregnancy.

The strength of your relationship: Is your relationship with your partner solid and loving? Are you having a child as a way to fix something that is amiss in your relationship? Having a child puts a strain on every couple, so it is essential that you both feel as close to each other without having a baby as you anticipate feeling when you do have one. Do you both feel a family of three (or more) can be as fulfilling as a relationship between two people? Do you feel supported in your relationship? If not, you may want to seek individual or couples counseling before considering pregnancy or as soon as possible.

The safety of your relationship: Sadly, it is not uncommon for women to feel pressured or coerced by their partners into becoming pregnant or making decisions about their pregnancy. If a woman is in a relationship with a domineering or controlling partner, she may not feel that she can freely choose when or whether to have a child. Some women are sexually or physically victimized by their partners before or during pregnancy. If you do not feel safe in your relationship for any reason, you can receive confidential help from community advocacy services that address domestic and/or sexual violence. The National Domestic Violence Hotline (1-800-799-SAFE) or the National Sexual Assault Hotline (1-800-656-HOPE) can provide you with information about free services in your own community.

Making time for yourself and for your partner: If you do not have family members available to babysit, will you both be comfortable leaving your child with someone else? Can you afford babysitting? If you cannot afford sitters often, how will you and your partner make time for each other?

Impact on your romantic relationship: Talk to your spouse or partner about how a child will affect your relationship. For a healthy family life, both parents must truly want a baby and recognize that their "dating life" will change after becoming parents. This is true for couples of all ages. Even if you have family members who are willing to babysit, it will take planning to enjoy a romantic weekend or

For Dads and Partners:

Participate in Pregnancy!

Get as involved in your partner's pregnancy and childbirth as possible! Even though you are not actually carrying the baby, you can take part in this miraculous adventure in a variety of ways. If the mom-to-be is trying to eat healthy foods and exercise, join her! Get informed by reading books like this one to understand how your baby is developing and what your partner is experiencing as her body and emotions change. Talk to other dads or partners about how they handled pregnancy and birth, and even ask your own dad what it was like when your mom was carrying you. Be supportive of your partner and plan your role as parents together! Remember, you are just as important in the birth and parenting of your child as you allow yourself to be. And it will not hurt if you rub your partner's feet once in a while!

I was 54 when my girlfriend of 14 years became pregnant. I accepted the fact but was angry and resentful about it, certain that my life and all the plans I had for it were ruined. I was so wrong! All I can say to any dad out there who is not planning on having a child and finds there is one on the way is this: What you think is going to be worst thing in world can turn out to be the best thing in the world. It happened to me! And if it happened to me, it can happen to anyone. —Richard, 55, dad of one

even an intimate evening at your favorite restaurant. Differences in parenting styles and ideas about how a child should be raised can also cause marital stress. Are you prepared to make changes in your relationship to accommodate a newborn? Are you and your partner clear about what you expect your roles as parents will be, and how you plan to divide the day-to-day responsibilities of raising your child?

Other family considerations: Today's families take many different forms. Your baby may be the first child for one parent, but not the other. You may have extended family nearby, or you may have a circle of friends who are your "chosen family." Consider how having a baby may affect all these relationships. Will you need to be especially considerate about reserving space in your home for a visiting stepchild now that you need a nursery for the baby? Do you want to be closer to where your parents or in-laws live, because they are supportive (or do you want to be much further away, because they are intrusive)?

Balancing family and work: How will you feel when you have to split your time between work, relationships, and caring for a baby? Do you or your partner want to stop working and stay home with your child? Is this financially feasible? If not, how will you feel leaving your child in daycare or with a caregiver? If you have a partner, have the two of you discussed in detail how you will handle the day-to-day responsibilities of having a child? You may envision a 50-50 split of duties, while your partner is expecting you to shoulder the lion's share of caring for your baby.

Job flexibility: What might it be like when your child gets older and there are daycare and school issues to deal with? Is your job flexible enough that you can stay home if a child is sick? Will you be able to attend school conferences and events such as plays and family breakfasts? Will you or your partner need to find a more flexible workplace? Will your partner be able (and willing) to alternate staying home when needed, or will that responsibility fall to you?

Handling the Unintended Pregnancy

What about the unexpected pregnancy? Despite today's birth control options, more than half of all pregnancies are unplanned. An unplanned pregnancy brings a number of challenges. While you may not have been able to prepare as well as you would have liked, it is just as crucial for parents whose pregnancies are unintended to consider how having a baby will change their lives. Increased knowledge can help prospective parents to handle this major life event. An unintended pregnancy may be a welcome surprise. Some couples, after having failed to conceive for years, may have accepted a childless relationship or have chosen to adopt. Sometimes these couples can find themselves pregnant. This situation can send the newly expectant mother and her partner on an emotional rollercoaster, which runs the gamut from delight to terror. The best thing to do in this case is slow down and take everything into account. The couple should talk things through to be clear about their respective apprehensions and excitement.

Physical and Health Considerations

You do not have to look like a supermodel or exercise like an Olympic athlete to have a healthy pregnancy. However, before becoming pregnant, it is beneficial to consider your overall health. In fact, it is a great idea for every woman to see her gynecologist or family physician prior to becoming pregnant. You can discuss your feelings or concerns about pregnancy, get information on how to determine the most fertile days of your menstrual cycle, and have a general exam to identify any health concerns that need to be addressed. Before trying to conceive, consider the important health-related items that follow.

Your Preconception Visit to Your Healthcare Provider

Even if you think you are in excellent health, it is really very important that you be examined by your healthcare provider before trying to get pregnant. This visit is crucial to a smooth pregnancy, benefiting both your health and the healthy development of your fetus.

Your healthcare provider should do a complete physical exam, including an evaluation of your thyroid gland. He or she should also check for any sexually transmitted infections or other illness. Your provider will take a personal and family history to uncover any genetic diseases that run in your family or are more common in your ethnic group. If you have an ongoing health issue, such as diabetes or asthma, you should create a healthcare plan with your physician that will guide you throughout your pregnancy. If you are diabetic and are not in optimal control, it is essential that you get control of your diabetes

---

Things to Think About: Finances

Money is not everything, but it does not hurt to consider the financial impact a child might have on your life. For example, what will happen if one working parent stays home and your family income is reduced? Will you have to move to a new home to accommodate a child? Will having a baby demand changes in your current spending habits? There are expenses like car seats, childcare, babysitters, food, and clothing that will increase as well. You will also want to save for college and other big life events like marriage. Sitting with your partner and going through questions like these will help you both become realistic about your finances. While money worries may not stop you from having a child, it is essential to be on the same page with your partner when it comes to family finances.

Be honest, open, and realistic—and be positive!

---

before becoming pregnant. Obese women benefit greatly from losing even 10 to 20 pounds before conceiving. Doctors generally recommend that all women of childbearing age take 400 micrograms of folic acid (a B vitamin) daily at least one month prior to conceiving to support the development of a healthy neural tube in the fetus. The neural tube is the structure from which the brain and spinal cord develop. Women who have previously had a baby with a neural tube defect will be advised to take a higher dosage of folic acid.

The government website WomensHealth.gov offers resources on how to improve your health and manage chronic conditions. The book *The Healthy Woman: A Complete Guide for All Ages* is available without cost to view or download from the website.

Do You Have a Healthy Body?

As we explained above, before you and your partner try to conceive, consider your overall health and ways to improve it. This does not mean starting a crash diet or training for a marathon. Simply exercising at least three times a week for a half hour and eating a diet

Calculating Your Body Mass Index (BMI)

Although there are many helpful BMI calculators online to help you, the formula is actually fairly simple. BMI is basically calculated by dividing your weight (in pounds) by your height (in inches) *squared*, then multiplying that number by a set conversion factor (703):

$$\frac{\text{weight (pounds)}}{\text{height (inches)}^2} \times 703 = \text{BMI}$$

For example, a 5'5" (65 inches)-tall, 130-pound woman has a BMI of 21.63, based on the following calculation:

$$\frac{130}{4225} \times 703 = \text{BMI}$$

So, what's your BMI?

rich in fruits, vegetables, and whole grains is a simple and smart way to improve your health. An established healthy lifestyle will make it easier to continue taking good care of yourself during your pregnancy. Chapter 2 provides more detailed information about diet and exercise during pregnancy.

Women who have a normal body mass index (BMI) tend to have the healthiest pregnancies. Your BMI is calculated from your height and weight. A normal BMI is between 18.5 and 25. A BMI of 30 or higher is considered obese. While obese women can have healthy pregnancies, they may also have more complications and do better if they lose excess weight before getting pregnant. Check with your healthcare provider if you are unsure if you have a healthy BMI.

How Much Stress Do You Have in Your Life?

We all know that life can be more stressful at certain times than others. Take a good look at what is going on in your life and evaluate how much stress you are under. Are you caring for an elderly parent? Is your job stretching you beyond your limits right now? Are you overscheduled or sleep-deprived? Both you and your partner should reduce stress as much as possible before getting pregnant. While the research on the effect of stress on fertility shows mixed results, it is clear that trying to become pregnant can be stressful and can take a toll on couples' relationships. Therefore, improving your stress management skills can be very helpful.

There are many ways to reduce stress. Some include saying "no" to demands on your time, cutting back on hours at work, or getting help with things like housecleaning or yard work to make more time for yourself. You may also want to try talking with a supportive therapist, getting more regular exercise, or doing yoga or meditation.

Where Is Your Positive Mental Attitude (PMA)?

Any time you embark on a major life change, having a positive mental attitude (PMA) enhances your chances for success and enjoyment. If you and your partner can stay upbeat and positive, your relationship will benefit and your health may benefit as well. Just consider how much better everything seems when you have a positive outlook.

Are you a glass-half-empty or glass-half-full person? In what ways can you improve your outlook? Aligning a healthy body and a positive mind can give you a leg up in beginning parenthood. You may want to give yourself six months to improve your health and psychological disposition before trying to conceive. Improved health may increase your chances of getting pregnant in the months that follow.

Your Psychological History

While focusing on staying positive is generally helpful, you may wish to address any major mental health challenges that you have experienced up to this point. If you or your partner have a history of serious depression, anxiety, bipolar disorder, psychosis, or substance abuse, it is important to have access to appropriate mental health resources before you get pregnant. Many women (one in four) have a history of sexual abuse in childhood. These experiences, as well as any other history of psychological trauma, may make the healthcare procedures of pregnancy and childbirth a challenge. More and more professionals are learning how to support women through these challenges. You may wish to

Iron and Folic Acid: Critical *before* You Conceive

Get screened for iron deficiency anemia before getting pregnant. If necessary, your healthcare provider can prescribe iron to bring your levels to normal. As mentioned before, women should take 400 micrograms of folic acid daily for at least a month before they become pregnant in order to protect the neural tube, which will become the brain and spinal column in your developing embryo. Some providers recommend taking folic acid or prenatal vitamins for at least three months before getting pregnant. In addition to taking dietary supplements, folic acid can be found in leafy green vegetables, citrus foods, legumes like peanuts, fortified breakfast cereals, and fortified breads.

find a healthcare provider who has a trauma-informed approach and will work with you step by step to ensure that you are as comfortable as possible throughout your pregnancy and birth experiences. Some women find that a specially trained doula (a nonmedical support person) makes all the difference in their ability to relax and participate fully in the childbearing year. (See Chapter 3 for more information about doulas.)

Are You Anemic?

Having your blood tested is an important thing to do before getting pregnant. Of utmost significance will be your levels of hemoglobin, a complex protein-iron compound in the blood that carries oxygen to the cells from the lungs and carbon dioxide away from the cells to the lungs. If there is a decrease below the normal range in hemoglobin, this is known as anemia, which can put your health—as well as the health of your fetus—at risk. If possible, see your healthcare provider to determine whether you are anemic prior to conceiving. Because pregnancy makes anemia worse, you will want to have a normal red blood cell count during pregnancy. Anemia is easily treated with prenatal vitamins taken before (or after) conception or with iron supplements you can get over the counter at your local pharmacy.

Does Your Partner or Donor Have a Healthy Sperm Count?

The prospective father should do what it takes to maintain a healthy sperm count before and during your attempts to conceive. Men must maintain a relatively low sperm temperature at all times to keep the sperm viable and healthy. If he soaks in hot tubs or spends too much time in saunas, the temperature of his sperm will increase and negatively affect their motility. Sperm motility basically has to do with the *quality* of the sperm, particularly their ability to move towards an egg. If there are any questions about Dad-to-be's sperm motility, have him see an urologist for a complete sperm count and evaluation.

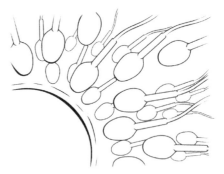

Improving sperm quality

Your partner may be able to increase sperm quality and motility by certain lifestyle changes:

- Eat a healthy diet, including organic fruits and veggies.
- Check with his healthcare provider about any medications or health conditions.
- Decrease alcohol intake.
- Stop smoking.

Preconception Genetic Testing and Counseling

Whether or not to have genetic testing before trying to conceive is a very personal decision. In general, the following factors increase the risk for genetic abnormalities:

- Any couple that has a family history of a certain birth defect
- Greater maternal age
- A couple with a child who was born with an intellectual disability, a birth defect, or any other inherited disorder

- A woman who has had three or more miscarriages or who had a child that died in infancy, even if the cause was not found
- Men and women who work in occupations that expose them to radiation, drugs, infectious agents, medications or chemicals
- Ethnic groups that have higher-than-average risk for certain diseases, such as African Americans, people of Mediterranean descent, and Ashkenazi Jews
- Couples who are first cousins or other close blood relatives

If any of these apply to you and/or your partner, you may wish to consider genetic testing and counseling with a genetic counselor before starting your family. Some genetic disorders, such as cystic fibrosis, must be passed along by both parents. Other genetic abnormalities, such as Huntington's disease, can be transmitted by only one parent. A third set of genetic abnormalities are caused by mutations that happen during the development of the embryo. See Chapter 4 for more complete information about genetic screening.

The best part about becoming pregnant is the loving, gentle focus the world encourages you to have with yourself. It's no time to stress about your weight or all the potential things that can go wrong. Every day, wake up and say "I'm going to love myself silly!" It's what's most important for you and your baby. —*Allison, 33, mother of three*

possible. Once you discontinue using birth control, follow all the health and safety guidelines that pertain to early pregnancy. This is the time to consider any job changes that may be advisable if your job places you in a toxic or super-stressful environment, discontinue the use of alcohol and recreational drugs, discuss all your prescription or over-the-counter medication with your healthcare provider, and avoid sick people to the extent possible. The early days and weeks of pregnancy are times when the developing embryo is quite vulnerable, so if there is a possibility you may be pregnant take into account the pregnancy health considerations in Chapter 2.

Safety while Trying to Conceive

Because you will not know that you are pregnant immediately after conception, during the time period when you are trying to conceive you will want to avoid anything that could possibly harm a tiny embryo. This means that you should follow the guidelines in Chapter 2 regarding medications, toxins, and avoiding infection to the extent

Pregnancy and Chronic Illness

If you have a chronic illness such as an autoimmune disorder or diabetes, preparation can help you to have a healthy pregnancy.

Evaluate Your Situation

Many women fear becoming pregnant if they are dealing with a serious or ongoing illness. You need facts to determine whether these fears are justified. Talk to your primary care practitioner and any specialists that you see to find out whether pregnancy will bring additional challenges. Hold on to your PMA (positive mental attitude) and get informed about your particular situation.

Line Up Your Support System

You will probably need to develop a trusted medical team to have a healthy pregnancy. For example, if you have an autoimmune disease and want to become pregnant, work with an obstetrician and a rheumatologist together in order to create a plan that provides you with the optimum reduction in your symptoms and the maximum safety of your pregnancy. You will also want to be sure that your partner or another support person is

Nutrition Tip: Eat Well

One of the most wonderful things about becoming pregnant is the encouragement you will receive about taking excellent care of yourself. From your mother to your physician to perfect strangers, you will find everyone asking how you are feeling and supporting your efforts to take extra-special care of yourself and your body. It is the perfect time to begin exercising and eating healthier. Start by reading labels and removing processed foods from your diet. Eat organic whenever possible and think about getting the most nutrition for your calorie buck. Simple things like eating brown rice instead of white or choosing a banana over a cookie are great ways to begin. Do not be hard on yourself and do not obsess about what you eat. Remember that whatever you eat or drink you are sharing with your baby! (See Chapter 2 for more details on healthy eating for pregnancy.)

prepared to advocate on your behalf if you are not well enough to do so and to help you with the challenges you will encounter.

Gynecological Issues

If you have gynecological issues, it is important that you keep talking to the professionals. Before you conceive, your gynecologist can guide you through any conditions that may impact conception or pregnancy. The following are three common gynecological issues that women encounter.

Polycystic Ovarian Syndrome (PCOS)

It is estimated that about 10 percent of women have this condition. Symptoms include irregular or no periods, ovarian cysts, oily skin, and obesity. Though it is possible to become pregnant if you have PCOS, women generally need considerable help from their obstetrician to do so, and it may take years to conceive. Sometimes PCOS can make conception impossible. Talk to your healthcare provider if you think you have polycystic ovarian syndrome so you can get the maximum treatment possible and increase your chances of becoming pregnant.

Cervical Cancer and Cervical Dysplasia

If you have had cervical cancer, you may encounter some unique obstacles to pregnancy. First, you do run the risk of the cancer returning, which could obviously endanger your life and your baby's life. Additionally, cervical cancer puts women at risk for pre-term labor. You may not have had a cancer diagnosis but have been treated for cervical dysplasia, or abnormal cells on the cervix. Certain procedures used to treat cervical cancer and cervical dysplasia (such as a cone

I knew it could be difficult for me to conceive since I had been diagnosed with PCOS years before, so I proactively sought the help of my OB/GYN and a fertility specialist when we wanted to start a family. After months of medications, doctor visits, and nightly injections I was physically and mentally drained from the experience. I needed a break, and my husband and I decided to take a "vacation" from trying to get pregnant. Three months later, before starting up fertility treatments again, I took a pregnancy test that came back positive! I'm sure that all of the treatments contributed to my ability to conceive but taking the mental burden off was just as important. —*Michelle, 43, mother of two*

biopsy) can weaken the cervix, causing problems carrying a fetus to term. Women who have cervical issues from treatment of cancer or dysplasia can lose their pregnancy at around 16 weeks' gestation. Talk with your physician about your options and any concerns if you have had cervical cancer or dysplasia.

Double Uterus

Some women are born with abnormalities in the shape of their uterus—a condition called "double uterus." As a girl with this condition grows into a woman, her uterus grows into an abnormal shape. Once she is pregnant, her fetus can grow in an abnormal position as well, and the fetus' head may not be down. A "double uterus" creates the possibility of preterm labor and a difficult delivery.

Pregnancy in Later Life

Forty years ago, the majority of women had children in their late teens or early twenties. There were few pregnancies after age 35. But today, many women have placed increased emphasis on their work life and personal goals and are choosing to have children later in life—even into their late thirties and early forties. A healthy woman can have a successful pregnancy at any age, but there are indeed increased risks in attempting to have a child later in life.

35 Is Not a Magic Number

Age 35 is not a "magic number" at which complications begin, but it serves as a guideline for the maternal age at which additional testing might be recommended. Any of the complications mentioned below gradually increase in frequency as women get older. If you are in your mid-thirties or above, then the following will be helpful information to have in your back pocket as your pregnancy proceeds.

Reduced Ability to Get Pregnant

Women are actually born with all the eggs they will ever have. As women age, the number of eggs in the ovaries diminishes and the eggs can lose the healthy qualities they possessed when they were younger. This can pose a greater risk of miscarriage in the first three months of the pregnancy due to maternal genetic issues and a higher risk for genetic diseases in general.

Reduced Cycles Lessen Chances of Pregnancy

Women over 35 also do not ovulate as regularly as women under 35, so the opportunities to become pregnant are diminished.

Increased Risk of High Blood Pressure

High blood pressure can exist before pregnancy or can occur as part of the pregnancy in a condition called preeclampsia. Preeclampsia occurs at a higher rate in women who are older than 35. When a woman develops preeclampsia she often has to go on bed rest in order to reduce her blood pressure. Occasionally medications are necessary to control the condition, and sometimes the infant must be delivered early before negative effects occur.

Increased Risk of Placenta Previa

Placenta previa is a condition in which the placenta grows over the opening of the cervix. Women with placenta previa can have bleeding any time during pregnancy, and, in some cases, the bleeding can be severe. As long as the placenta is overlying the cervix, a vaginal delivery is not safe and a woman must deliver by cesarean section. Many women with placenta previa deliver safely but require careful attention throughout the pregnancy, frequent ultrasounds, and intermittent hospitalizations if the bleeding becomes dangerous. (See Chapter 8 for a detailed discussion of placenta previa.)

Higher Risk for a Cesarean Section

Often women over 35 have more difficulty tolerating labor and pushing the baby, which can result in the need for cesarean section

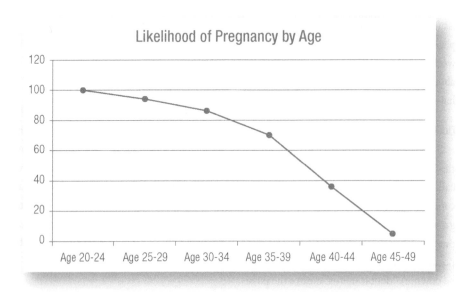

This graph shows the likelihood of pregnancy for women in good health, having unprotected sex, at various age ranges. (Source of data: M. Sara Rosenthal, *The Fertility Sourcebook*, 3rd edition, 2002.)

Never make a decision not to have a baby because you are afraid of what might happen. Of course there are millions of things that can go wrong in any pregnancy, but compare that to the 10 million things that go right every day for all those moms and babies no matter their age or health issues. Ask your questions, do your homework, and consider any major obstacle you think you might have. Then have faith and make your decision from a place of love, not out of fear.—*Jenny, 37, mother of two*

(or C-section). Even if you have a healthy, normal pregnancy, if you are older you should be especially mindful of the possibility that you will need a C-section.

Premature Delivery

Women over 35 are more likely to deliver prematurely. The reasons for this are unclear, but if you are older than 35 be aware that preterm contractions might indicate an early birth. Notify your doctor right away if you have any abnormal pelvic pain, backaches, or bleeding.

Higher Risk for Stillbirth

Stillbirth refers to fetal death after the twentieth week of gestation and occurs in about 1 percent of all pregnancies. There are many causes for stillbirth. Genetics can play a role, but there are a number of factors that can result in stillbirth, including infection, maternal health issues, and problems with the placenta.

Baseline Medical Conditions

Older women are more likely to have medical issues such as diabetes or high blood pressure and more likely to be on some type of long-term medication that could interfere with the health of their pregnancy. If you have a chronic condition, work with your healthcare provider to manage your condition and monitor the risk to your fetus if the condition is not in perfect control.

Need to Consult Fertility Services

If you are over 35 and cannot get pregnant after six to twelve months, you should seek the advice of a fertility specialist. There are many techniques fertility doctors can use to improve your chances of getting pregnant, such as intrauterine insemination and in vitro fertilization.

Prenatal Care: Love Yourself to Good Health

It is important for every woman to take excellent care of herself. But older moms have even more reason to be mindful of their health. If you are especially careful to follow healthy guidelines for eating, weight gain, exercise, and rest, your body will be more resilient through the stresses of pregnancy and childbirth.

Also, talk early on with your pregnancy healthcare provider regarding prenatal screening. Although most babies are born healthy, the risk of abnormalities increases when a woman over the age of 35 decides to have a baby. Generally, genetic screening can bring you peace of mind as most tests turn out to be normal. Prenatal screening involves blood tests to determine if there is the chance that your baby may have genetic abnormali-

Six Keys to a Successful Pregnancy—At Any Age!

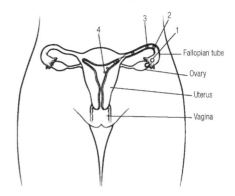

- Eat healthy foods.
- Gain 20 to 30 pounds throughout your pregnancy.
- Exercise regularly.
- Avoid alcohol, tobacco, and any illegal drugs.
- Avoid herbal supplements unless approved by your healthcare provider.
- Get as much rest and relaxation as you can.

ties such as Down syndrome. If there is an issue, you can discuss your options with your partner and healthcare provider. (Prenatal genetic screening is covered in Chapter 4.)

Most important, be positive and as stress-free as possible. Your attitude and emotional state are both a part of good health. Feeling happy and positive is as useful for you and your baby as eating right and taking prenatal vitamins. Surround yourself with loving, positive friends and family or even join a support group for pregnant moms. Love yourself and enjoy your journey into motherhood!

Getting Pregnant! Throw Out the Birth Control and Don't Throw In the Towel!

OK! You are ready to take the exciting leap into pregnancy and parenthood. Many couples believe that all there is to getting pregnant is getting rid of the birth control and increasing sexual activity, but it may not be quite that simple. It may take a little knowledge and practice for a couple to become successfully pregnant. There actually is some science behind the process, and

when armed with the information you need you can increase your chances of becoming pregnant sooner. Remember that even if you do everything the "right" way, couples have only a 20 to 25 percent chance of conceiving a pregnancy during any one menstrual cycle.

As you begin, remember that it can take, on average, up to a year to become pregnant. Stay positive and relaxed, and communicate openly with your partner. There may or may not be bumps in the road, but if you remain optimistic you will be less stressed and you will also enjoy the entire process!

How conception occurs

Each month during a woman's reproductive years, an ovary releases an egg into the fallopian tube (1). The egg starts traveling down the fallopian tube (2). If the timing is right, sperm travel up the vagina and uterus into the fallopian tube. If one fertilizes the egg (3), then the embryo starts developing as it travels toward the uterus, eventually implanting in the uterine wall (4) around day 5 or 6.

Know When You Ovulate

Ovulation is the process of releasing a ripe egg from cysts in the ovaries into the area near the opening of the fallopian tube. Because the ovaries are not directly attached to the fallopian tube, cilia (tiny hairs that line the tubes) provide a suction effect that draws the egg into the fallopian tube and down to

> When you are trying to get pregnant, don't let sex become only functional. Keep it as exciting as it ever was even if it can't be spontaneous. —*Tyrone, 35, dad of two*

its inner portion where fertilization can occur. Usually only one or two eggs are actually released at the time of ovulation.

There is a very short span of time when fertilization can occur—a six- to eight-hour window! After that, the egg begins to die and your body begins the process of menstruation, resulting in your period. To increase your chances of becoming pregnant, it is essential to determine when you may ovulate.

Calculate your most fertile days: Your menstrual cycle begins on the first day of your period, and this is referred to by doctors as "day one." On average, a woman's menstrual period lasts for five to seven days, during which time her estrogen level rises. Estrogen is a female hormone produced by the ovaries that causes the stoppage of the previous menstrual bleeding and a thickening of the uterine lining. This prepares the uterus to accept and hold onto a fertilized egg.

In a usual cycle, ovulation occurs 14 days before a woman gets her period. A normal cycle can be 23 to 35 days, which means ovulation can occur anywhere from day 9 to day 19 (remember, we are counting from the first day of your period). One of the most effective ways to increase your chances of conceiving is to try every other day, from day 9 to day 19. The egg degrades rapidly after ovulation, so timing is essential! These are the days it is most important to have sex with your partner.

In order to keep sperm count high, it is generally recommended that you have sex every other day during this time frame. If you have sex multiple times per day, or even every day during this time, it can deplete the quantity of sperm and actually decrease your chances of becoming pregnant.

So mark your calendar, and remember to have fun! Timing is essential, but you don't want to make your partner feel like he has to perform on command, and you don't want your relationship to feel mechanical.

Women are less likely to conceive later in their menstrual cycle. During ovulation, the cyst from which the egg emerges begins to make progesterone, which changes the features of the lining of the uterus so that the lining will not accept a fertilized egg. The uterine lining ripens and prepares to shed again on day one of the next cycle.

Exercise Idea: Walk

Women considering pregnancy should stay active! If you already exercise, doctors recommend you continue doing what you are already doing. If you are not exercising, begin with something mild like walking. All you need is a pair of comfortable shoes! Find a walking partner and you will increase the fun. Exercise three times a week for 30 minutes per day, and you will help keep your weight stable, feel energized, and maintain good health. (Once you become pregnant, remember to avoid hot yoga, jacuzzis, and saunas.)

Irregular cycle? Help is on the way! If you are lucky enough to have a regular 28-day menstrual cycle that runs like clockwork, you can simply use a calendar to determine which days you are most likely to get pregnant. If your menstrual cycles are irregular, fear not! There are a number of tools available to help you calculate your most fertile days. These include ovulation test kits, ovulation calculators found online at many pregnancy websites (such as www.marchofdimes.com), and tracking your basal body temperature.

Basal body temperature: Taking your body temperature first thing in the morning before you get out of bed is referred to as taking your basal body temperature. When you ovulate there is a shift in your basal body temperature. By tracking your temperature through your menstrual cycle you will be able to predict the day you ovulate.

Basal body temperature monitoring is effective but takes persistence and an accurate eye for fluctuations in body temperature. If your body temperature stays at baseline (97°F–97.5°F) throughout your entire cycle, it might mean you didn't ovulate at all that cycle. If you find you are having many cycles where you don't ovulate, you may want to see a fertility specialist.

Ovulation test kits—easy PEEsy! Ovulation test kits are relatively inexpensive and may help clarify your exact date of ovulation. These tests kits are readily available in drug stores. According to the Food and Drug Administration, they are 90 percent accurate if administered correctly. A kit contains numerous testing strips, each with a porous end. Most kits recommend that you urinate

Tracking Your Basal Body Temperature

Tracking your basal body temperature is a quick and simple process. You will need a digital thermometer, pen, and calendar to chart your temperature readings. Keep all these next to your bed. It is essential that you take your temperature as soon as you wake and before making any major motion with your body. If you move around too much your temperature will rise and skew the accuracy of your readings.

You can begin on any day in your cycle. Simply take your temperature immediately upon waking and write it on your chart. During the first half of your cycle, your temperature will fluctuate slightly but will hover between 97°F and 97.5°F. The very day you ovulate, your body temperature will decrease slightly but not by more than a half degree. Once you determine this drop in temperature, you will know you are ovulating and are most fertile, and you should try to conceive on that day.

The next day, you will find that your temperature has risen to around 97.5°F–98.5°F. The temperature will stay in that range until a day or so before your period, when it drops to baseline levels again. When your temperature makes the sudden rise again just after ovulation, you are no longer fertile. You are only fertile during the day the temperature takes a dip and for the few days before that temperature dip.

into a cup first thing in the morning and then hold one of the porous strips in the urine for a predetermined amount of time before removing the strip. When the ovulation line on the strip is a darker pink than the baseline, you are ovulating.

If you have irregular cycles or if you just want confirmation that you are ovulating, these kits may be helpful. However, it is not a good idea to rely solely on a kit, and you should *not* wait for the results to turn positive in a cycle (you should start trying before the kit turns positive). If you wait for positive results, sometimes you have waited too long, because your chances of conceiving are high the few days before ovulation as well as the specific day of ovulation.

What to Do if You Can't Seem to Conceive

Most couples trying to get pregnant are successful within a year. Couples over the age of 35 generally take longer to get pregnant. However, there is a general rule of thumb about seeking the help of a fertility specialist. If you are under the age of 35 and have not conceived within a year or if you are over 35 and have not conceived within six months, it is recommended you seek the guidance of a fertility doctor.

A fertility specialist will examine you and your partner, ask you both questions about your medical history, and perform a number of tests including the following:

- A sperm analysis will be performed on Dad-to-be to insure his sperm look healthy and are motile (that is, they move a lot).

- Your cervix will be swabbed to test for infection and pH levels and to examine how thin and stringy your cervix is around the time of ovulation.

- You will be given a blood test to determine if enough progesterone is in your blood during the last half of your menstrual cycle; progesterone is needed to keep the uterine lining healthy during the last half of the menstrual cycle so that the fertilized egg "sticks."

- A fertility specialist will perform an FSH test on both men and women. The follicle stimulating hormone (FSH) is an indirect indicator of a woman's estrogen level. If elevated early in the menstrual cycle, it may indicate a poor quality egg. Women are usually tested on day 2 or 3 of their

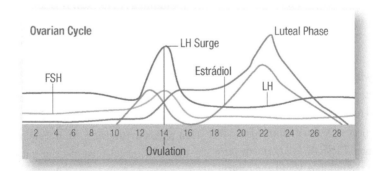

Hormones surging during ovulation
Your ovulation cycle tells you when you are most likely to conceive.

menstrual cycle. In men, FSH is essential in the production and transportation of sperm.

- Also on the third day of your menstrual cycle, an estradiol test is performed. Estradiol is a form of estrogen that is necessary for ovulation to occur. Estradiol is made by the ovaries and helps thicken the uterine lining.
- A luteinizing hormone (LH) test may be performed on both you and Dad-to-be. In women, LH helps the ovaries produce hormones and is important in the maturation of eggs. In men, LH affects sperm production. A woman cannot

We had been trying to conceive for about nine months, and I began to notice that I seemed more into the whole process than my husband. I decided to confront him honestly. I expressed that I felt unless he was really 100 percent on board we would not be successful. This was a turning point for him. He got on board and we conceived that very month! There may be a lot of science to getting pregnant, but positive attitude and clear intentions matter too! —*Gina, 33, mother of two*

ovulate without LH, so an LH test is performed at the time of projected ovulation.

- A prolactin test is also performed on men and women. Prolactin is a hormone produced by the pituitary gland and contributes to the production of milk in women. For women, prolactin can interfere with conception because it can prevent menstruation and hence ovulation. In men, prolactin can cause problems with sexual desire and cause erectile difficulty.
- Your doctor will test for androgens—in particular, testosterone. Androgens influence sexual ability and function of both men and women. Without testosterone, men often have trouble with their erections, may have dysfunctional sperm, and have a low sex drive. In women, too much testosterone can affect the menstrual cycle, and too little testosterone can result in a low sex drive.

Common Recommendations for Enhancing Fertility

Many couples find that, after all the fertility tests are completed, there is no apparent medical reason why they are having trouble conceiving. Conversely, it can be common to find that the fallopian tubes are blocked, causing infertility. Whatever the findings (or lack thereof), there are several common recommendations and procedures couples can follow to increase their chances of becoming pregnant.

Clomiphene (Clomid): It is sometimes recommended that women take clomiphene citrate, or Clomid, in order to enhance chances of getting pregnant. Clomid is a medication taken once daily on days five through nine of your menstrual cycle. Clomid stimulates the ovaries to release more eggs. More eggs mean you have a better chance of having a fertilized egg as part of your cycle. Clomid is generally considered safe, but there is a 5 to 12 percent chance of conceiving twins on a Clomid cycle.

I had been trying fertility treatments for ten years before finally trying IVF. Although I was successful after my fourth cycle of treatment, I feel there is something no one really emphasizes for women. IVF works only about 30 to 40 percent of the time. That means a whopping 60 percent of women will not conceive using IVF. Statistically, that's huge! I think being realistic is so important when trying IVF—or any fertility treatment for that matter. Be positive, but research adoption as an option as well. —*Barbara, 33, mother of twins*

Intrauterine insemination (IUI): This can be done with or without stimulating the number of eggs a woman produces. Sperm is processed and inserted directly through the cervix and into the uterus. With the excess of sperm and the stimulation of the number of eggs produced, the chances of getting pregnant are higher than average.

In vitro fertilization (IVF): IVF is performed when a woman's fallopian tubes are blocked. The process begins by stimulating the ovaries to produce numerous eggs. The eggs are harvested and mixed with sperm, creating a number of viable embryos. The doctors evaluate each embryo to make sure it is healthy. If it is, the embryo is saved. A small number of fertilized embryos are then inserted in the uterus at the time of ovulation. IVF success rates vary from clinic to clinic but generally are 30 percent per cycle.

When I found out I was pregnant and told my grandmother, she said: "Life is full of little surprises, but nothing's more surprising than finding out you're having a little one!" She was so right—even the second time around!
—*Anna, 30, mother of two*

Chapter 2

Pregnant! Now What? Ensuring a Healthy Pregnancy

Take a deep breath…you and your partner did it! You are pregnant! Maybe it happened the first time you tried, or maybe you have been trying for months or even years. No matter how you have reached this point, a new journey is just beginning. Like most newly pregnant women, you are probably experiencing a range of emotions from elation to fear! Your mind may be racing with thoughts about what doctor to choose, when to purchase diapers and a car seat, or how you will look in maternity clothes. But, as with every journey, you have to begin at the beginning and take one step at a time.

Rome was not built in a day, and neither is a baby! Right now you can just enjoy these early moments of pregnancy when everything is a possibility, you still feel like yourself, and your body still looks familiar! Then read this chapter and know it will guide you in which steps to take next. Like any journey you embark on, there is a logical process to follow.

My period is very irregular so I was taking early pregnancy tests every month. We'd been trying for about six months, and I'd gotten used to being disappointed. My husband, however, is a total optimist! This time I was planning to wait one more day before taking my early pregnancy test. But, when my husband, who's an ER doctor, left for work at 5:00 a.m., he begged me to take the test that day and call him with the results. He said he had a "good feeling," but I told him not to get his hopes up as I kissed him goodbye. After he'd left, I went to put on my running shoes and spotted the pregnancy test on the dresser. I decided to go ahead and get the disappointment over with. I'll always remember the shock and awe of seeing that plus sign! My usually glass-half-full husband was right! I went for my run and savored having such a secret all to myself—for just that moment, only my baby and I knew. I didn't ponder the laundry list of things I now had to think about, like calling my doctor, genetic testing, or throwing out all the nonorganic food in the fridge. All I remember is how the sun was rising in golden slivers behind the city skyline, the sound of the river lapping against the shore, and the tingle in my cheeks from the cold autumn air. Three stars hung low in the dawn sky, and I thought they were the first sign of me, my husband, and our baby as a new family! It was amazing. —Carmen, 28

When you go on vacation, you do not get on the plane first and then think about packing your suitcase! If you can allow yourself to go step by step and not jump ahead, you can keep yourself happy, relaxed, and informed during your pregnancy. In this chapter, you will take your first pregnancy steps by answering the following questions:

- Which foods should I eat and which should I avoid now that I am pregnant?
- How much weight should I gain?
- What exercise is safe, and what if I haven't been exercising at all?
- What medications are safe and which should I avoid?
- Should I worry about toxins and infections in my home or at work?
- How can I have a healthy pregnancy while working outside the home?
- How do I keep my partner feeling involved in the pregnancy?
- What are some tips for my partner as we begin this journey?

Start by Taking Great Care of Yourself!

If ever there is a time to truly take excellent care of yourself, it is when you become pregnant. From now on, everything you do or consume will affect not only you but also your baby. That includes everything from eating and how you exercise to whether or not you are thinking positive and feeling happy. For the moment, you can think of you and your baby as one.

We will start your pregnancy journey with nutrition and exercise information. But please use this information as a loving guide to taking good care of yourself and not as a weapon to induce guilt or negative feelings about yourself. This is not a time to bemoan the fact that you wished you lost those 20 pounds before now, nor is it a time to lose those 20 pounds. Pregnancy is simply a time to treat yourself with genuine love and respect and to take the best possible care of yourself right now. As the saying goes, yesterday is gone. Today, you can be happy and healthy for both yourself and your baby.

Nutrition: Shift Your Thinking

Women in particular can have many issues around food. We are bombarded with images of how we think we are supposed to look and messages about what we are supposed to deny ourselves to get that way. It is all nonsense. Every body is different and every woman is beautiful—right now, right this moment! Especially now that you are pregnant!

It may seem radical, but the first step in eating healthy is shifting your thinking. Food is your friend, not a foe. We literally cannot live without it. For our bodies to function properly we need nutrients from the food we consume. Eating is meant to be one of the greatest pleasures of being human. We are not meant to deny ourselves food but to thoroughly enjoy everything we choose to consume. There is nothing wrong with any single food. After all, eating a cookie is a luscious joy; but eating a dozen cookies is simply not a healthy way to offer your body other nutrients it truly needs.

Becoming pregnant is the perfect time for making a shift in your thinking about food. It is easy to understand that your baby will be consuming what you consume. And, like you, the fetus needs a variety of nutrients to be as healthy as possible. So no hating yourself for eating ice cream and no more negative thoughts about how much you should or should not weigh! Simply think of food as an essential ingredient to keep you and your baby healthy. Take the following information and use it to make eating a joy. And the next time you are tempted to criticize yourself about food, stop! Then remind yourself that loving yourself is the best way to take excellent care of you and your baby.

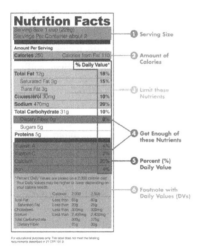

Nutrition during pregnancy
The first step in eating healthy is shifting your thinking! It's important to read nutrition labels and plan healthy meals and snacks.

If Only It Were True: You Are Not Eating for Two

Humor me for a moment and imagine your developing embryo sitting at the dinner table with you. Now, how much food do you think he or she needs to consume for dinner?

A crumb perhaps? Anyway, not much! This image may help you dispel the myth that pregnant women are eating for two, especially in your first trimester (the first three months of your pregnancy).

Women need to consume only about 300 additional calories per day in order to maintain a healthy weight gain for pregnancy and to keep the developing baby healthy. In your first trimester, you need only eat about 50 additional calories (the amount in an average apple). So keep that in mind as your pregnancy progresses, and you will also keep from gaining unnecessary weight.

The Joy of Food: Healthy Eating

Simply put, everything you consume during your pregnancy eventually ends up going through your placenta to feed your child. So eating as many natural and organic foods as possible and increasing your intake of fruits, veggies, and whole grains is the place to start. (This also means you should avoid eating anything that you do not want your baby to consume, including tobacco products as well as all alcohol and illicit drugs.)

Here is a quick overview of why certain foods are so important for overall good health:

Fruits and vegetables: Fresh fruits and vegetables are loaded with vitamins, antioxidants, and healthy carbohydrates that promote growth and healthy brain development in your fetus. Raw fruits and vegetables generally contain the most nutrients, because heat from cooking destroys some of the vitamins and antioxidants. Still, it is better to eat them cooked than not eat them at all! Fruits in particular are best eaten raw as they are high in vitamin A and vitamin C, important

My mother gave me some simple wisdom about eating and gaining weight during pregnancy. She said: "Eat when you're hungry and don't eat when you're not. If you have a food craving, give in to it in moderation and let your doctor worry about your weight." I took all these tips to heart and gained a healthy amount of weight, and stayed happy and stress free every pregnancy! —*Joann, 40, mother of three*

components for fetal growth and development. It is ideal to have at least five to eight servings of fruits and vegetables each day. (One serving equals a half-cup of raw or cooked veggies or fruit or one cup of leafy greens.) You can eat fruits and vegetables alone or serve them as part of a rice or pasta dish, casserole, or side dish.

Whole grains: This is no time for a low carb/no carb diet! The carbohydrates and nutrients found in whole-grain foods—such as brown rice, whole-wheat bread or crackers, and whole-grain oats—are full of nutrients and provide fiber for your digestive tract. Every woman needs carbohydrates throughout her pregnancy, and getting them through whole grains is the healthiest way.

Protein: Every pregnant woman needs protein in her diet. Choose lean meats like chicken or turkey, or consume nuts, soy products like tofu and soy milk, eggs, and low-fat dairy products. Fish is also a healthy choice, but try to choose cold-water ocean fish. Farm-raised, river-caught fish and fish from some

lakes can contain too much mercury. High levels of mercury should be avoided during pregnancy. Be sure to fully cook all meats and eggs and avoid any raw fish such as that found in sushi. (For more details on what to avoid, see the next page.)

Sweets: It is true that sweets like candy, cookies, cake, and ice cream are generally low in nutritional value and high in calories, but you do not have to give them up altogether. If you want to have an occasional sweet treat, go ahead—just do so in moderation. You can even boost the nutritional value of your treat by adding fresh fruit topping to ice cream, making cookies and cakes with whole-wheat flour instead of white, or reducing or replacing some of the fat used in any recipe. Applesauce is a great replacement for recipes calling for vegetable or canola oil. Whatever you choose to eat, enjoy every bite!

Healthy Nutrition: What to Avoid

There are some foods you will have to give up during your pregnancy because they have the potential to harm you or your fetus. Some can even cause birth defects or pregnancy loss. Be sure to read the information provided below thoroughly, and remember, if you are wondering whether or not a food is safe to eat, err on the side of caution and do not eat it!

In general, you will want to follow these guidelines:

• Avoid eating raw sprouts or consuming any foods that are unpasteurized, such as unpasteurized milk, milk products, and soft cheeses.

- Wash your hands regularly before and during cooking and wash all produce extremely well, including organic fruits and vegetables.
- Keep all raw meats separate from all other foods in your refrigerator.
- If you remove a food from the refrigerator, it should not be kept out at room temperature for longer than two hours.
- To ensure food safely, check the temperature of your refrigerator and keep it between 35°F and 40°F.

You will need to avoid foods that, because of their preparation, carry the potential for either bacteria or parasites. Some also are high in certain minerals or are derived from plant-based ingredients that can harm the fetus. Your healthcare provider will be able to provide you with a more complete list, but the following categories of foods should be avoided.

Soft, unpasteurized cheeses: This group includes feta cheese, Camembert cheese, Mexican *queso blanco*, blue cheese, and Brie cheese. Because they are unpasteurized, they can contain Listeria, a bacterium that can only be killed through pasteurization. Listeria can cause preterm delivery or even a miscarriage. Check packaging to make sure your cheese is pasteurized before eating it.

Cold cuts and deli meat: Cold cuts from your deli also carry the risk of Listeria because they are not pasteurized. Even whole cooked rotisserie chicken and turkey should be avoided, unless they are hot and have not been refrigerated. Eating deli meat is safe only if you microwave it to kill any potential bacteria. Sealed

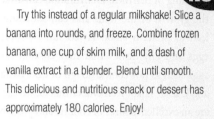

Frozen Banana "Shake"
Try this instead of a regular milkshake! Slice a banana into rounds, and freeze. Combine frozen banana, one cup of skim milk, and a dash of vanilla extract in a blender. Blend until smooth. This delicious and nutritious snack or dessert has approximately 180 calories. Enjoy!

cold cuts found in the refrigerator section are pasteurized and are safe to eat in moderation, but are not necessarily the healthiest choice.

High-mercury fish: Certain types of fish are relatively high in mercury and should be avoided. These include: shark, tilefish, swordfish, king mackerel, grouper, orange roughy, saltwater bass, and canned white albacore tuna. If you must eat tuna, the chunk light version is preferable and can be found in the canned fish section at the supermarket. Salmon, haddock, cod, flounder, catfish, sole, tilapia, and scallops are also safe to eat in reasonable quantities. Aim for a total of 12 ounces of acceptable fish each week.

Sushi and sashimi: Raw fish contain bacteria and parasites that have not been killed through cooking. Parasites can cause unpleasant health problems and are difficult to treat, especially when you are pregnant. Certain sushi rolls, such as spicy tuna rolls, can also contain fish that are high in mercury. Avoid all uncooked fish and any sushi made with cooked fish that is high in mercury.

Raw or runny eggs: Uncooked eggs can be contaminated with the bacteria Salmonella.

Salmonella can cause dehydration due to vomiting or diarrhea. Dehydration can affect the growth of the fetus and can sometimes lead to preterm labor. Avoid raw or runny eggs and any dishes that may contain raw eggs such as raw cookie dough or cake batter and Caesar salad. Remember that *cooked* eggs are an excellent source of choline and protein, so they can be enjoyed any time.

Caffeine: Consuming too much caffeine while pregnant can increase your risk of preterm labor, miscarriage, and a low birth weight baby. One study has found that consuming only 200 milligrams of caffeine per day resulted in twice the risk for miscarriages. Coffee is not the only beverage that contains caffeine. Many diet and regular sodas, energy drinks, certain teas, and even chocolate contain caffeine. To be

I drank at least three 16-ounce coffees a day. So, when I became pregnant, I had to make a drastic change! Here's what I did: I had two eight-ounce decafs in the morning and then drank eight ounces of skim milk with coffee-flavored syrup as a treat in the afternoon. I also avoided going into any coffee house until my second trimester, so I didn't feel tortured! It wasn't easy, but knowing that it was essential to the health of my baby kept me motivated. —*Paula, 38, mother of one*

safe, skip the caffeine altogether. But if you must have your morning joe, doctors recommend one cup or less of coffee per day. (Just remember: One cup equals eight ounces, not a giant mug!)

Artificial sweeteners: There are a variety of artificial sweeteners to choose from, and some are deemed safer than others. If you have specific concerns, talk to your healthcare provider.

- *Saccharine* (Sweet'N Low): This is an artificial sweetener found in individual packets and in many food products that claim to be "sugar free." Although there is no hard evidence that artificial sweeteners can cause harm to your fetus, saccharine will cross the barrier of the placenta and reach your baby.

- *Rebaudioside A* (Stevia): This plant-based sweetener has been recognized by the U.S. Food and Drug Administration (FDA) as safe during pregnancy.

- *Aspartame* (Equal or NutraSweet): This artificial sweetener is used in cold foods

What NOW?

Mercury Poisoning

Because consuming even small amounts of mercury can cause serious harm to your developing baby, the Environmental Protection Agency (EPA) has developed guidelines for avoiding foods that carry the risk of methyl mercury poisoning. But just because there are mercury risks from consuming certain fish, this does not mean you should avoid fish altogether. Fish contain high levels of healthy omega-3 fatty acids and provide a good source of protein. Eating up to 12 ounces of tuna, salmon, shrimp, catfish, or pollock per week is considered safe. There are published advisories on the mercury content of locally caught fish, so be sure to check before preparing for a meal.

and liquids. The FDA regards it as safe when used in moderation in pregnancy. Women with PKU, a metabolic disorder, should not use aspartame.

- *Sucralose* (Splenda): This sweetener is derived from sugar but has no calories. It is regarded as safe for pregnant women.

Herbal teas: Herbal tea can be made from any herb that exists in nature. Some herbs are perfectly safe, but others have medicinal properties that can be dangerous during pregnancy. Because herbal teas are not regulated by the FDA it is difficult to determine which products are safe. It is widely known, however, that some herbs found in tea can increase the risk of miscarriage or preterm labor. Sassafras and comfrey are two such herbs. If you must drink herbal teas, read the labels carefully or speak with an herbalist before consuming a particular tea

Spicy foods: Foods containing jalapeño peppers or other spicy peppers can cause heartburn during pregnancy. Heartburn is not dangerous to your pregnancy but it can cause considerable discomfort and the need for antacids. But if you like it hot, go ahead and indulge. Keep some Tums handy just in case!

Unwashed fresh vegetables: All fresh vegetables, even those that have been grown organically, should be washed thoroughly before eating to remove any potential allergens, chemicals, or bacteria.

Alcohol: It is a fact that drinking alcohol during pregnancy can cause mental and physical birth defects in your baby. It was once believed that small amounts of alcohol were safe in pregnancy, but we now know that even small amounts of alcohol taken regularly during pregnancy can lead to a condition known as fetal alcohol syndrome. This is a condition in which infants are born with the potential for cognitive impairments, unusual facial features, and behavioral issues. There is no cure for fetal alcohol syndrome except to avoid alcohol during pregnancy. Do not kid yourself: Moderate consumption of alcohol is as unsafe as excessive alcohol use. In fact, most doctors agree that pregnant women should avoid the consumption of alcohol altogether.

How Much Weight Gain Is Enough?

Fifty years ago, doctors often scolded women if they gained more than 20 pounds

For Dads and Partners:

Unusual Food Cravings

Macaroni and pickles? Hot sauce on celery? Chocolate-covered steak? Believe it. Unusual food cravings are common in pregnant women. Some doctors believe cravings are due to nutritional deficiencies, and others think hormones play a role. It is generally okay to give in to and accommodate your pregnant partner's food cravings. And, as you run out the door for ice cream and peanut butter, it will not hurt if you can avoid saying, "Yuck! Really?" Try to smile and remember what your partner is going through physically and emotionally. Mom-to-be simply cannot help herself!

during their pregnancy. Many women had a hard time sticking to this guideline, and babies were often born too small or with low birth weight.

Today, guidelines have loosened up. Doctors take an individual approach to the issue of weight gain during pregnancy, based on a woman's weight and body type when she becomes pregnant. Women who are slim and have a Body Mass Index (BMI) of less than 22 can benefit from gaining more rather than less weight during their pregnancy. Doctors generally consider a weight gain of 35 to 40 pounds appropriate. This will result in a healthier pregnancy for the mom-to-be and provide the extra nutrients needed by her fetus. For average women with a BMI of 22 to 26, doctors recommend a weight gain of 25 to 30 pounds. For women with a BMI greater than 26, gaining less than 20 pounds is recommended. If your BMI is 30 or over, gaining 15 pounds or less is healthiest. (See Chapter 1 on how to calculate your BMI.)

Things to Think About: Do No Harm

There is a lot to think about in the first month of pregnancy, and even more to get used to. Focus on beginning a healthy diet, taking prenatal vitamins, and limiting any harmful activities, foods, or toxins you need to avoid over the next nine months (such as smoking and drinking alcohol) in order to maximize the health of your baby. If your pregnancy is high risk from the beginning, make sure you make the appropriate appointments with your specialists, and keep them!

Rate of Weight Gain

Try to gain weight at an even rate during your pregnancy. Sometimes women make the mistake of eating too much in their first trimester (remember the myth about eating for two?) and gain unneeded pounds. An average weight gain of five pounds is plenty in those first three months and will help build your growing placenta and blood volume. Remember that, at the end of month three, your fetus will weigh far less than a pound. So be conscious of not overdoing it during your early pregnancy, and know that you will still gain plenty of weight in the second and third trimesters—half a pound to one pound per week!

The good news is that you can expect to lose about 15 pounds immediately after your baby is born. Any additional weight you have gained will come off over time as you continue your healthy eating and exercise habits. The important thing while pregnant is not to stress about weight gain! Instead, focus on giving yourself and your baby the best nutrition possible through healthy eating. Enjoy the beauty of your swelling belly!

To Weigh or Not to Weigh: That Is the Question

How you keep track of your weight during your pregnancy is up to you. Some women find it useful to keep a weekly record of weight gain in order to keep on course with their eating habits. Other women find it a nuisance or even depressing to check that scale each week. At each prenatal visit, your healthcare provider will weigh you and keep a record of how much or how little you are gaining, and for many women that is enough. Others may want to take advantage of weight gain calculators found online. They take your current weight and calculate for you, week by week, how much you should weigh as you progress through your pregnancy.

If you want to use an online weight-gain calculator, try www.indiacurry.com/women/pregcalc.htm.

The point is not to stress about weight, so think carefully about what will work best for you. If you are the type of woman who will obsess over every ounce you gain, better to let your healthcare provider keep track. Otherwise, use your scale or an online pregnancy tracker as a tool to enjoy your progress, and congratulate yourself for feeding yourself and your baby the nutrients you both need!

The first question I had for my doctor was: "How much weight should I gain?" I'd always kept myself in good shape, and was having a hard time wrestling with the idea of eating too much and, frankly, getting fat. I'll always remember her answer. She said: "Listen, eat healthy, stay active, and don't worry about it. Do you even want to know how much weight you're gaining?" I thought about it and I really didn't. I told her only to tell me if there was a problem and, to this day, I have no idea how much weight I gained while pregnant! I do know I had a seven-pound, 13-ounce healthy baby boy, and that's all that mattered! —*Sara, 36, mother of one*

Exercise: Just Do It— But Don't Overdo It!

It is not only safe to exercise during pregnancy but such physical activity is a sure way to keep your body healthy as it changes over the next nine months. If you already exercise, good for you! Keep doing what you are doing and check with your healthcare provider for any adjustments you may need to make to your regime as your pregnancy progresses.

If you have not been exercising, no worries! Now is the perfect time to begin a simple program that will strengthen your muscles, increase your aerobic capacity, and improve your sense of well-being. Choose something you think you will enjoy and start small. You can begin with walking. This, along with biking and swimming, is a perfect exercise—easy on your joints and easy to do with friends.

The following tips for keeping in tip-top shape will help you maintain an exercise program throughout your pregnancy.

- **Maintain a mild to moderate exercise regime:** Excessive exercise can divert blood and oxygen to your muscles and away from your baby. It can also lead to a low birth weight baby. Start slow and do not do any activity in which you are markedly short of breath.

- **Stay hydrated!** Remember to stay hydrated while exercising and do not become overheated. Too high a body temperature can cause spinal and brain defects in your baby. Wear lightweight clothes and avoid exercising during the hottest part of the day.

- **Listen to your body:** If you feel strain, dizziness, or fatigue or have any vaginal bleeding or discomfort, stop exercising right away.

- **Get your heart rate up:** Make sure your physical activity includes some form of aerobic exercise to bring your heart rate up—but not to the point of palpitations!
- **Let your balance guide you:** Your balance changes as your uterus enlarges. Keep track of your balance as you get further along in the pregnancy and adjust your exercise routine as necessary.
- **Make exercise enjoyable:** Choose an activity you genuinely enjoy—it is the only way to keep up your routine!

Healthy Exercise Ideas: Keep On Keeping On

As part of your healthy pregnancy plan, it is very important that you find physical activities that you enjoy doing. Remember, exercise is something that will benefit both your health and that of the fetus. Of course, because of changes to your body, you will need to modify your exercise regime as your pregnancy progresses. Again, your

Exercise Idea:

Kegels to Strengthen the Pelvic Floor

It is never too early to start doing Kegel exercises. Kegels work the muscles of the pelvic floor, including the urethra, rectum, and vagina. Strengthening these muscles will help you better tolerate your baby passing through the birth canal without ripping or tearing. To locate those muscles, imagine urinating and stopping your urination midstream. The great thing about Kegels is that you can do them anytime, anywhere and no one will know—even at work! Try doing three sets of ten Kegels once daily, working up to three sets of ten, three times per day.

My husband always joked that it was better to look good than to feel good. But I have to say, don't underestimate the power of cute maternity workout clothes! There's no reason to feel dowdy when you're putting so much effort into keeping healthy. Find something cute that you feel good in and wear it! Even if it is the same outfit over and over. Looking good makes you feel good, and you deserve it! —*Yolanda, 33, mother of three*

healthcare provider will suggest when it might be time to switch gears or exercises. The important thing is to make exercise a fun and safe part of your day throughout your pregnancy.

Biking: This exercise strengthens your leg muscles and increases your aerobic capacity. Be sure to wear a helmet, and aim to bike for 30 to 60 minutes at a time, at least three times per week. Bring a water bottle and stay hydrated. You will be thrilled at how easily you can become acclimated to this activity, and it may make you feel like a kid again! Biking is a great solo activity or one you can do with a friend or in a group.

Running or walking: Start by setting small goals for walking or running such as twice around the block or walking the dog for 15 minutes. Then increase your distance and pace as you acclimate to your routine. If you want to start running, begin by walking for two minutes, then running at a reasonable pace for two minutes. Gradually increase your running time while decreasing your

Swimming was the best exercise while I was pregnant. It was such a relief to get in the water and not feel the weight and awkwardness of my body for a while. There is also something so calming about flowing through the water. Whenever I was stressed or feeling down about the size of my body, I hit the water and all bad feelings washed away! —*Tina, 28, mother of two*

walking time until you are only running. Keep track of your breath, and slow down if you become winded. Work your way gradually to your goals and have fun. If you choose walking as your main exercise, a pedometer can help you track the distance you walk and increase your motivation to stick with the program—and a portable music player can make you want to dance, not just walk!

Swimming: This is an excellent activity during pregnancy. It is easy on your joints, provides an excellent aerobic workout, and as a bonus allows you to feel weightless while in the water! Swim for at least half an hour three times per week.

Weight lifting: Weight lifting during pregnancy should be done at your gym with skilled spotters. Whether you use free weights or weight machines, you will improve your muscle strength and tone, and stay strong throughout your pregnancy. There may be some safety considerations, so check with your healthcare provider to see if you should modify your routine.

Softball: This great group activity is excellent exercise during pregnancy. As long as there is no sliding into home plate, you will enjoy the camaraderie with your teammates and keep yourself healthy.

Tennis: This court sport provides a safe aerobic workout during pregnancy. Whether playing singles or doubles, you will improve muscle tone and stamina that will serve you well during labor and delivery.

Soccer: The "beautiful game" also provides a great aerobic workout, but it is best played only in your first trimester. Accidental injuries to the uterus are too great a risk later in your pregnancy. After your first trimester, you can switch to running or biking to keep your aerobic capacity high.

Basketball: Whether you play one on one or with a team, basketball is a fun way to keep in shape while pregnant. Just remember to play safe—no throwing elbows—and keep hydrated!

Nutrition Tip: Address Constipation!

The production of progesterone during pregnancy relaxes the intestinal muscles, causing many women varying degrees of constipation. Although uncomfortable, constipation does not pose any threat to your health or to the health of your baby. To help with constipation, drink plenty of fluids, especially water, and eat a diet high in fiber. Fiber is found in whole grains as well as in most fruits and vegetables.

Running group: Ideally, it would be fun to meet with other expectant women (or at least one other mom-to-be) and go running for a half hour or an hour, if you are skilled. If you cannot talk freely with your running mates, you are probably running or walking too fast.

Prenatal yoga or Pilates: These days, many yoga or Pilates studios offer targeted classes for pregnant women, which are safe and quite popular. Remember that hot yoga is not a safe option.

Fluid Retention: Another Reason to Keep Moving

Regular exercise and keeping active can alleviate fluid retention in your feet and legs. If you work at a desk, be sure to get up once every hour and move around. Sitting for three hours or more at a stretch will contribute to fluid retention.

Additionally, some women will have fluid weight gain as a result of developing pregnancy-induced hypertension (PIH). If you find you have a great deal of fluid retention, see your healthcare provider to make sure you do not have high blood pressure as well, which is consistent with PIH and pre-eclampsia (also known as toxemia) and which is a serious condition requiring close medical attention.

Health Issues of a High-Risk Pregnancy

Not everyone starts out healthy when they become pregnant. Many women have underlying health issues that need to be addressed throughout pregnancy. In addition to special-

I have type 2 diabetes and wanted to get pregnant, but my doctor said I had to get my blood sugar under control first. Having new motivation, I worked really hard changing my diet and exercising. I lost some excess weight and felt really great physically for the first time in years! I went into the pregnancy confident and healthy, and have twin boys to show for it! —*Catherine, 32, mother of two*

ized medical care, anyone who has a chronic illness can benefit from additional emotional support during pregnancy and practical support after the baby is born. Discuss your concerns with your partner if you have one and with other people who care about you.

The following are some health conditions that need extra attention during pregnancy.

Diabetes in Pregnancy

Type 2 diabetes has become epidemic in recent years, and so it is not uncommon to be diabetic and pregnant. While type 1 diabetes is less common, pregnant women with this condition need additional care as well. It is a good idea to see a diabetic specialist or endocrinologist if you find out you are pregnant and have diabetes. Type 1 and type 2 diabetes are usually diagnosed before pregnancy, but some women develop gestational diabetes, which only occurs during the pregnancy, usually in the last trimester.

Risks associated with diabetes: The biggest risk for women who have diabetes and do not take care of their blood sugar levels is that the baby can get too big; this means that you will not be able to deliver naturally. The baby can have severely low blood sugar after birth. Your baby can also have an increased risk of birth defects or be born too early. Your diabetes side effects—such as heart disease, visual problems, and kidney failure—can get worse if you do not care for yourself during pregnancy. You can have an increased risk of stillbirth or miscarriage. Fortunately, doctors have determined that keeping your blood sugar level normal in pregnancy eliminates these risks.

Additional care needed: If you are diabetic, you will need extra medical attention before you get pregnant to make sure you are ready to conceive. The doctors will examine your eyes for diabetic retinopathy and will check your blood pressure, your heart and blood vessels, your kidney function, your thyroid function, the function of your nervous system, and your Hemoglobin A1C level. The Hemoglobin A1C level is important since it represents an average of what your blood sugar levels have been for the last three months. In a sense, it measures how sugar-coated your red blood cells have been over their lifespan, which is 120 days or about three months.

Besides an obstetrician skilled in diabetic care and a diabetologist or endocrinologist, it is a good idea to see a nurse educator who will help you manage your blood sugar and other pregnancy issues. A registered dietician can help you with food choices that will support your own health and that of your baby. If you see any other specialists for health concerns related to your diabetes, you should see them more often in pregnancy. You may wish to see a counselor, clinical social worker, or psychologist to help you cope with the stress of pregnancy and having a baby. It is not too early to find a good neonatologist (a doctor who works with newborns) who is skilled in managing children of high-risk mothers or a good pediatrician who often can do the same.

Monitoring glucose levels: Monitoring your glucose (blood sugar) levels may require more effort during your pregnancy. Your doctor will usually have you check your blood sugar and write that value down at least four times per day. This makes sure you are on the right track and helps determine how much medication you need to take. If you are on pills for diabetes, you will likely work with a diabetic educator to learn how to use insulin. Insulin is considered the "gold standard" (or best and most effective treatment) for women who are diabetic and pregnant.

Diabetic? Monitor Your Blood Sugar!

If you have type 2 diabetes, it is important that you keep your blood sugar as normal as possible—even before you find out you are pregnant. This might involve changing your diet, your physical activity, and even your medications so you have normal numbers going into the pregnancy. Diabetes often worsens during pregnancy, so it should be monitored throughout your gestation.

High blood sugar is most dangerous in the first eight weeks of pregnancy. Because most women do not know they are pregnant until past the fifth week, there is precious little time to get blood sugar to normal levels. This is why it is a good idea to have normal blood sugar levels before you get pregnant.

Ideally, you should check your blood sugar when you first wake up, after having fasted for eight hours. You should check your level before each meal, an hour or two after a meal, and at bedtime. Severe diabetics may also need to check their blood sugar at around 2 a.m. or 3 a.m.

The American Congress of Obstetricians and Gynecologists (ACOG) has slightly different diabetic guidelines for pregnant women than those for women who are not pregnant. ACOG recommends fasting levels under 105 mg/dL and levels of 110 mg/dL before meals. If it is an hour or two before another meal, your level should be between 135 mg/dL and 155 mg/dL. It should not go below 65 mg/dL during the nighttime.

You should know that having such tight control over your blood sugar means you will run the risk of having low blood sugar. You may feel sweaty, dizzy, or have low energy. Keep orange juice or candies to suck on handy to bring up your blood sugar. You can also buy injectable sugar that you can take to bring up severely low blood sugar. One injectable is called glucagon. It raises the blood sugar when injected by you or by family members.

Your blood sugar can get too high if you do not match your food intake with the right amount of insulin, if you suddenly decrease your activity, if you become ill or overly stressed, or if you overeat. High blood sugar plus extra physical activity can make your sugars go higher. Watch out for weight loss, increased urination, and increased thirst.

High ketones: When you have persistent high glucose or are eating less than your body needs, your body may make certain chemicals called ketones. Ketones occur when you do not have enough insulin and your body uses fat in place of glucose. This can be harmful to your baby and to you. Fortunately, you can check your urine for ketones and make the proper adjustments as required. One condition you can develop if you have high ketones for a long time with diabetes is called diabetic ketoacidosis. If you develop this dangerous condition, you will experience frequent urination, heavy thirst, abdominal pain, tiredness, nausea, vomiting, confusion, muscle aches or stiffness, breath that smells fruity, or rapid breathing.

Ketones should be checked on a fasting basis, when you are ill, when your blood sugar runs high, or whenever you feel symptoms of hyperketosis. Your doctor may have other recommendations about when you should check your ketone level.

High Blood Pressure in Pregnancy

There is a significant difference between having pregnancy-induced hypertension (PIH) and having high blood pressure before you become pregnant. Preexisting high blood pressure makes for a high-risk pregnancy. You may be on medications that are not appropriate in pregnancy, and you may need to change your medications and your lifestyle in order to have a healthy pregnancy.

High blood pressure means there is excess force of blood going through your arteries. Your blood pressure is considered too high when the first number, the systolic blood pressure (the pressure when the heart is taking a beat), is more than 140 mm Hg and the diastolic number (when the heart is at rest) is more than 90. Due to the way blood flows in pregnancy, most women have much lower blood pressure than this during gestation.

The overall risks of high blood pressure or hypertension include strokes, heart disease, kidney failure, and heart failure.

High blood pressure in pregnancy does not automatically mean you will have a child with birth defects. Uncorrected high blood pressure can cause fetal distress and birth defects in children, especially if the high blood pressure was present before the pregnancy.

About six to eight percent of pregnancies are affected by high blood pressure. Most commonly, this problem occurs as gestational high blood pressure (PIH), and it is more common in first pregnancies. Women who are older than 35 when they become pregnant are more likely to have preexisting high blood pressure.

Rheumatic and Autoimmune Diseases and Pregnancy

Having an autoimmune disease—like systemic lupus erythematosus, scleroderma, or rheumatic joint disease—used to mean that you were advised not to get pregnant. More recently, it has been possible for a woman who has an underlying rheumatic or autoimmune disease to have a baby. It takes careful management by an obstetrician or perinatologist and an internist or rheumatologist to make the pregnancy successful. These are high-risk pregnancies, but they can be successful.

Pregnancy can make the inflammation in your joints and tissues worse, and medications used to treat these conditions are not always safe during pregnancy. The good news is that women with rheumatoid arthritis actually feel better during the pregnancy. Systemic lupus erythematosus and antiphospholipid syndrome can flare up and be worse, especially in the latter half of the pregnancy. Flares of

High Blood Pressure: Deal With It Early

The best time to deal with high blood pressure is before you get pregnant. Talk to your healthcare provider about your blood pressures and how you will keep them down during the pregnancy. Very few medications work in pregnancy; however, methyldopa is one of them. Your blood pressure should be under control before you get pregnant. To help ensure it is, keep the level of salt in your diet low and maintain a regular exercise program. If you are on an angiotensin-converting enzyme (ACE inhibitor) or Angiotensin II (AII) medications before pregnancy, talk to your healthcare provider about switching away from these before conceiving. It may be possible to go off medications altogether during pregnancy because your blood pressure is likely to drop in the first half of pregnancy or if you maintain a really healthy lifestyle during the pregnancy. Do not smoke or drink alcohol during the pregnancy as these activities elevate blood pressure.

lupus are painful but do not usually affect the baby. Flares of antiphospholipid syndrome increase the risk for blood clots in the arteries and veins. This can lead to miscarriage or stroke. Pregnancy-induced hypertension (PIH) is more common in antiphospholipid syndrome and can cause permanent kidney and liver damage in the mother as well as fetal distress and prematurity.

Some autoimmune diseases, such as Sjögren's disease or scleroderma, can actually affect the fetus. If you have these or any other autoimmune diseases, it is best to check with your rheumatologist before conceiving.

Rheumatic Diseases: Medications during Pregnancy

What NOW?

Ideally, women with rheumatic diseases who are pregnant should not take any medication at all. However, there are medications that can be taken safely and others that must be avoided. It is always wise to check with your doctor. He or she will determine the risk versus the benefit in order to decide which medication, if any, you should use.

Safe Medications	Unsafe Medications
• nonsteroidal anti-inflammatory (NSAID) medications*	• mycophenolate
	• methotrexate
• sulfasalazine	• cyclophosphamide
• antimalarials (certain ones only)	• anti-tumor necrosis factor
• corticosteroids	• rituximab
• cyclosporine	• warfarin
• heparin	
• azathioprine	
*Safe taken before 32 weeks	

Many rheumatic diseases put you at high risk for PIH, which can have a negative effect on the fetus. If you have a rheumatic disease and already have high blood pressure or kidney disease, you probably should not become pregnant. Women with antiphospholipid syndrome will likely be placed on low-dose aspirin and heparin in order to thin the blood. Some rheumatic diseases will cause birth defects that affect the heart rhythm of the baby.

You should be in good rheumatic control for at least three to six months before trying to get pregnant. Work with your doctor to determine what you should do about your medications. If you have a flare-up, you should be on no more than 10 milligrams of prednisone per day. Instead, hydroxychloroquine should be used as it is very safe in pregnancy. If you develop high blood pressure, this should be treated, too. Antiphospholipid syndrome should be treated with low-dose aspirin and/or heparin. Warfarin should be used after delivery to reduce the chance of blood clots.

Avoiding Teratogens

A teratogen is a substance that causes a higher-than-average rate of miscarriage or birth defects. There are medications, toxins, and foods that can act as teratogens in pregnancy. A teratogen can be a drug, infection, chemical, medication, radiation, or even a maternal health condition such as diabetes or high blood pressure.

Some teratogens are dangerous throughout the whole pregnancy, but most have their greatest effect on the embryo between weeks five and ten of gestation. This is when the embryonic organs are forming rapidly, including the circulatory system, nervous system, and skeletal system.

Thalidomide is an infamous teratogen used in the 1960s for treating nausea in women during their first trimester and for the prevention of miscarriage. It was later found that when given from days 21 through 36 of pregnancy, a fetus's limb development was affected; as a result, many children were born with stunted or absent limbs.

Another common teratogen is alcohol. Unlike thalidomide, alcohol can affect fetal development throughout the pregnancy. The major body parts that are affected are the brain and the facial features.

OK, here comes the part where you may feel like you need to live in a bubble for the next nine months—eating nothing but organic vegetables and brown rice while running on a treadmill, breathing through an oxygen mask. Not so! If you are generally living in a healthy environment, there is little that you will need to change now that you are planning to become (or already are) pregnant. However, it is important to make yourself aware of known chemicals, medications, and toxins that could be potentially harmful to your unborn child. Potentially unsafe foods were addressed earlier in this chapter; now we will consider medications and environmental hazards in light of their safety during pregnancy.

Medications and Pregnancy: Play It Safe

When you first find out that you are pregnant, it is time to take immediate stock of the medications you are taking—both over-the-counter and prescription. Before this moment, you may not have thought twice about taking a medication. Now is the time

Teratogens to Avoid during Your Pregnancy

- Accutane (acne medication)
- Alcohol
- ACE Inhibitors (like certain blood pressure medications or angiotensin-converting-enzyme inhibitors)
- Androgens (for instance, testosterone)
- Carbamazepine
- Cocaine
- Warfarin or Coumadin
- Methotrexate (an anti-folic acid medication)
- Diethylstilbestrol (DES)
- Lead
- Mercury
- Lithium
- Phenytoin
- Tetracycline (acne medication)
- Streptomycin
- High doses of vitamin A
- Valproic acid (a medication for seizures)

to shift your thinking; remember that everything you consume has the potential to affect your baby. Talk to your healthcare provider immediately about your medications and find out what is safe to take now that you are pregnant. But be sure not to stop your medication unless directed to do so.

There are many medications that you may use safely during pregnancy, and many that you must absolutely avoid. The following are guidelines, but be sure to tell your healthcare provider about all the medications you are taking—both over-the-counter and prescription—so that he or she can keep you and your baby safe during pregnancy.

Don't get lost in information overload! And don't let any of the information scare you. You will only be pregnant with this one baby one time. Be informed, be healthy, and be positive. Enjoy every single minute of your pregnancy— morning sickness and all! —*Jan, 32, mother of three*

Determining Medication Safety

The Food and Drug Administration (FDA) has categorized medications with regard to their safety for use during pregnancy. A medication is categorized based on the amount of research done on the drug and what the medical field has learned from experience prescribing the medication. New medications and medications with little research when used during pregnancy rank lower.

Below are the categories that reflect the safety of medications in pregnancy:

Category A: There have been controlled studies on pregnant women indicating no risk to the fetus.

Category B: Either well-designed human studies show no risk, despite animal studies that show adverse effects, or animal studies show no risk to the fetus, but there are not adequate studies done on humans. This category contains a slight possibility of risk to the fetus, but is generally considered safe.

If a medication has not been listed in pregnancy Category A or Category B, it should be used with caution and only under the advice of your physician. Many medi-cations may carry more benefit than risk. Others clearly have risks that outweigh the benefits. This risk/benefit balance varies from person to person.

Category C: No good human studies have been done. Animal studies have shown adverse effects on the fetus. However, in some circumstances, the benefits of these medications may outweigh the risks.

Common Category C dilemmas are those such as using Compazine during pregnancy, taking Diflucan for fungal infections, and using some antide-pressants (see below).

Category D: Studies have shown adverse effects on human fetuses, but in select cases, the benefit of taking the medication may still outweigh the risk.

For Category D drugs, the benefits are generally not superior to the risks of taking the medication. One Category D drug is alcohol; another is lithium, a drug used to treat bipolar disorder. Many chemotherapy drugs used for cancer treatment are consid-ered Category D.

Category X: Studies have shown birth defects in humans, and these drugs should never be taken during pregnancy.

Category X drugs carry such a significant threat to the fetus that they should never be used during pregnancy. These drugs include Accutane, used to treat cystic acne; Tegison or Soriatane, used to treat psoriasis; and thalidomide, which is fortunately not used anymore but was formerly prescribed for first trimester nausea or the prevention of miscarriage.

Medications Requiring
Careful Consideration

If you take any of the following medications, you may want to talk with your healthcare provider.

Antidepressants and other psychiatric medications: Paxil is a commonly used medication for the treatment of depression and anxiety disorders. The FDA rates Paxil as a Category D drug, which means that research studies have shown some problems in babies whose mothers took these drugs during pregnancy. Even Category D medications may sometimes be used during pregnancy if the benefit outweighs the risk.

If you are a woman who is taking Paxil or another antidepressant during pregnancy or just before pregnancy, it is a good idea to talk to your healthcare provider about the risk versus the benefit of taking the medication. Some women can get by without taking medication during their pregnancy, while other women have severe symptoms and may need to change to a safer antidepressant. Don't stop taking any antidepressant medication abruptly without medical supervision. If you suffer from depression or other mental health problems, it is crucial for you to receive treatment and support during pregnancy and after childbirth. This may involve carefully monitored medication but also may include psychotherapy, prenatal support groups, and other forms of help that will allow you to feel as well as possible throughout your childbearing experience.

The same is true for women who are pregnant and are taking antipsychotic medication. If the psychosis is severe enough to

I paid two teenagers who lived across the street to change my cat's litter box each day. They loved our two cats, so the cats benefited from playtime as well. It may seem silly for me to have gone to such lengths, but do not put your health at risk and potentially jeopardize the health of your baby by touching that litter box!
—*Joann, 31, mother of two*

greatly impact the mental health of the mother so that she cannot function, the choice to take the antipsychotics may need to be made. If, on the other hand, the woman is relatively stable, she might get by with therapy and close monitoring and be able to stop the medication.

Aspirin and nonsteroidal anti-inflammatory drugs (NSAIDs): Taking these drugs carries a risk of lowering blood platelet count and increasing bleeding time. Commonly used products under this category include aspirin, naproxen (Aleve), and ibuprofen (Advil and Motrin). Many women substitute acetaminophen (Tylenol) for NSAIDs because acetaminophen works for pain without carrying the risk of bleeding problems. You should only take NSAIDs on the advice of your healthcare provider.

Antihistamines: These are commonly used for the treatment of hay fever, allergies, and sometimes respiratory infections. They constrict the blood vessels and reduce stuffiness, itchy or watery eyes, and runny nose. Unfortunately, there is some thought that these drugs can constrict the blood vessels supplying the placenta and fetus, causing risk to the fetus. Antihistamines commonly taken include Benadryl, Claritin, Allegra, and Zyrtec. Consult your healthcare provider before taking any of these medications.

Oral contraceptives: It is usually a good idea to stop using the pill and use another form of contraception until you have at least one normal period before trying to conceive so that you have can have a better idea of when you become pregnant. If you discover you are pregnant while still taking oral contraceptives, discontinue taking them, but don't be alarmed, as they have not been shown to cause birth defects.

Safe Medications

When it comes to any medication, never go it alone. Always ask your healthcare provider about the risks versus the benefits of taking any medication, prescription or otherwise. However, the following list will give you an idea of what is considered safe to take during pregnancy.

- **Tylenol (acetaminophen)** is a good pain medication for things such as headaches or muscle aches.
- **Aldomet (methydopa)** is one of the few medications safe for the treatment of hypertension during pregnancy.
- **Actifed** is a medication that should be avoided during the first trimester, but after that it can be used for nasal congestion, especially from allergies.
- **Budesonide** is an appropriate medication for asthma or allergic sinusitis.

Handy, Safe Medications: What NOW? Keep in Stock!

Rather than send your partner on a midnight run to an all-night pharmacy, keep the following in your medicine cabinet in case you need them!

- **Tylenol:** For fever and for pain such as a headache or body aches.
- **TUMS:** They're kind of chalky to chew but they work fast for heartburn.
- **Ranitidine:** If your heartburn is unrelenting, your obstetrician might recommend that you take ranitidine once or twice a day to prevent heartburn from occurring in the first place.
- **MiraLAX or milk of magnesia:** Constipation is common in pregnancy and can be treated using either of these medications.
- **Ginger:** You can take ginger pills or consume candied ginger for the treatment of nausea.
- **Claritin or Benadryl:** If you suffer from allergies or hay fever, you should have these medications on hand to use sparingly.
- **Monistat cream:** Yeast infections are common in pregnancy and are easily treated with Monistat, which comes in many different forms.
- **Loperamide:** This is a good drug for occasional diarrhea. See your healthcare provider if you have persistent or bloody diarrhea.

- **Chlorpheniramine or Diphenhydramine** are commonly used drugs for hives or for hay fever symptoms.
- **Pseudoephedrine,** while not used as commonly as before, is a drug you can get from the pharmacist for nasal congestion.
- **Claritin or Benadryl** can be used sparingly in pregnancy to treat internal allergies or hives and hay fever.
- **Hydrocortisone Cream or Benadryl Cream** can be used to treat various rashes.

- **Bacitracin or Neosporin** are ointments that are used to treat skin infections.
- **Clindamycin** is an antibiotic that can be used for bladder infections and other types of infections in pregnancy.
- **Erythromycin** is an antibiotic commonly used for the treatment of respiratory infections.
- **Penicillin** (including Amoxil, amoxicillin, Augmentin, methicillin, and carbenicillin) are all antibiotics that are used for a number of bacterial infections.
- **Macrobid, Penicillin, Cephalosporins, and Augmentin** are antibiotics commonly used in pregnancy for bladder infections.
- **Flagyl (metronidazole)** is an antibiotic used for gastrointestinal or urinary tract infections.
- **Zithromax (azithromycin)** is an antibiotic commonly used for respiratory infections.
- **Zovirax (acyclovir)** can be used to treat cases of herpes during pregnancy.
- **Dextromethorphan** is a cough medication that comes in products like Robitussin DM.
- **Dramamine (dimenhydrinate)** is a common treatment for motion sickness.
- **Ginger, Pyridoxine, and Metoclopramide** are safe medications to take for nausea.
- **Metamucil, Colace (Docusate), Dulcolax, milk of magnesia, and MiraLAX** are common treatments for constipation that can be used throughout pregnancy.
- **TUCKS, Preparation H, and Anusol** can be used for the management of hemorrhoids in pregnancy.
- **Senekot** is a common treatment for constipation.

- **Imodium AD (loperamide)** treats temporary diarrhea.
- **Kaopectate** is a perfect treatment for women with diarrhea.
- **Gas-X (simethicone)** is a medication used for gas or bloating.
- **Ranitidine and Cimetidine** are used in pregnancy for the treatment of heartburn or indigestion.
- **Maalox and Mylanta** are liquid medications you can use for the treatment of heartburn or indigestion.
- **TUMS** is a chewable medication often used for the treatment of heartburn.
- **Parlodel or Carbergoline** is a good treatment for high prolactin levels.
- **Insulin, Micronase, and Glucophage (metformin)** are treatments for diabetes type 1 or diabetes type 2. Your doctor will know which medication is appropriate for you.
- **Thyroid Hormone or Levothyroxine** is a good treatment for women who are also dealing with a low thyroid condition

Things to Think About: Cord Blood Banking

In cord blood banking, some of your infant's cord blood, which contains many stem cells, is isolated at the time of birth and stored at a facility for a yearly fee. This cord blood is used if your child later develops blood cancer or other diseases in which stem cells are needed to treat the ailment. Sometimes siblings can also be helped through this cord blood. Spend some time considering cord blood banking with your partner and be sure and tell your healthcare provider if you are planning to bank your baby's cord blood.

(hypothyroidism) during pregnancy.

- **Unisom (doxylamine)** is about the only medication that is safe for insomnia.
- **Monistat** is a commonly used medication for the treatment of yeast infections.

Environmental Hazards and Toxins to Avoid

As you may discover, the world can look very different to you when you are pregnant. Environmental hazards you may have never noticed or thought about are important to consider now that you are pregnant. Let's take a virtual look around you and sort through those things in your environment you should avoid while pregnant.

Beware of Infections

Viruses and bacteria can be environmental hazards. There are a number of infections that can result in birth defects or death of the fetus if they occur during pregnancy. While you may not have complete control over your exposure to illness, you should try your utmost to avoid these particularly serious infections. The rubella virus, sometimes known as German measles, is generally a mild illness in children but can cause serious birth defects when contracted during pregnancy. Another infection, cytomegalovirus or CMV, is commonly carried by adults without symptoms but can also cause birth defects, fetal death, or illness in the newborn. Pregnant women can get CMV through sexual contact or through contact with the saliva or urine of infected children. Toxoplasmosis is caused by a parasite and is transmitted through contaminated or undercooked food or contact with the feces

What NOW?

Precautions against Infections during Pregnancy

- Wash your hands thoroughly and frequently, especially after using the bathroom and before eating.
- Avoid unnecessary contact with anyone who is ill. Seek advice from your healthcare provider if you have a child who is ill.
- Get tested for sexually transmitted diseases and abstain or use condoms unless you are in a monogamous relationship with someone who has tested negative for sexually transmitted infections.
- If you have a cat, have someone else clean the litter box, and wear gloves when digging in garden soil.

of an infected cat (see next page). It can be transmitted to your baby if you are infected while pregnant. Sexually transmitted diseases such as syphilis, gonorrhea, and chlamydia are treatable before and during pregnancy but can cause grave consequences to mother and baby if they go undetected. Tell your healthcare provider immediately if you believe you have been exposed to any of these infections or any other serious illness.

Radiation Exposure

Radiation exposure is also dangerous during pregnancy. This includes the radiation that might be needed as part of cancer treatment, or even radiation exposure that comes from having too many X-rays, especially if the uterus is not protected with a lead shield. Radiation can cause a variety of birth defects, depending on the length of the exposure and the stage of pregnancy when the radiation exposure occurred.

Housecleaning Products and Related Chemicals

General household cleaning products are safe, but harsh cleaning products, such as oven cleaners or products containing bleach, need to be avoided. You may wish to avoid excessive exposure to fresh household paint (although studies about any possible harm have mixed results), and pesticides or insecticides are to be avoided.

Cat Litter

Cat feces can contain toxoplasmosis, a parasite that is dangerous in pregnancy. You can have a blood test to determine if you are immune to toxoplasmosis. To be safe, if you have a cat, have someone else in your home change the litter. (Lucky you!) If you must change the litter yourself, wash your hands thoroughly afterward!

Foods That May Contain Bacteria or Mercury

See page 29 for information on foods to avoid.

Hair Perms and Dyes

There are strong chemicals in these hair products. Hair dyes generally are considered safe during pregnancy, but it is usually recommended to delay their use until after the first trimester.

Insect Repellent

It is better to stay indoors than use insect repellent; if you use insect repellent containing DEET, however, know that it has been well researched and found to have no effect on the fetus during the second or third trimester. There has been no research on DEET and breast-feeding. Because mosquitoes and ticks can carry disease, limited use of insect repellants may be necessary.

Products Used in Hobbies and Crafting

If you engage in hobbies and crafting in which paint thinners, oil-based paint, lacquer, cleaning solvents, varnish remover, lead (in stained glass), adhesives, and certain plastics are used, you should reduce their use during your pregnancy. There is no hard-and-fast research indicating that these products definitely cause birth defects, but experts still agree their use should be limited.

Phthalates

Phthalates are found in plastic bottles (such as water bottles), floors, toys, and shower curtains. Phthalates have hormonal effects on the body, including the unborn fetus.

Bisphenol A (BPA)

This chemical agent is also found in bottled water and in certain food

BPA numbers

Choose safer plastics:

1 PETE | 2 HDPE | 4 LDPE | 5 PP

Plastics to avoid:

3 V — PVC or vinyl can contain phthalates | 6 PS — Polystyrene Foam | 7 Other — Can contain Bisphenol A

Read the recycling numbers on the bottom of cups and bottles so you can choose safer plastics and avoid BPA.

What NOW?

Seatbelt Alert!

Although you might be shocked to even consider them as an environmental hazard, seatbelts can pose a danger to your fetus as you progress in your pregnancy. Luckily, however, this is one environmental hazard over which you have a great deal of control. As your pregnancy advances, you need to make sure that the lap belt of the seatbelt fits low, in the area of your pubic bone. You should always wear the shoulder harness while pregnant.

and beverage containers. Bisphenol A is considered toxic to the unborn fetus to a small degree. BPA-free bottles and plasticware are commonly sold now. (Looking ahead, BPA-free toothbrushes are even available for children!)

Teflon Chemicals

These are used in stain-proofing of carpet, food packaging, and clothing. Your greatest risk is in working in a factory that uses this chemical regularly.

Tough Habits to Break

Much of our health relies on our habits and lifestyle. Your baby's health before birth is affected by your habits and lifestyle as well.

Smoking

Smoking is one of the most difficult habits to break, but if you smoke, it is critical to the health of your baby that you stop.

Your baby is smoking, too: When a pregnant woman smokes, it can damage her baby's lungs and deprive the fetus of oxygen. Smoking can cause or contribute to a long list of birth defects and dangerous conditions that affect mother and baby. These include low birth weight, which creates serious risks for the baby, and disabilities that can last throughout the child's life. You should be aware that your own smoking is dangerous for the baby, but so is secondhand smoke, which comes from being around others who smoke, and even "thirdhand" smoke, which is the residue left in carpets, clothing, and other items in a home or car where someone has been smoking. There is research to suggest that smoking and breathing secondhand smoke can cause genetic damage to the fetus.

Breathing free for everyone's sake: If you are struggling to stop smoking, the website smokefree.gov has some excellent resources specifically for pregnant women who want to quit. If your partner or another household member is a smoker and is reluctant to quit, ask him or her to accompany you to your healthcare provider to discuss the issue. When you, your partner, or other family members quit smoking, you give your child the added bonus of your improved health and life expectancy—and you will all smell better!

Recreational Drugs

If you use marijuana, cocaine, or any other recreational drug, you need to stop (preferably before conception). Get help if you can't stop using on your own or if you have painful personal issues that underlie your drug use. If you are reading this book, you must care about your pregnancy and your baby. Be honest with your healthcare provider and get the help you need. Street drugs can cause birth defects, serious behavioral and physical dis-

Safety First at Work

You need to know when your job is hazardous to your health and take measures to avoid those things that could be bad for you or your baby. Proper precautions can help you avoid miscarriage and preterm birth. These are things you should do:

- Keep your work hours at a reasonable level.
- Avoid exposure to toxins and other harmful substances. Read labels when in doubt.
- Avoid repetitive heavy lifting as this can trigger preterm labor.
- Keep noise levels to a minimum.
- Avoid prolonged exposure to cold or heat.
- Avoid high-stress environments.

Remember that your balance and agility are greatly reduced as your pregnancy advances. This means that jobs that require you to be graceful and well balanced are to be done carefully—or not at all—during the third trimester.

abilities, miscarriages, and developmental disorders. Remember, alcohol is a drug with devastating effects in pregnancy as well, and if you are unable to stop drinking, you need to seek help.

Pregnancy on the Job: Be Safe, Be Comfortable

Working at your job while pregnant may call for some some modifications such as adjusting your work schedule or environment to stay safe and comfortable. Most women continue working throughout most or all of their pregnancy, and there are things you may wish to consider to make this a pleasant experience.

Nausea

In their first trimester many women experience nausea and vomiting that can interfere with your productivity and comfort if you are at work. To minimize nausea, avoid anything that you know triggers it, such as certain smells or the sight of certain foods. Consuming small amounts of food frequently during the day can be helpful. Don't let your stomach get too empty or too full. Keep simple snacks handy, like crackers or bread, which can help settle your stomach. Ginger is a natural way to ease nausea. Drinking ginger ale or ginger tea or nibbling on candied ginger can help. Nausea is worse if you are dehydrated, so make sure you keep a steady supply of water available at your desk or workspace. See Chapter 4 for more information about handling morning sickness.

"I'm Sooooooo Tired!": Fatigue at Work

Think about it—your entire body has suddenly shifted gears and its entire purpose is to grow and house another human being. That is hard work—especially in the first trimester—and many women have to handle frequent fatigue. If you do not work outside your home, you may be able to rest when you need to. Most women in the workplace need to use some creativity to find ways to stay productive and alert.

Try some of the following to stay rested and productive at work:

- Eat foods that have plenty of protein and iron in them. This improves your hemoglobin and fortifies your cells.

- If possible, allow yourself to take frequent breaks. Rest and close your eyes or take a short walk before going back to what you were doing.

- If your job requires a lot of physical activity, you may have to cut back a bit. This holds true at home, where everything doesn't need to be perfectly clean all the time.

- Pay attention to fitness and get enough exercise to increase your energy level but not so much that you deplete your energy level.

- Get plenty of sleep. Go to bed as early as you can and try to get seven to nine hours of sleep nightly. Make sure you rest on your left side as much as possible since this maximizes blood flow to the uterus and minimizes swelling of the legs.

No Heavy Lifting

Whether lifting boxes at work or groceries and toddlers at home, while pregnant you need to pay attention to proper lifting. Lift with bent knees and try not to lift more than 30 to 40 pounds, especially at the end of the pregnancy. When you take a rest from heavy lifting, try to move around so your muscles and tendons stay loose. When sitting, rest your arms on a back rest and use adjustable armrests for the most comfortable sitting experience. Get up at least once per hour so you can maintain circulation in your legs and minimize edema (swelling). Sometimes a small cushion or pillow behind your lower back can ease back pain.

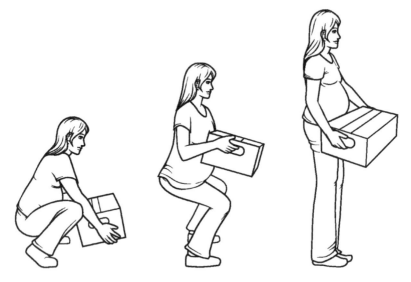

Proper lifting technique

While you should not be lifting heavy objects, if you have to lift anything at work, it is best to know how to do it safely. Don't lean over to pick up an object. Bend your knees to squat close to the item. Keep your back straight and your legs and feet apart. Tighten your stomach muscles and use your strong leg muscles to lift. Avoid twisting or reaching. Ask for help when you need it. You may need to talk to your supervisor about adjusting your job responsibilities if you normally are required to lift heavy items.

Take a Load Off

If you have a job where you stand for hours at a time, you may begin to have blood pool in your ankles, feet, and lower legs, which is known as edema. Standing is also hard on the back, and you may have more backaches. One good method of avoiding edema is to put your leg up on a crate or box for an hour or so and then switch to the other side. This should be done along with wearing comfortable shoes and wearing supportive hose to put pressure on the fluid in the legs and keep them energized.

Bending should also be done carefully while pregnant. Make sure you begin by bending at the knees and not at the waist. Carry any load as close to your body as you can and do not twist your back while lifting objects, especially heavy ones.

Occupational Exposure to Toxins

If you work at a desk behind a computer, you have little to be concerned about at work. However, industrial jobs, jobs in high pollution areas, and agricultural jobs in which there is exposure to pesticides can all potentially affect your fetus. Minor or occasional exposure to household chemicals or pesticides is generally considered safe. But if you are exposed daily at work to herbicides and pesticides or you have a factory job where you are exposed to high-risk chemicals, you will need to make some changes.

Getting your nails polished in pregnancy carries almost no risk, but if you work in a nail salon during pregnancy, you may need to change your profession until after your baby is born. Prolonged daily exposure to salon chemicals can be dangerous for your

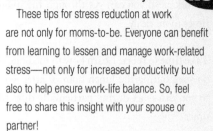

Stress Reduction Is for Everyone

These tips for stress reduction at work are not only for moms-to-be. Everyone can benefit from learning to lessen and manage work-related stress—not only for increased productivity but also to help ensure work-life balance. So, feel free to share this insight with your spouse or partner!

fetus. Consult your healthcare provider with specific questions about potential workplace toxins.

Work Stress Reduction

Many women have stressful jobs. Whether managing a multichild household or keeping up with work deadlines, overtime, and complex interaction with other coworkers, you will want to adjust your work life to reduce stress. Stress can adversely affect anyone, including you—and your fetus. While working, try some of the following ideas to reduce your stress level:

Learn to prioritize: Prioritize your tasks, manage your workload, and take control of your life. If you have a job with many responsibilities, talk to your manager about what can be done to help keep your workload reasonable and safe as you progress with your pregnancy. Some things can be delegated or eliminated altogether so you have less to do.

Keep communication open: If you stay calm when talking with others and negotiate difficulties as soon as they happen, you will experience less stress. If you find yourself frustrated, share these things with caring coworkers so you can get through the rough times more easily.

Take time to relax: Learn how to meditate or do yoga during the lunch hour or after work so you can relax during particularly difficult times.

Learn to say "no": Say no to events, projects, and demands on your time that are not essential or that create rather than relieve stress.

Other Miscellaneous Risks

There are several things you may need to avoid to keep you and your baby in excellent health throughout your pregnancy.

Dry-cleaned maternity clothes: Make sure your dry cleaner is reputable and uses chemicals within established guidelines. Better yet, save yourself the worry and money and buy only washable maternity clothes.

Bottled water in plastic containers: These contain phthalates, which can be harmful to the fetus. If the bottle is open, throw it away after a week. Do not reuse bottles because there is always a chance of bacterial contamination of the reused water. Tap water from municipal water systems is generally considered safe.

Plastic wrap: This carries the chance of breaking down into dangerous plastic particles when heated with food. Use parchment paper or waxed paper instead.

Nonstick cookware: If Teflon-lined cookware is used at low temperatures and with utensils that aren't abrasive, it should be completely safe.

Partners Are Pregnant, Too!

Remember that even though your partner is not carrying the baby, he or she is pregnant too! Your partner is experiencing a unique set of concerns, thoughts, and feelings about your pregnancy. While you may be garnering all the attention and well wishes, remember to take time to find out how your partner is feeling and pay attention to his or her needs, too.

Because your partner is not experiencing the same physical and emotional changes that you are, the pregnancy might not feel as real to him or her. Issues can arise in many areas of your life together. Exhaustion and nausea can interfere with your social life, and it is common for issues to arise around sex as a partner may often worry about hurting you or the baby during sexual activity.

Your partner may have concerns about money and about how much caring for a baby will cost. Your role as a life partner is changing and may be disconcerting to your spouse or partner. Joy and excitement may give way to ambivalence and anxiety. So work together and communicate! Keep your partner involved in your pregnancy.

The bond between the mother and her unborn child begins in early pregnancy, and you may find that this bond is getting in the way of your relationship with your partner. If you see this happening, talk about it with your partner and schedule some quality "alone time" as a couple.

Helpful Tips for the Other Expectant Parent

What NOW?

It is important that both Mom-to-be and her partner are involved in the pregnancy. To this end, here are some tips for the one who may not be physically carrying the baby but who is equally invested in the journey!

- Try to involve yourself in the pregnancy as early as possible. It may be especially helpful to read about first trimester pregnancy issues, because they seem less obvious than the changes in later pregnancy.

- Take part in selecting who will deliver the baby and where you will go to have the baby. If you are planning a home birth, make sure you are prepared to handle the extra responsibility.

- While you do not have to go to all prenatal visits, go to some of them so you can see the progress of the pregnancy and listen to the heartbeat!

- If your partner has an ultrasound, by all means attend. If the ultrasound is at 18 weeks or later, you and your partner can decide if you want to know the sex of the child.

- Read a book on pregnancy—like this one! You will understand what is going on as your baby develops and understand the changes Mom-to-be is going through emotionally as well as physically.

- Know that it costs a great deal of money to have a baby. Make sure your insurance will cover the pregnancy and delivery and make sure you are financially prepared for the diapers, formula, toys, and baby furniture.

- Talk about any issues that arise in your sex life and seek help from a counselor or therapist if you cannot work things out together.

- Keep the lines of communication open so that neither of you feels isolated or unheard.

Sex and Pregnancy: A Game Changer

A couple's attitude toward sex can change with pregnancy. This is especially true if there has been a previous miscarriage, which is sometimes mistakenly thought of as being related to sex in pregnancy. But a happy, satisfying sex life is as important during pregnancy as it was before pregnancy. Be sure to be open and honest with your partner about any issues, fears, or feelings you may have regarding your sex life. Here are some things to consider:

- When pregnant, a woman's breasts enlarge and become tender, especially during the first trimester of pregnancy. Partners need to be aware of the increase in tenderness of the breasts and should be gentle.

- The first trimester often comes with extreme fatigue, nausea, and vomiting. If this is the case, a woman may simply feel too miserable to have sex. On the other hand, the increase in blood supply to the sexual organs of the woman make the sexual experience more intense and enjoy-

Once a week, I sat down with my husband and our pregnancy book. I explained what was going on in my body and how the development of the baby was progressing. It became a really special time for us to bond over the pregnancy, and I think he felt much more a part of things. It was great for our relationship, too!—*Tamara, 40, mother of three*

able, especially in the second trimester. Talk about your feelings during this time and find creative ways to adjust to the situation.

- In the third trimester of pregnancy, the belly is very large and this interferes with typical sexual intercourse. Be as creative as possible and try different sexual positions that may work better for both of you.

- A pregnant woman's hormones are increased in pregnancy. This can result in a marked increase in vaginal secretions. Some women, on the other hand, have decreased secretions, so the couple may need to use a vaginal lubricant (such as K-Y Jelly) to make sex easier.

- Women who are pregnant are at greater risk of urinary tract and vaginal infec-

tions—some of which cannot easily be treated with typical medications during pregnancy. In order to combat this, it may be advisable to cut back on sex or use condoms to prevent infections.

- Sex may cause a small amount of bleeding during the first trimester. Don't assume that sex is the cause, however: *Call your healthcare provider if you notice bleeding at any point during the pregnancy.*

- Intercourse is generally safe for the baby in pregnancy, so couples need not worry that their activity will do any harm, except in the specific circumstances mentioned below. In fact, the baby is well protected by the cervix, the cervical plug, muscular tissue, and the amnion—so don't worry!

For Dads and Partners: Ask for Wisdom

While the journey of pregnancy is a shared joy, it can also strain your relationship with your spouse or partner. Partners may hesitate to share their fears, questions, or concerns. If you are the partner of a pregnant woman, look for role models—friends or family members who have already gone through the birthing process and understand what you are going through right now. Such persons can provide a wealth of support and information for you. Take these individuals aside and ask them a few questions about their own experiences. Remember, people differ in their willingness to share openly, so be sure to ask respectfully and don't press for answers if your role model seems reluctant.

These are questions you may want to ask:

- How did you have an adequate sex life during the pregnancy?
- What was labor like, and how did you best help your pregnant partner?
- What is your role in the family now that you have children?
- How has your love life changed since you became parents?
- Were there any aspects of pregnancy and delivery that surprised you?
- How did you take care of yourself during the pregnancy and in the days after the delivery?
- What were you afraid of during the pregnancy and delivery?

My husband was sincerely afraid of hurting the baby during sex. No matter how many times I told him that just wasn't true, he couldn't get past it. Finally, I asked him to come with me to one of my OB appointments to talk with the doctor about it. She was awesome, and even used illustrations to explain why sex was perfectly safe for our baby. Life was good after that! —*Bonnie, 31, mother of two*

- If you suffer from placenta previa (where the placenta blocks the cervix), sexual activity is prohibited. Sexual activity should also be avoided if a woman has a risk of preterm labor. This is because women who are pregnant have longer orgasms that can contract the uterus for too long a time. If you know you have ruptured your membranes, do not have sexual intercourse and see your healthcare provider right away!

My husband and I had just begun talking about having a baby. So when I started throwing up every morning and became utterly exhausted, I thought I had the flu. My flu turned out to be a healthy baby boy! My husband and I still joke that we can't talk about "you know what" or we'll have another four kids!

—*Sally, 32, mother of four*

Chapter 3

Month One—Weeks 1 through 4

If a journey of a thousand miles begins with a single step, then your pregnancy journey begins with a single incident—conception! Whether you are completely surprised by your pregnancy or have been trying to conceive, the first few weeks are generally an anticipatory time of ovulating, having sex, and waiting it out to see if you miss your period. Since you usually ovulate after the first couple of weeks of your cycle, you spend the next couple of weeks anticipating whether or not your pregnancy test will be positive because it is already week four before you can find out if you are pregnant!

But whether you are prepared for pregnancy or surprised by your current condition, there are some interesting things to know about what is happening with your body and your baby during this first month. In this chapter, we will answer the following questions:

- What do I do if I've missed my period but my pregnancy test is still negative?
- How will I know I'm pregnant, and at what point am I actually considered pregnant?
- What happens at the very beginning of pregnancy?
- What causes twin or triplet pregnancies?

My husband and I had been trying to conceive for about nine months, and I confess I was beginning to lose hope. We were away on vacation when I was next ovulating, and had sex on all the right days. The night we returned home, I remember waking up out of a sound sleep because I'd rolled over on my stomach and my breasts were so tender and sore. I figured my period was coming, but I'd never felt such soreness before. I'd started to urinate more as well, but it was summer and I simply thought this was the result of drinking lot of fluids. I'd so convinced myself I'd never get pregnant that, when my period was about three days late, I didn't think about that either. I happened to mention it to a friend at work who was also trying to get pregnant and she said, "You know, silly, you might be pregnant. Take the test!" I just knew she was wrong. I waited two more days, and when my period still hadn't arrived, I took the home pregnancy test. I was shocked to see it was positive! Now I know that my body was showing me all the signs, but my mind was somewhere else. Pay attention to the signs and never give up hope! (And if your breasts are as tender as mine were, wear a sports bra to sleep in for support!) —*Trista, 31*

- How do doctors calculate the age of the embryo or fetus?
- How are my emotions and hormones changing?
- How can I find the right healthcare provider to help me throughout pregnancy and delivery?
- What are some common questions that women and their partners have in early pregnancy?

From Ovulation to Pregnancy: Playing the Waiting Game

Determining whether you're pregnant can take time—and patience.

Am I Pregnant?

Once you have ovulated and tried to conceive, you have to play the waiting game for nearly two more weeks before you can find

> When my wife came out of the bathroom with that pregnancy test and told me it was positive, I lifted her up and twirled her around the room. I felt like we had won the lottery. Then I realized getting pregnant *is* winning the lottery! —*Dennis, 40, dad of two*

out if you are pregnant. Two weeks can seem like two years when you are wondering if you have achieved your goal! While cramping and bloating are common symptoms during this phase in pregnancy, you may find yourself worrying that your period is in your future, not a baby.

At the end of the fourth week you can take an early pregnancy test. Some tests can detect a pregnancy as early as five days before you miss your period. If the test is positive, you are likely pregnant. If the test is negative, wait a few days and take the test again—it may be positive later in your pregnancy. If the test is negative on the first day after your missed period, it is likely you are not pregnant. When in doubt, book an appointment with your healthcare provider to have a blood test for human chorionic gonadotropin (hCG), a hormone made by the developing placenta—which will confirm that you are indeed pregnant!

Missed Period but Negative Pregnancy Test?

If you miss your regular period and your pregnancy test is not positive by week five, consider how you are taking the test. You need to follow the directions on the pregnancy test box exactly. You also need to make sure that you do not drink a large quantity of water or other beverage before the test. Remember, the pregnancy test measures the level of human chorionic gonadotrophin (hCG—the telltale hormone present in pregnancy) in your urine. So drinking a lot of water before the test only dilutes the amount of hCG in the urine, and this can give you a false negative result. In the same way, taking the test at any time of the day other than first thing in the morning, before you have had anything to drink, can reduce the perceived levels of hCG in your urine, and the test will be falsely negative.

If you reach your fifth week and believe you are pregnant but have not been able to

If Your Pregnancy Is Unintended

If your pregnancy test is positive and it is an unplanned pregnancy, you may feel elated or you may be devastated. You may be wondering whether you will have an abortion or keep the baby, and whether you will put your baby up for adoption. How will you tell your spouse, partner, or the rest of the family? In this case, it is best to seek professional guidance from your healthcare provider, a therapist, or a health clinic. There are many avenues for adoption, and many organizations can help you sort through the emotional decision about whether to have an abortion. Be sure to also seek supportive friends and family as you go through the process of making decisions about your pregnancy.

get a positive pregnancy test at home, see your healthcare provider for a blood test that measures hCG. Blood tests for hCG are far less likely to be affected by any other outside influence, and you can trust that your blood test results will be accurate.

Pregnancy Begins

According to medical convention, you are not pregnant during weeks one and two of gestational age (see page 61). This is the time when the uterine lining begins to thicken in preparation for conception and for the ultimate imbedding of the fertilized egg. Your estrogen levels rise throughout this stage of your cycle, which triggers the thickening of the uterine lining. At the time of conception, the female hormone progesterone rises dramatically and, in a healthy pregnancy,

will remain elevated until you deliver. The progesterone is initially made by the ovaries but, at a certain point in pregnancy, production switches over so that the placenta makes the progesterone. If the pregnancy is to end in miscarriage, the progesterone level drops and the pregnancy is lost.

When Does Conception Occur?

In the first few days of the third gestational week, the egg is fertilized, usually while it is still in the fallopian tube. A zygote is the single cell that is formed by the merging of the sperm and the egg. Amazingly, this one little cell contains all the genetic material that will create an entire human being—your child!

During the two-cell stage through the eight-cell stage, each cell carries the ability to form a whole human being. So, if one breaks off and goes its own way, you get identical twins. Identical twins come from one fertilized egg and thus are identical in every way. Fraternal twins come from two different eggs that are fertilized separately.

Development in the First Few Days

By about the third day after the egg is fertilized, it has divided into 12 to 16 cells. These cells begin to form a ball known as a morula. The morula makes its way through the fallopian tube, arriving in the uterus at about day 4. The cells begin to form a ring around an inner cavity, and the morula transforms into the next stage of development, called a blastocyst.

The blastocyst develops an inner mass, which becomes the embryo, and an outer layer that develops into the placenta. By about day 6, the developing embryo begins to attach to the uterine wall, which contains water and

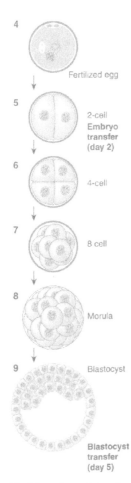

4 — Fertilized egg

5 — 2-cell
Embryo
transfer
(day 2)

6 — 4-cell

7 — 8 cell

8 — Morula

9 — Blastocyst

Blastocyst
transfer
(day 5)

First few days of development
The fertilized egg develops into a blastocyst.

By the second week after conception, the blastocyst begins to form three separate layers. The first layer will become the skin, hair, and nervous system of the embryo. The second layer develops into the muscles, bones, blood, circulatory system, teeth, connective tissues, and kidneys. The inner layer becomes the baby's internal organs such as the heart and the lungs.

Before you may even suspect you are pregnant, an incredible process has taken place. Within the first two weeks after conception, the single cell that is created by your egg and your partner's sperm has divided several hundred times, traveled into the uterus, and is now implanted inside the uterus.

From Embryo to Fetus

The embryo stage includes all the phases from the formation of the first few cells through the tenth week of gestation. The term "fetus" is used after the tenth week.

Embryo at four weeks of development
Your embryo at four weeks is approximately half an inch long and weighs less than one ounce. Arms and legs, brain and spinal cord, and heart and lungs are beginning to form. By the end of the month, the heart begins to beat.

nutrients, and the implantation of the embryo is normally complete by day 12. All this time the blastocyst has been encased in a shell known as the zona pellucida. By the time the blastocyst reaches the uterus, it "hatches" from the zona pellucida. The underlying blastocyst is sticky, and the blastocyst is now able to find a spot on the uterine lining onto which to attach. At this point in time, when the blastocyst imbeds into the uterus, you may have a bit of spotting.

Evolution and Embryonic Growth

Doctors and researchers have spent a lot of time studying embryonic development in the different species of animals. What they have found is that those things that developed earliest in early prehistoric animals also develop the soonest in human embryos. The backbone, for example, was one of the first things to develop in early fish and reptiles. This also happens to be the body part that develops soonest in human embryos.

Embryonic Age versus Gestational Age

Doctors define the weeks of pregnancy by two methods. There is the gestational age, which is calculated from the first day of the last menstrual period. There is also the embryonic age, which begins at the end of week two of the gestational age, and is approximately the time of conception. At the beginning of the embryonic age, there is actually an embryo (about the size of a poppyseed), and you are actually pregnant. In this book, we are using the gestational age to mark the phases of pregnancy.

Your Changing Body in Early Pregnancy

Because your embryo is microscopically tiny, your uterus will not be enlarged in the first four weeks of pregnancy. Most women in weeks three and four of pregnancy feel fairly normal. Some have all the same symptoms they would have if they were about to get their period. You may feel bloated and crampy, but this usually goes away or improves when you finally miss your period. Your body will have an elevated level of human chorionic gonadotropin (hCG), the pregnancy hormone produced by the embryo. This hormone usually causes mood changes and nausea; but, because the levels are low, you will not feel many symptoms.

There are a few very sensitive women who experience symptoms of hCG even though their levels are only somewhat elevated. These women can develop nausea and vomiting very early in their pregnancy. They tend to have these symptoms for a very long time, sometimes throughout the pregnancy. This is not a dangerous sign, and some say that the more pregnancy symptoms you have, the healthier the pregnancy is.

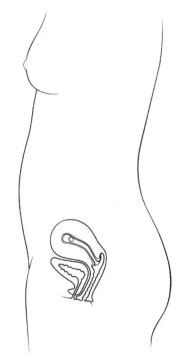

Your changing body: Month one
Your pregnancy isn't visible yet, but special changes are happening inside you!

Hang On! It's Going to Be a Bumpy Ride!

The hormones of early pregnancy, particularly hCG, can cause mood swings and spells of crying or depression. You may feel

> I wasn't prepared for the emotional roller-coaster I suddenly found myself on! I began crying for the silliest reasons and sometimes for no reason at all. I got angry at things I never even bothered about before, and all I wanted to do was lie down and go to sleep. Thankfully, my husband was a saint, and simply hugged me and said: "Hey, it's all part of the beauty of the little baby you are growing! Don't worry about it!" I still cried at commercials but I sure felt a lot better about it thanks to him!
> —Donna, 44, mother of two

more forgetful or frazzled during this time. You may get into more arguments with your spouse because he or she does not understand how moody you have become and may inadvertently hurt your feelings. If you have nausea or vomiting, you may be frustrated and wondering whether or not this pregnancy is worth how horrible you feel! Of course you know it is, but pregnancy side effects can be tough to take at times. Whatever you do, be gentle with yourself and take extra-special care to meet your own needs during this time.

Mood swings in early pregnancy are common and are nothing to worry about. You are not going crazy! Most of these mood swings will pass by the end of the first trimester. Deep inside your body, changes are occurring and hormones are increasing, leading you to feel out of sorts and downright crabby and weepy. Becoming angry or emotional over minor happenings is common!

Have your spouse or partner read this section of the book in particular. Both of you will benefit if he or she understands that changes in your mood can happen in early pregnancy. As a partner, it is important to recognize this is a normal part of pregnancy. Kindness and understanding are the best medicine.

Finding the Perfect Pregnancy Healthcare Provider

One of the first orders of business after learning you are pregnant is to find a pregnancy doctor, nurse practitioner, or nurse-midwife who meets your unique needs. Even though your baby's birth is nine months away, it is important to take some time now to think about what kind of delivery will be best for you.

Considerations in Choosing a Practitioner

As you think about finding a healthcare provider, consider the following questions:

- Do you definitely want to deliver at a hospital?
- Have you thought about a home birth?
- What are your thoughts on cesarean sections?
- What kind of pain control do you want during your labor?
- Do you want a female or a male healthcare provider?

I wanted to do something special to let my husband know that I was finally pregnant. I asked him to take me to dinner at our favorite restaurant. Earlier in the day, I'd ordered a special cake from our local bakery that had a pink baby shoe and a blue baby shoe on top, which I'd brought to the restaurant before our reservation. After dinner, the waiter brought over the cake and my husband burst out, "Oh, my God! You're having twins!" It took me a few minutes to explain that at the moment the fetus looked like a blob of cells, so he'd have to wait and see! Anyway, we'll always remember that moment! —*Emily, 34, mother of one*

- Do you want to see a family doctor, who will take care of both you and the baby, or do you want to see a pregnancy specialist, an obstetrician or midwife?
- Do you want to have your partner or other family members involved in the delivery process?
- Do you want to deliver at a hospital that has a neonatal intensive care unit (NICU) in case there is a problem after the baby is born?
- Do you want to go to a hospital that supports "rooming-in"—a situation where the baby stays with the mother twenty-four hours a day?

Matching your medical style and needs: If you like to be actively involved in your medical care, you will want to find a healthcare provider who enjoys explaining what is going on and is willing to take the time to do so.

If you have a chronic illness or other specific medical concerns, you may seek a specialist who can help you to have a safer pregnancy and delivery. Learn as much as you can about the individual or group of providers you are considering. Find out who may be doing the actual delivery, as you will want to feel comfortable with any provider who may potentially deliver your baby.

Cost and coverage: Your choice of a practitioner may also be affected by your health insurance coverage and the region in which you live. For example, you may have fewer options in a rural area, or your insurance may not cover a free-standing birthing center.

Your choice of delivery location: It is important to have some idea of where you may wish to deliver, because this decision affects your choice of a healthcare provider for your pregnancy and birth. Some women feel very strongly about delivering their baby at home. In such cases, they usually must hire a midwife who will do home deliveries. It is a good idea to have an emer-

Nutrition Tip: Early Pregnancy

Your baby weighs a fraction of an ounce at the beginning of pregnancy, and it needs very few calories for itself. Eat a healthy diet and begin to eliminate the unhealthy things in your life, including alcohol. You do not need to increase your calorie intake at this point; but, if you are underweight at the beginning of your pregnancy, you can start eating more in order to normalize your weight.

gency hospital and physician notified of the home delivery to make sure all goes safely. Other women feel more confident having their baby in a hospital. Some women prefer the additional backup of a hospital neonatal intensive care unit (NICU), or have medical conditions that make this a wise choice. Women who choose hospital deliveries often feel that the ability to have an emergency C-section is important should the situation arise. Women who deliver in hospitals also have access to pain medication, including an epidural anesthetic, which makes the birthing process much less painful. Still other women choose to deliver in a hospital but decide to have the baby "naturally" without any pain medication used during the delivery. Another delivery option is a birth (or birthing) center, which may be either free-standing or attached to a hospital. Birth centers strive to provide a home-like atmosphere with the safety of medical backup.

Today, there is a wide variety of healthcare professionals for you to choose from. Below are the various options you can consider.

Obstetrician

An obstetrician is a medical doctor specially trained in women's health issues, including pregnancy and delivery. Much of their practice involves pregnancy and childbirth, and they have a great deal of experience in these areas. They have the skills to do a C-section if this becomes necessary during the labor process.

Family Practice Doctor

This is a doctor who is skilled in dealing with all aspects of family healthcare, including the process of labor and delivery. Not all

Possible Physical Symptoms of Pregnancy

During this first month, you may experience the following:

- missed period
- possible staining or spotting (when fertilized egg implants in your uterus)
- fatigue
- nausea, with or without vomiting
- breast tenderness
- bloating, flatulence
- more frequent urination
- food cravings or aversions
- sensitivity in pelvic area; cramps

family practice doctors deliver babies, so you need to ask whether the doctor of your choice also does obstetrics. Family practice doctors will also take care of the baby after he or she has been born. Most family practice doctors do not do C-sections. The benefits of this are that fewer C-sections happen when a family practice doctor does the delivery; in general, these babies do just fine. The downside is that if a C-section is definitely required during the delivery process, the family practice doctor must refer you to an obstetrician to perform this procedure.

Midwife

A midwife is a nurse or other healthcare professional who has had extra training in delivering babies and caring for women during pregnancy. Certified nurse-midwives (who have nursing degrees) and certified midwives (health professionals without nursing degrees) earn master's degrees and must pass an accreditation test offered by the American College of Nurse Midwives. Midwives who attend home births may only be certified by the North American Registry of Midwives and have a range of educational backgrounds. The midwife often works with a doctor or obstetrician who can provide consultation and backup in case of emergency. Some hospitals allow midwife deliveries. Other midwife deliveries are done at free-standing birth centers staffed by midwives. Still other midwives will do home births with backup from a nearby hospital and doctor. Midwives do not have the skill or training to do C-sections, but, as with family physicians, their rate of delivering without the need for C-section is lower than for obstetricians.

OB Nurse Practitioner

An obstetrical (OB) nurse practitioner is a registered nurse who has additional specialized training to work with pregnant women and those who are giving birth. The OB nurse practitioner works both independently and in collaboration with physicians as part of a healthcare team.

Perinatologist for High-Risk Pregnancies

If you have a preexisting serious illness (such as an autoimmune disease) or are diagnosed with one during pregnancy, you may want to use a perinatologist during your pregnancy. Perinatologists are doctors skilled in managing high-risk pregnancies. In a high-risk pregnancy, either the mother or the fetus may have problems which need to be managed. The perinatologist will manage medications given to you during pregnancy

When my partner told me she wanted to have a home birth, my immediate response was a mix of panic and terror! How would we manage? Would Cheryl's OB still be present? What if something went wrong? Would we need special equipment in the house for her to deliver safely? If we went the way of a doula [a nonmedical support person], would I have even less of a role to play during the birth? As it turned out, everything went smoothly and beautifully. It was such a special event for my partner, for me, for everyone involved! We met with the midwife well in advance of the delivery date. In speaking with her about all possible case scenarios, and because our OB was positive and fully on board, my worries soon faded. The minute Cheryl started contractions, I knew my role in relation to the midwife, and I was able to enjoy the entire experience. I actually think that having a home birth for our son ensured that I was an active participant in the blessed event. —*Alex, 38, mother of one*

and closely follow your health and the health of your developing fetus. Using a perinatologist can greatly enhance the success of your pregnancy and provide you with peace of mind.

Doula

A doula is specially trained individual who supports women through pregnancy, childbirth, and during the period after the baby is born. Doulas work with women to help them tolerate the pain and stress of labor and delivery. They usually play a complementary role to the medical professional by offering a continuous, reassuring presence for the mom-to-be and her partner. A doula is usually hired along with the healthcare provider who performs the delivery. Doulas can be especially helpful for women who are anxious about medical procedures or childbirth because of experiences in their past. They can also help new mothers with breast-feeding concerns.

Don't go wild buying maternity clothes once you find out you're pregnant! You'll be surprised what regular clothes you can get away with for quite some time. Also, a girlfriend of mine told me that maternity clothes were cut so generously she ended up eating way more than she needed to because she had the room to expand! Eat well and wear what fits—don't try to fit what you wear! —*Inge, 32, mother of two*

Following Your Pregnancy: Chart Your Course!

Believe it or not, the next nine months are going to fly by! At this point, it is a great idea to begin charting your pregnancy. As mentioned above, your healthcare provider will use a pregnancy wheel, a little cardboard gadget that uses the date of your last menstrual period, to point to your due date. You can also subtract three months from the first day of your last menstrual period, and add a week. This will be sufficient to give you a due date as well. If you have very long cycles, tell your healthcare provider, and your due date may be adjusted for that. You can easily find online calculators to help you determine your due date.

Once you have a due date, buy a calendar, especially a pregnancy calendar if you can. With this calendar, you can mark the date of your last period, and then mark each pregnancy week as it progresses. This allows you to track how far along you are. Everything up to the end of week 12 is the first trimester. Everything from week 13 to the week 28 is called the second trimester. Everything from week 29 to week 40 is your third trimester.

You can also use your calendar for fun! Mark down things like when you first feel your baby move and any symptoms, cravings, or emotions you may experience. Be sure to write down all your doctor appointments so you do not forget to go. A large calendar may also give you room to write down your thoughts, concerns, joys, or worries.

Exercise Idea: Keep Moving!

Do not be afraid to exercise as normal, especially during this first month. If you wish to begin exercising for the first time or want to start something new, ask your healthcare provider if it is appropriate for you. Avoid vigorous activity if you are not used to it. Instead, start a walking or biking program in which you increase your distance or time in small increments until you reach your goal. Your body and mind will both benefit from exercise, and you will feel better about yourself and your pregnant body.

I decided to make my pregnancy calendar more like a scrapbook of the next nine months. I used stickers and markers, wrote vignettes about my feelings and thoughts about the baby, recorded when I stopped vomiting and when the baby first kicked. I even wrote down wishes and dreams for his life. Not only did I remember important doctor appointments, I also had a complete history of what it was like to be pregnant. It is so much fun to look back on! —*Georgia, 44, mother of three*

your due date within a day or two. Even better, you can find many due date calculators online. (Try the one at lessonladder.com.)

Question: I had some spotting when I should have gotten my period, but I still had a positive pregnancy test. Do I have to worry?

Answer: Bleeding and spotting in the first trimester occur about 20 to 30 percent of the time. There may be slight cramping or none at all. If you get bleeding that is minor, do not use tampons but instead use sanitary napkins or panty liners. Do not douche. Contact an emergency room or your healthcare provider if you have ANY bleeding or cramping. It is true that

Common Questions about Being Newly Pregnant

With nine months ahead of you before you deliver, you likely have loads of time to conjure up a thousand pregnancy questions that you would like answered. While it is always a good idea to write down your questions and bring them to your healthcare provider, below are answers to some common questions newly pregnant women have.

Question: How does the doctor know my due date?

Answer: The length of a pregnancy is 40 weeks from the first day of your last menstrual period. Your doctor has a special wheel that uses the first day of your last menstrual period to determine your due date. Without a wheel, you can approximate your due date by taking the first day of your last menstrual period, subtracting exactly three months, and adding exactly seven days. This will be

For Dads and Partners:
Moods and Understanding

Early pregnancy is a time of celebration with your partner, but know that your partner's physical and emotional states are changing. Her body is now focused on growing and housing another human being, and with that comes a vast hormonal shift. These changes affect the way your partner acts and feels both physically and emotionally. This is a time to be empathetic and patient. Follow her lead, help her get rest when she can, and give her some extra TLC (tender loving care)! It's really important not to discount your partner's emotions just because she is pregnant. That feels disrespectful to many women. Some of these emotional changes will pass by the time she reaches her twelfth week, but in the meantime offer her a hug and plenty of understanding.

bleeding can be a sign of miscarriage. If you are concerned in any way, contact your healthcare provider immediately.

Bleeding can also be a sign of an ectopic pregnancy, where the fertilized egg has settled in the fallopian tube and will ultimately rupture the tube. It can also be a sign of a condition known as a molar pregnancy, which is a pregnancy that does not produce a healthy fetus but instead grows irregular tissue that makes the pregnancy hormone. Again, if you have any bleeding, contact your healthcare provider.

Around six to twelve days after you conceive, you can get spotting that is from implantation of the embryonic tissue into the uterine wall. Occasionally an infection of the pelvis or urinary tract can result in what appears to be uterine bleeding. Some women get bleeding during intercourse because the cervix is more vulnerable in pregnancy and bleeds on contact more often. While this can be scary, you need to know that normal intercourse does not cause miscarriages.

Prenatal Testing: Testing for Progesterone Levels

As you are in the very early stages of pregnancy, you do not normally need any prenatal testing. The most common test done at this stage of pregnancy is testing for your progesterone level to make sure your ovaries are making enough progesterone to sustain the pregnancy. If needed, this test is done at the end of the third week of your cycle.

After I became pregnant, I decided to do something to keep my husband involved in the pregnancy. After each four-week increment, I had a little party with my husband. He would cook something special for dinner and I would make dessert. I called it "Baby Night." Then we would sit at the table and celebrate where we were in the pregnancy, and talk about what was coming next and any issues or feelings we had about it. Not only did we stay on the same page in terms of the baby's development, we were able to catch early any issue that one or the other of us had and deal with it before it got buried or out of hand. It really brought us closer, and I think it helped my husband feel like he was really part of the process! It worked so well, we decided to do it every month until our son graduates from college! —*Donna, 30, mother of one*

Question: What is a miscarriage like?

Answer: A miscarriage can occur anytime from conception to about 12 weeks' gestation. While there are pregnancy losses after 12 weeks, many doctors do not consider them to be miscarriages; these are instead called second trimester losses or preterm births. When a miscarriage occurs in the first trimester, you will likely experience uterine cramping (like a heavy period), bleeding from the vagina that can get very heavy, and the passage of tissue of various sizes that represents the passage of the products of conception. In most cases, you should see your healthcare provider when you have a miscarriage to make sure the products of conception have passed and to discuss when you can try to get pregnant again (if you are ready to have that conversation).

Question: When should I start taking prenatal vitamins?

Answer: Many doctors recommend you begin taking prenatal vitamins for at least one month before you get pregnant so your nutritional status is as good as it can get. It is especially important to take folic acid (400 mcg), which is usually included in prenatal vitamins, before you become pregnant. You can find prenatal vitamins at your local pharmacy or health food store.

Question: Should I take supplemental calcium?

Answer: Your healthcare provider will talk to you about how much milk you drink and the amount of other dairy products you consume per day. If your intake is not adequate, he or she will recommend you take 1000 to 1200 mg of calcium with vitamin D per day. You can still drink milk and eat dairy as you cannot overdose on calcium supplements. Calcium supplementation should continue throughout the pregnancy so as to maintain your bone mass and build bone mass in the growing fetus.

Question: When should I first see the doctor now that I am pregnant?

Answer: Doctors and clinics that take care of pregnant women have different policies on this issue. Some clinics hold off on the new OB visit until the woman is at 10 weeks' gestation. The reason behind this is that, if an early miscarriage should occur, there is nothing that can be done to prevent it and a new

OB visit will be wasted. Other clinics have no such guidelines and will allow you to come to a new OB visit as early as six weeks. Some of the decision is up to you. If you have lots of worries or expect to have a high-risk pregnancy, see the healthcare provider earlier in your pregnancy. The best practice is to call for an appointment as soon as you know you are pregnant. The office will help you determine when you should be seen.

Question: Which hospital should I go to?

Answer: This can be a complex question. Some couples want to make sure the hospital is close to their home, especially if they have a history of fast labor. Other couples simply go to the hospital where their doctor delivers. Some doctors deliver babies at more than

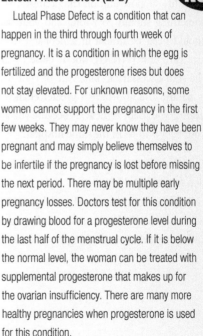

Luteal Phase Defect (LPD)

Luteal Phase Defect is a condition that can happen in the third through fourth week of pregnancy. It is a condition in which the egg is fertilized and the progesterone rises but does not stay elevated. For unknown reasons, some women cannot support the pregnancy in the first few weeks. They may never know they have been pregnant and may simply believe themselves to be infertile if the pregnancy is lost before missing the next period. There may be multiple early pregnancy losses. Doctors test for this condition by drawing blood for a progesterone level during the last half of the menstrual cycle. If it is below the normal level, the woman can be treated with supplemental progesterone that makes up for the ovarian insufficiency. There are many more healthy pregnancies when progesterone is used for this condition.

As soon as I became pregnant, a friend of mine suggested I start a pregnancy journal. She said that she didn't do it until her second baby because she initially hadn't realized how much she would forget about her experience. There are so many changes happening and so many thoughts and feelings you experience that it is wonderful to record them, and then go back to remember what it was like. So I did keep a pregnancy journal! I even added copies of my ultrasound pictures and other little mementos of my pregnancy. It's a wonderful record of a truly magical time! —*Joyce, 30, mother of two*

one hospital, giving you choices. Another option is to consider choosing a hospital that has a neonatal life support unit on the premises. If something should go wrong and your baby should need treatment at a neonatal intensive care unit (NICU), one is close by and the staff necessary to take care of your baby is handy. You also have a greater chance of visiting your baby right away because you and your baby will be in the same hospital.

Question: What options do I have in addition to a hospital birth?

Answer: Some women choose home birth with a nurse-midwife and a backup plan, and others deliver at birthing centers that are either free-standing or attached to a hospital. If you are considering either of these options, it is important to learn as much as you can about these birth settings because they may influence your choice of healthcare provider and your preparation for childbirth.

Question: When will I hear my baby's heartbeat?

Answer: At five and a half weeks, the fetal heartbeat can usually be seen using a transvaginal ultrasound. This test, however, involves putting a probe into the woman's vagina and is not normally performed unless there is a reason for concern. Using a Doppler device on the mother's abdomen, the healthcare provider can usually hear the heartbeat at around 12 weeks. You will be able to hear the heartbeat as well!

Question: When will I feel my baby move?

Answer: You have a long way to go before that big event happens. In the first trimester and part of the second trimester, the fetus is just too small to feel from the outside. You will feel the thrill of those first kicks at around 18 to 20 weeks' gestation. At first, it will feel like gas bubbles or butterflies in your abdomen. Over time, the kicks will be more obvious and closer together. Kicks will be visible from the outside or by putting your hand on your abdomen over the uterus at about 21 to 22 weeks' gestation.

Notes:

My friends hate when I say this, but I didn't have any unpleasant symptoms during my first months of pregnancy. It was a little anti-climactic. I wanted to feel something—nausea, exhaustion, crying over spilled milk—anything. I looked the same, and pretty much felt the same. It was hard to believe I was actually carrying a baby. —*Vicki, 26, mother of one*

Chapter 4

Month Two—Weeks 5 through 8

By week five, nearly every woman who is pregnant should have a pregnancy test that gives a positive result. Hooray! With the good news, you may expect to see your belly immediately swell, anticipate becoming irritable and weepy, or have nausea and vomiting. Not necessarily so. Even during weeks five through eight, your baby is teeny-tiny. No need for maternity clothes at this point! And, unless you tell someone, no one is going to suspect a thing from looking at you. While many women experience some form of pregnancy side effects, others have no symptoms at all at this point.

And then there is the idea of sharing the good news. Some women share the information that they are pregnant as soon as they discover a positive pregnancy test and others wait—sharing the information with no one or only with their partner. The decision about when to tell others about your news is a personal one. You have only this time in pregnancy to be truly alone with the idea that you are pregnant. So, it is up to you to decide

All I remember about the second month of my pregnancy is how utterly exhausted I was. Before my pregnancy, I never closed my office door at work. But I was suddenly so tired and cranky that I spent most of the day with the door shut, trying to work without having to deal with anyone else. One night after working late, a coworker dropped me off at the train station to take the subway home. As luck would have it, the circus had just let out and hundreds of kids and parents were crowded onto the train platform. It's funny to think about now, but I was so utterly exhausted I made up my mind to beat all those kids to a seat on the train! Obviously, at seven weeks along, I didn't look pregnant so I knew no one would give up their seat. I didn't know how I was going to explain taking a seat from a child but I knew there was no way I could stand up all the way home! When the train pulled up I lost my nerve but, thank God, a kind man offered me his seat out of chivalry! The next day at work, my friend in the office across from mine knocked on my door, and I let him in. He had two kids. He asked, "You're pregnant, aren't you?" I was shocked and started crying. "Hormones," I laughed. He handed me a tissue and said, "I knew when you kept shutting your door. My wife had to do the same thing. Just let me know how I can help." I will always be grateful for those two men who were able to have empathy for me! Little things mean so much during those first months! —*Jules, 33* when to take this information from being private knowledge to something friends, relatives, and coworkers can celebrate with you. See Chapter 5 for more considerations about when to share your news.

Weeks five through eight can be a time of excitement and a time of mystery. You know there is life inside of you, and you may feel irritable or exhausted; but it may also seem like nothing has really changed. Rest assured, however you are feeling, there are amazing things happening in your body. In this chapter, we will address the following questions:

- How is my baby developing at this early point in my pregnancy?
- What changes can I expect in my emotions?
- How can I deal with symptoms like heartburn and morning sickness?
- What should I expect at my first prenatal visit to my healthcare provider, and how can I prepare?
- What tests will I have at this first visit?
- What are some common questions and answers for the first prenatal visit?
- How do miscarriages happen, and can they be prevented?
- What should I do if I experience bleeding or spotting?

Your Baby's Growth and Development: Grow, Baby, Grow!

While still extremely small, the embryo in the fifth through eighth weeks is growing and changing rapidly. Key things are happening in the area of what is known as

"differentiation." Differentiation happens when each individual cell suddenly develops a mission. An ordinary cell becomes an eye cell and nothing else. The cells that make up the circulatory system begin as cells without purpose; then, within a week of your finding out you are pregnant, your baby's circulatory system is already developing. Each cell learns its specific functions, all of which are important in determining how your baby will look and how the organs will operate.

This phase of pregnancy is vitally important. Imagine if a toxin or chemical affected just one cell at week five. That single cell will divide millions of times before the creation of all the cells necessary for a newborn baby to be born. When that tainted cell divides, it passes on whatever damage it sustained from the toxin or chemical so that, ultimately, millions or more cells are negatively affected by the initial insult. This means that the earlier you take care of yourself, avoiding potentially toxic medications and staying away from industrial or other chemicals, the greater the positive effect on the fetus. Some early insults to growing cells can cause severe birth defects, possibly even a pregnancy loss. An insult to a cell that is further along in the pregnancy causes less of a ripple effect in terms of cell division, which then lessens the likelihood of birth defects.

Let's take a look at the amazing feats of differentiation, growth, and development your baby is going through during weeks five through eight of gestation.

Week Five

The embryo at this stage looks like a tube of sorts. The tube has three layers, each inside

Can't Say It Enough: Take Your Prenatal Vitamins!

What NOW?

Ideally, you were already taking prenatal vitamins (or at least folic acid) before you conceived. If not, remember that, regardless of when you have your first prenatal visit, you should start over-the-counter prenatal vitamins and get enough calcium in your diet as soon as possible. If you do not believe you can get enough calcium from food, begin taking 600 to 1200 mg of calcium with vitamin D. Your healthcare provider may have his or her own ideas of what prenatal supplements you should be taking, but it is still a good idea to begin a prenatal vitamin of some sort on your own and before seeing your doctor or midwife.

the next. The outer layer is called the ectoderm, and the cells of the ectoderm continue to develop into the neural tube. The neural tube will eventually become the baby's spinal cord, brain, skin, and hair. Inside the ectoderm is the mesoderm, which contains cells that will become the heart, arteries, veins, bones, reproductive system, muscles, and kidneys. Remember that these layers are changing both in their development and in size at the same time.

The inner layer of this tube-like structure is called the endoderm. The endoderm continues being a tube that, ultimately, turns into the baby's intestines, bladder, and pancreas.

The first system to develop in your growing embryo is the circulatory system. Your baby needs blood vessels and capillaries to move nutrients and other proteins around that are ultimately crucial to the embryo's growth. It is kind of like needing to build a roadway before you can put up buildings and other features.

At this point in time, your baby is the size of a sesame seed, or only about one-tenth of an inch long—barely visible to the eye.

Week Six

At this time, your baby is about the size of a pumpkin seed and is growing extremely quickly. It develops the umbilical cord and placenta that will be the baby's nutrition lifeline throughout the rest of your pregnancy. The very first beats of the baby's heart will begin by the sixth week, but they will not be strong enough to hear on the doctor's Doppler ultrasound until around week twelve.

By now, your baby has a head and is beginning to differentiate cells into those that become the ears and eyes. An opening for the mouth is formed this week. Arm and leg buds (without fingers or toes) will begin to appear in roughly their appropriate places, and will continue to grow into normal arms and legs. Internal organs are beginning to take shape, including the intestinal system and other abdominal and chest organs. The embryo is beginning to look somewhat like a person!

Week Seven

Your baby is continuing its pattern of extremely rapid growth. Cells are dividing almost continuously and continuing to differentiate into increasingly complex organs. The arms and legs are busy growing longer by week seven, but there are still no fingers and toes to count. Brain growth is particularly

I had miscarried before, so my husband and I were keeping my pregnancy to ourselves. I wasn't showing at all, but one day, around week six, my mom said she knew I was pregnant and asked how I was doing. "How did you know?" I asked. "Moms know everything about their kids," she grinned. "You'll see!" she added. "I hope so," I answered. Then, after a brief pause, I started to cry. "Don't worry, Linda," Mom assured me. "You'll see this time. Like I said, a mother knows." And she was right. I had a healthy baby girl, and I now know what she meant because I know everything about my little Lindsey! —*Linda, 29, mother of one*

important around week seven, creating your baby's nervous system, which allows for its ability to move, feel, see, hear, and taste. It may even be the foundation for laying down your baby's innate personality.

The lenses of the eyes develop during this week even though the baby would have no ability to see yet. Pigmentation that will determine your baby's eye color is being laid down. Along with this groundwork for the visual systems, the embryo is forming its nostrils, pancreas, intestines, and bronchi. Lungs begin to form and develop, yet do not allow for respiration. Your baby is now about a half-inch long, or the size of an average blueberry. The heart beats quickly at a rate of around 140 to 180 beats per minute.

Week Eight

The embryo's heart begins to get bigger by week eight, and can easily be seen on a prenatal ultrasound. The baby begins to look even more human, with fingers and elbows developing. The knees develop, while the toes are nothing but little nubs at the ends of the legs! For the first 20 weeks of development, average embryo or fetus lengths are measured from the baby's crown to its rump; after that, measurements are calculated from crown to heel. At week eight, your baby is still under an inch long and weighs less than half an ounce.

The face is doing a great deal of developing at this stage. The ears, eyes, eyelids, and even the very tip of the nose appear. This is a time of intestinal development as well. Intestines begin life in the umbilical cord and later migrate to the abdominal cavity. Tiny buds of teeth are beginning to form under the baby's gums. The baby is about two-thirds of an inch long— about the size of a raspberry.

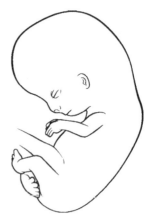

Fetus at eight weeks of development
An eight-week-old embryo is approximately two-thirds of an inch long (from crown to rump) and weighs less than half an ounce. Eyelids have formed, but the eyes remain closed. The inner ear begins to develop; bones appear; ankles, wrists, fingers, and toes form; and genitals begin to develop. By the end of the month, all of the major organs and body systems have begun to develop.

Your Changing Body: The Invisible Transformation

While inside your body amazing things are happening, most likely no one will notice anything happening on the outside. Let's take a look at what you may be experiencing during weeks five through eight.

Baby Bump? Well, Almost!

During the first few weeks of pregnancy, two factors come into play that will make you feel as though it is not just you in there. Most noticeably, your body is experiencing rising levels of blood progesterone and human chorionic gonadotropin (hCG) levels. The progesterone is coming from the ovaries, but by the end of the first trimester, the ovaries will be relatively silent, and the growing placenta will be making the progesterone necessary to support the pregnancy. This hormone comes from the embryo itself as well as the placenta. Both of these hormones are necessary but will give you symptoms you might perceive as uncomfortable.

The other factor affecting the way you feel is the growth of your uterus. The uterus itself reaches the size of a fist or a softball by the end of the eighth week, and if you are relatively thin, you may be able to feel a hard sensation just above the pubic bone when you press in that area. There is also an increase in blood volume that makes your abdomen a tiny bit bloated. You may also begin to feel as though your pants are too tight, and you may want to wear looser clothing or pants that have an elastic waist.

Breast Tenderness

One of the first symptoms you may experience is breast tenderness, often worse than the tenderness you might feel before your period. The tenderness can be there even if you are doing nothing. For example, your

> I had a pair of pants I wore right through my first trimester. They were pencil-leg khakis made from cotton and lycra, and had a flat front and side zipper. I called them my "magic pants" because no matter how my belly began to swell, they kept fitting—and they went with everything! —*Rhonda, 33, mother of two*

nipples might be tender just from touching your clothing. If you accidentally bump your chest, you may feel the tenderness. You may not be able to go without wearing a comfortable and supportive bra. Breast tenderness can last throughout the pregnancy, but in most women the symptom improves and even resolves during the second trimester.

Sense of Smell

By week six, you could have several pregnancy symptoms. You may notice your sense of smell is more acute, and you may feel nauseous when smelling certain odors. There may be foods that, because of their smell, you just cannot bring yourself to eat.

Fatigue

You may be experiencing significant fatigue. You may feel as though you always need to take a nap or that your brain is fuzzy and you cannot think straight because you are so tired. It might seem impossible to complete your usual work. This is the time to set aside expectations and simply rest, watch television, or take an afternoon nap if possible. Try to get your daily work done in small quantities with plenty of rest breaks in between. This symptom fortunately does not last, and you will feel better by the time you reach 13 weeks' gestation or so.

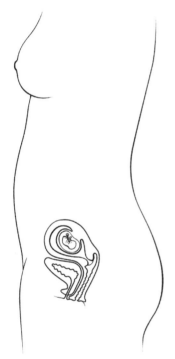

Your changing body: Month two
Your waistline begins to expand a little, but you still don't look pregnant despite the incredible development going on inside your uterus.

Heartburn

Heartburn can occur throughout your pregnancy, but it often begins in the first few weeks. Heartburn is also known as acid reflux or gastroesophageal reflux disease (GERD).

Pregnancy hormones affect the valve that controls acid flow between the stomach (where it is supposed to be) and the esophagus (where it does not belong). Reflux can also be caused by the pressure of the enlarged uterus, but this is not a factor in early pregnancy. Acid reflux or GERD can occur when your stomach is empty or after a big meal. The feeling is like a pressure or outright pain in your chest that begins at the upper abdomen and travels up to the throat. You may experience a sensation of fullness in your throat or the feeling of acid in your throat, and you may have bad breath. Asthmatics can notice an increase in wheezing when the GERD is active. All in all, heartburn is not serious, but it can certainly be one of the more annoying symptoms of pregnancy.

Heartburn can sometimes be relieved with a simple glass of water. However, you can talk to your healthcare provider about special medications for heartburn if it becomes severe. In the meantime, there are three excellent treatments you can use to protect your esophagus from the effects of the painful stomach acid. These include:

TUMS or other generic antacid: These are chewable tablets that can reduce the symptoms of GERD extremely quickly. They contain calcium carbonate, which is perfectly safe during pregnancy. While they have a nice fruity or peppermint taste, they are chalky, and women with morning sickness especially might find them difficult to take.

Maalox or Mylanta: These are basically identical antacids, which usually come in a thick, viscous fluid form. They contain calcium car-

> I never had heartburn before in my life. So, when I began to have severe pain and pressure in my upper belly, I panicked. I didn't know what was happening. I called my mom, and she said it was heartburn and to take an antacid. I didn't want to do this without consulting my doctor. I remember lying on the floor, doubled over, waiting for her call back! I wish I'd known it was safe to take an antacid before the pain became so intense!
>
> —Mary, 33, mother of three

bonate, aluminum hydroxide, and magnesium hydroxide, which are safe in pregnancy and act to neutralize the acid in the esophagus. Because they are thick, sticky fluids, some women, especially those with morning sickness, might have a hard time getting the liquid down. Fortunately, if you can swallow the medication, it can reduce your symptoms, right away.

Ranitidine: Ranitidine is what doctors call an H2 blocker because it works to reduce the amount of stomach acid by acting negatively on the histamine-2 chemical receptors in the stomach. These are pills that are generally recognized as safe during pregnancy. Ranitidine can be extremely successful in reducing symptoms, but it can take several hours to see any relief. Over-the-counter ranitidine generally comes in packages containing pills that are 150 mg or 300 mg. Start by taking 150 mg tablets once per day and contact your healthcare provider if you feel you need any more.

Morning Sickness: Polly Needs A Cracker!

Perhaps the symptom of pregnancy women fear most is the proverbial "morning sickness." Contrary to popular belief, morning sickness can happen any time of the day, and it can range from a mild case of queasiness to vomiting so severe that you cannot even keep even liquids down.

Morning sickness happens in about half of all normal pregnancies. Like many other symptoms of pregnancy, the symptom is due to the sudden change in the levels of the hormones estrogen and hCG in the blood and tissues. Doctors have traditionally been reassured to see some morning sickness in a woman because it means that the hormone levels are high, and the pregnancy has a better-than-average chance of being successful. Do not worry, however, if you do not get morning sickness at all. It simply means that your stomach is doing a better job of handling the stressors of the hormone changes.

Morning sickness generally shows up when you first wake up in the morning and is worse on an empty stomach. Some women only feel nauseous in the presence of certain smells. Exactly which smells trigger nausea and possible vomiting varies widely among women and can be different from pregnancy to pregnancy. Certain food smells, however, appear to be common triggers for many women.

The trick with morning sickness is to find the things that trigger your symptoms and take steps to avoid them. If you need to have something in your stomach all the time, make sure you are always prepared with snacks. If you cannot get out of bed in the morning

My partner loved fried eggs and bacon on Sunday mornings, but I suddenly could not stand the smell of either! I actually threw up one morning because of it. Reluctantly, he had to stop eating them until week 16, when the smell no longer bothered me. Boy, did he enjoy that breakfast when I gave him the go-ahead!
—*Michelle, 40, mother of three*

without vomiting shortly thereafter, find a remedy that works for you—like a cup of ginger tea before getting out of bed. Avoid those foods and smells that make your symptoms worse.

Morning sickness can be very severe at times, and you may need to see your healthcare provider or visit an emergency room if you believe you are getting dehydrated from vomiting. Fortunately for most women, morning sickness lasts only a few weeks, and by the second trimester, you should feel better. Particularly sensitive women may have this symptom throughout the pregnancy. If this is happening to you, see your healthcare provider for further advice and guidance.

Let's take a look at some strategies you might have on hand in order to deal with your symptoms of morning sickness. Not every strategy works on every woman so you should go through the list and try different things to see which ones work the best for you.

Eat smaller meals throughout the day: Nausea is worse on an empty stomach. It helps to eat small meals throughout the day rather than eating large meals and having long periods of time where your stomach is

empty. Carry packs of crackers or cookies to snack on and change your patterns of eating so you are eating five to six small meals every day.

Avoid dehydration: Do everything you can to avoid dehydration, which is actually much more harmful to you than to your baby. If you have to carry a water bottle around with your favorite beverage, do so. Frequent small drinks of water or a nonacidic liquid are best. Set a glass of water or water bottle at your bedside so you can take a sip during the night and keep water handy at your desk if you have an office job.

Do not mix liquids with solid foods: For some reason, morning sickness is better if you do not mix your liquids with your solids. Go ahead and have your meal as planned but skip the glass of milk or water until at least half an hour after your meal. You can also have your liquids half an hour before meals.

Wake up slowly—keep your head down: Some women literally cannot get out of bed in the morning in the first few weeks of pregnancy without heading to the toilet to vomit. In this situation, try this: When you wake up, keep your head down as much as possible and don't get out of bed. Keep a pack of soda crackers within reach by the bedside. After a few crackers and a quick rest, get out of bed and see if you feel better.

Limit exposure to cooking smells: As mentioned, smells are sometimes hard for women with morning sickness to tolerate. Cooking smells seem to be the worst. Try having someone else cook for you and keep fans going or open the window to decrease smells.

Get plenty of rest: Nausea and vomiting can take a toll on even the hardiest woman. Make sure you take the time to rest as often as possible and even schedule an afternoon nap if you have the time. The better rested you are during this part of pregnancy, the less likely you are to experience nausea and vomiting.

Keep cool: Morning sickness is definitely worse when you are stuck in hot, stuffy places. Try to avoid getting overheated and keep your surroundings as fresh and airy as possible.

Stock up on lemons: Lemons are a natural remedy for nausea that can be safely used in pregnancy. Keep lemons and lemonade in the house. Even sniffing a lemon will quell some women's symptoms of nausea. A tall glass of cool lemonade provides a nice relief from nausea symptoms.

Double-duty watermelon: Watermelon will help you stay hydrated and does a great deal to reduce the symptoms of nausea. A small bowl of cut-up watermelon will help.

Potato chip appetizer: If you find yourself too nauseated to sit down at the table for a meal, try having salty potato chips in the house and munch on a few. They will often settle your stomach so that you can sit down and have a normal meal.

Mild exercise: Exercise sounds like the last thing you would want to do when you're

I had morning sickness, and the one thing that helped me was that I never went anywhere without saltines and a can of ginger ale. As soon as the nausea hit me, I'd sip on the ginger ale and nibble the crackers—even on the subway or while in a meeting. It really helped.
—*Yolanda, 32, mother of one*

feeling nauseous, but a little bit of exercise can settle your stomach and make you feel better. Try a simple walk around the block and only go at a pace that makes you feel comfortable.

Stay upright after eating: Try not to lie down after you eat. Lying down can bring the acidic contents of your stomach into the esophagus. Not only can it give you a bad case of heartburn but it can also make you nauseated. Try to stay upright for at least a half hour after a meal.

Never skip a meal: An empty stomach is often an upset stomach. Even if you think it will help you keep your weight down, never skip a meal and allow your stomach to become empty. Acid builds up in an empty stomach and makes symptoms of nausea and vomiting much worse. (And skipping meals is not a good weight-control method, either.)

Watch the spices: Spicy food can be the worst thing for morning sickness. Even cooking spicy food can trigger nausea and vomiting in some women. If you happen to really like spicy food but can't eat it during this phase of

Try deep breathing if you feel nausea. Sit quietly and focus on breathing in and breathing out. Try it for 10 in-and-out breaths. It helps relax your body and take your mind off feeling sick! —*Janet, 41, mother of two*

pregnancy, the problem should be short lived, and you may be craving spicy foods by the middle of your second trimester!

Ginger tea soother: Ginger tea is an herbal remedy that works wonders. Ginger has anti-nausea properties, and is sometimes used in cases of motion sickness. Drink ginger tea warm or cold, and consider adding sugar or honey if you need the extra calories.

Frequent Urination

Frequent urination happens during pregnancy when hormones rise drastically and the blood volume flowing through the veins and arteries increases substantially. By the end of the pregnancy, you will actually have 50 percent more blood than you had before you were pregnant. All that blood is liquid that needs to be processed by your kidneys. Your kidneys make more urine, and you have to urinate more often. You may find yourself getting up more often during the night to urinate, and you will need to take more breaks to go to the bathroom than ever before. Many women experience frequent urination as early as the sixth week of pregnancy.

It is important that you remember to take bathroom breaks whenever you need to. If you allow urine to sit too long in your bladder, you can get a bladder infection. Bladder infections are common in pregnancy, and, while not generally dangerous to the embryo or fetus, they are extremely uncomfortable and can lead to a kidney infection, which is more serious. If your kidneys become infected you will land in a doctor's office or emergency room fairly quickly with extremely uncomfortable symptoms. Take the time to drink as much as you need to in order to feel well hydrated. This will further increase your need to urinate but can reduce the incidence of bladder infections and will keep you from being dehydrated, which can increase nausea.

Your Emotions: Rollercoaster Ride or Amusement Park?

You may be one of those lucky women who glide through their second month without any emotional changes. They are happy about the pregnancy and will have begun devoting their extra time to eating healthier and exercising. They may have purchased a pregnancy book such as this one and are eagerly lapping up the pages, learning all they can about their pregnancy. If you are one of these women, you may be in the minority! Most women experience emotional changes, some of which date from the moment they realize they are pregnant. Emotional changes vary greatly from one pregnant woman to the next and depend on a number of factors:

Circumstances of the Pregnancy

Was this a planned or unplanned pregnancy? Does your partner share your feelings about having a baby? Was this a pregnancy that resulted from violence or coercion? Are you currently living in an unsafe situation?

Fears about the Pregnancy

Do you chronically worry that something is wrong with the baby? Have you had a past pregnancy complication you do not want to reexperience? Have you had a pregnancy loss you do not want to repeat?

Stress

Do you work a full-time job that requires more than 40 hours a week? Do you have relationship issues that are causing you stress? Are there going to be financial worries once the baby comes, or do you already have financial worries that make this pregnancy difficult?

Physical Demands

Do you have a toddler at home you need to carry around or other children to care for? Do you have a physically demanding job that requires a great deal of stamina on a regular basis?

Resilience

Everyone is different. What is stressful and difficult to handle in the case of one woman might be a minor ruffle in another's life. If you find you are less resilient than others, get some professional help from a counselor or therapist to help you ride out the emotions. The happier you are, the happier your baby will be.

Being pregnant can make you emotional for many reasons, but the two most likely are: (1) hormonal changes, and (2) stress regarding your pregnancy. Let's look at both of these issues.

Stress Affects Your Emotions

How you feel about being pregnant is likely to lead to variable emotional responses. At week five, it may seem almost unbelievable that a life is growing inside of you. Certainly, an embryo at this stage cannot be felt, and the fact that you are about to become a mother can be overwhelming. Even though you may be overcome with happiness and excitement, thoughts about everything from what you will pick for baby furniture to how you will handle finances may be occupying your thoughts. You may feel suddenly inundated with everything that needs to get done before the arrival of your baby—and you may suddenly want to do everything as soon as possible. However, before you panic, remember that 40 weeks is a long time. Everything will fall into place. So, pace yourself, and try to enjoy each day of your pregnancy!

Conversely, you may feel more reticent about being pregnant if you have experienced a past pregnancy loss. These first weeks, the passage of time is both frightening and golden; each passing day you remain pregnant could mean that this pregnancy will be a healthy one. Yet you worry each day that it may not last. Some women carry this fear throughout their pregnancy, while others begin to feel better as weeks 5 through 8 carry over to weeks 9 through 12. Sometimes a well-timed fetal ultrasound can be performed in these early weeks of pregnancy. The identification of a heartbeat on the ultrasound machine can be both joyful and reassuring.

Whatever emotions your pregnancy is bringing up for you, it helps to talk about what you are experiencing. Discuss your feelings with your healthcare provider, a therapist or counselor, or your partner. You can also talk to other moms and to your friends and family. Whomever you choose to talk to, be sure that they are supportive and upbeat.

You can also search out blogs and other online forums to find like-minded women who are experiencing what you are or who have already been through it. Online forums exist on every pregnancy topic you can think of and provide an additional means of support. But a word of caution: Take what you read with a grain of salt. If you have serious questions or concerns, it is still always best to check with your healthcare provider.

Hormonal Changes

The first few weeks of pregnancy are a time of great hormonal changes in your body. The hormones progesterone and hCG are rising rapidly in response to the growing pregnancy, and these hormones act on the brain, the rest of the nervous system, and the endocrine (hormonal) system of the body. In early pregnancy, for example, the level of hCG can approximately double every two days until it quickly reaches thousands of International Units (IU) per deciliter in your body. A normal hCG level in a nonpregnant woman approaches zero. Such a change in the hormonal makeup is bound to begin to take an emotional toll on even the most placid woman!

Troublesome Emotions

Stress and hormonal changes can lead to some more disturbing feelings. Here are some common emotions you may experience:

I hate when my wife cries for whatever reason. So, when she became weepy during her first trimester, I had a hard time with it. I decided to lighten things up by keeping tissues in my pocket. And every time she began to cry over something silly, I just handed her tissues and said, "Tell me when it's over." It made us both laugh and kept things in perspective.
—*Ted, 35, dad of two*

Anxiety: You may be feeling anxious and fearful. Sometimes this fear is based on genuine reasons for concern. For example, you may feel anxiety about the health of the unborn baby. You may feel that it is too early to celebrate and that you might lose the pregnancy at any time. You can also feel a kind of anxiety or fearfulness that you cannot place. A fearful sensation can wake you in the night, or you may feel a vague sense of unease for no apparent reason. This emotion, like fatigue, often disappears by the time you reach your second trimester.

Sadness or depression: An increase in tearfulness is a common symptom of early pregnancy. You may find yourself getting emotional and crying over an ordinary gift card, or you may find that sad movies or those with strong themes send you into tears when, ordinarily, such a thing would not have occurred. Many women become disturbed by the sudden change in sentimentality because they feel as though they will be an emotional wreck the entire pregnancy. While emotions do run high throughout pregnancy, many women feel more like themselves—and less tearful—by the time they reach their second trimester. If you feel an unrelenting sadness or your mood is so low you have trouble functioning, seek help for depression. Talk to your healthcare provider and ask for a referral to a therapist.

Irritability: You might begin to experience an increase in irritability in these first few weeks of pregnancy. You may have more arguments with your partner, or you may find your children's behavior to be more bothersome than usual. You might be less tolerant

> I couldn't stand my sweet husband asking me every morning how I was feeling—and he was getting tired of having his head bitten off for being concerned. So, every morning, I stuck a word on the refrigerator door alerting my husband to how I was feeling. He could simply check the fridge, and if the word wasn't "cranky," "nauseated," or "exhausted," he could give me a hug and ask, "How are you feeling?" It took a lot of stress out of those first few months! —*Tabatha, 30, mother of one*

of the dish left out or your partner's impatient words and feel as though you might fly off the handle. These irritable feelings are a normal part of the first few weeks of pregnancy, and they do pass. Simple techniques such as deep breathing and counting to 10 before answering can be very useful.

Mood swings: Mood swings are common in this part of pregnancy. You may have the desire to do something, such as a shopping trip or another outing, and then change your mind at the last minute. You may find something someone said to be hilariously funny, only to start crying a few minutes later. When you are having mood swings, you cannot take much stock in what you are feeling because that feeling could change in a matter of moments. Mood swings are a common and normal part of the first weeks of pregnancy. By the time you reach your second trimester, most of these issues disappear. Keep your sense of humor and remember you are not going crazy!

Your First Prenatal Visit: Much Ado about Everything!

Your first prenatal visit is exciting and perhaps anxiety-producing.

When Should You Have Your First Visit?

Most women have their first prenatal visit sometime after six weeks' gestation, which is two weeks after they have missed their period.

Exceptions to this include women who might be having constant or intermittent bleeding and want some reassurance that everything is going to be fine. Women with recurrent previous miscarriages might want to see their healthcare provider immediately in order to be tested for the blood level of progesterone. Therefore, the first visit may be as early as six weeks or as late as twelve weeks. You should seek prenatal care before you reach 12 weeks' gestation. The best idea is to call your healthcare provider as early as possible and ask when you should schedule your first visit.

What to Expect at the First Visit

First, you will meet your obstetrician, family practice doctor, or nurse-midwife. He or she will examine you and ask about your current health and past medical history.

Remember that this first visit is your opportunity to decide whether this is the right healthcare provider and practice for you. Even if you have carefully researched your options, you may simply not "click" with the provider, or you may feel that you are not being treated respectfully when you are seen. Trust your instincts, and remember that you can find someone else if you are not comfortable with the first provider you see. The earlier you make the change, the better.

All pregnancies are different. This is your chance to ask your healthcare provider about your specific pregnancy: what to expect and what you should be concerned about, if anything. This will likely be your longest prenatal visit because blood needs to be drawn, you need a complete exam, and your past medical and obstetrical history needs to be reviewed. This is also the time to start asking questions. Take the time before your appointment to write down as many questions as you can for your healthcare provider so you leave your appointment informed!

The healthcare provider will ask you questions that determine your "dates" or the time frame for when the baby is likely to be born. He or she will use a special pregnancy wheel and, using the date of your last menstrual period or the known date of conception, determine the expected date of confinement

Prepare for Your First Prenatal Visit

- Allow plenty of time. This will probably be your longest visit, and you don't want to be stressed about the time it takes. Arrange for childcare if needed.

- If there are aspects of your history that you are not ready to share with your partner, you may wish to go alone. It is important that you respond fully to any questions your healthcare provider may ask, as this information can affect your pregnancy.

- Before your visit, write down any questions you want to ask. Remember that you can "interview" the healthcare provider to decide if he or she is a good match for your needs.

- Bring a small notebook to take notes—you will be surprised at how much information you will forget because of all the excitement!

- Make a list of all prescription and over-the-counter medications you take, including the dosage. Include anything you have taken since your last menstrual period.

- If you have a complicated medical history, write it out so that you are not struggling to remember dates and conditions during your visit.

- If you have had any genetic tests before conceiving, bring a copy of the results.

- Be sure you know the date of the first day of your last menstrual cycle, if possible.

(EDC). This is the estimated date of your baby's birth. Then you will be asked a series of detailed questions about your past and present health.

Your Past Medical History

Your healthcare provider will want to know about what your health has been like over your lifetime and in recent months. Some of these questions affect the management of your pregnancy, so it is important for you to be honest and complete in your answers.

General health and medical history: The healthcare provider will want to know if you have ever been in the hospital before. This reveals information about what kinds of conditions you have and if any of these conditions could interfere with the current pregnancy. The medical history of your family should also be discussed during this initial visit; this historical information includes diseases, psychological conditions, and obstetrical issues. At the very least, the medical histories of your parents and siblings should be included.

Existing or prior medical conditions: Your healthcare provider may ask if you have any medical conditions, such as liver disease, kidney disease, diabetes, a heart problem, or an autoimmune disease (such as lupus or rheumatoid arthritis). Some of these issues need to be managed intensively during the pregnancy, and you may need a specialist to work along with the OB doctor or other healthcare provider.

Mental health issues: You will also be asked about your past and present mental health. Mental health issues include depression, anxiety, eating disorders, bipolar disorder, and psychosis. Any medications you are taking need to be discussed. You will likely be instructed to consult with your mental health specialist (usually a psychiatrist or psychiatric nurse practitioner), who will change dosages, switch medications, or stop medications altogether if necessary. It is important that your

OB doctor or midwife and mental health specialist are in communication and work together during your pregnancy and that you have enough information to participate in decisions about your own care.

Relationship abuse: Healthcare providers now routinely screen for intimate partner violence, and some ask about sexual coercion, assault, or abuse as well. If you are not safe in your relationship, your healthcare provider should be able to connect you to community resources (such as confidential domestic violence and sexual abuse advocacy agencies) that can help. If you are not in danger currently but have a history of any form of abuse, this can also affect your emotions, reactions, and ability to participate in your prenatal care and enjoy parenting. The medical profession is learning more about the ways in which women are controlled by abusive partners, including interference with birth control and pressure about pregnancy, and you may be able to get support and referrals if you can talk about these difficult issues.

Gynecological history: The healthcare provider will want to know what type of birth control devices and medications you have used in the past and especially the most recent method of birth control you have used, including when you stopped using that form of birth control. If you have ever had an abortion or a miscarriage before, you need to say so. If you have had multiple miscarriages, the healthcare provider may perform a progesterone test to make sure your progesterone level is high enough. A cervical exam might show premature opening of the cervix. This may mean you are a candidate for a cervical cerclage, a procedure in which the cervix is stitched together so it cannot open prematurely.

Your Present Health

You will have a physical exam to assess your general health. Your healthcare provider will also listen to your heart and lungs and do an abdominal exam.

Baseline measurements: Your healthcare provider will be interested in your height, weight, and blood pressure. If you have high blood pressure at this time, your medical follow-up will be more intense, and you may need to see an internist to discuss using a safe blood pressure medication during the pregnancy. Your height and weight will allow your healthcare provider to determine your body mass index (BMI), which is a measure of whether you are underweight, normal weight, or overweight. The amount of weight you gain in pregnancy should differ according to your BMI. (For how to calculate your BMI and information about the meaning of this measurement, see Chapter 1.)

Gynecological health and exam: Your healthcare provider will do a breast exam for breast nodules or breast cancer and will examine the uterus and cervix by doing a bimanual exam, in which he or she places two fingers into the vagina and uses the other hand to "trap" the uterus between the two hands. The size and shape of the uterus are examined and the healthcare provider makes an educated guess as to how far along in the pregnancy you are. Your healthcare provider will also assess to see that the cervix is closed and firm. A Pap test will likely be performed to check for

The First Prenatal Visit

During this visit, your healthcare provider will

- ask detailed questions about your past medical history
- learn about any current medical problems
- find out what medications you are taking and discuss their safety
- talk to you about vitamins and nutrition
- perform an internal exam
- conduct a panel of blood and urine tests
- check your general health, including your blood pressure
- ask about your safety at home
- discuss what to expect in your pregnancy
- answer any questions you may have

abnormal cervical cells, and the cervix will be evaluated for sexually transmitted diseases. The uterine size will be evaluated and fetal heart tones may be assessed (if you are close to 12 weeks' gestation).

Medications: Your current and recent medications are important and will need to be reviewed. It's a good idea to prepare a detailed list before your first prenatal visit. Some medications can absolutely not be taken during pregnancy and will need to be stopped. If there are medications you cannot avoid taking (such as for chronic medical or psychiatric conditions), you will need to work with a specialist such as an internist or rheumatologist, and possibly with a perinatologist, so that you can take the safest medications possible throughout the pregnancy.

Medication allergies need to be noted. During times of distraction or emergency, you may not be able to tell your healthcare provider what you are allergic to.

Lab Tests

Blood will be drawn at your first prenatal visit. Some of these tests will be related to your general health, while others will specifically be related to pregnancy. Let's take a look at the various screening tests that will be performed during this first prenatal visit.

Hemoglobin: This is a test of your red blood cell count and will tell if you are anemic or not. Anemia is common in pregnancy, but it is not usually present early in pregnancy. If you are found to be anemic at the first prenatal visit, your healthcare provider will recommend that you buy iron tablets to take once a day. Iron builds up the blood count, and you will feel more energetic as well.

Blood type: Your blood type is O, A, B, or AB. Exactly what blood type you are does not affect the pregnancy. However, should you need blood due to some emergency, it is a good idea to know and record your blood type so that you will be given the right blood.

Rh factor: The Rh factor is important in pregnancy. Rh is a protein in blood, and you will be either Rh positive, meaning you have the protein, or Rh negative, meaning you do not have the protein. If you are Rh negative, and your baby is Rh positive, your baby can pass antibodies into your blood. These antibodies can affect future pregnancies and can be very harmful. If you are Rh negative, you should receive Rh immunoglobulin (RhIG) to prevent this from happening. If both you and the baby's father are Rh negative, the baby will be Rh negative and there is no risk. RhIG is given at 28 weeks of gestation and then after

childbirth if the baby is found to be positive. It should also be given within 72 hours of bleeding that occurs during pregnancy.

Rubella screen: Rubella—also called German measles—is a viral illness you can get as a child. While German measles is not very common, most children are vaccinated for the disease as babies. In some cases, however, you may have skipped getting the vaccine or it may not have "taken." If this is the case, the rubella screen will show up as negative, and you are vulnerable to getting rubella during pregnancy. Having rubella while pregnant is very dangerous to the baby and can result in fetal death.

Varicella screen: Varicella is also known as chicken pox. Most people have had the dis-

Prenatal Testing: The First Tests

Generally, doctors agree that your first obstetrical (OB) visit should take place between six and ten weeks of pregnancy, but many women call and make an appointment as soon as their home pregnancy test is positive. One of the first orders of business will be to have blood drawn to determine blood and Rh types and your hemoglobin level. Your healthcare provider can also confirm your pregnancy with a blood test, and will test for syphilis, HIV, and other sexually transmitted diseases; bladder infection; and your immunity to varicella (chicken pox). The provider will also check to see if you have had rubella or hepatitis B. Your healthcare provider will usually do a Pap smear during your initial visit. This visit is the first step to ensuring you have a healthy pregnancy!

ease and a varicella vaccination is available, although it is usually given to young children. You are screened for varicella because having this illness while pregnant can negatively affect your baby's health.

Cystic fibrosis screen: Cystic fibrosis is a disease caused by genes from both parents that results in thick sputum in the lungs and thickened mucus in the abdominal area. This is a disease that can result in chronic respiratory illnesses, recurrent blockage of the bowels, and early death as a teen or young adult.

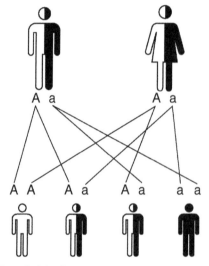

Genetic inheritance

Children inherit genes from both parents. Here the letters indicate a trait like the gene for Tay-Sachs disease, which requires that both parents have that gene and pass it on to their child (indicated as aa), who then is an affected individual. An individual who carries a gene for Tay-Sachs disease from one parent but did not inherit this gene from the other parent will appear normal (Aa) but can pass it on to his or her children, hence the need for prenatal genetic testing.

Hepatitis B surface antigen: This is a liver disease passed on through sexual activity and tainted blood. There is a vaccination against hepatitis B but not everyone has had it. A test for hepatitis B surface antigen tells the doctor if you have chronic hepatitis, which can be dangerous to the developing fetus.

Tay-Sachs and other Ashkenazi diseases: As many as one in four people who are of Ashkenazi (Eastern European) Jewish descent may be a carrier for a variety of genetic disorders. The most well known is the rare disease Tay-Sachs, but there are a variety of other genetic disorders in this group. The screen will tell you if you are at risk for transmitting one of these diseases. The odds are one in four that these disorders will be passed on to an individual child if both parents carry the gene.

Sickle cell disease (SCD) and other hemoglobin abnormalities: Sickle cell is a blood disease that is primarily found in the African American population. It is a condition that causes blood cells to deform and break, resulting in blockages in the arteries and veins. Anemia is common in this disease. During pregnancy, the disease can become more severe and pain episodes can occur more often. A pregnant woman with SCD is at a higher risk of preterm labor and of having a low birth weight baby. However, with early prenatal care and careful monitoring throughout pregnancy, a woman with SCD can have a healthy pregnancy. Beta thalassemia is another hemoglobin abnormality found primarily in those of Mediterranean and African descent. It can range in severity.

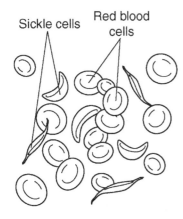

Normal cells versus sickle-shaped cells
Sickle cell disease can make a pregnancy more complicated.

HIV: Human Immunodeficiency Virus (HIV) is a serious virus passed through unprotected sex or contact with human blood, such as through shared hypodermic needles (for instance, drug use). If you have HIV, you have a high-risk pregnancy as the virus can be passed on to your fetus. Certain medications can be given during pregnancy that can decrease the risk of passing on HIV to your baby. Even if you do not have HIV, for the sake of the health of your fetus, it is best to be proactive by being honest with your doctor if you believe you are at risk for the virus.

Tuberculosis: This is a test done on high-risk patients, such as recent immigrants from countries where the disease is more prevalent and people who live with someone who has the disease. The test involves injecting a small amount of tuberculin protein under the skin. If a strong reaction occurs to the injection over the next three days, you likely have had tuberculosis.

Active tuberculosis can be harmful to the fetus.

Hepatitis C: This is a form of hepatitis that is usually transmitted by exposure to blood, although it can also be transmitted by sexual contact. The test for hepatitis C is done on patients who have been at risk for the disease.

Your First Prenatal Ultrasound

During this first prenatal visit, your healthcare provider will determine when you got pregnant and, most significantly, when you will deliver. To do so, working from the dates of your last menstrual period, he or she uses a "pregnancy wheel" for the calculations. If you do not know the dates of your last menstrual

Don't ask me why, but I thought I'd be able to hear my baby's heartbeat and get an ultrasound photo at my first visit! I wish I'd read a book like this before I went; then I wouldn't have had to deal with the embarrassment of looking shocked when my doctor said my baby was practically microscopic at the moment!
—*Jillian, 27, mother of one*

period, the healthcare provider will probably rely on an ultrasound to get a set of accurate dates.

The earlier an ultrasound is done in pregnancy, the more accurately your healthcare provider can estimate the gestational age and your due date. If you have your ultrasound at seven weeks, you have an accurate due date within a week. If you do not have your ultrasound until 20 weeks, the dates are only accurate to within two weeks.

Questions and Answers for Your Prenatal Visit

Your first prenatal visit is not just a time for your healthcare provider to question you about your health and medical history; it is also an important opportunity to ask any questions you may have about your pregnancy—from this early stage right to the birth of your baby! In fact, while labor and delivery are still a long time away, knowing your healthcare provider's opinions around the process of delivering a baby will be informative and helpful. Keep in mind that your first prenatal visit can serve as a screening interview of sorts. Every woman is unique and has specific issues and concerns about her pregnancy. The questions you ask and the answers you receive may help you decide if a particular clinic or practice is right for you. You should feel comfortable to ask a range of questions, such as those below. The answers represent typical responses you can expect.

Question: What do I do about dental care?

Answer: Good dental care is very important in pregnancy. You should have your teeth examined and cleaned by a dental hygienist at least once during your pregnancy. You should also practice meticulous dental care, including brushing and flossing twice daily. Obstetricians do not like you to have X-rays during pregnancy but may agree to it in a dental emergency, such as if a tooth abscesses. You should also have a dental appointment shortly after you deliver because pregnancy can make you prone to cavities.

Question: Can I eat my meat raw or very rare?

Answer: Meat often contains parasites that can affect you and your baby. The best precaution is to eat your meat well done. In particular, pork should be well cooked because it contains the Trichinella worm in its muscle. If eaten, the worm can get into your system and give you Trichinella, which can affect muscle development in the fetus.

Question: What if I get a fever?

Answer: Generally, low-grade fevers of 99.5°F or less are not dangerous to the embryo or fetus. The only really safe medication you can take in pregnancy for a fever is Tylenol or acetaminophen. Take it at the recommended dose of 500 to 1000 mg every four to six hours. Do not take any other medication for fever. The important thing is to find out why the fever is occurring so you can take measures to cure the underlying condition. Be sure to call your healthcare provider if you have a fever.

Question: What kinds of environmental hazards should I avoid?

Answer: There are many types of environmental hazards that can be harmful in pregnancy. If you work in an environment that employs a lot of solvents like toluene and hexane, try to limit your exposure to them as much as possible. You should definitely avoid pesticides and herbicides, commonly used in gardening, as these can cause genetic deficiencies in your embryo and, later, birth defects to your baby. You can still use most cleaning products, but it is a good idea to wear gloves. (See Chapter 2 for detailed information.)

Question: Can I travel during pregnancy?

Answer: Travel, including by plane, train, and car, is generally safe through much of the pregnancy. Your healthcare provider may recommend that you not travel by plane after your seventh month—and absolutely

> I had a long list of questions for my first prenatal appointment. When my doctor began getting annoyed and rushing me, I knew I needed to find another doctor. So I did, and then sent a polite note letting my former doctor know why I had done so. She actually appreciated the feedback. If you are not happy with your choice, make another one! Nine months is a long time! —*Kelly, 34, mother of two*

no plane travel during the ninth month. This is because you could rupture your membranes or go into labor during your flight!

Question: How can I avoid having a miscarriage?

Answer: The vast majority of miscarriages cannot be prevented because they are genetic in origin and often happen because there is something wrong with the pregnancy. If you have recurrent miscarriages, check with your healthcare provider about whether you have progesterone deficiency syndrome, and get treated for it to prevent pregnancy loss.

Question: What should I do about my diet?

Answer: You should eat a healthy diet containing lots of vegetables, fruits, whole grains, and lean meats. You should eat the same number of calories you normally eat (about 2000 to 2300 calories) until you reach your fourth month of pregnancy, when you should add about 300 calories per day.

Question: Should I take prenatal vitamins, any other supplements, or herbal remedies?

Answer: You should begin taking an over-the-counter or prescription prenatal vitamin that has the recommended extra doses of iron and folic acid when compared to normal vitamins. If you don't consume adequate amounts of milk or other dairy products, take 1200 milligrams of calcium with vitamin D every day. Ask your healthcare provider about the dose and timing of supplements, since your body can't absorb too much calcium at once. Your healthcare provider may also recommend iron pills if your hemoglobin comes back low. There are no herbal remedies specifically recommended for pregnancy, and research on herbs in pregnancy is scant. Be sure to consult with an herbalist about what to take during pregnancy and be sure to inform your doctor of any herbal supplements you are taking.

Question: Can I exercise while pregnant?

Answer: Of course! You can generally continue any exercise you have been doing prior to pregnancy. As your pregnancy progresses, you may have to alter your activity to accommodate your growing belly. Avoid contact sports that can injure the uterus, especially past the fourth month of pregnancy. If you are going to try a new sport, be sure to get the OK from your healthcare provider before beginning.

Question: Are there midwives in this clinic?

Answer: Some clinics have midwives that work alongside the doctor. Often the doctor and midwife will alternate visits until the end of the pregnancy. In these clinics, you will often have the option of having a midwife deliver your baby with obstetrical backup.

Question: Whom do I call when I have a question, and when will my question be answered?

Answer: Some clinics set up a special line staffed by nurses trained in obstetrics and gynecology. You can ask them questions 24 hours a day. Many women feel relieved to have such quick access to help. On the other hand, some clinics have answering services that call the doctor for you. You then wait for the on-call physician to contact you directly. Either approach provides you support, but some women hesitate to contact the doctor for what they perceive as a minor question. You will have to decide what works best for you.

Question: Who will be delivering my baby?

Answer: Many practices have group coverage and the arrangements for the person who will perform the delivery vary. It would be worth finding out early if the arrangement suits you.

Question: What do I do if I experience bleeding or cramping?

Answer: You can call the doctor or nurse line to get advice. If the bleeding and cramping are severe, you will probably have to go to the emergency room (ER) to be evaluated and treated by the ER doctor or the on-call obstetrician.

Question: What constitutes an emergency?

Answer: Every healthcare provider has his or her own definition of what is an emergency. A good clinician will tell you that any kind of heavy bleeding or cramping or severe back pain that comes and goes constitutes an emergency. Some doctors consider it a medical emergency if you do not feel the baby move for a few hours. In most cases, you will be asked to report to the ER or the hospital's

Exercise Idea: Prenatal Yoga

Yoga has tremendous health benefits for everyone! By combining your breathing with gentle stretching and a variety of poses, yoga helps your body become strong, relaxed, and energized. Yoga is growing in popularity in the United States. Most health clubs and even some hospitals offer prenatal yoga classes. If you want to try something new or begin a new exercise program, give yoga a try; but be sure your class is prenatal. Some yoga poses, such as twists, are not healthy for your baby. A prenatal instructor will avoid any poses inappropriate for pregnant women. He or she will also know how to adjust poses depending on how flexible you are and how far along you are in your pregnancy!

labor and delivery unit for further evaluation. Bladder infection symptoms are very painful and need prompt treatment. Some doctors would consider this an emergency, too. *If you are at all concerned about anything, however, call your healthcare provider and let him or her decide on the urgency of the matter. Do not try to self-diagnose!*

Question: When will I need to change my habits regarding exercise, sex, and nutrition?

Answer: Your healthcare provider will probably tell you that you should begin adding healthy foods to your diet right away and start taking a multivitamin the minute your pregnancy is confirmed. Unless you have a placenta previa, your sexual activity can remain the same—although you may need to be creative as your baby grows and you expand! With few exceptions, you can exercise as usual until it becomes uncomfortable to do so or if you could be at risk for miscarriage.

Question: Do you have experience working with abuse survivors, and will you work with me to be sure I feel safe and comfortable during pregnancy and childbirth

Answer: Some healthcare providers have specialized training in what is called trauma-informed care. They understand that women who have a history of domestic violence or sexual abuse or assault may find medical procedures to be very challenging. If you are a survivor, you can find resources at the Pandora's Project website (http://pandys.org/quickinfocards.html) that will help you to explain your needs to your provider.

Question: How do you feel about including a doula in my care?

Answer: If you have decided that a doula (see Chapter 3) will be helpful to you, you want to be sure that your healthcare provider will welcome and work cooperatively with this individual rather than feeling uncomfortable with the doula's presence. Some doctors and nurse-midwives routinely include doulas in their practices.

Question: When will my next prenatal visit be?

Answer: Your healthcare provider will probably tell you that you will have prenatal visits every four weeks until you reach 28 weeks. One of these visits should fall between 18 and 20 weeks because this is when you will have another ultrasound to check the fetus and to find out the sex of the baby if you want to know. After 28 weeks, you will have appointments every two to three weeks until you reach 36 weeks. After 36 weeks, you will have weekly visits until you deliver. If you have a high-risk pregnancy, your visits will be closer together.

Question: What testing will I have later in pregnancy?

Answer: Most of the testing will be done on the first prenatal visit. After that, you will have an additional test for hemoglobin levels to see if you are becoming anemic. Urine samples for sugar, blood, or infection are tested every visit. Your weight and blood pressure will be checked, as well as the fetal heartbeat. At 26 to 28 weeks, you will have a one-hour glucose tolerance test (GTT) test, which measures the amount of glucose in your blood after one hour. If it is elevated, you

My doctor was world renowned and no-nonsense and so was her clinic. I thought I liked this approach until one day she had an emergency and I saw one of her colleagues for my prenatal check-up. This doctor was so loving and kind and excited for me that I wished I could switch to her practice! My advice is shop around before you settle on a doctor. Know what you want and don't settle for anything less! —*Zoe, 36, mother of two*

might have a condition known as gestational diabetes, which can be treated.

Question: What are your ideas about natural labor versus medically aided labor like an epidural or, possibly, narcotic pain relief?

Answer: Most doctors are open to a wide variety of labor and delivery choices, but some will have preferences. The first option is natural labor, for which you have no medications to control or lessen pain and instead use techniques like controlled breathing, walking, taking a shower, or sitting on a ball. The epidural, a common option, involves putting medicine into a catheter in the outer part of your spinal canal. It anesthetizes the abdomen and legs so that you have almost complete pain relief throughout your labor, without drowsiness. You can also receive injections of a narcotic pain medication. Such narcotic medications are injected into your muscle (usually in your buttocks, but sometimes in the thigh or upper arm) and give you partial relief for one to two hours.

Question: In what situations would you consider doing a cesarean section?

Answer: It is of interest to note that family practice doctors do fewer cesarean deliveries than obstetricians. One reason may be that a C-section is performed when there is a failure to get the baby out after several hours. There is some variation in doctors' willingness to consider a C-section, but it is generally agreed that fetal distress, hemorrhaging, and placenta previa are reasons to undergo a C-section.

Question: When should an episiotomy be performed?

Answer: An episiotomy is a small incision the doctor makes between the outside of the vagina to down near the anus. It opens up the vagina so the baby passes through more quickly. Some doctors perform this procedure out of convenience, to speed the delivery. Others do it because the baby is truly stuck and needs help to pass through the birth canal. In cases of heavy bleeding or fetal distress, most doctors will not hesitate to do an episiotomy. Very often if an episiotomy is not performed, the woman will tear anyway. This actually is preferred over doing an episiotomy and tends to be better for short-term and long-term healing.

Question: How long past my due date will I be allowed to go?

Answer: This all depends on the condition of your pregnancy. If you are having complications, such as high blood pressure or gestational diabetes, you may be induced before your due date or on your due date. If your pregnancy is considered normal, few healthcare providers will allow you to go two weeks past your due date. Delivering more than two weeks past your due date is associated with an increased risk of fetal distress and placental insufficiency. For this reason, many providers will only let you go one week past your due date.

Question: How do you feel about induced labor?

Answer: Induction of labor involves giving Pitocin by IV, using Cervadil (a medication inserted into the cervix), misoprostol (another medication inserted in the cervix), or a cervical bulb procedure. These procedures are done to bring on labor when it does not start naturally and there is a medical reason to do so. (See Chapter 12 for more details on induced labor.) Some healthcare providers prefer to let nature take its course because there is a slightly higher risk of C-section when the labor is induced. Other doctors will just do inductions of labor if the pregnancy has gone on too long or if it is medically necessary for the mother or fetus. Labor should not be induced for convenience only.

If everything is as expected and the results of the exam are normal, you will be given an appointment to see the doctor in four weeks.

Is My Pregnancy Healthy? Should I Be Worried?

You are living with a new body. For the first time (or second, or third, or...), your entire being is changing to accommodate the growth of a new life. With new sensations in your body and possible side effects of early pregnancy, like nausea, spotting, or exhaustion, it is completely natural you might worry. The following are some things you can do to ease your concerns and things you should immediately tell your healthcare provider about if they occur:

You May Have Your hCGs Checked

Your doctor may do a series of tests called serial hCGs. The testing itself is simple. The doctor draws your blood for the level of human chorionic gonadotropin (hCG). These levels vary greatly among different pregnancies, and a single test is not enough. In a healthy pregnancy, the levels of hCG double within two days. If you have your hCG level tested 48 hours after the first test, the doctor can compare the two numbers to see if the hCG has, in fact, doubled. If the hCG level has doubled, the doctor can tell you that at this point the pregnancy seems to be growing properly. Miscarriages are possible for other reasons, but a doubling of the hCG is a reassuring sign. If the hCG does not

For Dads and Partners:
The Power of Patience
In these early weeks, your partner's body is adjusting and changing to the demands of its new purpose: growing and housing a baby! Remember that you are adjusting, too. Your partner may be irritable, exhausted, and even vomiting. Try to remain patient and flexible. If the smell of steak makes her sick, be gracious about not eating it for now. Give her opportunities to nap, and be forgiving if she snaps at you! Most of this will pass by week 12, when you will likely be able to return some normalcy to your everyday life!

approximately double after two days, this is a concerning sign, and there is a possibility that ultimately you may have a miscarriage.

Hyperemesis Gravidarum: A Case of Extreme Vomiting

If you are among the unlucky few who have nausea and vomiting that become so severe that you run the risk of becoming dehydrated, then you may have a condition known as hyperemesis gravidarum. If you think you are having hyperemesis gravidarum, you should contact your healthcare provider immediately for advice and possible treatment. Hyperemesis gravidarum is generally considered to be a problem of the first trimester of pregnancy, and, in fact, most cases of this condition occur during that time. There are, however, cases of women who are so sensitive that they have hyperemesis gravidarum throughout the entire pregnancy.

Hyperemesis gravidarum is believed to be caused by the high blood levels of hCG that the embryo and the placenta are producing. Women who are pregnant with twins or who have a molar pregnancy (explained in Chapter 3) have higher levels of hCG in their bodies and are more prone to getting the excessive nausea and vomiting involved in this condition. Fortunately, intravenous fluids can be given to restore blood volume and improve symptoms. In general, it is only the fluids that are replaced. It remains up to you to try to get solid nutrition into your body. If you still have trouble keeping food down and continue to lose weight, you may be miserable, but your baby will be able to survive on your body's fat and sugar stores, and your condition will not endanger your baby's life.

Remedies for hyperemesis gravidarum: Think about drinking nutritional beverages like Ensure, which can provide a number of calories and nutrients in a few short gulps. Other beverages like Gatorade can keep your blood volume up and keep your electrolytes in working order. Anything you can do to get nutrition into your body will help your baby and make a difference.

Some women have a single episode of hyperemesis gravidarum and, after treatment by a physician, can continue drinking and eating enough to prevent further episodes of dehydration. Other women need repeated treatments with intravenous fluids in order to feel better. Even if you have already gone to the emergency room for intravenous fluids this pregnancy, don't be afraid to go back again if you need to.

You can try to prevent hyperemesis gravidarum in the same way you fight off symptoms of ordinary morning sickness. Eat plenty of small meals each day, keep crackers

Nutrition Tip: Nausea

If you have nausea and vomiting it can be a problem during this month. To keep getting calories and help keep your food down, try foods like crackers, salty potato chips, toast, or rice. Ginger in many forms helps reduce nausea naturally. Sometimes nausea is worse on an empty stomach, so try to eat something, even if it is only a few nibbles of a saltine. If you have morning sickness and begin to lose weight, you needn't worry unless the weight loss is accompanied by dehydration or an inability to take in fluids. If this should happen, contact your healthcare provider for further advice or head to the emergency room for IV fluids.

handy at all times, and hang onto the water bottle or drink multiple glasses of water each day in order to prevent becoming dehydrated. It would not be unusual to drink up to ten glasses of water each day if your stomach and symptoms of nausea can handle it. Women who have trouble drinking water might do better by drinking carbonated beverages, such as sparkling water or ginger ale.

Another remedy for hyperemesis gravidarum is the use of vitamin B6 supplements, taken at about 50 to 100 milligram per day. If you are experiencing hyperemesis gravidarum and think you want to try vitamin B6 supplementation, talk to your healthcare provider before starting the product.

Occasionally, hyperemesis gravidarum is linked to psychological or emotional problems. If you think you might be suffering from an underlying psychological problem that is making your nausea and vomiting worse for you, do not hesitate to see your healthcare provider or mental health specialist as soon as you can.

Spotting during Pregnancy

Perhaps nothing can be more alarming than vaginal spotting—with or without uterine cramping—during these first few weeks of pregnancy. It is natural to begin to worry about miscarriage. For the most part, you can relax. Up to 30 percent of women with perfectly healthy pregnancies will experience spotting during their first trimester. Usually, the incidence of spotting lessens as your pregnancy progresses, but it is something no woman wants to experience. *While spotting is not uncommon, you should definitely call your healthcare provider if you have any bleeding at all.* It should not be taken lightly. Bleeding

After our first two children, we wanted a third. Sadly, I had three miscarriages in a row. It was a very painful time for me. At one point, I wanted to quit trying, and my husband said something I will always remember: "If it's meant to be, it'll happen. It just hasn't been the right time yet. Have faith." I agreed to keep trying, and our fourth pregnancy ended in a full-term, healthy little girl whom we named Grace. She was meant to be. It's so hard to keep trying, but don't give up just because you have a miscarriage. So much of pregnancy is out of our control. Just have faith. —*Lisa, 45, mother of three*

may indicate an ectopic pregnancy (a pregnancy growing outside of the uterus), which must be addressed. Once it is determined that the pregnancy is properly inside the uterus, there is less cause for alarm.

There are some situations in pregnancy when the phenomenon of spotting is considered to be normal. Around the end of week four, the embryo implants itself into the uterine lining by attaching to the lining and creating the first tender blood vessels that connect your baby to your own body. When blood vessels are first forming, their connections are tenuous and it is normal to have some vaginal bleeding.

Again, when the placenta begins to spread out and grow in the first few weeks, blood vessels are also being connected to you and forming a bridge that will keep the baby alive throughout the entire pregnancy. The placenta grows extremely fast and in an outward direction to form something that will look like a pancake. During this rapid placental growth, blood vessels can temporarily break and give you anything from a few pink spots on your underwear to a temporary flow like a light period.

Anytime you are having spotting during the first few weeks of pregnancy, you need to wear a panty liner or menstrual pad and keep track of how much you are bleeding and whether you are having light pink spotting or a heavy dark flow with or without clots. This way you will be able to provide accurate information to help your healthcare provider know whether you should be seen in the office or emergency room. Don't forget to report any bleeding or spotting. Don't try to determine how serious it is yourself.

When you are having vaginal spotting, you should avoid any sexual intercourse because it could make the bleeding worse. You should not use tampons to hold back the bleeding; tampons left in too long are breeding grounds for infection. Call immediately if you have cramping associated with moderate to heavy bleeding.

Miscarriage Symptoms

The main symptoms of a miscarriage include vaginal bleeding, which can be very heavy, cramping pain in the lower abdomen that feels worse than the cramps of a menstrual period, and the eventual passage of the tissue that was the embryo through the vagina. Once that happens, your bleeding will slow considerably and the miscarriage will be complete.

While bleeding or spotting may have normal causes, they can also signal trouble. Always call your healthcare provider if you are spotting, cramping, or bleeding.

Miscarriage

It is a sad fact that miscarriages do happen. Half of the 20 to 30 percent of women who suffer bleeding complications during early pregnancy will go on to lose the pregnancy. Most miscarriages happen in the early weeks of pregnancy. Past 12 weeks' gestation, miscarriages are far less common, although they can still occur.

"Chemical Pregnancy": Very Early Pregnancy Loss

While about 10 to 15 percent of pregnancies result in detectable miscarriages, experts also believe that fully half of all fertilized eggs are actually miscarried. These very early miscarriages occur in what are known as "chemical pregnancies," which are detectable by testing minute levels of hCG in the woman's body.

Apparently, half the time a pregnancy begins and the hCG begins to rise, the pregnancy is lost—usually right around the time you expect your period, so you do not even know you were pregnant. This chemical pregnancy can only be detected by measuring the hCG levels, and the only way you would know it was lost would be if you had a positive pregnancy test followed by what seemed to be a menstrual period.

Because you do not know you are having a chemical pregnancy, the term "miscarriage" is usually reserved for situations in which a

Causes of Miscarriage

- Genetic mutations
- Autoimmune diseases like rheumatoid arthritis and lupus
- Uterine structural problems, such as having a uterus that has a septum down the middle of it or having a condition known as a bicornuate uterus
- Heavy smoking
- An infection in the uterus
- Heavy alcohol use
- Heavy caffeine use
- Diabetes mellitus, especially if it is not in good control
- Antithyroid antibodies in the bloodstream
- Certain uncommon blood diseases
- A syndrome of low progesterone known as luteal phase deficiency

woman has had a pregnancy test, the test is positive, and she goes on to lose the pregnancy at a later time.

Understanding Miscarriage

Miscarriages are both sad and confusing. As a woman, you wonder what happened and if you could have done anything to prevent the miscarriage. The truth is, however, that almost all miscarriages are completely unpreventable. Miscarriages, in most cases, represent the body's natural process of ridding itself of a pregnancy that was unhealthy or somehow genetically unable to survive. In less common situations, there may be something about your health that you may not have known that caused the pregnancy to end. Women who have more than one miscarriage could have a genetic reason behind their inability to carry a pregnancy to term.

What to Expect if You Need to Go to the Emergency Room

While you should call your healthcare provider even if you have light bleeding, you may be advised to go to the emergency room if you are bleeding through a pad every hour, if you have symptoms of dehydration, or if you have a great deal of cramping along with your bleeding.

At the emergency room, the nurses and doctors will check your vital signs to make sure you are not suffering from dehydration. If you are bleeding heavily or are showing signs of dehydration, the doctor may order IV fluids. You may also have a vaginal exam and may have a test for fetal heart tones. Doctors will also draw your blood for testing. Common blood tests for heavy bleeding in early pregnancy include the following:

Hemoglobin or hematocrit: These tests will determine if you are becoming anemic from blood loss and will estimate the amount of blood you have lost in this episode.

Cause for Alarm? When to Call Your Healthcare Provider

Call your healthcare provider if you experience any of the following:

- Nausea and vomiting that is so severe you cannot keep anything down for at least 24 hours
- Signs and symptoms of dehydration such as feeling faint, dry mouth, and rapid heartbeat
- Losing more than ten pounds during the month
- Any vaginal bleeding or spotting
- Passing anything that looks like tissue, which tends to be lighter and more varied in color than a blood clot

hCG level: Since hCG levels can vary widely in both normal and abnormal pregnancies, a single hCG level may not tell you everything. However, your healthcare provider can repeat a second hCG in two days; if the value has doubled, your pregnancy is likely to be healthy even if you are having bleeding. Normally, hCG levels double until about 10 weeks' gestation and can actually climb from 0 to as high as 290,000 in the first 10 weeks! Then hCG levels begin to decline until week 20. Between week 20 and delivery, the hCG level generally remains stable.

Vaginal ultrasound: Because you are early in your pregnancy, an abdominal ultrasound may not be able to provide adequate information regarding issues with your pregnancy. A vaginal ultrasound can provide more accurate

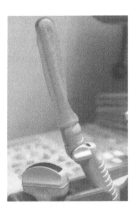

The only way to get a clear ultrasound image in the first few weeks of pregnancy is by inserting a lubricated probe like this one two to three inches into the vagina. For this exam, you will empty your bladder first, then lie down on the examining table. The lubricated probe is smaller than a speculum. Most women find the procedure only slightly uncomfortable.

Pregnancy—like all of life—is filled with mystery, joy, and sometimes heartbreak. Know that you have the strength and love to provide whatever it is your child needs. Stay in the moment. Don't worry about things that haven't happened, and embrace whatever comes. It's all part of the parenting journey. Even if it means saying "good-bye."—*Julie 42, mother of one, with six miscarriages*

information at this point. For a vaginal ultrasound, a technician uses a rod-like transducer that can detect your baby's heartbeat as early as about six weeks. If you are less than six weeks along, the ultrasound will be able to tell if there is something resembling a small berry in your uterus. It can also detect if your uterus is filled with blood or if it is completely empty of pregnancy contents. In addition, the ultrasound examines the fallopian tubes and ovaries to make sure you do not have an ectopic pregnancy, where the embryo is growing outside of your uterus.

If your pregnancy shows no obvious signs of being inevitably lost and you are medically stable, the doctor or midwife will send you home to wait and see what happens. If you do in fact miscarry, your healthcare professional can do a number of things, including waiting to see if you pass pregnancy-related tissue (called the products of conception), performing a vaginal evacuation, or checking another hCG in two day's time.

Notes:

I had just given birth to our second child, and my husband and I were grateful and satisfied. We were pretty strapped financially, and two kids were exactly what we wanted. Well, as life would have it, three months after our little girl was born, I became pregnant for the third time. Surprise! We dreaded telling our families because they knew our financial situation. We waited until the last minute of my twelfth week to tell everyone—and, much to our surprise, no one was negative. "God will provide," my mother said. And she was right! —*Tess, 47, mother of three*

Chapter 5

Month Three—Weeks 9 through 12

Whew! Some of the roughest waves of pregnancy should be subsiding as you enter weeks 9 through 12. You will probably be feeling less morning sickness and more energy. You may be anticipating telling family and friends your big news, and you may be beginning to think about maternity clothes and baby gear! Perhaps one of the best things is that you will begin to actually feel and even look a little more pregnant!

If you have been concerned about miscarriage, you may be allowing yourself to feel some relief as these final weeks of your first trimester come to a close. You may also be considering when to tell your employer and whether you plan to return to work after your baby is born. Breathe and enjoy this time because big things are happening inside your body—your little baby is growing, and you are well into your pregnancy journey!

I was heading toward week 12 of my pregnancy and, at five feet, ten inches tall, I wasn't showing at all. I couldn't wait to explain to my boss and coworkers why I'd been so exhausted and cranky. Trouble was, another coworker who was only five feet, two inches tall was clearly pregnant (she was even wearing maternity clothes) but had not told anyone yet. She wasn't married, and I figured she just wasn't ready to break the news—but she looked at least five months along. And of course, in the workplace, no one could ask her. One afternoon in the ladies room, she confided in me that she was pregnant and was going to tell our boss that afternoon. Her due date was only one week before mine! I didn't tell her my news and I spent the rest of the day dreading telling my boss the following week. We would both be on maternity leave at the same time! Fortunately, my boss took it well. And when I told my colleagues in a meeting, everyone was floored that my due date was only one week after my coworker's—especially her! Although everyone meant well, my coworker and I spent the next six months listening to everyone compare how we carried our babies. It was annoying to say the least, and I often felt sorry for my normally petite coworker because she always looked so much bigger than I did and everyone felt an odd compulsion to mention it. Turns out, she had her baby three days before me, but because she had a C-section, we were in the hospital together. We could finally laugh about all we'd had to put up with at work—and holding our babies made it all worthwhile! —*Monica, 36*

In this chapter, we will cover answers to the following concerns related to the last month of your first trimester:

- How will my body look and feel at this point?
- How is my baby growing?
- When can I hear its heartbeat?
- What if I am carrying multiples (twins or triplets)?
- Should I go ahead and have a genetic test?
- Should I find out the sex of my baby?
- How and when should we tell other people I'm pregnant?
- What about ectopic pregnancy?

Things Are Beginning to Take Shape—Even You!

So much is happening now! By week 12 you will likely begin to feel the little baby bump as your uterus expands, and perhaps you will begin to look pregnant, too. The following is an overview of what might be happening to you this month:

- By now, you may have overcome the urge to keep the pregnancy to yourself and are officially pregnant to everyone you know. On the other hand, you may still be keeping your secret for fear of pregnancy loss and may have only told one or two close friends or relatives that you are pregnant. With week 12 approaching, you may be anticipating spreading the joyful news!
- The risk of having a miscarriage is still present but diminishes with every passing day. Women can still have some cramping and spotting until approximately the twelfth week. Your healthcare provider

should be notified of any bleeding and may be able to reassure you.

- This is still a time when toxins, infections, chemicals, smoking and drinking, and other exposures can cause a birth defect including an insult to your baby's delicate and differentiating brain. Anything that attacks the brain at this stage of pregnancy could have drastic results.
- Your symptoms of fatigue and morning sickness should be subsiding or may have passed completely by now. This means you can begin to redouble your efforts toward eating a healthy diet and exercising to the best of your ability. Your nutrition is very important at this stage and your fetus needs every molecule of healthy calories, vitamins, and minerals you can give him or her.
- While the average person will still not be able to tell you are pregnant, you may notice that your favorite pair of jeans does not zip up properly, and you often can feel a hard lump just above your pubic bone in your lower abdomen. By your twelfth week, your uterus is the size of a large grapefruit and is continuing to grow. You might be wistfully looking at maternity clothes at this stage, but you won't need them for at least another month.
- You may have had your first prenatal visit by now. (For detailed information about what to expect and ask at the first visit, see Chapter 4.) If you have had the first visit, you will have discussed with your healthcare provider any preexisting or pregnancy-related conditions that increase your risk of complications. If your pregnancy is expected to go normally and everything is

Once I heard the baby's heartbeat and my doctor reassured me that everything was going well, I was so relieved. I picked up the phone and called my mom! I'll always remember staying up with her for two hours talking, crying, and reminiscing about my own childhood! It was such a special moment! —*Asacia, 30, mother of two*

happening on schedule, you can sit back and enjoy the journey of being pregnant. If your pregnancy is expected to be high risk, follow your doctor's instructions to the letter while remaining as positive and stress-free as possible!

Your Baby's Growth and Development: Hello Little Person!

During weeks 9 through 12 your baby's growth and development continues at an extremely rapid pace. At this point in the pregnancy, development is more important than growth. As mentioned, any kind of chemical or genetic insult to the embryo or fetus at this stage in development could contribute to a serious birth defect. So keep up your good work eating healthy and avoiding toxins.

Week 9

Getting enough calcium—either in your diet or through a supplement—is increasingly important during this week of development. Your baby is beginning to grow cells

that make the cartilage and bones that will continue to grow throughout the pregnancy. The eyes are developing and the eyeballs can be recognized. Your baby is busy growing a tongue. The intestines, which actually begin their existence in the umbilical cord, start to migrate out of the umbilical cord and into the abdomen, where they belong. The baby has grown a thumb and all of its fingers, which are still very short and are connected by webbing.

The baby's reproductive organs begin to develop at this stage, but, on inspection, you would not be able

Nutrition Tip:
Increase Calories and Calcium

While your baby still weighs less than an ounce, you can begin to increase your calorie content so that you are eating about 300 extra calories per day in foods that are nutritious and healthy for you. This month, you should focus on getting enough calcium in your diet. You should be getting around 1200 milligrams (mg) of calcium through things like yogurt, leafy green vegetables, and, of course, milk and cottage cheese. A single cup of milk contains 300 mg of calcium and a half cup of cottage cheese contains about 65 mg of calcium. If you feel unable or unwilling to take in that amount of calcium in your diet, do not be afraid to supplement your diet with pills containing calcium and vitamin D. Vitamin D is included in most calcium supplements because it is known to help increase your body's ability to absorb the calcium. If you opt to take calcium supplements, take 600 to 1200 mg of calcium daily.

to tell whether it is a girl or a boy. In fetal reproductive development, all babies start with external reproductive features that look like a girl's, but in boys, the genetic makeup makes this configuration temporary. Soon he will form a penis and scrotum, and you will be able to tell that, in fact, he is a little boy.

Your baby is no bigger than the size of an olive. At this stage of pregnancy, doctors measure the size of the baby from the top of the head (the "crown") to the rump, because the legs are curled up tight and hard to measure.

Week 10

Your tiny little baby has begun to move and is wiggling and swimming around the uterus. Even though your baby is moving, you will not be able to feel its movements until around 20 weeks. It has developed all its joints—including its wrist, knee, shoulder, elbow, ankle—and even the hands, fingers, and toes. Your baby's cells have moved to the correct location in the body, and the brain and muscles are growing and developing at a breakneck speed. Your baby has grown a teeny bit and is about the size of a grape— about 1.25 inches long.

Week 11

Happily, most of the critical differentiation and development your baby had to do is now complete. Your baby begins a period of extremely rapid growth, and can grow up to three-quarters of an inch in just this week alone! The baby's head is out of proportion to the rest of its body, taking up about half of the total length. While your baby has had eyelids for several weeks, they begin to fuse into a closed position and will not open again for several months. The irises, or colored part

of the eye, begin to develop at this stage. Eye color is determined by the baby's genes.

Perhaps the most significant development this week or the next is the increase in importance of the placenta. Until now, the ovaries have been producing the progesterone that has kept the pregnancy healthy. It is at this time that the tiny blood vessels in the umbilical cord connect you to the baby, and the placenta begins to produce the hormones you need to support your baby's growth and development.

As mentioned above, the baby is measured in terms of its crown-to-rump length (CRL), or the length from the top of its head to the baby's little bottom. The CRL at week 11 is about 1.5 to 1.7 inches, and your tiny fetus is about the size of a walnut.

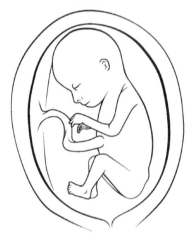

Fetus at 12 weeks of development

At approximately 2 inches long and just one-half ounce in weight, a 12-week-old fetus is beginning to look like a real baby. Twenty buds for future teeth appear; all internal parts are formed but are not fully developed; fingers and toes continue to grow and soft nails begin to form; bones and muscles begin to grow; intestines begin to form; the backbone is soft and can flex; the skin is almost transparent. Note that the hands are more developed than the feet; the arms are longer than the legs.

Week 12

With the differentiation of your baby's tissue complete, there are still many things left for your baby to develop as he or she continues the process of becoming a whole human being. The fingers and toes have lost their webbing and tiny little fingernails will begin to grow. At last, the genitals start changing, and soon you will be able to tell if you are having a boy or a girl.

The amount of amniotic fluid that bathes the baby for the rest of the pregnancy begins to increase. In part, this is because your baby's kidneys have begun to start working and will actually produce urine that becomes part of the amniotic fluid. If your baby were actually eating real food through his or her mouth, his intestines would be able to gurgle because the muscles in the intestines responsible for pushing food and gas through the intestines have begun to contract.

Your baby continues his or her meteoric increase in weight and size and is now about the size of a small kiwi fruit.

Your Changing Body: Looking and Feeling Pregnant

By the end of the twelfth week of gestation, you will have begun losing some of the more annoying signs of early pregnancy. Things like breast tenderness, fatigue, nausea, and vomiting will have passed—or will be rapidly improving—as you approach your second trimester. You will have begun to gain weight and will begin to feel that you are actually pregnant!

Weight Gain

Weight gain varies widely from woman to woman, particularly in the first trimester. This is partly because some women begin to eat more than recommended, thinking they no longer need to watch what they eat or that they need to give extra nutrition to their growing baby. (Remember: You are not really eating for two!) Unfortunately, what these women do not realize is that their baby weighs just a few ounces and is really tiny. In general, doctors recommend a total weight gain of only two to four pounds during the entire first trimester. That amount of weight primarily comes from an increase in blood volume in your body. A small percentage of weight gain is from the increase in the size of the uterus, and an even smaller fraction is due to the actual size of the embryo.

If you have gained more weight than needed at this point, do not worry. Every day is a new beginning and you can start now to normalize your eating. Most importantly, focus on healthy, nutrient-dense calories when you eat.

Prenatal Testing: The Basics

If you wait to have your first prenatal visit until this last half of your first trimester, you will likely have the entire panel of tests done at this time, including an HIV test, rubella screen, blood typing, and Rh factor (see Chapter 4 for information about the first prenatal visit). If you have already had at least one prenatal visit, the doctor will check your weight and blood pressure and the baby's heartbeat. A urine sample with be obtained, as is the case with all prenatal visits.

Frequent Urination: Please Pee!

As we have talked about in Chapter 4, you may have to urinate frequently. Just as was the case earlier in your pregnancy, your increased blood volume is creating more work for your kidneys as well as your bladder. In this part of the pregnancy, the growing uterus, which sits just behind the bladder, is causing increased pressure on the bladder. The bladder gets more irritable, and you will find yourself going to the restroom more often.

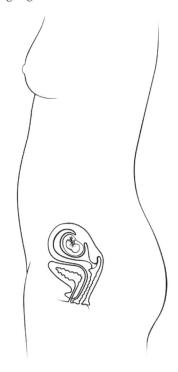

Your changing body: Month three
By the end of the first trimester, you will probably notice that your breasts are significantly fuller and your nipples may darken.

You need to take the time out of your busy day to pee! Try to go every hour or two—and more often if you need to. Be sure not to deny yourself fluids as a way to control or even prevent these frequent trips to the restroom.

Doing so could lead to dehydration, or you could get a bladder infection from having stagnant urine sitting in your bladder.

Vaginal Spotting: Call Your Healthcare Provider

A full third of all women will have spotting at some point in the pregnancy, and although it may be normal, this is something for your healthcare provider to determine. Most spotting happens early in the first trimester and sometimes is the result of the placenta attaching to the uterine wall and the blood vessels of the growing placenta bleeding as they develop. Because any spotting or bleeding can signal an impending miscarriage (see Chapter 4) or an ectopic pregnancy (see page 121), don't delay making that call.

Keeping track of the amount of bleeding you are having will help your healthcare provider determine how to proceed.

Increased Energy Level: Is That the Eleven O'clock News?

By this point in your pregnancy, your energy level probably will have returned to near normal. You are approaching the magical time of the second trimester when you feel you have all the energy in the world. You probably will feel better able to keep up the demands of work, school, and family life. Even so, you might still find the need to take a nap in the afternoon or at the end of a long day. Indulge yourself in sleep whenever you can. It is healthy for you and your baby!

If you are still feeling sluggish at this point of the pregnancy, you can improve your energy level through exercise. If you are exercising, keep it up. If you got sidetracked or have not started, go ahead and begin walk-

My husband is a camera nut and wanted to document every single moment of my pregnancy! I was used to his photo-taking and actually thought it was cute. But when he wanted to photograph me not being able to zip up my favorite pair of jeans, it wasn't cute anymore! He got the message when I hid his camera and wouldn't tell him where it was until he agreed to ask permission to take my picture!

—*Kelly, 28, mother of one*

ing, biking, doing prenatal yoga, or swimming. These activities are perfectly safe to do while pregnant and will help you feel better both mentally and physically.

Decreased Breast Tenderness

Your breasts may be less tender than they were when you first found out you were pregnant. Breast tenderness normally decreases as your pregnancy progresses. Breast tenderness is still common in the last half of the first trimester but it often improves over time.

Your Emotions: Still Some Ups and Downs

Pregnancy is an emotional time for many reasons. Not only are your hormones in play but the reality of bringing a child into the world can also raise a number of questions, concerns, and even fears. Even if you are elated and feel prepared, you will likely hit an emotional bump or two along your pregnancy journey. Remember: It is vital to talk about your thoughts and feelings with your partner, close friends and family, or a therapist.

Time to Stop Worrying about Miscarriage?

The risk of miscarriage lessens considerably after the first trimester, but the 12-week mark is not a magic boundary and women do miscarry later in pregnancy. It is certainly reassuring if you have already heard the beat of your baby's heart. Many women do begin to relax about being pregnant around this time. You may begin to look over maternity clothes with some purpose, and you might allow yourself to make a purchase or two!

Fears about pregnancy loss may have hindered your sexual relationship with your partner. While such fears have been proven to be scientifically unfounded, they may have prevented you and your partner from experiencing the kind of sexual relationship to which you had become accustomed. This is the time to rekindle your sexual relationship with your partner and to begin to settle into the idea that you are about to bring a new life into the world.

For Dads and Partners: **Help Out!**

This is a good time to take on more responsibility at home. Your partner's body is busy creating a new life, and she needs to spend some extra time each day to care for herself and the new life growing inside her. Try to take over chores that may have been hers, like cooking dinner, doing laundry, or walking the dog. Your thoughtfulness will go a long way in keeping your relationship healthy and happy and will be remembered fondly for years to come!

Feeling Stressed Out? Talk It Out!

If your pregnancy is unplanned, if you are facing a medical complication that makes your pregnancy high risk, or if you are still facing the possibility of a pregnancy loss, you may be feeling anxious, sad, or lonely—even if other people are around you. It may be hard for you to allow yourself to be happy about your pregnancy. These feelings may be challenging to share with others, and you may be suffering from keeping all these emotions to yourself.

Stress during pregnancy is a common problem, so there is no need to feel alone! Your body, your hormones, and your life itself are changing rapidly. In fact, pregnancy is considered one of the top five causes of stress a woman can experience in her lifetime. You may feel tearful and unable to watch sad movies, look at babies, or deal with the changes your body is going through. You may also have a constant feeling of nervousness that no amount of rest can shake. You may be wondering why what should be the happiest time of your life is not.

Setting aside a regular time for meditation or relaxation each day can help you manage stress throughout your pregnancy. Some women find yoga or tai chi to be helpful; others learn meditation techniques through a class or a video; and others simply take time each day to read, write in a journal, or listen to calming music. The key is to develop the habit of relaxation, so that the inevitable stresses of pregnancy don't hit you so hard.

Sad and stressful feelings are common during pregnancy. But, if they are severe, you may require the intervention of a skilled therapist or counselor in order to ease your stress. It takes courage to seek the help you need. Ultimately you can be motivated by the thought that what you do for yourself to feel good you are also doing for your baby! Do not hesitate to find a therapist. Talking with him or her will prove to be very helpful. You deserve to be happy and to feel like yourself throughout pregnancy.

The period after birth is difficult for some women and establishing a therapeutic relationship during the pregnancy can be helpful if issues arise after the baby is born. If you have a history of abuse in your life, being pregnant and facing childbirth can stir up troublesome emotions. Remember that unfortunately these are very common experiences for women. Seek a therapist with specialized expertise in these issues and consider connecting with a domestic violence or sexual assault advocacy program for individual help or a support group. Your healthcare provider should be able to refer you to an appropriate person or agency.

Please don't be afraid to seek a therapist if you are having particular emotional issues around your pregnancy. So many things can come up for you when you become pregnant. I was terrified of the idea of being responsible for another human being's survival—so much so I couldn't eat or sleep. I found a wonderful therapist to help me, and I was able to overcome my fears and actually enjoy my pregnancy. Get the help you need—you deserve to enjoy your pregnancy! —*Sharon, 34, mother of two*

In addition to a therapist, or if your emotional stress is not severe, you can talk with your partner or even trusted friends and family about what you are going through. Some communities offer support groups for pregnant women as well. You may even find that taking an exercise class specifically for pregnant women provides you with an informal support network. Gradually, as you approach your second trimester, you will begin to feel better about being pregnant—and your hormones will begin to work positively to improve your overall outlook.

Your Prenatal Visit: Par for the Baby Course

If you are having your first prenatal visit this month, see Chapter 4 so you will be prepared. The most exciting part of this month's prenatal visit will be hearing your baby's heartbeat. As part of the exam, you will have a urinalysis, which generally checks for glucose (sugar) levels in your urine as well as for the possibility that you have a hidden bladder infection. As always, your doctor will check your weight and blood pressure.

Your Expanding Uterus

While it might not be evident to you, it is also during this third month that changes in the size of your growing uterus can be perceived, at least by your healthcare provider. So, he or she might perform a bimanual examination to check the size of the uterus. This exam involves the physician placing two fingers inside the vagina while using the other hand to feel the size and shape of the uterus. By the twelfth week, however, the doctor will be able to feel the top of the uterus just above the pelvic bone, and this is usually sufficient to determine the size of the uterus.

Hearing and Seeing Your Baby's Heartbeat

Anytime you hear your baby's heartbeat is reassuring! With every prenatal visit once the heartbeat is detectable, aside from joy, the sound of your baby's heartbeat will also provide valuable information about the health of your pregnancy. Starting at 10 to 12 weeks, and occasionally earlier, fetal heart tones should be able to be heard at your exam. If the healthcare provider cannot hear the heart tones this month, an ultrasound will be ordered to confirm that the heartbeat is visible on an abdominal or vaginal ultrasound. Hearing your baby's heartbeat for the first time is one of the most exciting moments of your pregnancy!

Things to Think About:
Sharing Your Good News

This month is a time when most women think about telling friends and relatives that they are indeed pregnant. Some women choose to tell everyone, including the checkout person at the grocery store. Others will choose to tell a select few members of their family and social group, waiting until it becomes obvious that they are pregnant. What you choose to do about telling friends and family is up to you and your partner, but be sure you are both on the same page about it! Also consider the effect on your work situation if the news gets to your boss before you have a chance to discuss it.

Baby Beat: What's Happening with Your Baby's Heart

Your healthcare provider will check your baby's heartbeat using a handheld device every time you have a prenatal visit. If, at any time, he or she cannot hear the heartbeat, the healthcare provider will likely order a quick ultrasound evaluation to check that the heartbeat can be seen. In most cases, the ultrasound technician will let you see what's happening inside the uterus on a monitor screen. You will be able to see the valves of the heart flapping—or the movement of the fetal heart—as it beats an approximate 110 to 180 beats per minute.

At this point in your pregnancy, you may notice that the heart rate will be on the higher end of normal, in the range of 160 to 180 beats per minute. As the pregnancy progresses, the heart rate will decrease over time so that it is more in the range of 110 to 140. This is because your baby is getting bigger and will naturally have a lower heart rate because bigger babies tend to have lower heart rates. One exception is when the baby is very active. Just as your heart rate goes up when you exercise, your baby's heart rate will do the same.

Can Your Baby's Heartbeat Tell You Boy or Girl?

There is an old wives' tale that says if a fetal heartbeat is faster than average, in the range of 160 to 180 beats per minute, the baby is going to be a girl. Or, if the heartbeat is slower than average, in the range of 120 to 140, the baby is going to be a boy. This is truly an old wives' tale!

In the first trimester, if the heart rate is a bit above 180 beats per minute, you do not need to worry. This is just how your baby's heart happens to be and it does not represent anything harmful. Later in pregnancy, especially in the third trimester, a rapid heart rate above 180 can mean your baby is in some distress due to problems with the placenta (infection or insufficient ability to provide oxygen and nutrients to the baby). It can also mean that there is some kind of infection going on inside the uterus. Your doctor may want to further investigate the situation to make sure nothing is wrong.

Is Genetic Testing Right for You?

This month, your doctor will likely have a serious conversation with you about the possibility of detecting genetic abnormalities in your fetus. You may already have had blood tests for certain genetic disorders, either before conception (Chapter 1) or during your first prenatal visit (Chapter 4). While genetic defects cannot be changed or manipulated, this is the time in pregnancy when you have the option of knowing whether or not your baby has certain genetic abnormalities.

Off the bat, some women choose not to have genetic testing because, no matter what issues their baby may have, they would not terminate their pregnancy. Conversely, some women choose to undergo genetic testing because they would indeed elect to abort their pregnancy if the fetus was found to be affected with a serious genetic disease. In addition, women and their partners may wish to have information about genetic abnormalities so they can be better prepared for the future,

Procedure for Chorionic Villus Sampling (CVS)

The chorionic villi are small extensions of the growing placenta that can be removed for analysis without endangering the nature of the placenta. The CVS procedure is done during the tenth through the twelfth week of gestation—early enough for you to make a decision about what you want to do regarding the ongoing status of your pregnancy.

The test is performed by inserting a thin tube called a catheter through the vagina and cervix and into the uterus. Ultrasound is used to find the placenta and to take a sampling through the catheter. Some doctors will do this procedure by inserting a tiny needle into the abdomen and taking a sample of the placenta through the inserted needle.

even though they are ruling out termination. Either way, you should be thoughtful about your decision and discuss the ramifications with your partner.

Obstetrical Ultrasound or Nuchal Translucency (NT) Screening

This test can be done at 10 or 11 weeks' gestation. It may show problems with the liver, kidneys, and limbs and can measure the transparency of what is known as the nuchal ridge. A thicker nuchal ridge means there is a thicker space between the back of the baby's neck and the spine. This can indicate the possibility that the baby has Down syndrome. The NT screening is considered along with blood tests and can be a good reason to go ahead and check further with chromosome testing.

Chorionic Villus Sampling (CVS)

The doctor will offer you the chance to undergo chorionic villus sampling (CVS) in order to determine the genetic makeup of the fetus. This test, for example, can determine whether your fetus has a genetic abnormality such as Down syndrome, Tay-Sachs disease, hemophilia, or cystic fibrosis (see Chapter 4 for more information about certain genetic abnormalities). What the CVS test cannot do is determine the presence or absence of diseases like neural tube defects, which cause spina bifida and anencephaly—both very serious conditions. On a positive note, the CVS technique can tell you whether your baby is a girl or a boy, although of course it is not performed for that reason.

The placenta develops from the same cells as your baby and therefore contains the same genetic code. A biopsy of the placenta will determine the genetic makeup of your baby and detect the presence or absence of common genetic diseases, although it will not detect every possible rare genetic abnormality.

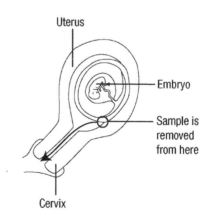

Chorionic villus sampling

In chorionic villus sampling, a piece of the placenta tissue is removed through the cervix.

Advantages of chorionic villus sampling: CVS has its advantages over the amniocentesis test (see Chapter 6 for more on amniocentesis), which is another test doctors can use to determine the genetic makeup of the fetus. Amniocentesis is generally performed at around 15 to 20 weeks. For some women, testing this late may make the decision to terminate more difficult, especially since they may have felt fetal movement by this time.

Disadvantages of chorionic villus sampling: This procedure for genetic testing is not without its risks. You may experience a leakage of amniotic fluid or some vaginal spotting that may last up to two days. If you had a needle sampling through the abdominal wall, you may experience some pain in the area where the needle was inserted. In addition, you can develop a serious uterine infection as a result of having had a foreign object inserted into the uterus.

You also have a slight but increased risk of miscarriage with a CVS. The rate of miscarriage is about 1 in 100 to 1 in 200 and somewhat depends on the experience of the person performing the test. When a skilled perinatologist performs the procedure, the risk of miscarriage is about 1 in 400. CVS can also result in the fetal loss of a digit (a finger or a toe). This may occur in approximately 1 out of 2000 to 3000 cases.

Having a test such as a CVS is completely up to you. If you do not want to know about the possibility of genetic disease, if you feel you are at a very low risk for having a baby with a genetic disease, or if doing the test will make no difference in what you will do regardless of the results, you can skip the test

and rest in the knowledge that the chance your baby has a significant genetic condition is very low.

On the other hand, if specific genetic diseases run in your family or if you have another child with a genetic condition, you might feel better knowing the status of this pregnancy, whether or not you choose to abort a pregnancy that turns out to be abnormal. You may wish to consult a genetic counselor to help with this decision or to assist you in understanding the options and consequences if a genetic abnormality is detected.

Are You Pregnant with Multiples?

Perhaps you knew it all along due to fertility treatments or the way your healthcare provider looked when he or she commented that your uterus is bigger than expected at this stage in your pregnancy. Or perhaps it is simply a huge surprise that you did not expect! But either way, discovering you are pregnant with multiples puts a new perspective on your pregnancy—and on your life!

The first thing to know is that you are officially considered to be a woman with a high-risk pregnancy just because you have two or more babies inside you. If you have been seeing a nurse-midwife or OB nurse practitioner for your prenatal care, you will probably need to transition to working with an obstetrician and perhaps a perinatologist (a specialist in high-risk pregnancies). The frequency of ultrasounds and your visits to the doctor will increase, and it is common to eventually be put on weeks or even months of bed rest to carry your pregnancy as long as possible.

My wife's pregnancy wasn't planned—and neither was the news that we were having twins! I'll always remember the sheer terror that pulsed through my body when she told me. It wasn't until our two little girls were born that I was able to feel joy about it. If you don't know any different, there's nothing to having newborn twins. —*Jason, 33, dad of twins*

Fraternal or Identical?

Whether you are having twins, triplets, or more, there are two types of multiple pregnancies: fraternal and identical.

Fraternal multiples: In fraternal multiples, each fetus comes from its own fertilized egg. This means that your ovaries released more than one egg at the same time, and each egg was fertilized by sperm cells. The result is two (or more) babies growing in the same uterus. Each baby has its own placenta and each baby can be a boy or a girl. Each is genetically different from the others, and the twins or triplets are considered to be as similar to each other genetically as any other brothers and sisters. This type of pregnancy is called a "fraternal twin" or a "fraternal triplet" pregnancy.

Identical multiples: The second type of multiple pregnancy is identical multiples. This occurs when a single fertilized egg divides into two cells that separate from each other. Each of the two cells then has the capability to create a complete and healthy human being. Interestingly, the embryo can be as big as eight cells before a cell breaks away from

the others to form a complete human. This type of pregnancy is called an "identical twin" or "identical triplet" pregnancy, and results in siblings that are genetically identical. They will look alike and be the same sex. The embryos can share a single placenta or can each have an individual placenta.

Some Things to Know about Risk

A pregnancy with more than one baby involved carries a higher risk of complications. The more babies you are carrying, the higher the risk. The main risks of having a multiple pregnancy are the following:

- You can develop pregnancy-induced diabetes, a condition known as gestational diabetes. This can happen in single pregnancies as well but is more likely in multiple pregnancies.

Multiple Pregnancies: Causes and Predispositions

The following are the main causes of (nonidentical) multiple pregnancies:

- The use of fertility drugs or taking fertility treatments such as in vitro fertilization (IVF)
- Being older than 35
- Being of African descent
- Having a history of delivering fraternal twins in the past

You can have an increased chance of a twin pregnancy if twins happen to run in the family or if you get pregnant shortly after discontinuing birth control pills. However, these factors only apply to fraternal twins or other multiples. Identical twins don't run in families, and the odds of having identical twins do not vary with the factors above.

- You are more likely to develop a pregnancy-induced condition associated with high blood pressure and swelling of your tissues. Such a condition is called preeclampsia or pregnancy-induced hypertension (PIH) and can result in prolonged bed rest, medication to control blood pressure, and possible harm to the babies.
- You run a much higher risk of delivering your babies before they have developed enough to live outside the uterus without a great deal of medical support. This is called prematurity. To prevent a premature birth you may be put on bed rest and medication to settle down the irritability of the uterus.
- Multiple pregnancies have a greater incidence of miscarriage. You can lose a single baby and go on to carry the other baby or babies to term, or you can lose the entire pregnancy.

Multiples: What Are Your Chances?

The incidence of fraternal twin pregnancies is rising because of the increased use of fertility treatments, in which doctors usually implant more than one fertilized egg in order to increase the chances of a successful pregnancy. Because fertility treatments are not available in every part of the world, the incidence of fraternal twin pregnancies is different depending on where you live. On average, however, fraternal twin pregnancies occur 22 times per 1000 live births. Identical twin pregnancies are far less common. The rate of occurrence has not changed over time and is about 4 identical twin pregnancies per 1000 live births.

- In multiple pregnancies, there is a greater risk of having an infant with a genetic defect. Doctors may do a chorionic villus sampling (CVS) or amniocentesis of each baby's placenta or amniotic fluid to see if they have any genetic problems if you consent to these procedures.

Multiples: A Life Changer!

The knowledge that you are having a multiple pregnancy can be both exhilarating and frightening. You have to now think in double or triple! Even in your elation, you may be worried over how to continue to work or financially support the babies once you deliver. You might also be concerned about what lies ahead for the rest of your pregnancy and what it will be like to care for more than one baby at the same time, especially if they are born prematurely.

If you can, relax! There are many things you can do to ensure the best possible outcome for the pregnancy:

- Increase your diet to include an extra 600 calories per day. Those twins or triplets need more energy and nutrients than a singleton pregnancy, so you will have to work hard to get in those calories.
- Your doctor will probably ask to see you more often. You should attend every appointment and carefully follow your doctor's directions.
- Use only the herbs, medications, and supplements your doctor recommends.
- Find out what activity level is right for a woman at your stage in pregnancy. Carrying multiples is harder on your system than carrying one baby, so you will need to get extra advice from your doctor

Let everyone know you are having multiples! It's a great way to get the news out there that you are ready and willing to accept clothing and baby gear in good condition! Costs add up quickly, so don't be tied to wanting only new items. Every penny you save now is a penny you can put away for your babies later!

—Evelyn, 29, mother of twins

on the amount of exercise you can do without provoking early labor.

- Get as much rest as possible. Carrying more than one baby absorbs more calories from you and depletes your stores of energy. Allow yourself to be a sort of "human incubator" right now and indulge yourself in plenty of naptimes.

- If you have financial concerns, research consignment shops, thrift stores, and organizations that have clothing, toys, and baby equipment (such as strollers or high chairs) at reduced cost. Most of these outlets will not take items unless they are in good condition.

- Accept help! When friends and family offer to be there for you to care for your multiples, help with household chores, or offer items you can use, just say yes!

Prepare to Care for Your Multiples at Home

It is worthwhile to consider that after your newborns come home from the hospital, they may have added healthcare demands due to prematurity. They may have spent weeks or even months in the hospital before growing large enough to bring home. Conversely, if you carried your multiples far enough into your pregnancy at the time of your delivery, you may be able to take your newborns home within a few days of their birth. The average weight of a twin infant at the time of his or her birth is about five and a half pounds, while the average weight of a triplet newborn is about four pounds. But whether premature or full term, you will be caring for very small infants!

In addition, while the occasional twin pregnancy is able to be delivered vaginally, most twin and virtually all triplet pregnancies are delivered by cesarean section. The only time a vaginal delivery of twins is allowed is when both twins are nearly full term and both are in the head-down position. There is the rare doctor who has retained the skill to deliver twins vaginally who are not in the head-down position, but a delivery like this is considered too high a risk to take, and finding a doctor who is willing to perform such a delivery would be extremely difficult.

At this point, you cannot prepare for every contingency, but you do have the opportunity to seek additional support and resources so you can care for and enjoy your babies. When you get home with your newborns, you will be very exhausted and may still be in pain, whether you have had a vaginal delivery or a C-section. It can feel like a very overwhelming experience to take care of more than one baby at a time. Be sure to ask for help from your partner and other family members, and get rest whenever you can. Round up any help that is offered or you can afford to hire (for the present or after the babies are born) and try to become as organized as possible!

Pink or Blue? Finding Out Your Baby's Sex

This month you will want to consider whether or not you wish to know your baby's sex. As discussed above, the only way to find out during weeks 9 through 12 is by having a chorionic villus sampling (CVS) (see page 115), which can reveal the baby's sex. This test looks at the genetic material (chromosomes) inside the cells of the placenta, which are identical to the baby's chromosomes.

If you choose not to have CVS during this month, the next opportunity to find out the baby's sex will be during weeks 15 to 20, if you have an amniocentesis. Or, most commonly, you will have an abdominal ultrasound at 18 to 20 weeks. At that time, a skilled ultrasound technician will be able to visualize the scrotum and penis of the male fetus as well as the vulva seen in a female fetus.

While trying to decide whether or not you want to know your baby's sex, use the lists below to help you weigh the pros and cons.

Why You Might Want to Find Out Your Baby's Sex

• You can begin to shop for clothing and baby accessories that are specific to your baby's gender. No being inundated by green and yellow! It may also help you feel more prepared to have decided on gender-specific décor for the nursery and to choose clothing and baby equipment specifically for your boy or girl. Because you will receive baby gifts, it enables you to tell others what you need as well.

• You can begin a focused search for your baby's name without having to come up with an alternative name for the opposite sex. You may have already picked out a name, even before you knew you were pregnant, or you may find yourself poring over baby name books looking for something you like. If you know your baby's sex and have picked out a name, you can begin to call your growing belly by the name you have picked out.

If you do not want to know the sex of your baby, be very clear with all the medical staff with whom you come into contact. Many people assume that you do know or that you want to know, and they may inadvertently blurt out the secret. Every time I went to a prenatal visit or had an ultrasound, the first thing I said was, "I don't want to know the baby's sex." And it was a wonderful surprise in the end!
—*Tobi, 37, mother of six*

• If you were desperately hoping for a boy and feel you need time to get used to the idea that, in fact, you are having a girl (or vice versa), knowing the baby's sex early in the pregnancy can help you begin to bond with the child you are having. Bonding increases when you know the sex of the baby you are having—even if it is not the sex you originally wanted. If you feel you are going to have problems coping with having a child of the sex you did not prefer, find out earlier in the pregnancy so you can begin to get used to the idea and so you can get professional help in talking out your disappointment and bonding issues.

- You may have an older child who needs more time to get used to the idea of having a little brother or sister. Siblings may have their own preference of what sex the baby is going to be, and knowing the sex may help the sibling with his or her own bonding experience. When you have picked out a name, you can help your older child further bond by calling the fetus by its selected name. Big brother or sister can also help you pick out infant clothing and accessories with this knowledge.

Why You Might Want to Wait to Find Out Your Baby's Sex

- You may find yourself delighted with the idea that you will have a surprise at the end of a long pregnancy. Some say there are few surprises left in life, and knowing your baby's sex when you finally see his or her face and hold the baby in your arms for the first time is one of the last real surprises out there.

- The idea of not knowing the baby's sex and having an upcoming surprise might make life more bearable in the last few weeks of pregnancy when you are otherwise increasingly uncomfortable, sleeping less, and generally feeling like you are finished with being pregnant!

- You may enjoy imagining what life would be like with either a boy or a girl.

- You may be feeling protective of your baby and might feel that knowing the baby's name and sharing it with others makes your baby too exposed to the world even before it is born. By keeping the baby's sex a secret to you and everyone, your baby has time to grow and be born before making his or her presence known!

- You may be frustrated with the stereotyping of girl and boy babies—every boy's outfit seems to have a football logo, while the girls' clothes are pink, pink, pink! It may be important to you and your partner to consider your child as an individual who may or may not like football or the color pink.

Ectopic Pregnancy: What to Know

An ectopic pregnancy occurs about once in every 100 pregnancies. It happens when the embryo attaches itself to the fallopian tubes, cervix, or inside the abdomen itself instead of into the uterine wall where it belongs. Most of the time, an ectopic pregnancy attaches itself to the lining of the fallopian tubes where it begins to grow and develop.

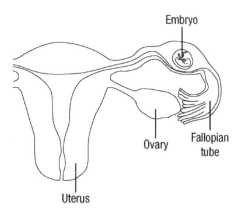

Ectopic pregnancy
An ectopic pregnancy usually grows in the lining of the fallopian tube.

An ectopic pregnancy can happen in a normal fallopian tube; however, there is often something wrong with the fallopian tube that causes the fertilized egg or zygote to become blocked in its passage to the uterus.

Common Causes of an Ectopic Pregnancy

- A prior ectopic pregnancy, which has scarred the fallopian tubes.
- Past surgery to the fallopian tubes.
- A prior infection such as pelvic inflammatory disease (PID), which damages the fallopian tubes. (Half of all women with an ectopic pregnancy have suffered from some kind of pelvic or uterine infection.)
- Smoking may be a contributory factor.

Rare Causes of an Ectopic Pregnancy

- An abnormal shape or size of the fallopian tubes due to a birth defect
- Having had a ruptured appendix in the past
- Suffering from endometriosis, a condition in which uterine cells grow where they don't belong

Factors That Increase the Risk of Ectopic Pregnancy

- Being older, especially over the age of 35
- Having had many sexual partners over the years
- Conceiving via in vitro fertilization (IVF)
- Having a reversal of a tubal ligation (a sterilization procedure)

If the ectopic pregnancy is not caught early, and the embryo grows bigger, it may rupture the fallopian tube, resulting in internal bleeding. Symptoms of a ruptured fallopian tube include feeling faint from blood loss and low blood pressure, feeling a sensation of severe pressure or pain in the rectum, pain that is felt in the shoulder area, or severe and sudden pain in the lower portion of the abdomen. About 1 out of every 10 ectopic pregnancies results in internal bleeding.

Ectopic Pregnancy: Warning Signs and What to Do

What NOW?

How do you know if you have an ectopic pregnancy? There are some warning signs. For instance, you will often have some kind of vaginal bleeding, and you may experience low back pain and mild cramping on one side of the lower abdomen or pelvis or pain all over the lower abdomen. You might also have all the other normal signs of a pregnancy.

Call your healthcare provider if you experience any of the following:

- A fever greater than 100.5°F.
- Vaginal bleeding of any sort, including light spotting.
- Cramping that does not go away after a day.
- Dizziness, lightheadedness, or shoulder pain—these are possible signs of a ruptured ectopic pregnancy, which is an emergency.

Some ectopic pregnancies have no symptoms, particularly in the very early stages of the process, and are discovered during a routine pelvic ultrasound. Even these smaller ectopic pregnancies need treatment. If a tube ruptures, it is considered a medical emergency and you should go to the emergency room immediately.

Treating an Ectopic Pregnancy

If an ectopic pregnancy is small and has not ruptured, it can be treated with medicine, and surgery can be avoided. If surgery needs to be performed on an early ectopic pregnancy, the contents of the pregnancy can be removed, and the fallopian tube can be rescued. This can often be done by laparoscopy, a procedure in which a tiny camera is inserted in the abdomen. Sometimes a large incision can be avoided by using this procedure. If your fallopian tube is saved you could indeed still have a normal pregnancy from that tube in the future, but there is an increased risk of ectopic pregnancy in that tube. Experts say that about two-thirds of all women who have had a single ectopic pregnancy are able to have a normal pregnancy afterward.

Sharing the News with Friends, Relatives, and Your Workplace

There are as many ways to announce your baby news as there are pregnant couples! Some couples enjoy keeping the news to themselves for as long as possible. Others cannot wait and tell everyone as soon as they know! Some couples even make events out of telling family and friends through a surprise party or special dinner. How and when you choose to tell the world your news is a personal decision, but here are some things to consider.

Mum's the Word: Reasons You May Want to Keep Your News to Yourself

- In the first trimester, there is still an elevated risk of miscarriage.
- If this is an unplanned pregnancy, you may still be worried about telling anyone that you have become pregnant. You may feel a bit lonely being the only one who knows you are having a baby, but at the same time, you may feel conflicted about telling anyone at all until it becomes obvious. Take this time to come to grips with the idea of being pregnant. Consider

talking to a professional therapist or your doctor so you can feel confident about revealing your pregnancy.

- The more people you tell, the more likely

My husband can't keep a secret to save his life! But he promised he wouldn't divulge our news until I'd hit week 12, and he promised we'd tell people together. Well, when I got to week 12, he gave me a charm bracelet with two charms: a little baby shoe encrusted with diamonds and a pair of lips encrusted with rubies. I looked up at him and laughed. "Who'd you tell?" I asked. He looked down at me with a boyish grin and said, "Just about everyone! Even the lawn guy knows." I wanted to be mad but the whole thing was just too funny! And what woman could be angry staring at a diamond-encrusted baby shoe! —*Virginia, 31, mother of one*

your news will spread—even if you do not want it to. Someone else's pregnancy is a hard secret to keep! If you tell even the most trusted friend or relative, you run the risk of that person telling someone else—or posting the news on Facebook.

- If you choose to tell only a select group of people, you may hurt someone's feelings if they find out they were not among the first to know.
- If you think many of your family and friends will be disappointed in your news—perhaps because they do not believe you have the financial resources for a

child or think you have too many children already—you may want to find a way to feel more secure and supported in your news before you let your naysayers know.

Baby News at Work

Many women are concerned about telling their employer about their pregnancy. It is important to remember that you are not the first pregnant women in the workplace and you will not be the last! Pregnancy is something all employers have to handle, and yours has likely done it many times before. Some supervisors will be more understanding than others. Some will be elated for you, and some may show no emotion at all. Your supervisor's reaction is not the most important thing.

Five Great Reasons to Let The World Know You Are Pregnant!

- You may have been waiting a long time for this pregnancy to happen and you might feel the urge to tell everyone you know so they can share in your joy and success.

- Telling all your friends and family will provide you with supportive people to share your elation, fears, and concerns about being pregnant.

- Telling many friends or relatives about your pregnancy can make it all feel even more real, ridding you of the secret you have been holding back for the last month or so.

- Even if a miscarriage were to occur, you would rather have people know so they could offer you support.

- You and your partner are just the kind of couple that cannot possibly keep a secret—especially one this big!

What is most important is that you maintain a professional demeanor at work, be upfront with your supervisor and coworkers if you need any special accommodations or assistance due to your pregnancy, and continue to maintain your level of performance as best you can. Let your supervisor know your plans for maternity leave and when (or whether) you plan to return to work. This will help him or her prepare appropriately for your upcoming absence.

Now is a good time to begin researching your health insurance policy for information on pregnancy coverage as well as your employer's policies on the amount of time allowable for pregnancy leave and whether or not you will be paid for your leave. If you are planning to return to work after your baby is born, calculate the time you will be able to take off during or after the pregnancy, keeping in mind you may have vacation time you can add to your maternity leave.

Many employers have parental leave policies that cover fathers or other partners as well as new mothers. If your partner can take some time after the baby is born to enjoy your little one and help you as you recover from childbirth, this can be very special for all three of you. Another possibility is that your partner may wish to take parental leave after your maternity leave is used up, so that the baby will be with a parent for a longer period of time. This is an excellent time for you and your partner to discuss these options and to see what may be practical in your situation.

I was definitely planning on returning to work after my baby was born. But once I held her in my arms, I knew there was no way I was going back. I felt so guilty because I had assured my boss I was returning. I dreaded telling her but decided just to be honest about how I hadn't expected to feel this way. I was so surprised by how understanding she was. She said the same thing happened to her sister. Honesty is the best policy when it comes to the workplace!
—*Shelby, 35, mother of three*

In addition, you will have to begin the process of finding appropriate daycare for your infant after you return to work, if you are planning to do so. It may be as simple as beginning to find a good nanny, asking a relative to watch your infant, or having your partner take time off from his or her job in order to take part in the infant-rearing process. Note: Many childcare programs have waiting lists, so it is never too early to find one with which you are happy—and sign up! If you are planning on using a childcare program for the care of your infant, you will need to research programs now. Be proactive about finding what you think will be best for your child.

If you are not planning on returning to work, you will have to decide how and when it is best to let your workplace know. If you are aware that it will take many months to find an appropriate replacement for your position, then be courteous and tell your employer as soon as possible.

Sex during Pregnancy: Keep Your Bond Strong

Early in your pregnancy, the issue of sex between you and your partner will come up. Either you or your partner might feel fearful that having sexual intercourse or having an orgasm will somehow adversely affect your baby. You need to know that there is absolutely nothing about the process of sexual intercourse or having an orgasm that will do any harm whatsoever to a healthy pregnancy, nor will intercourse or orgasm cause or contribute to a miscarriage. If you are spotting and/or cramping at this stage of the pregnancy, your healthcare provider will tell you not to have sexual intercourse because doing so will irritate the vagina, cervix, or uterus,

Exercise Idea: SEX!

Make your sex life a priority during your pregnancy. Right now especially, you are still not showing and your uterus is still tucked away neatly behind your pelvic bone. At this stage, you can engage in your normal sex life without the need to alter anything! It is so important as a couple to maintain, if not improve, your sex life and intimacy during pregnancy. Once your baby arrives, demands on your time and energy will shift. So, keeping a strong, stable sex life now will help you maintain your intimacy during those stressful first months adapting to your new life with a baby!

and you might feel worse as a result. The only condition where sexual intercourse is specifically prohibited because of the pregnancy itself is placenta previa, which will be discussed in greater detail in Chapter 8.

If you are tired and nauseated, however, you may not feel much like making love. Some couples handle this issue very well because they have a solid and loving relationship with each other, while others will feel a decline in the feeling of closeness they once shared. If your partner is thoughtful and understanding, the likelihood is that you will resume an enjoyable sex life as soon as you feel better.

Sex with your partner should be mutually enjoyable. If your partner pressures you, makes you feel guilty, or won't take no for an answer, your relationship needs some help before you have a child together. If you feel unsafe in any way or your partner won't participate in couples counseling, seek help yourself. While most women who are pressured or forced into sexual activity by their partner don't think of this as sexual assault, it is. A domestic violence or sexual assault advocacy agency in your community can usually provide free, confidential help in this situation.

I remember the end of my first trimester so well. My morning sickness was gone, I suddenly felt a surge of energy, and I loved how many of my pants and skirts weren't quite fitting me anymore! It was like someone flipped a switch and I finally felt joyously pregnant instead of miserably sick and exhausted!
—*Beatrice, 42, mother of two*

In a healthy relationship, sex during pregnancy can be as much fun as ever. As your belly gets bigger, you will have to be more creative about sex, experimenting with sexual positions that feel right and are possible late in pregnancy. Right now is a great time to enjoy a normal and healthy sex life with your partner! This intimacy is not only safe but it will also help you maintain the love and affection you have enjoyed with your partner.

Most importantly, keep the lines of communication open regarding sex. Tell your partner what you are feeling and encourage him or her to do the same. It is essential to keep talking about any issues either of you might be having and to offer each other understanding and support!

Notes:

I felt like an eagle during my fourth month—as if the entire world were new and spread out before me like a forest of possibilities! I felt somehow powerful and connected to the flow of life, like I had never felt before. I was soaring and happy and hopeful! It was a wonderful time, and I tried to embrace every moment of it!
—*Suzanna, 40, mother of two*

Chapter 6

Month Four—Weeks 13 through 16

Congratulations! You have graduated into the second trimester of your pregnancy and can begin to relax about the health of the fetus growing inside of you. The many uncomfortable symptoms of pregnancy you may have experienced in the first trimester have probably subsided, and you are left feeling a sense of relief as well as renewed energy. You may finally be able to enjoy being pregnant.

During this month, you will begin to "show." This means that the uterus will have grown above the level of your pubic bone and is officially in both the abdomen and the pelvis. People will begin to notice the telltale baby bump that says you are pregnant. Likely, you feel better about telling people you are pregnant now that it is more obvious to the casual observer and fears about miscarriage have dropped significantly.

While you still cannot feel your baby move, it is growing and moving frequently—although it sleeps more than 90 percent of the time. This rest provides your baby with the energy to do all the growing and developing it

I knew there was a lot to consider during my fourth month of being pregnant with genetic testing issues and, for me, the possibility of gestational diabetes. And needless to say, I'm a worrier by nature. I was with a dear friend one day for coffee and she was listening patiently as I went through my laundry list of worries. Eventually, she stopped me and said, "You haven't mentioned clothing." "What?" I asked. She replied, "You love clothes, and you haven't mentioned your plan for maternity wear. I have an idea. You should make a game of this and see how long you can go without buying actual maternity clothing!" Suddenly I had something to focus on that I loved—bargain shopping and finding inexpensive clothing! We immediately came up with a plan. And, once a week, I started shopping at consignment stores and thrift shops for regular clothing that would double as maternity wear. I remember buying a black shift dress that was four sizes bigger than my normal size. It cost $2 at the thrift store. I wore it with a white turtleneck underneath (it was fall in New England!), and my favorite black boots. I got so many compliments on that outfit! Thanks to my friend, I found a way to focus on something other than pregnancy worries and had a blast bargain hunting for nonmaternity wear. (By the way, I made it through my seventh month in regular clothing!) What I learned about being pregnant—and really life itself—is that there's always something positive to focus on if you allow yourself! —*Trina, 37* needs to do this month. Also this month, there is a shift away from differentiation of body parts toward the process of growing and refining the function of the various organs within your baby's body. You may still find it hard to really believe you are pregnant this month, but your belly will tell you otherwise!

These are some of the questions we will answer in this chapter:

- How is my baby developing at this point?
- Should I purchase maternity clothes yet?
- What should I expect at my prenatal visit?
- How do I know if I am depressed? What can I do about depression?
- Should I consider amniocentesis or blood tests to screen for genetic abnormalities? And if so, what will amniocentesis be like?

Your Baby's Growth and Development: Things Are Starting to Work!

Your baby is not simply a miniature person that needs to grow bigger in order to be born. Important processes are happening inside your baby this month that will allow all of his or her body parts to work properly and sufficiently outside of your body.

Week 13

As you begin your second trimester, your baby is beginning to form the vocal cords that will allow you to hear his or her first cry in just five short months. The baby's face looks like a human face, except the eyes are far apart and the ears have not yet moved into the right place. During week 13, the eyes and ears begin to move into their proper positions.

By now, if your baby is a boy, his reproductive organs have differentiated into those that look exactly like male genitals. If ultrasound technology were just a bit better, we could tell your baby's sex. Currently, most healthcare providers wait until 16 to 20 weeks for the reproductive organs to become big enough to see with the best degree of accuracy.

As mentioned above, the baby's organs are formed and are beginning to do their job. For example, during this week, the baby's liver begins to secrete the necessary bile for digestion, and his or her pancreas has begun to secrete insulin for blood sugar metabolism.

The arms and legs twitch as the muscles learn how to do their part in creating a human being that can move and change positions at will. Your baby is about the size of a large egg and is about three inches long when measured from the crown of its head to its rump (CRL) and it weighs about 1 or 2 ounces, or less than an eighth of a pound.

Week 14

During week 14, the baby begins to practice breathing movements, although it is not possible for it to breathe outside the womb. The parts of the brain that control breathing are becoming active and the baby inhales and exhales occasionally. It still does not have a regular pattern of breathing.

The baby's face is still changing shape as the eyes and ears continue to travel to their respective places. Your baby's neck begins to elongate so that the chin is not sitting squarely on the chest. The baby can now move his or her hands and is reflexively moving them. The baby can have episodes of vigorous movement, but because of its small size, these movements cannot be felt.

The placenta continues to be the sole source of the baby's nourishment. While there is a mechanism to allow the passage of important calories and nutrients, the same mechanism acts as a filter to prevent the actual mixing of blood between the mother and her fetus. The fetus has his or her own blood type and the mother has her own blood type; in most cases, they do not mix.

Your baby is beginning to grow something called lanugo. This is pale, fine hair that develops all over the baby's body. It is believed to help the skin develop and remain anchored as the cells of the skin divide and grow. Hair is beginning to form on the scalp and eyebrows. The baby may actually hiccup at this stage, although you won't feel it.

Your baby is now about 3.5 inches long (crown-to-rump length) and is about the size of a lemon. It weighs only about 1.5 ounces.

Week 15

During week 15, an ultrasound may show that your baby is sucking his or her thumb. Even fetuses have a natural sucking reflex, and this is the time the baby has to learn to suck so that it can suck at your breast, a pacifier, or a bottle.

The skin of the fetus is still extremely thin and is actually transparent enough to reveal the tiny blood vessels beneath the skin. The lanugo (fine hair) has been produced and will continue to thicken as the skin becomes thicker and tougher. The lanugo will disappear by the time you deliver, unless your baby is extremely premature (between 24 and 26 weeks' gestation).

The baby's bones are lengthening so that they are more in proportion to the rest of the body. These bones are helping to form limbs that contain joints and cartilage. The baby's elbows may begin to bend at this age, and he or she will continue to have episodes of increased movement mixed with episodes of sleeping. During an ultrasound, the fetal heart rate will increase if your baby is moving vigorously.

Your baby is continuing to grow but has little body fat. He or she is about the size of a small apple, weighs about 2.5 ounces, and is about four inches long from the crown of the head to the rump.

Fetus at 16 weeks of development

At 16 weeks' gestation, the fetus is not ready to live outside its mother's body but is growing rapidly. It is approximately 4.5 inches long and weighs 3.5 ounces. Eyebrows, eyelashes, and fingernails form; arms and legs can flex; the neck and external sex organs are formed; the skin is wrinkled and the body is covered with a waxy coating (vernix) and fine hair (lanugo); the placenta is fully formed; and the outer ears begin to develop. Kidneys are functioning and beginning to produce urine. The fetus can swallow and hear.

Week 16

Some women will experience the first flutters of the baby's movement by week 16, while others will not feel movement until the next month. The baby's bones become harder so that kicking movements are easier to feel. Women who are overweight during pregnancy will generally feel movement later in pregnancy than thin women. When movement is felt also depends on where the placenta is located. If the placenta is in front of the baby, it might take longer to feel movement.

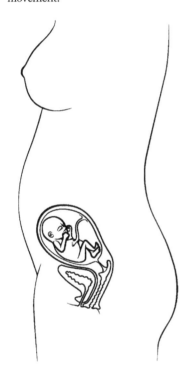

Your changing body: Month four
By the fourth month, your uterus is actually moving up within your abdomen to make room for expansion, and you finally have a baby bump!

The arms and legs are growing at such a rate now that, finally, the arms are shorter than the baby's legs. Frequent movements are happening between fetal naps. There is a great deal of extra amniotic fluid surrounding the fetus so that it is able to literally swim inside your uterus. The fluid provides a protective cushion around the fetus.

The baby's kidneys are continuing to develop. The baby produces urine that is excreted into the amniotic fluid. More hair is produced on the fetal scalp, and facial muscles have begun to develop. This means that the baby can now open and close his or her mouth and can reflexively smile. The baby can also swallow amniotic fluid.

Your baby weighs about 3.5 ounces and is the size of an avocado. It is about 4.5 inches long.

Your Changing Body: Finally a Baby Bump!

This is the month that you will finally look (at least a little) pregnant. Over the course of the month, your normal clothing will seem tighter and by week 16, about half of all pregnant women are in maternity clothes. Beyond your physical appearance there are a myriad of changes taking place inside your body. Let's take a look at some of them.

Mood: Much Better, Thank You!

The fatigue you felt during the first trimester will begin to abate as you start to feel a bit more energized doing your daily activities. Some women are so energized that they begin to purchase maternity clothes, baby clothes, and baby accessories with abandon. Many women also feel a surge of joy and empowerment as they begin to embrace their pregnancy without uncomfortable side effects!

On the other hand, being pregnant is still stressful, and some women are prone to episodes of sadness and depression. The American College of Obstetricians and Gynecologists (ACOG) reports that between 14 and 23 percent of all pregnant women will develop some symptoms related to depression. We will talk about depression in pregnancy later in this chapter.

Breast Care

You will experience much less tenderness in your breasts than you had in the first trimester as your body becomes accustomed to the elevated estrogen level of pregnancy. Nevertheless, your breasts are probably bigger in size than they were before you got pregnant. This is the time to get a larger-sized bra!

At this point in your pregnancy, your breasts may begin to leak and you will notice spots of yellowish or clear discoloration on the inside of your bra or clothing. If you squeeze your breasts or nipples, you will notice more fluid coming out. This fluid, called colostrum, is not actual breast milk but is a substance that precedes breast milk.

Keep your breasts clean and protected with a firm, supportive bra now and throughout the pregnancy. If you are planning to nurse, your breasts will soon have a new purpose and you will want to take good care of them.

Frequent Urination Continues: Where's the Bathroom?

The increased frequency of urination does not go away in the second trimester, and in fact, it usually worsens. You may begin to find yourself waking up one to three times during the night to void, and frequent trips to the bathroom will be part of your day. Your uterus is getting bigger, making for less room for your bladder to fill with urine before you feel the urge to urinate.

Holding back on fluids will not help the problem, and you run the risk of dehydration if you try to restrict your fluid intake in order to urinate less. Dehydration can give you symptoms of lightheadedness and dry mouth and maybe some contractions. Remember: Your baby needs all the liquid you can get into your body. Because you are developing a greater blood volume, you should drink at least 10 glasses of a nutritious liquid or water each day.

Sleep Issues: Find a Way to Nap!

During this month, it will become difficult for you to sleep comfortably on your stomach. The stressors of pregnancy and hormonal influences may make it difficult to get the amount of sleep you are used to. You may need to adjust your sleep position. For example, if you are normally a stomach-sleeper, you may be more comfortable lying on your back or side. Some women find they need pillows between their legs or behind

Nutrition Tip: Get Your Healthy Calories
By now you should be consuming 300 extra calories per day, or about 2300 to 2600 calories per day total. It is not essential that you track every calorie and write it down; but instead, be mindful of adding additional healthy calories to your diet each day. On average, you should gain about a pound a week. Keep up the habit of eating a wide variety of foods each day in order to get the best possible nutrients.

their back in order to feel comfortable enough to sleep, and other use large "body pillows" for support.

There is an old wives' tale that says that sleeplessness in pregnancy prepares you for the sleep interruptions that are inevitable with a new baby. Certainly, you will be more accustomed to an erratic sleep pattern by the time you finish the pregnancy.

Try to sleep the best you can and do not use any prescription sleep aids or over-the-counter products advertised to help you sleep. Instead, you need to be prepared to nap during the day if possible and to rest as much as you can to compensate for lost nighttime sleep.

Is It Called Pregnancy Brain or Baby Brain? I Can't Remember!

"Pregnancy brain" or "baby brain" are semi-joking terms that represent what happens to the thinking and behavior of many pregnant women. "Pregnancy brain" involves behaviors like dropping objects you thought you had a grip on, going to a business meeting on the wrong day, or forgetting what the date is. In short, you may become a bit scatterbrained this month, and symptoms of "baby brain" may last throughout your pregnancy. This is due to the hormonal changes occurring inside your body and your preoccupation with the miraculous developments going on inside you, and your fuzzy-headedness will go away when you are no longer pregnant.

In order to cope with "pregnancy brain," you need to take it easy on yourself. Buy a set of note cards or a small notebook and be prepared to write down lists of things to do, reminders related to your active day, and even your grocery list. Ask your partner or a friend to help you remember important things (sometimes just asking out loud gives your own memory a boost). Do not worry that you have suddenly become forgetful and that this change is permanent. This is a natural, normal part of pregnancy, and you will get through it! After you give birth, your memory will go back to normal. So hang in there and keep your sense of humor!

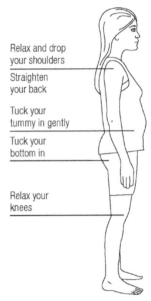

Relax and drop your shoulders

Straighten your back

Tuck your tummy in gently

Tuck your bottom in

Relax your knees

One-minute posture check
Maintaining good posture can prevent backache and headaches. As your body changes, remember to take a minute to check your posture.

Your Center of Gravity: Steady as She Goes

As your uterus grows, you become heavier in the front of your body as compared to the back. Basically, you are becoming front-heavy! During this month (especially toward the end of week 16), you may notice an increased tendency to stumble or may experience the feeling of losing your balance. This is a matter of simple physics and will only get more challenging as your belly grows.

You will also begin to have trouble traveling through crowds or getting around small or narrow spaces because your belly will not let you fit. Note: You will not hurt the baby if you have to squeeze through a narrow space or if you bump into someone in a crowd. Just be aware of the fact that you are now a bigger person and will have to adjust your behavior accordingly. Also remember to adjust any exercise regime you have to prevent falling or other injuries.

Water Retention

Water retention is a natural part of the second and third trimesters of pregnancy. Your feet may swell or your fingers may thicken. As your pregnancy progresses, you may not be able to wear your favorite rings. One way to cope with this is to try to remove your rings every day. Then, if the day comes that you have trouble putting the rings back on, put them away in a safe place until you are no longer pregnant or wear them on a sturdy chain around your neck.

Water retention generally does not mean that anything is wrong. But if you experience a sudden increase in water retention, check with your doctor within a day or two in order to make sure the swelling is unrelated to preeclampsia. (Ecclampsia is a condition that causes seizures in some women during pregnancy; it is related to high blood pressure and can be life-threatening.) Remember that hot weather and standing on your feet for long periods of time will naturally increase the amount of fluid retention you experience. It should also be noted, however, that some women do not experience water retention at all.

Loosey Goosey: Relaxed Joints

This month you may find you have increased flexibility or that your skin has greater elasticity. In fact, your muscles, skin, and joints begin to lose their rigidity and stretch or bend increasingly. This is because, during pregnancy, your body produces a specific hormone called relaxin. Relaxin is made to allow the skin of the belly to grow and expand as the uterus increases in size. A side effect of this is that your joints and muscles are affected as well.

Relaxin also allows one specific joint to expand more easily. This joint is called the pubic symphysis and is located in front of the pelvic bones. This joint normally does not move at all. However, in the labor and

My hands began to swell in my second trimester and, instead of removing my wedding rings, I kept telling myself the swelling would go down. Well it didn't! And I actually had to have my rings cut off! My advice is to remove your rings and put them back on only when your swelling goes down. —*Alisha, 33, mother of one*

delivery process, it must stretch out and expand to allow your baby to pass through the birth canal. The pubic symphysis is able to expand because of relaxin.

Be mindful that your body is becoming more limber and flexible. Also, remember to modify your exercise plan if necessary. Be attentive to any balancing you have to do during your routine or while holding any kind of equipment like weights. Be sure to have a firm grip on exercise equipment.

Heartburn: Tum-Ta-Tum-Tum

Heartburn can worsen in pregnancy due to the increase in intra-abdominal pressure from the expanding uterus as well as the effects of hormones on your esophagus and stomach. As mentioned in Chapter 4, heartburn can be treated by taking TUMS, Maalox, or ranitidine. You can also focus on eating smaller meals and avoiding acidic foods like tomatoes, coffee, ketchup, and citrus products.

The other thing you can do to alleviate heartburn is to raise the head of your bed by a few inches and prop up your head and torso with extra pillows. These steps will help avoid the effect of gravity on your digestion while you are lying down, which results in having stomach acid travel up into the esophagus, creating heartburn.

Your Emotions: Good, Better, Stressed

Now that you are in your second trimester, you may find that your mood has lifted enormously. Your energy level has returned to normal or maybe even improved, although you may find yourself taking the occasional nap on a busy day. You may feel so good that you are beginning to plan the space that will become the nursery and may allow yourself the time to buy a few items you will need for the baby. Your body will still feel familiar to you, yet you will also experience the excitement of showing just a little. In short, you should expect to feel really joyful and energized this month!

The second trimester, however, is not always so blissful for every woman. Women can still have negative emotions or moods that interfere with the enjoyment of their pregnancy during this time.

Stress: Demands on Your Time

If you are in your second trimester of a healthy pregnancy, you may suddenly want nothing more than to stay at home and prepare for your baby's arrival. Nevertheless, many pregnant mothers are facing the demands of keeping up a household, caring for other children, and/or performing in their workplace.

For Dads and Partners: Keep the Fire Going

Great news! Now that your partner's mood has improved, her sex drive is likely to increase. This is a good time to rekindle your sexual relationship or continue your already steady intimacy. Remember, having intercourse or your partner reaching orgasm will do nothing to hurt your baby—so just relax and enjoy each other! As your partner's belly expands, you can increase the sexual excitement between you by trying different positions that can also enhance your sex life. As always, be sure to discuss any issues or concerns you have with your partner—and listen to hers as well!

Workplace demands can be particularly stressful. During your first trimester, your fatigue may have affected your productivity so that you are working under the added stress of constantly having to hustle to keep up or, worse, catch up. You might also feel overwhelmed by the amount of work you have to do, and all this can lead to increased anxiety and feelings of stress.

If you work in a retail job or in jobs such as industrial work, cashiering, or waitressing, you will be on your feet much of the time and will feel more tired doing your job now than when you were not pregnant. You may have increased swelling and aching in your legs and feet and feel overwhelmed by the physical demands of your job.

How will you be able to continue your physically demanding job as your belly grows and your stamina decreases? Questions like these can make you wonder how far into your pregnancy you will be able to go before the physical demands make it inevitable that you must stop. This could lead to financial worries and increased stress.

Remember: If you need help with your emotions, fears, or stress, talk it out with your partner, a trusted friend, a family member, or a therapist. Keep exercising and try prenatal yoga and meditation to relax. Try your best to keep a positive mental attitude and do not be afraid to ask for help.

Boost Your Mood

If you are having mild mood dips, self-care and support from others often will help you feel better. Daily exercise, such as a half-hour walk, will work wonders. Talking to your partner or a trusted friend, watching a comedy on TV, listening to upbeat music, or reading an inspirational book may help you improve your mood. Think carefully about the people with whom you spend your time, and take a break from the "Debbie Downers." Many women find that keeping a journal or a private blog helps them to sort out their thoughts and feelings. There have even been research studies showing that smiling at yourself in the mirror can lift your mood. If nothing else, it may make you laugh!

Your Prenatal Visit: Keep Yourself Healthy

As your pregnancy progresses, you will begin to get into the routine of seeing your healthcare provider. The doctor, nurse practitioner, or nurse-midwife will continue to see you every four weeks until you reach 28 weeks. This means you will likely have only one prenatal visit this month unless you have a high-risk pregnancy.

Blood Sugar and Routine Checks

Your doctor will check your urine for evidence of infection or increased blood sugar, and you will be weighed and have your blood pressure taken. The baby's heartbeat will be checked.

Uterine Measurements

Your doctor will also perform an exam of your abdomen to see if your uterus is the appropriate size. A vaginal exam will likely be unnecessary. By the sixteenth week, your doctor will make a measurement of your uterus by checking the distance from the pubic symphysis (the joint between the pubic bones) to the top of the uterus in the abdomen. Ideally, the number of centimeters in this measurement will be about the same as the number of weeks of gestation, but this can differ if you are carrying multiples or just have a large or small baby.

Fetal Monitoring

The healthcare provider will also have a discussion with you about fetal monitoring. There are certain maternal blood tests and uterine tests, such as amniocentesis, that can be done between weeks 15 and 20 to see if your baby has a genetic abnormality. You may have already had a chorionic villus sampling (CVS) test; however, having an amniocentesis is far more common. We will discuss prenatal testing further later in this chapter. Your healthcare provider will explain to you the pros and cons of having these sorts of tests.

By the time you finish this appointment, you can expect to have an appointment for an abdominal/pelvic ultrasound and possibly for an amniocentesis.

Prenatal Testing:

The Alpha-Fetoprotein Blood Test

This is the month where your healthcare provider may ask you if you want an alpha-fetoprotein (AFP) blood test as part of a panel of blood tests called a quad screen test. The AFP is primarily a test that can indicate an increased possibility of Down syndrome and other conditions. Alpha-fetoprotein testing will be discussed later in this chapter. The decision to have this testing is up to you.

Depression during Pregnancy

Many women experience pregnancy as an exceedingly happy time of life, but others experience mood swings, sadness, and even depression during pregnancy. The American Congress of Obstetricians and Gynecologists (ACOG) estimates that 14 to 23 percent of pregnant women will experience depression during pregnancy.

Depression is a disorder of mood and behavior that affects 25 percent of all women in their lifetime. Stress can contribute to depression. In pregnancy, depression can be triggered by the high levels of certain hormones in the body or simply by being unhappy about the pregnancy or the sex of the child you are carrying, or being stressed out by the demands of work, home, and pregnancy combined.

Depression in pregnancy can have an adverse effect on you and your baby and can be dangerous if it interferes with your ability to care for yourself or if suicidal feelings begin to take hold. Sometimes known as antepartum depression (literally, "before birth" depression), this mood disorder can be triggered at any point in your pregnancy.

Symptoms of Antepartum Depression

There are several signs of antepartum depression. Doctors become concerned when you have some of the symptoms below for at least two weeks or longer:

- *Feeling much sadder than normal.* You may cry more often, worry more, and generally have a negative outlook on life.
- *Problems with concentration.* Even though "pregnancy brain" can affect your concen-

tration, this is much worse with antepartum depression. You may have trouble following a conversation or concentrating on television programs or movies. You may be ruminating on sad thoughts to the point that concentration becomes difficult.

- *Loss of interest.* You may lose interest in activities you usually enjoy, including talking with friends or relatives, or hobbies you normally participate in.

- *Disrupted sleep pattern.* While pregnancy normally interferes with having a solid night's sleep, if you are depressed, you may have trouble falling asleep and you may wake up early and not be able to get back to sleep. Conversely, you may feel like sleeping the day away.

- *Increased anxiety and disturbing thoughts.* You may feel more anxious than normal—over and above the anxiety women usually experience when carrying a child. This can keep you trapped in your house for fear of going out in the world, or you may have irrational feelings regarding your baby and your pregnancy.

- *Recurring thoughts of hopelessness, death, or suicide.* If you begin to have thoughts of this nature, you should seek professional help right away. If you are feeling suicidal and you have some kind of plan to kill yourself, this is an emergency situation.

- *Eating disruption.* You may realize you are eating all the time or find that you have no appetite. You may even begin losing weight. Should this happen, it is important to get help so that your baby continues to receive needed nutrients and you can take care of your own physical needs as well.

- *Feelings of guilt or worthlessness.* You may feel that you are undeserving of the expected joys of motherhood or that you are overwhelmed by having a baby. You may experience irrational guilt about things you have done that you believe might have affected the fetus.

The following factors may contribute to antepartum depression:

- A past history of depression unrelated to pregnancy
- Trouble in your personal relationships, especially with your partner
- Previous experience with infertility treatments
- Loss of at least one pregnancy in the past
- Pregnancy complications that interfere with the enjoyment of the pregnancy
- Work or other life stressors
- A history of sexual, physical, or emotional abuse
- Being in an abusive relationship during pregnancy
- Experience with trauma of any kind

You may think that being depressed will only harm you and will not do anything to hurt the baby—but unfortunately, this may not be the case. If depression is left untreated, it can result in poor nutrition, smoking, drinking behaviors, and suicidal thoughts or actions. All of these things together can cause your baby to be premature, have low birth weight, and possibly have developmental problems. The baby is at increased risk for attention problems, irritability, and decreased physical activity in the uterus. These consequences are highlighted not to make you feel even more guilty or unworthy but to help you realize the importance of seeking and receiving help for depression during pregnancy.

Getting Treatment for Antepartum Depression

Depressed people, in general, have difficulty taking care of themselves, and depressed pregnant women may struggle to properly care for the fetus inside them. This is why you need to seek urgent treatment if you think you may be suffering from depression during your pregnancy.

Treating antepartum depression medically is more difficult because many medications used in the treatment of depression have not been proven safe during pregnancy. There are some medications that may be used if you and your doctor are comfortable with this choice. Your doctor will likely recommend treatments like psychotherapy, group therapy, and support groups.

You may be worried because you don't know what psychotherapy will be like. Television and the movies often portray therapy inaccurately. Most therapy for depression involves your identifying the stressors that are making life difficult and working with your therapist to try to reduce your stress and bolster your coping skills. Your therapist will help you identify any negative thought patterns that are making you feel worse and increase your positive behaviors. Therapy can be hard work, but it can also be very rewarding. In addition to helping resolve the depression that affects your pregnancy, therapy can help you address emotional issues, reactions, and behaviors that will improve your ability to be a great parent once your baby is born.

Your healthcare provider may be able to recommend a therapist, or you may find one at a local mental health center, a college counseling center, or a women's center. Several

Natural Remedies for Depression

- Exercise.
- Plenty of rest and sleep (eight hours per night).
- Setting a small goal for each day, such as doing a load of laundry or calling a friend.
- Things that lift your mood, such as watching a comedy or listening to upbeat music (temporary but helpful).
- A diet low in caffeine, processed carbohydrates, artificial preservatives, and sugar.
- Acupuncture, meditation, and prenatal yoga—all have been shown to have a positive effect on the symptoms of depression.
- Omega-3 fatty acid supplements such as fish oil.
- Herbal remedies containing St. John's wort, SAM-e, 5-HTP, magnesium, or vitamin B6 (some herbal remedies may interfere with other medications, and many have not been studied enough to ensure safety during pregnancy).

Note: As always, talk to your healthcare provider or psychiatrist before taking any herbal remedy or supplement, and seek advice if you find your depression to be severe.

professional associations sponsor listings of qualified therapists. Your therapist may be a psychologist, a clinical social worker, or a mental health counselor, but he or she should be licensed by the state to practice and have experience in treating antepartum and postpartum depression.

Meditation and prenatal yoga, in addition to therapy, can help to alleviate depression. Exercise, in general, has been shown to have a surprisingly powerful ability to lift mood. If you are struggling with your moods, a daily walk may be more helpful than you can imagine. Try to find another person who will walk with you, since this will make it more likely that you will get out every day even if you are not feeling very lively.

More Genetic Testing Options

Last month, your healthcare provider most likely had a conversation with you regarding possible genetic abnormalities in the fetus. If a genetic disorder is detected, you will have the opportunity to begin coping with having a child with special needs or to consider having an elective abortion. Chorionic villus sampling (CVS), a screening test, was discussed in Chapter 5. The conversation about genetic testing will be repeated this month as you approach the time when an amniocentesis or quad screen test can be done to demonstrate the presence or absence of several different genetic abnormalities.

Detecting Neural Tube Defects

The overall risk of a neural tube defect is about 1 in 1000 living children. This defect involves the failure of the embryonic neural tube (within the tube-like structure of the tiny blastocyst, which is the early embryo) to close. This can result in the tailbone portion of the spinal cord failing to close, giving rise to a condition called spina bifida. If, on the other hand, the head portion of the neural tube does not close, it can result in a condition called anencephaly, in which a large portion of the brain is missing.

Maternal Serum Alpha-Fetoprotein Test (MSAFP)

In some cases, neural tube defects can be detected via ultrasound, but, in general, a specific noninvasive test called a maternal serum alpha-fetoprotein test is used. This is a harmless test that determines the level of maternal alpha-fetoprotein (AFP), which is elevated in certain genetic disorders. While it is an easy blood test for doctors to perform, there is a high risk for false positives, causing unnecessary worry in an otherwise normal pregnancy. If the test is normal, however, you can be reasonably sure that the fetus does not

Things to Think About: Baby Gear for Less

Many new parents want everything for their baby to be brand spanking new! But baby gear is expensive and adds up quickly. You may be surprised at how used items can often be just like new. Take a look online or by shopping in consignment or thrift stores for gently used baby clothes, equipment, and toys. Yard sales and garage sales can also yield treasures. Also ask friends and family for hand-me-downs. Remember that everything can be washed or cleaned and will many times look practically brand new afterward. Because babies grow so quickly, used baby clothing is often as good as new and sometimes can be found with tags still intact. As you'll see, sometimes your baby outgrows clothing before having a chance to wear it! There may be items that you will want to purchase new, like a car seat, to be sure they are up to current standards. But you can save a great deal of money by being open-minded about used items. Think about it!

> Genetic testing is such a big decision. I was 38 when I became pregnant, and my doctor wanted me to have every test in the book. My husband and I talked it over and we decided on only having an amniocentesis. We knew we would not terminate the pregnancy but felt it would help us prepare if we were going to have a child with a genetic disease like Down syndrome. My advice on genetic testing is talk it over with your partner, and do what makes sense to you—no matter what your doctor may suggest. —*Mariah, 44, mother of one*

have a defect in the neural tube. The MSAFP can be followed up by doing the same test on amniotic fluid during an amniocentesis.

Quad Screen Test (Using MSAFP)

The MSAFP is often part of the quad screen test that is done between 15 and 20 weeks' gestation. The quad screen test measures the maternal levels of alpha-fetoprotein; human chorionic gonadotropin (hCG); a hormone called estriol, which is produced by the fetus and placenta; and inhibin A, a marker for Down syndrome.

The quad screen test—and the MSAFP in particular—can increase the healthcare provider's suspicion for a neural tube defect but cannot determine for certain that something is wrong with the baby. The American Congress of Obstetricians and Gynecologists recommends that all pregnant women be offered this test, but it is ultimately your decision whether or not to have it.

High levels of MSAFP can raise the suspicion for a neural tube defect. High levels can also indicate the possibility that a fetus is developing an abnormal esophagus or that the baby's abdomen has failed to close properly. High levels of MSAFP mean that the patient needs a careful ultrasound to make sure that none of these conditions exist.

If, on the other hand, the quad screen test shows low levels of hCG, alpha-fetoprotein, and estriol, it may indicate Down syndrome. As with neural tube defects, the test cannot say for certain that the condition actually exists but may sway the healthcare provider to order a confirmatory amniocentesis if the patient agrees.

You should know that the quad screen and MSAFP test are screening tests that do not actually diagnose a specific condition and may have false positive results. The most common cause of abnormal results is the presence of multiple fetuses. Abnormal levels can also point to incorrect gestational dates, which could mean that the pregnancy is more or less advanced than expected. An accurate date of conception is often crucial for determining the probability of having a fetus with these genetic abnormalities.

Choosing to have a quad screen is completely up to you. Talk to your partner about the various choices you have regarding prenatal testing and, together, decide what you would do if the tests showed an abnormality in the fetus. Would you, for example, have an elective abortion if your fetus had spina bifida, anencephaly, or Down syndrome? Or do you feel you would like extra time to get used to the idea of having an infant with a genetic defect? Chances are that you would want to know as far in advance as possible, even if it would not change what you would

Common Genetic Testing Using Amniocentesis

What NOW?

Amniocentesis may reveal some common genetic disorders:

- Trisomy syndromes, such as trisomy 21 (Down syndrome), trisomy 18, and trisomy 13 (rare disorders that affect physical and mental development)
- Sickle cell anemia, often seen in people of African descent
- Hemophilia, a sex-linked blood disorder
- Cystic fibrosis, a disease of the gastrointestinal tract and the respiratory system
- Tay-Sachs disease, a disorder that causes progressive deterioration of mental and physical abilities and is more common in Ashkenazi Jews, along with other genetic disorders that disproportionately affect this ethnic group
- Duchenne muscular dystrophy, a disorder of the muscles
- Turner syndrome, in which one of the two X chromosomes that normal females have is either missing or abnormal, possibly causing physical and reproductive disturbances
- Klinefelter's syndrome (or XXY syndrome), in which males have an additional X chromosome that may not cause any symptoms or may cause disturbances of physical, social, and/or language development
- Rh sensitization, an immune rather than a genetic disease that affects women who are Rh negative and who are having an Rh positive baby (discussed in greater detail below)

actually do during the pregnancy. Knowing in advance about some genetic abnormalities can help the doctor prepare for any possible delivery difficulties that may be associated with these problems.

Amniocentesis

An amniocentesis is done at 15 to 20 weeks' gestation. Besides detecting genetic abnormalities, the test can show whether you have an infection in your uterus. It is performed by using ultrasound to find a large and accessible pocket of amniotic fluid within the uterus and inserting a needle to draw out a small amount of the fluid.

The fluid is then placed in a Petri dish to check if infectious organisms are growing, and the rest of it is used to detect genetic diseases by looking at the fetus' genetic material or chromosomes. Amniocentesis cannot detect the presence of structural changes in the baby. It can tell the sex of the baby and whether it has a genetic abnormality. Amniocentesis can also reveal any neural tube defects (that affect the brain and spinal column), which cannot be identified with CVS. While there are approximately 200 known genetic diseases, the amniocentesis will only check for a few of the more common diseases unless there is a specific disease you already have in the family.

When to consider amniocentesis: As mentioned, amniocentesis is elective and often is considered when one or more of the following conditions exist:

- You are older than age 35, when the risk of chromosomal defects rapidly increases.
- You have had a previous birth of a child with a specific genetic birth defect.
- You have a strong history of birth defects in your extended family.
- You have had a quad screen test with abnormal results.

- You are a carrier of a known X-linked birth defect.
- You are known to carry the gene for a recessive disorder (such as Tay-Sachs disease or cystic fibrosis).
- You take some type of seizure medication, such as valproic acid (Depakote) or Tegretol (carbamazepine).
- You are suspected of having Rh sensitization.
- The ultrasound was suspicious for having a neural tube defect.

Although I knew I would carry my pregnancy to term no matter what, my doctor recommended amniocentesis because I was nearly 40 years old. She said the results would help us to be prepared if there were any concerns, and that sometimes there are things that can be done to help a fetus in utero or in the delivery room. We decided to go ahead and have the test so that we could have as much information as possible. —Fran, 42, mother of two

Risks of amniocentesis: The risk of miscarriage with amniocentesis is 1 out of every 300 to 500 procedures. This is about three to five times safer than the typical chorionic villus sampling (CVS), although the risk of miscarriage with CVS may be lessened with a highly skilled practitioner. You can reduce your risk by going to a facility that has a doctor who has done many amnioceteses in the past. Ask about the rate of miscarriage

for the facility in which you are having your procedure. You will also want a registered ultrasonographer to do your pre-amniocentesis ultrasound.

You should have a visit with a genetic counselor before having the amniocentesis, and, in fact, many doctors require it. A genetic counselor is a professional with at least a masters' degree and highly specialized knowledge of genetics. He or she will ask about your family and personal history of genetic diseases and can tell you what your estimated risk is for the various diseases. You can then decide for yourself whether or not it is worth the small risk of having the test performed.

The amniocentesis procedure: Amniocentesis is an outpatient procedure that is performed in a clinic or hospital. First, you will have an ultrasound to check the status and structure of the baby's features. For this, you will lie down and expose your belly. A nurse or doctor will clean your abdomen with iodine solution or alcohol, and the ultrasound machine will be used to locate a satisfactory pocket of amniotic fluid.

Then, under ultrasound guidance, the doctor will insert a long, thin needle with a hollow core through the abdominal and uterine walls into the pocket of fluid. About two tablespoons or one ounce of amniotic fluid is drawn out of the uterus. Your body will soon replace the amount of fluid lost during this procedure.

The procedure may not bother you at all or you may feel some kind of pressure on your abdomen during the test. The needle might feel like a pinch, and you could have some cramping sensations. Local anesthesia can be used to numb an area of your abdomen.

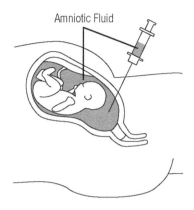

Amniotic Fluid

Amniocentesis

Along with detecting chromosomal abnormalities, amniocentesis can reveal the sex of the baby.

Because amniocentesis may involve an exchange of bodily fluids between you and your baby, if you are Rh negative your doctor will give you a shot of RhoGAM after the test so that you do not get sensitized by your baby's red blood cells.

After the procedure, you will need to rest for the remainder of the day. You should have someone else drive you to and from the procedure. If you experience any vaginal bleeding or worsening cramps, you should contact your healthcare provider. Do not engage in vaginal intercourse, heavy lifting, or travel by air for the next two to three days. Minor cramping is normal; resting will help it abate.

It generally takes one to two weeks until you receive the results. The laboratory that is working on your sample will measure the levels of alpha-fetoprotein in the amniotic fluid and will remove cells from the baby's amniotic fluid, grow them until they are greater in number, and then evaluate the chromosomes using a microscope and by doing tests to see if certain genes are present. Be sure you are with your partner or other supportive family member or friend when you receive the results. If your baby is found to have a genetic abnormality, be open to discussing options again with your partner and possibly with the genetic counselor.

Maternity Clothes: Friend or Foe? It Is Up to You!

Some women are put off by the idea of having to wear maternity clothes, afraid that they will have to buy tent-shaped dresses with little bows at the neck. It may help if you approach the idea of maternity wear much like you do your regular clothing: Fit is everything, especially in maternity wear. Granted, there are not as many options in maternity clothing as there are in regular clothes, but you can still approach your purchases with an eye for what looks good on

Whatever you do, make sure that you tell your wife or partner how great she looks (and she does) in her maternity clothes. Actually, you should be prepared to be pleasantly surprised. My wife looked amazing! I even went shopping for maternity clothes with her. It's important for women to feel good about their bodies—especially when they're pregnant and expanding every day. —Cameron, 40, dad of three you and what does not. Here are some tips for shopping for maternity wear:

- Start with basics, like black pants and skirts, in stretch fabric. These will likely take you through your entire pregnancy. They also go with everything!

- If you find basics you love, buy them in more than one size so you will have them handy as you inevitably expand during the course of your pregnancy. Natural fabrics usually feel better than synthetics.

- Only buy a few items at a time. You will be surprised how your bust, hips, buttocks, and thighs may grow along with your belly!

- Ask friends for hand-me-downs. Most women are thrilled to hand off their maternity wear to someone else.

- Try before you buy. While it is always easy to find a bargain online, this is not a time for blind purchasing. Go to the stores to make sure you like the fit of the clothing you purchase. Just like regular clothing,

Do not buy any maternity clothing believing you will wear it after the baby is born. Believe me, once you deliver, you will practically want to burn the items you lived in for those six months of pregnancy! Shop wisely, stay within your budget, and do not kid yourself about how you will use those clothes again! But, by all means, donate them to someone who will appreciate them. —*Maryellen, 39, mother of three*

 maternity wear can slim you or make you look larger—it all depends on how the garment fits you.

- Accessories—like a bold necklace or earrings—can make you feel pretty, put together, and more like yourself. They can even change the way an entire outfit looks. Buy a few accessories to spruce up your maternity wear. As a huge bonus, they will always fit!

- Remember your feet! Shoes can make an outfit, too. But be aware of any balance issues you may have, and adjust your heel height accordingly. Also, be mindful if your feet swell; have a shoe option available to accommodate—and support—your tired, swollen feet. (No need to wear sneakers with skirts. There are plenty of pretty options out there that are comfortable and stylish!)

- Buy regular clothing in larger sizes at consignment or thrift stores like Goodwill. This is inexpensive and often more stylish than maternity wear.

Exercise Idea: Reward Yourself!

As your body continues to change, you may find it just a little harder to be motivated to exercise. A remedy for this is to keep track of each day you exercise and, after five days, give yourself a reward! You can purchase that cute maternity dress, take yourself out for a nice lunch, or get a pedicure. Whatever you choose as a reward, be sure to be consistent about giving it to yourself. It is so important to treat yourself well throughout your pregnancy, and you deserve a little something for continuing to do what is healthiest for you and your baby.

- If you need suits for work, buy one or two basic ones and change their look with pretty blouses and accessories.

- If money is tight, limit yourself to only one maternity splurge. Just make sure it is something you love and that it can take you through your pregnancy. A little (or not so little) black dress, a stunning top, or a sexy date night outfit will fit the bill. It is important that you allow yourself to feel good no matter what size you are!

- Avoid anything that makes you feel dowdy, frumpy, or "little girlish." Unless you regularly wear bows on your clothing, avoid them now.

- Shoulders should fit properly. This is a key to looking stylish, not sloppy.

- Be sure your blouses are longer than usual to cover stretch panels in pants and skirts. Allow for plenty of expansion in the breast area. Wear a stretchy t-shirt underneath if you are showing more cleavage than you want to.

- If you need a winter coat, buy a regular one at a discount or thrift store in a size that will accommodate your belly, and then have the shoulders altered to fit you.

- Have fun shopping! If you find yourself getting depressed over the options out there or how things are fitting, remember your pregnant body is a temporary condition. Ask a friend or family member to help you shop—a little support will make the process less burdensome.

It is more of a challenge to find maternity clothing if you are a plus-sized woman. The best option for plus-sized new moms is to purchase roomy tops that are one or two sizes bigger than your pre-pregnancy size. Pants are also best purchased at a plus-size store and fit best if you buy polyester or polyester-blend

I loved my second trimester of pregnancy! I felt happy, excited, energized, and still cute! I loved the challenge of finding regular clothing that could still work with my growing body, and I didn't have to give up my high heels and boots! It was a wonderful few months!
—Jessica, 35, mother of one

pants that have an elastic waist.

You, too, may have the problem of changing sizes during the pregnancy so be prepared to buy bigger pants that better fit your hips and bottom. And most of all, keep a positive attitude. Every woman's body is beautiful no matter what size it is!

I took the subway to Boston every day for work. I was so miserable my first three months, and no one ever gave up their seat because no one could tell I was pregnant. When I hit my fifth month, I was so happy to finally look obviously with child! I was offered a seat every day. There was one older gentleman who actually saved me his seat all winter because no one could tell I was pregnant under my coat! My last day of work before I had my baby, I gave him a gift card to Starbucks to thank him. Now we chat all the way into Boston. I show him photos of my daughter and he tells me about his grandchildren. It was a nice way to meet a great friend! —*Liza Marie, 32, mother of one*

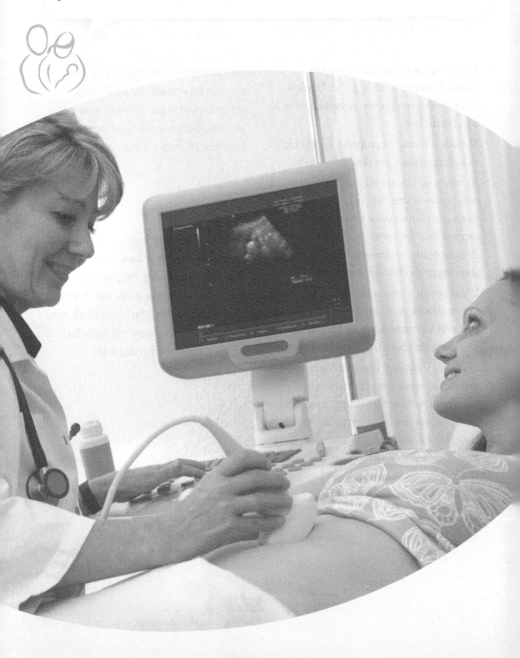

Chapter 7

Month Five—Weeks 17 through 20

In the middle of your second trimester you have reached the halfway point in your pregnancy—congratulations! And, most likely, you are feeling pretty good. The risk of miscarriage or fetal loss has become extremely low, and you will have heard the delightful sound of your baby's heartbeat at least two to three times by now. Symptoms you may have experienced in the first trimester will have abated, and your focus can finally be on enjoying your pregnancy—and all that goes along with preparing to be a parent.

Because you are clearly showing at this point, you are probably getting attention from everyone, from your partner to the grocery clerk. You may be the center of attention at work, in your neighborhood, and with friends and relatives. People will begin opening doors for you, carrying heavy objects for you, and you will likely not have to stand up on a bus or train because people will give up their seat. In short, you may be feeling a bit like rock star! And why not? The birth of another human being is the greatest miracle on Earth!

In addition to enjoying your celebrity status, you will also be making some important decisions this month. If you did not have an amniocentesis last month, you will need to decide if you wish to have this genetic test now. You and your partner will want to be

I remember vividly the day I reached week 18 of my pregnancy—May 29th to be exact—and here's why: I was taking a walk during my lunch break at work and passed by a McDonald's. I suddenly had an irresistible craving for one of their chocolate milkshakes. I hadn't eaten in a McDonald's since I was 15 years old! I remember standing there looking and trying to decide what to do—it wasn't exactly on my list of healthy calories, but the craving was so intense. I can't tell you how badly I wanted to go in. But guess what? I didn't give in to that craving. Instead, I walked back to work. I then spent the rest of the day wishing I'd had that milkshake. To this day, when I think of standing there desperate for that chocolaty treat, I can see the door, feel the sun, remember the people walking by, and feel the intensity of that craving all over again! I still ask myself: "Why didn't you just get one?" Now, in retrospect, I obviously should have! So, now, every May 29th, I go to McDonald's and get a chocolate milkshake with my son, and I tell him this story! It's a fun ritual. But believe me when I say: Don't ignore your cravings! —*Elisabetta, 29* clear about whether or not you wish to know the sex of your baby. You may also want to think about preventing stretch marks, travel concerns, and some health-related issues. But best of all, for the first time, you may experience your baby kicking inside of you. This is, quite possibly, the most exhilarating, thrilling, and indescribable part of being pregnant!

In this chapter, we will help you with the following questions and concerns:

- How is my baby changing and growing?
- Can I prevent stretch marks?
- What concerns should I discuss with my healthcare provider?
- When will I feel my baby kick, and what is it like?
- Can I still travel by airplane?
- When should I start purchasing baby items, and which ones?

Your Baby's Growth and Development: Can You Hear Me Now?

Your baby is developing by leaps and bounds at this point. Let's take a look at what's happening during your fifth month.

Week 17

Your baby truly looks like a tiny human being, with a slightly bigger head in proportion to the body. The baby's circulatory and urinary systems work now. Only very small amounts of fat exist in the baby's body, so it could not possibly regulate its own body temperature outside of the womb.

The placenta is now more proportionate to the size of the baby. Prior to this, the placenta was bigger than your baby. The baby's heart

Using a book like this one, I would read about the growth of my baby week by week and loved the analogies of what size my baby was at various stages: a blueberry, a red onion, a grapefruit! To help my husband visualize what was going on, I got a "baby bowl" and would put in it whatever size item was the equivalent of our baby's size that week! My husband couldn't wait to wake up on Sunday morning to see what was in the bowl! —*Christa, 34, mother of two*

pumps an incredible 25 quarts of blood through its system every day, providing a way to get nutrients to every cell in his or her body.

Neurologically, the brain is continuing to develop, and basic infant reflexes are in place. Your baby is able to swallow amniotic fluid now as the stomach and intestines practice working. The eyelids are no longer fused, and your fetus is able to blink using its tiny eyelids.

The ears and brain are adequately formed so that your fetus can begin to hear loud sounds. He or she can hear your heartbeat fairly clearly, and this becomes a comfort to your baby—as are the sounds of intestinal rumbling! Your baby can hear loud external sounds, and he or she is beginning the process of recognizing your voice. Your baby can hear music, if loud enough—although it is not recommended to blast constant music at your uterus in the hope of giving birth to another Mozart!

Your baby weighs about five ounces at this time and is about five inches from its crown to rump. He or she is now is the size of a very large red onion.

Week 18

Your baby is busy forming tiny pads on the tips of its fingers and toes, so that it has its own set of fingerprints. The eyes finally look forward, and what you see on ultrasound is the face your baby will have—minus the chubby cheeks. The baby is able to make meconium, which is the equivalent of fetal baby stool, but doesn't usually expel the meconium until after birth.

If you are having a male child, he will begin to develop his prostate gland deep within his pelvis; this gland will later become important to him for procreation and sexual functioning. Your baby will have developed the ability to have diaphragmatic spasms, also known as hiccups. When you begin to feel your baby move, which is around this time, you may even feel his or her hiccups as rhythmic movements in your belly.

As external sounds become increasingly easy for your fetus to hear, you will want to discourage exposure to very loud sounds. Playing music for your baby is always fun and will increase fetal movements—just watch the volume!

Your baby is about 6.7 ounces in weight, 5.5 inches long, and the size of a big grapefruit.

Week 19

Vernix caseosa, the greasy or cheesy substance that protects the baby's skin from drying out in the wet environment of the uterus, is beginning to form. So, if your baby were to be born at this time, he or she would be covered in the white substance. Organs are growing bigger inside your baby's body, and they are performing their functions fairly well. This means that your baby's liver is working at near normal capacity, and the kidneys, pancreas, stomach, and intestines are functioning. Your baby's heartbeat is strong enough to be heard with a normal stethoscope placed upon your abdomen. Usually, you can hear the heart tones in the lower rather than the upper portion of your uterus.

Your baby is about 6 inches long and about 8.5 ounces. In the fetal position, the baby is approximately the size of a mango.

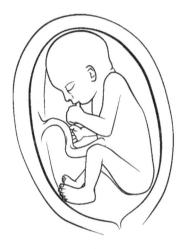

Fetus at 20 weeks of development
At approximately 6.5 inches long and 10.5 ounces in weight, a 20-week-old fetus is beginning to fill out the uterus. The sucking reflex develops: If the hand floats to the mouth, the fetus may suck his or her thumb; the fetus is more active. You may be able to feel the fetus move; he or she sleeps and wakes regularly. Nails grow to the tips of the fingers; the gallbladder begins producing bile needed to digest nutrients; in girls, the eggs have formed in the ovaries; in boys, the testicles begin to descend from the abdomen into the scrotum.

Week 20

The baby is beginning to pick up weight at a slightly faster pace. It sleeps about 80 to 90 percent of the time as it stores energy for growing and developing. Nevertheless, many mothers will have felt the baby move on occasion by now. If you are carrying a female fetus, her uterus is starting to develop the features it may need to perhaps make you and your partner grandparents some day!

If your baby were born today, it would have a somewhat alien appearance due to its lack of body fat. This will soon change as the weeks go on. Just as female fetuses have begun their reproductive development, in most cases the testes of males will have reached their expected position. Brain development continues at a rapid pace. The teeth have finally grown beneath the gums. So, remember that your continued calcium intake is not only contributing to your baby's bone growth but is also now crucial for his or her dental health.

The baby is about 6.5 inches long (from crown to rump) and weighs a remarkable 10.5 ounces. It is the size of a small cantaloupe.

Your Changing Body: Stay in Balance!

While pregnancy is something you have likely gotten used to and while the second trimester is generally the happiest and most delightful part of pregnancy, you will still have symptoms that remind you every day that you are pregnant.

Weight Gain: Don't Stress about It— It's Healthy!

Of the 25 to 35 pounds most women gain during pregnancy, you should have gained about 10 pounds so far. Your baby still weighs less than a pound so most of the extra weight goes into your increased blood volume, fluid retention, the weight of the placenta, and the increased mass of the uterus. If you suffered from significant morning sickness, you may have to play "catch up" and should gain a little extra weight so you have reached the 10-pound mark of total pregnancy weight gain.

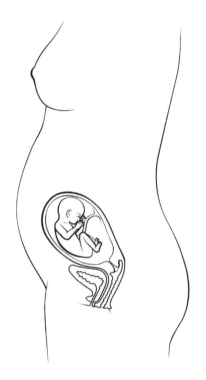

Your changing body: Month five
In month five, your tummy begins to announce your pregnancy, and don't you look wonderful!

If, on the other hand, you have gained more than 10 pounds over your pre-pregnancy weight, you need to talk to your healthcare provider or a nutritionist about ways you can slow down your rapid weight gain without harming the body. If you are right on target with the 10-pound weight gain by 20 weeks' gestation, you should continue to eat an extra

300 calories each day in order to provide nutrition for both you and the baby.

It is important to remember not to obsess about weight gain but focus instead on healthy eating and nutritious calorie intake. If you are gaining a little more or less than average, it is not a problem. Just keep taking good care of yourself and your baby.

If you have any body image issues, this may be a time when they come to the forefront. Regardless of the amount of weight you gain, it is important to maintain your focus on healthy eating and caring for yourself and your baby. If you find yourself limiting your food intake too much or being particularly negative about your expanding body, please talk to your healthcare provider or find a good therapist to guide you through this time. Accepting the beauty of your body in any state is vitally important to your pregnancy and to your own health and well-being.

Dizziness: Watch Your Step

You may find yourself feeling dizzy, having head rushes when you stand up, or having a general feeling of lightheadedness. These symptoms, while normal, can be both annoying and frightening—and they sometimes relate to blood pressure. Do call your healthcare provider if the symptoms persist.

While a woman's blood volume increases during pregnancy, her blood pressure goes down. Women with higher-than-normal pre-pregnancy blood pressure will find their blood pressure is more in the normal range. Women who have normal to low blood pressure before pregnancy are more likely to experience problems with low blood pressure.

I really had a tremendous fear of gaining weight with my pregnancy. In college, I had struggled with anorexia, and some of those old feelings and habits began to surface. I immediately sought help from a program at our local hospital before things got out of hand. With therapy and a support group, I was able to eat healthy and manage my issues around eating and body image. If you need it, don't wait to get help! You and your baby both deserve it! —Marissa, 36, mother of one

Normal blood pressure has a wide range—from 100/60 to about 130/80. Any time the top number is below 100, which can happen in pregnancy, you may experience symptoms of lightheadedness, dizziness, or fainting episodes. Normally, blood pressure drops when you stand up suddenly from a lying or sitting position, and this is when you will experience the most symptoms.

To keep yourself from getting dizzy, make sure you are well hydrated and that you stay out of extremely hot or stuffy conditions. Sit up for a few seconds before rising to your feet after lying down. If you have a wave of dizziness, stand still until it passes and then go about your business. Take your time and just be aware of taking things a little slower than normal.

Stretch Marks: Maybe, Maybe Not

Stretch marks can begin as early as the start of the second trimester. It is nice to think that using a cream or lotion on your abdomen will make some difference in the number of stretch marks you will get in the future. To that end, we will discuss remedies for treating stretch marks later on in this chapter. But the best way to avoid stretch marks is by gaining weight at a steady pace. Gaining too much weight too rapidly will likely result in increased stretch marks.

Uterine Changes: Stay Balanced

By this time, your uterus will have risen to the level of your belly button, and the distance between your pelvic bone and the top of your uterus has grown to about 20 centimeters. What this means for you is that the front part of your body is increasingly larger and heavier. Potentially, this can cause you to feel more off-balance and to have backaches if you stand for long periods of time.

Be mindful of being off-balance as your center of gravity changes for the remainder of your pregnancy. Hold hand rails when taking stairs or escalators and take it slow. As your belly protrudes, it will become harder to see the ground you are walking on. Watch for cracks in sidewalks or uneven pavement as well as toys on the floor if you have children already. Be aware of your expanding girth

Prenatal Testing: Amniocentesis?

Besides the usual urinalysis, your doctor may offer to perform an amniocentesis this month if you did not have one in month four. This genetic testing is often performed at about 15 to 20 weeks, and is explained in detail in Chapter 6. The decision to have this testing is up to you and your partner, so have the discussion about whether or not to have the test before you see the doctor for your monthly visit.

as you maneuver through crowded places as well.

Energy Level: Use It Before You Lose It!

Great news—your energy level will be at an all-time high during this month! Use that extra power to maneuver through the demands of being pregnant, home responsibilities, and workplace projects. You will likely have the excitement and energy you need to begin planning for your hospital stay, to begin buying items for your newborn, and to attend to the details of the nursery. Even with all of this wonderful energy, you need to continue to get as much sleep as possible to stay alert and healthy.

Do not feel frustrated if those around you at home do not feel the spurt of energy you do or the same need to get things done regarding preparing for the new baby. Try to involve your partner, and explain to him or her how you are feeling. Knowing that you will have less energy as your pregnancy progresses and it will be more of a challenge to accomplish things might help your partner pick up the pace with you this month! Use this time to get things done before the sleep deprivation and the uncomfortable aspects of advanced pregnancy take hold. Continue to exercise whenever you can since physical activity likely will become more uncomfortable for you as time goes on and your energy diminishes!

Pigment Changes

Now is the time when you will begin to notice increased darkening (more pigmentation) of both your nipples and the line that extends from your belly button to your pubic region. This line is called the linea nigra and will go away after you deliver your baby. Your

My husband didn't understand my sudden urge and energy to get the baby's room ready and purchase the items we needed. He felt we had so much time left to get all that done. But eventually I helped him understand that I had the energy now for a reason, and later on I was going to be more tired and not accomplish as much. He got on board and we had a blast preparing! *—Marci, 28, mother of two*

nipples may be a soft, dark brown now (regardless of your race), but they will begin to return to your more natural coloring after the baby is born. Note: For most women, the nipples will not return completely to the pinkish color they were before pregnancy; in other words, expect your nipples to be a bit darker following pregnancy.

You may also notice increased numbers of freckles and other skin spots. Some women will notice a darkening of their face as if they had recently been tanning. This change in facial pigment is called melasma, and it occurs most often in pregnant women who already have a darker skin tone. It is a normal part of pregnancy and will gradually go away after you have your baby. We will look at possible ways you can treat melasma in Chapter 9. Meanwhile, because during pregnancy you are more sensitive to the sun due to increased hormones, take extra care to use sunblock every day. This will reduce the likelihood of sunspots and freckles as well as melasma.

Your Emotions: Beginning to Feel like a Mom

With regard to your emotions, the big news this month is feeling your baby move (see "First Time Baby Moves," below), which makes the reality of having a baby seem more—well, real! Although you have certainly known in your mind that you are going to have a child, feeling the sensation of movement in your body brings this brand-new relationship into sharp focus.

Dream, but Be Flexible

Every parent has wishes and dreams for his or her child, but smart parents know that they cannot predict or determine every aspect of their child's life. Don't get stuck on your vision of a future NFL quar-

---

For Dads and Partners: Attention Deficiency?

Now that the pregnancy is official and your partner is definitely showing, her pregnancy is often the main topic of discussions at work, home, and with family and friends. Everyone's focus is on her condition more than anything you will say or do. At this point, it is natural that you might feel envious, and then you may feel negative about yourself for feeling this way! Know that your feelings are totally normal, and try to allow your partner to thrive in the limelight. If you can, talk with your partner about your feelings. All pregnant women get a lot of attention, just as your baby will get a lot of attention after it is born. Continue to do activities you enjoy so that you can feel as if things are as normal as possible and so feelings of envy can take a backseat in your relationship.

---

terback or an artist with the talent of Picasso. Focus, instead, on the values that are of most importance to you and your partner, and think about how you will create an environment where they will flourish. Do you want your child to be a thoughtful, kind person? Practice your own thoughtfulness and kindness, because that is how your child will learn these qualities. If you are raising your child with your partner, talk together about your goals for your child's character and the type of family atmosphere you want to create. Cultivate your own sense of optimism, because an optimistic outlook is one of the most important contributions you can make to bolster your child's mental health.

Give Yourself Time to Reflect about Being a Mother

Taking the time to think things through will help you enjoy your developing relationship with your baby. Use a journal (either a paper notebook or an online journal) to chronicle your thoughts and feelings, or write a letter to your baby to put in the baby book. Perhaps one day your child will be starting his or her own family and will cherish knowing your thoughts before you gave birth.

Take note of the positive behaviors of mothers you know. What do you admire? What aspects of motherhood make you smile? What challenges do you think you will have? Can you think of any resources that will help you to meet those challenges?

Focus on Fun with Your Partner or Friends

Relish your freedom! Go for a spontaneous hike with your partner just because the weather is perfect, or stay up late watching a movie on TV with a friend. If you feel moody or cranky, rev up your sense of humor and laugh a little about your grumpiness. Try your best to keep little irritations in perspective and to be mindful of the phenomenal process of nurturing a new little person within your body. You are doing a wonderful job, and you deserve to enjoy this special time in your life.

Your Prenatal Visit: Picture That!

Your prenatal visit this month will likely be routine. Your healthcare provider will check a urine sample and your weight and blood pressure, measure your uterus, and listen to fetal heart tones. You will more than likely have a prenatal ultrasound this visit as well. Your prenatal clinic may have an ultrasonographer and an ultrasound machine right in the office.

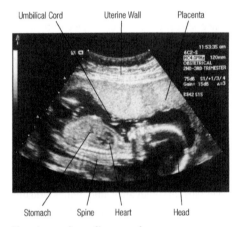

How to read an ultrasound
Ask the ultrasound technician to help you identify what you see on the screen or in the picture you are given to take home.

If you do have an ultrasound, this is the time that you will see your fetus appear more like a "real" baby. During the ultrasound, you likely will be able to see your baby's nose, eyes, mouth, and ears. Your ultrasonogra-

My favorite part of my wife's pregnancy was feeling the baby kick. I remember we would watch television at night and I would keep my hand on her belly the whole time. I have to say I was a little envious that I didn't know what it felt like from the inside like she did—but I loved it anyway! —*Jorge, 37, dad of three*

pher will generally point out those things that are harder for you to identify. Perhaps the easiest organ in your baby's body to identify is his or her heart, which is beating at a rate of approximately 140 to 160 beats per minute, although an active baby can have a faster heart rate. You will also be able to recognize your baby's spine, which curves around in the environment of the uterus.

The ultrasonographer will find and look at your baby's upper lip to make sure it does not have a cleft lip or palate. The technician will then look for the presence of the kidneys and liver to make sure they appear normal. The ultrasonographer will then assess the base of the baby's spine to make sure there is no evidence of spina bifida.

If you want to find out the sex of your baby, let your ultrasonographer know *before* the test begins. And if you do not want to know, be certain to inform everyone in the office associated with the appointment—the receptionist, the nurse, the doctor, and the ultrasonographer—of your decision! If you are interested in learning the sex, at some point your ultrasonographer will show you the baby's genitals. The testes and penis can be easily seen if the baby is a boy. Girls' geni-

tals are a bit more difficult to visualize unless you are well trained in ultrasonography. What you will be directed to observe will be the telltale presence of tiny lines—at least three in a row—that will represent the female child's vulva or genitals. When you see these lines, you will know you are having a girl!

Genetic Testing

If you did not have the quad screen blood test or an amniocentesis for the detection of genetic abnormalities last month, you may be offered the opportunity to have them this month. See Chapter 6 for information about these procedures.

Some hospitals and ultrasound offices are equipped with software to create 3D images of your baby. Make sure to ask for one of

Things to Think About:
Announcing the Sex of Your Baby

Parents who choose to find out the sex of their baby before birth have many creative ways of announcing the news! Some parents choose to just have one parent know and not the other, with the idea that the parent who knows will keep the secret until the baby is born. Others choose to have the ultrasound technician write down the sex on a piece of paper to be sealed and shared with friends or relatives and the expectant parents all at the same time! Sometimes parents will plan a special party to open the envelope. These types of creative announcements can make finding out the baby's sex a fun and less clinical experience and perhaps even as exciting as waiting to find out until giving birth! Think about it!

these amazing photos. If your hospital does not offer this, there are independent 3D ultrasound offices that will produce such a picture of your baby for a nominal fee.

First Time Baby Moves: Oh What a Feeling!

This is most likely going to be the month you feel the baby move for the first time! For some women, it is the most exhilarating feeling you will ever experience. That first kick is one of the most amazing moments you will have in your life! The movements represent the first reflexive kicks of your fetus. What a lot of strength for a baby who does not even weigh a whole pound yet!

The first kicks feel as though a butterfly has flown inside your stomach, or that a

> I remember sitting in a meeting at work and feeling the first flutter of my baby kicking. I actually yelped out loud and stopped my boss mid-sentence. I blurted out an apology and told everyone what had happened! The meeting happened to be with all women and there was so much excitement that we had to postpone the rest of the meeting until the next day! —Veronica, 31, mother of one

tiny fish is swimming within the uterus. You generally feel it when you are quiet and resting. Around weeks 17 through 18, you can create opportunities for this exciting phenomenon to happen. For example, you could drink a bit of orange juice in order to give your baby some extra stimulation from sugars, and then lie down and wait. You might be rewarded with the faint fluttering of your baby's first obvious movements!

Do not worry if, after you first feel the baby move, you do not feel your baby kick for several days at a time—especially if you are busy. The kicks are very faint at this point, and you might miss them just by being preoccupied. By the last part of the second trimester, however, not only will you feel the baby move on a regular basis but others will feel the movement from the outside as well. These fetal movements will change from a fluttering sensation to the sensation of something rolling around inside your uterus, punctuated by the kicking of arms and legs on occasion. Later on in pregnancy, your healthcare provider will give you some guidelines about how many kicks you should feel

Nutrition Tip:
Brown Rice Pasta with Feta Cheese and Spinach

Begin cooking 16 ounces of brown rice pasta (found in all major grocery stores, or use whole wheat pasta) in boiling water. While the pasta cooks, heat one tablespoon of olive oil in a large frying pan on medium heat, then add freshly minced garlic (one to two cloves) and sauté one bag of fresh baby spinach until it is cooked down. Add about one cup of pitted chopped kalamata olives and one cup of chopped fresh tomato; warm through. Crumble 8 to 10 ounces of feta cheese and set aside. Drain pasta, add spinach mixture and feta cheese to pasta, and combine. Salt and pepper to taste, then serve and enjoy!

in a given hour. For now, enjoy the occasional flicker of activity and expect more wonderful movement to come!

Dealing with Stretch Marks

Stretch marks are a skin condition that affects up to 90 percent of all pregnant women. While some women get stretch marks from their upper legs to the upper part of the abdomen, others get none at all. Stretch marks, though annoying, are a normal part of many pregnancies.

Whether or not you get stretch marks is partly hereditary. In fact, Dr. Leslie Baumann, who wrote *The Skin Type Solution,* indicated that if your mother was prone to stretch marks, you are more than likely to get stretch marks as well.

Nonetheless, there are treatments for stretch marks that you can consider trying. Because stretch marks can be prevented to some degree, this is the time in your pregnancy to begin preventative care if you are concerned. Once stretch marks develop, they are unlikely to disappear without treatment, which can be expensive and should only be done after you give birth. Let's take a look at some of the available stretch mark preventative remedies and treatments.

Stretch Mark Prevention

The following tips and products help prevent stretch marks from occurring.

Avoid rapid weight gain: Rapid weight gain stretches the skin too quickly, and a portion of the internal skin structures splits open, leaving a pink, purple, or red thin line in

I don't really know if the creams that I tried actually worked, or if it was just good genes, but I didn't get any stretch marks at all. And whether or not they worked, I enjoyed the ritual of my husband rubbing on the cream every day! —*Lenore, 34, mother of two*

the skin that does not bleed but is unsightly. The line in the skin spreads apart as weight gain and uterine size progress.

Stay well hydrated: Drink at least 10 glasses of water or other beverages per day.

Moisturize your skin: This does not mean you have to go out and purchase an expensive stretch mark cream, although many such creams exist. There is a big difference between a "lotion" and a "cream." A lotion generally contains a form of alcohol that ultimately dries out your skin, while a cream does not contain alcohol and is a better moisturizer for your skin. Read the ingredients on the label and avoid any products that contain alcohol.

• *Eucerin cream.* This is a moderately priced product that contains no alcohol and is good for your skin. It has no color or fragrance for those who might have skin allergies, and it has a thick consistency. Put it on your skin two to three times per day. Be sure you get the cream and not the lotion. Check labels for identical ingredients in generic versions at lower cost.

• *Products with shea butter or cocoa butter.* These lower-priced products are really healthy for your skin. Apply to your

Buyer Beware:
Products Containing Peptides

What NOW?

If you read about peptide-containing products that claim to reduce the appearance of stretch marks by repairing the skin using creams, do not make the purchase. There is no evidence that peptides work for the treatment of stretch marks—and these products can be very expensive!

breasts, hips, buttocks, and belly two to three times per day. Try to find a cream and not a lotion.

Reducing the Appearance of Stretch Marks

These products are believed to have some effectiveness in reducing the appearance of stretch marks. Note: Some are home remedies that have not been studied in a laboratory or research setting. For information about how to reduce the appearance of stretch marks after your baby is born, see Chapter 15.

Wheat germ oil: This treatment is considered a folk or home remedy that has not received much scientific attention. Even so, at least one research study found improvement in newly occurring stretch marks.

Vitamin C: This oral supplement can be purchased over the counter and can help stretch marks heal through increased collagen production. Vitamin C is believed to work on stretch marks that have recently emerged. Take with glycolic acid for increased effectiveness. Vitamin C supplements are generally taken in doses of 500 milligrams, three times daily or less. The recommendation is not to exceed 2000 milligrams (two grams) per day during pregnancy.

Traveling while Pregnant

Many pregnant women continue to live full lives, taking vacations, remaining active, and traveling for work. You should ask your healthcare provider whether or not travel is appropriate for you during any given month of pregnancy. Unless you have complications, there should be no problem with normal travel during this time.

Increased Risk of Deep Vein Thrombosis (DVT)

Pregnant women in general will be at a greater risk for deep vein thrombosis (DVT) than non-pregnant women. A DVT is a blood clot that occurs in the deep veins of the legs. The rate of DVT is about 1 out of every 1000 pregnancies, and travel can play a big role in developing this condition. It causes pain in the back of the calf (sometimes severe), redness or discoloration of the calf, and swelling of the lower leg.

DVTs occur during situations where the blood is not flowing properly. The high circulating levels of estrogen in pregnancy make the blood clot more easily. In addition, the uterus sits on the vena cava—the great vein that goes from your heart to your pelvis—and this can reduce blood flow in the legs.

A DVT becomes dangerous if a piece of the clot breaks off and travels up the vena cava to the lungs. A blood clot in the lungs is called a pulmonary embolism (PE), and it can have drastic consequences for your health. If the clot is big enough, it can straddle the openings to both lungs, resulting in imme-

I had to fly cross country for work while pregnant in my fifth month. When I checked in, the airline representative asked how far along I was. She then bumped me up to first class so I could stretch my legs and more easily walk around for breaks. I think she also wanted the staff to be able to keep an eye on me. I would suggest asking for an upgrade if you are pregnant—the airlines want you to be safe on their flights as well! —*Holly, 37, mother of three*

diate cardiovascular collapse and death within a few seconds. In fact, three percent of all cases of sudden death are due to a PE rather than some kind of heart condition.

Prevention of DVT

So how do you prevent a DVT or PE from occurring? You should try to avoid long-distance airline flights, and, if you have to fly, consider flying first class instead of coach; that way you have room to stretch your legs. Stretching your legs increases the muscle tension in the lower legs, which allows blood to flow more easily through the veins. The veins themselves have valves to keep blood flowing in one direction but have no muscle power to push blood through without your leg muscles doing the job.

If you must fly coach on an airplane, get up and stretch your legs after every hour if conditions allow. You can also move your legs as if you were walking in place while seated. If you feel you cannot do that, consider buying thigh-high compression stockings or TED

(thrombo embolytic deterrent) stockings from your local pharmacy or medical supply outlet center. These keep the blood flowing by compressing the lower leg veins.

You should also stay well hydrated while traveling. FAA guidelines currently do not allow you to bring in your own bottle of water, but you can purchase bottled water and other beverages after you pass through the security checkpoint. Aim to drink at least an eight-ounce bottle of water every hour. The environment on a plane is especially dry, so you will need the extra fluids.

Remember that a DVT/PE can happen any time you sit for approximately four hours or more in any situation, including taking a long car ride, bus ride, or train ride. Even sitting at your desk without getting up every hour or so could put you at risk for getting a DVT or PE. Be sure to keep moving wherever you are!

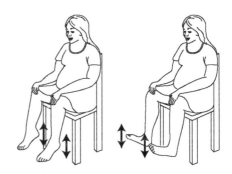

DVT-prevention exercises
Pump your feet to prevent DVTs.
This simple exercise may help prevent the formation of blood clots. You can do it while traveling in a car or plane or while sitting at your desk. First, put your toes on the floor and pump your heels up and down. Then rest your heels on the floor and pump your toes up and down. Don't try this while driving!

Reminder: Do Your Kegels!

If you haven't been doing your Kegel exercises, now is a great time to start! Kegel exercises work the muscles of the pelvic floor so that you will have strong muscles in your perineum (the area between the vagina and the rectum) and vaginal area—so important when it comes to the labor process. Those women who practice Kegel exercises during pregnancy will likely have an easier labor and birth process.

Kegel exercises also improve your ability to control urine flow, and you will have fewer hemorrhoids after the baby's birth. The perineum will heal faster if you have done Kegels, and you may have a reduction in the chances of having an episiotomy, the surgical cut sometimes made to enlarge the birth opening.

How to Do Kegel Exercises

There are several ways to learn how to do Kegel exercises. First, you can begin to urinate on the toilet and, during the middle of the stream, try to stop your urine flow. Hold the urine for about 5 to 10 seconds and then continue to void. Repeat this one more time during urination so you can understand what muscles you are contracting.

You can also locate your perineal muscles by inserting your finger into the vagina and attempting to squeeze your finger with the surrounding muscles. Then remove your finger and try to squeeze those same muscles. Once you have located and used the appropriate muscles, you can exercise them any time you're sitting down. Contract muscles for 5 to 10 seconds, and repeat the exercise 10 to 20 times.

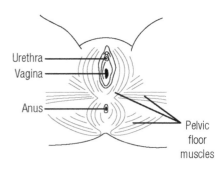

Pelvic floor muscles
These are the pelvic floor muscles you use when doing Kegel exercises.

The beauty of Kegels is that you can do them anywhere at any time, and no one will know! Try to do these exercises when you're sitting down at the breakfast table, in line at a drive-thru service, or when you are waiting to see your doctor or midwife.

Buying Baby Items: Ladies, Start Your Engines!

Yes, now is the time to begin researching and purchasing baby items! But do not go crazy—which is easy to do when you hit a baby store and see all the adorable clothes and accessories available for infants.

If you can, start by researching what you want and what you need, and make a plan. What items are you planning to purchase yourself and which items might your put on a registry for others to purchase for you as a baby shower gift? Do you really need that $50 pair of leather baby booties that look like little doggies? Are you planning to nurse, or do you need to stock up on baby bottles? If you are nursing, are you planning to go back to work and therefore need a breast pump to pump milk in the office?

Once you have thoughtfully made a list of what you need and have made a plan for how to acquire those items, it is best to create a budget and stick to it! Here are some things to consider:

- Go to consignment stores, thrift stores, and garage or yard sales looking for baby items.
- Check out your local Craigslist. It often lists the locations and times of local garage or yard sales and can tell you when and where consignment sales are offered, which are usually held in the spring and fall. Craigslist also lists a variety of baby items for sale.
- If you are really struggling financially, find out if there are any local organizations that assist new parents with baby items. Often, these programs are aimed at single mothers. Your county department of social services should be able to

> Be wary of registering for items that you don't really need! I remember returning a baby wipes warmer after discovering how ridiculous it was! I couldn't take it with me when we were out, and I didn't want my baby getting used to it and then screaming when I used a non-heated wipe when we were out! —*Josie, 28, mother of one*

direct you to programs in your community.

- To start, infants will often wear onesies (little t-shirts that snap in the crotch), so stock up on those. And do not try to guess your baby's size six months to a year down the road. No one knows just how big her baby will be and how fast he or she will grow. Buy as you go.
- Register for baby items at superstores like Babies "R" Us, Target, or Walmart. If you purchase an item on that list yourself, be sure to delete it from the list. Do not put an item on more than one list. Several large retailers will offer discounts (usually 10 percent) on unpurchased items that remain on your registry 30 days after the "event" (the due date). Check it out.
- Avoid buying used car seats, since they may not meet current safety standards.
- Always wash or sterilize any item you purchase used.
- Ask friends and family for hand-me-downs!
- Buy cribs and changing tables that can be used as your baby grows. Many cribs will convert to a toddler bed, and you can use changing tables later as standard dressers.
- If you have a list and a plan, you will be less tempted to make impulse purchases. But then again, have fun and be flexible if your budget allows!

Planning Your Baby Items List

Here are some tips to help make shopping easier.

Clothing sizes: Think back to the first time you had to buy a shower gift for an infant and found yourself pondering what size clothing to buy. It can be a little confusing trying to sort out age-appropriate sizes. So, here is a guide to relieve you of the guesswork for your own baby:

- **Preemie:** For newborn infants around five pounds or less who are able to come home from the hospital.

- **Newborn:** For infants up to about 10 pounds. If you are expecting a big baby, you may skip this size and go onto the next!
- **0–3 months:** For babies around 7 to 12 pounds.
- **3 months:** For babies around 12 to 14 pounds, or who are about two to three months old.
- **3–6 months:** For babies around 12 to 17 pounds.
- **6 months:** For babies around 14 to 17 pounds, or who are about four to six months old.
- **6–9 months:** For babies around 16 to 19 pounds.
- **9 months:** For babies around 18 to 19 pounds, or who are around seven to nine months old.
- **12 months:** For babies around 20 to 22 pounds, or who are about 9 to 12 months old.
- **18 months:** For babies over 22 pounds, or who are about 12 to 18 months old.

Exercise Idea: No Contact Sports, Please!

Your uterus is now big enough that contact sports are out of the question. You need to avoid sports where falling down is probable as well, like ice skating, snow skiing, or even water skiing. If you normally are a runner, you can continue running with the caveat that you be mindful that your center of gravity is different now and you are more likely to trip and fall. Many women stick with brisk walking, prenatal yoga, biking, swimming, or Pilates—all of which are good activities for this stage of the pregnancy. But whatever you choose to do, keep moving!

Every baby is different in size and shape so the above guide is just that—a guide for you to select clothing for an average-sized baby. Also, each manufacturer has a somewhat different size standard, so you have your work cut out for you!

Clothing items and accessories: Just like you, your baby will need basics for his or her closet or dresser. So work from this handy list to plan for your baby's wardrobe.

- **Onesies:** Babies wear these snap-crotch t-shirts underneath sleepers or alone during warm months. Stock up on these, especially for your newborn.
- **Sleepers:** Be sure the sleeper is not too complicated to put on.
- **Pants and tops:** Some people find that these are harder to put on and remove while changing the diaper unless the pants have snaps in the inseam. The advantage of these separates is that you can mix and match the outfits for a better selection.
- **Socks:** Babies kick off their socks on a regular basis. Buy socks snug enough to fit their tiny feet.
- **Bibs:** Some parents like a bib on their baby at all times to prevent drooling and spitting up on clothing. Others just use bibs for feeding their baby when they start solids around six months of age. You will go through a lot of bibs, believe me!
- **Pacifiers:** Select the type of pacifier you believe will be best and stick with the same brand.
- **Pacifier connectors:** These handy little devices are good for clipping the pacifier to your baby's clothing. That way, you do not have to pick the pacifier up off the

floor and wash it whenever your baby spits it out.

- **Hats:** Depending on your climate, you may need to buy some knit hats or sun hats for your baby.
- **Snowsuit or jacket:** Depending on the time of year and your climate, you may need a warm garment for your baby to wear outside. Buy one online if you cannot find the one you want in the stores.

Essentials for the nursery: You and your partner can plan and shop together for nursery furnishings.

- **Crib:** You can purchase cribs new or used. Do not buy a crib with drop sides or one that is more than 10 years old. (We discuss setting up the nursery in Chapter 9.)
- **Crib mattress:** Buy a new one if you possibly can. Crib mattresses run about $80 to $150.
- **Crib sheets, blanket, mobile, and bumper pad:** You can purchase these so that they all match or you can work with whatever you can find. It is always a good practice to have at least two sheets in case of accidents.
- **Bassinette or co-sleeper:** Some people choose to have the infants up to three months old in a bassinette that can be placed by your own bed so you can be close to your baby. A co-sleeper is similar to a three-sided bassinette that attaches to the side of your bed, so you can reach your baby easily while he or she has a safe space in which to sleep.
- **Changing table:** Some people buy a special changing table on which to change the baby's diapers. Others just buy a mat and change the baby on the floor or a bed.

- **Lamp and/or nightlight:** You may like a lamp in the room so you can turn it on when baby wakes up for feedings or needs a diaper change in the middle of the night. You may prefer a dim nightlight that can stay on all night.
- **Dressers:** These can be purchased cheaply at furniture or outlet stores. Consider the size you will need for storing your baby's clothes.
- **Blankets:** You will need a few receiving blankets (light flannel blankets), which

It may be hard to understand now, but enjoy the beauty of how you are feeling this month! As you move forward in your pregnancy you really are going to become increasingly tired and uncomfortable. Like everything in life, enjoy the moment and embrace it! Everything changes—and change is good, especially when there is an actual baby waiting for you at the end of the journey! —*Shirley, 42, mother of two*

can also double as burp cloths. You will also need warmer blankets for outdoors or for cool-weather situations.

- **Baby monitor:** You may want to purchase a monitor so you can more easily hear when your baby wakes up during the day or night or is crying in his or her crib. Video monitors are also offered at various retailers.
- **Diapers:** Find diaper coupons online or in newspaper circulars, and buy size NB, 1,

2, and 3 diapers when you can find them on sale. Newborn diapers only fit infants up to about 10 pounds at most, and you will often only need to purchase two to three packs of this size.

- **Baby wipes:** Buy these on sale or when you have a coupon, or go to a warehouse-type store and purchase a big flat of baby wipes. You will need them for a long time!

Essentials for the bath: While all moments you spend with your baby are precious, one of the most cherished is bath time.

- **A tub:** Purchase a sturdy tub that fits into your own bathtub, preferably one that is convertible and adjusts to fit both the needs of newborns and those of older babies.
- **Washcloths:** For cleaning your baby's body.
- **Baby towels:** These soft terry cloth towels have hoods to keep the baby's head from getting cold when he or she gets out of the tub to dry off.

Midpoint Monitor

Although you have reached the midpoint of your pregnancy and the risks for miscarriage have lessened greatly, you should still monitor your health closely.

Call your healthcare provider if you experience any of the following symptoms:

- A fever greater than 101.5°F
- A painful abdomen, whether it is a steady ache or crampy in nature
- Bleeding or spotting of any sort

- **Baby soap:** You can buy a combination baby wash and baby shampoo that can be used to clean your baby's head and body. There also are separate baby washes and baby shampoos if you prefer to use them.
- **Grooming tools:** These can range from the comb your baby gets in the hospital to a complete nail grooming kit. You will need to clip your baby's nails on a regular basis so your little one doesn't scratch himself or herself.
- **Lotions and oils:** Babies can get dry skin quite easily. Have some lotion or oil on hand to keep your baby's skin supple. Put it on daily or after a bath. You can also use baby oil for cradle cap (see Chapter 14).

Get ready for playtime: You can find toys at a great price at garage sales and consignment sales. Purchase gently used toys and books for your baby's health and development. A product such as the Mr. Clean Magic Eraser (slightly dampened) works really well for removing marks from vinyl or cardboard books.

- **Books:** Babies especially love cardboard books or those made of vinyl. The vinyl ones can be chewed on as well as read. Touch-and-feel books or books that are musical will expose your baby to new things.
- **Toys:** Focus on small things like rattles, manipulative toys that will stimulate the baby's ability to hold onto and manipulate objects. These toys will come in handy when your baby is about three to six months old.
- **Musical toys:** Any toy that plays music will be fun and soothing for your baby. Be sure the tune won't drive you a bit nuts!

- **An ExerSaucer:** This serves the same purpose as the old walkers babies used to have, but it is much safer because the baby cannot move around and get into trouble elsewhere in the room. This item usually has interactive toys on a ring in which your child sits supported by a sling chair. It will be useful for a baby that is as old as four months of age.

- **Play mats:** These are colorful quilted mats with a "gymnasium" of toys dangling above them. The baby can just look at the dangling toys or pull on the rings that many of them have on them.

- **Johnny Jump Up:** This is a chair-like item that hangs from a door frame. It can help the four to six month old learn to use his or her legs.

- **Teething toys:** When your baby is teething between four and twelve months, he or she can chew on the toys, or you can freeze them (they contain sterile water) to cool down swollen gums.

- **Swing:** Swings can sit low to the ground or can be as tall as four feet. They can soothe a fussy baby, or can just be fun and enjoyable for you and your child.

- **"Bouncy chair":** These are good devices for strapping the baby in on a table or floor. The device can bounce the baby a little, and some can be set to vibrate gently to soothe the baby.

Have baby, will travel: Here are the things you will need for keeping you and baby on the go:

- **Car seat:** You should purchase a bucket-style car seat for your baby's first six through seven months. These are designed for you to be able to carry the baby around. Many have a frame that stays strapped in the backseat and you simply snap the bucket into it.

Babies need to ride in a rear-facing car seat (in the backseat of the car) until they are at least 20 pounds or one year old. The American Academy of Pediatrics suggests using rear-facing seats until age two. It is important that the seat be installed properly in your car, according to the manufacturer's instructions. The National Highway Traffic Safety Administration website (www.nhtsa.gov) has a Child Care Seat Inspection Station Locater to find a nearby inspection station where certified technicians will inspect your car seat and teach you how to install it safely. There is usually no charge for this service.

- **Diaper bag:** You will need a sturdy bag to hold your baby's necessities—diapers, wipes, powders, and creams—when you are out shopping, visiting with friends, or out on an errand. You don't have to by a traditional diaper bag—a backpack or messenger bag may be more your style, and your partner may be more willing to tote it.

- **Infant carrier sling or pack:** You can buy a cloth baby sling to carry your baby around with you. It looks like a big circular scarf. You can also buy a more complex front carrier that allows you can do errands or household chores with your baby safely resting on your abdomen and chest. Backpack-type carriers are available for older babies who can sit up on their own.

- **Stroller(s):** Stroller/car seat combination sets use the car seat atop the bigger stroller. Later, the baby or child can just sit in the stroller without the bucket car seat. These are helpful when your baby falls asleep in the car seat, since you don't have to wake the baby to put him or her in the stroller. You can purchase an umbrella stroller that is much cheaper and lighter. These are not very supportive and are not recommended for babies less than six months of age, but can be convenient for an older baby.

Notes:

Be prepared for complete strangers to want to touch your belly and to actually do so without asking permission! There's something about being pregnant that makes people feel connected to you—as if the life you are carrying belongs to the whole world. I guess in a way it does if you think of it as part of carrying on the human race. But don't be shy about setting boundaries if this kind of attention makes you feel uncomfortable. Be polite but firm!
—*Alexandra, 33, mother of two*

Chapter 8

Month Six—Weeks 21 through 24

Woo Hoo! You have made it to the last part of your second trimester, and are two-thirds of the way to bringing your baby into the world! Your energy level is likely continuing to soar even as your uterus is growing by leaps and bounds. Lucky you—you can still see your feet and tie your shoes! Hopefully you still feel pleasantly pregnant and are enjoying this period of relative comfort before entering into the final stretch of your journey where all things—including you—become weightier.

At this point, you can feel your baby kicking on a regular basis, and the intense delight of bonding with your child is in full swing. While preterm labor, miscarriage, and gestational diabetes can still occur, ideally weeks 21 through 24 will be a continuation of the energized, smooth sailing you have been experiencing. This is the perfect time to continue planning for your baby's arrival by attending childbirth classes, scheduling a tour of your hospital or birthing center, and preparing for your baby at home.

In this chapter, we will answer the following questions:

- How fast is my baby growing this month?
- How can I cope with body changes, like lack of sleep and bladder infections?
- What is gestational diabetes, and how will I be tested for it?

Coincidentally, my two best girlfriends and I all became pregnant within a month of one another! When we hit our second trimester, we began to take photos together from the side. We stood in the same order in each photo and faced the same direction. We even wore similar outfits—jeans in month four, dresses in month five, overalls in month six. It was amazing to see how our bellies progressed and how, some months, one of us was so much bigger than the other two and vice versa. I gathered the photos and, as a surprise, made scrapbooks for each of my friends (and one for myself). I wrote down how much we weighed and how big around we were each month through to month nine. I also recorded my thoughts about our journey together and funny things that happened to us along the way. When each of my friends gave birth, I brought the scrapbook to her in the hospital. It was such a thrill to see their joy and laugh over how we looked! There was one empty space for a photo to be taken after we had all given birth. It was each of us with our little bundles of joy still standing in the same order and to the side wearing similar outfits—and our babies (all three boys!) wore matching outfits as well!—*Carolyn, 32*

- What is placenta previa, and how serious is it?
- Are childbirth classes useful? Which ones are right for my partner and me?
- How do I choose a hospital or birthing center?
- What is cervical incompetence, and should I be concerned about it?

Your Baby's Growth and Development: Kicks and Hiccups!

Believe it or not, by the end of this month, your baby will weigh about one and a half pounds! He or she is rapidly developing into the little person you will soon hold in your arms—and just to prove it, your baby is now kicking with some oomph! Let's take a look at what else is happening in weeks 21 to 24.

Week 21

The fetus is growing quickly, but not as quickly as in the last month. The legs and arms are in proportion to one another and the heart becomes strong enough to pump blood around the fetal body. The taste buds are beginning to work so that your baby can distinguish between different flavors. Fat layers begin to form, and this fills out your baby's appearance. This fat is necessary for the baby to regulate his or her body temperature after birth.

Hiccups are more common from this point on. Your baby may have hiccups several times a day as the diaphragm gets ready to "learn" the process of breathing. The fetus is growing in length and weighing more. At this point in the pregnancy, the baby is measured from the crown of the head to the heel, instead of from the crown to the rump as earlier. By this method, he or she now measures about 10.5 inches long, weighs approximately 13 ounces, and is the size and contour of a large banana.

Week 22

The baby has well-developed internal organs but is still very thin. The eyelids open and close, and your baby now has eyebrows. The brain continues to develop at a rapid rate, with billions of new brain connections being made every week. Because brain growth is very important, your diet should continue to be as good as you can get it. The testes of boy fetuses are descending into the scrotum, where they belong. Your baby also has identifiable nipples, whether it is a boy or a girl.

In ultrasound images, babies at this stage can often be found sucking their thumbs, a popular activity for many babies. He or she can wiggle fingers and can touch his or her face. While the lungs are continuing to develop, they do not contain enough surfactant, which is the substance that makes lungs pliable. The swallowing mechanisms have developed.

Your baby is about 11 inches long (from crown to heel) and weighs about 15 ounces—almost a pound! For the next three weeks, he or she will be about the size of a papaya.

Week 23

Your baby's proportions are nearly normal for an average newborn, and the bones of the middle ear, which will contribute to hearing, begin to harden. Your baby can actually hear, touch, taste, and smell.

Babies born at 23 weeks have a chance of survival, but the risk for medical conditions related to prematurity is high. So, if born prematurely at this time, your baby would need a great deal of medical support for several months in order to be able to survive and go home. About 25 to 35 percent of all babies born at 23 weeks can survive, according to data from the March of Dimes. Every day and every week your baby stays in your uterus is important and necessary for the best birth outcome.

Your baby weighs 1.1 pounds by now and measures 11.5 inches from crown to heel.

Week 24

Your baby is gaining weight quickly. If born during this week, he or she would have a 50 to 60 percent chance of survival. If these odds do not look good to you, do everything you can to insure that the baby stays within the womb. Most of the baby's weight is in its muscles and its organs. It still needs to develop more body fat.

The baby now has eyelashes, possibly hair on his or her head, and tiny fingernails that will continue to grow indefinitely for his or her life. Rapid eye movements, indicative of dreaming, can be seen on ultrasound as the brain develops further.

Your baby weighs about 1.3 to 1.5 pounds and is about 12 inches long. It is gaining about one-tenth to three-tenths of a pound per week.

Because the fetus is taking up an enormous amount of your iron for making blood and growing cells, your iron levels may be deficient even if you are taking an adequate amount of iron.

For this reason, you might become anemic, which is defined as a hemoglobin level of less than 10. If you are even close to reaching that number in pregnancy, your doctor might recommend that you take an iron supplement every day in order to bring up the hemoglobin level.

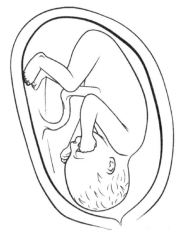

Fetus at 24 weeks of development
At approximately 12 inches long and weighing 1 to 1.5 pounds, a 24-week-old fetus can live outside the uterus but needs more maturing to ensure survival. Real hair begins to grow; the brain is rapidly developing; the eyes begin to open; you can see finger and toe prints; and the lungs are fully formed but not yet functioning.

Your Changing Body: Big and Beautiful!

This month you will notice tremendous growth in your belly, and you may find yourself beginning to fill out your maternity clothes or needing to give in and purchase them for the first time! While the changes outside are more apparent, there are even more interesting changes happening inside your body! Let's take a look.

Heartburn: Still an Issue

Heartburn tends to get worse during this month because the uterus is now pushing on the stomach, increasing the pressure and allowing acid from the stomach to enter the lower esophagus. See Chapter 6 for more information about heartburn and how to minimize this unpleasant problem. Small, frequent meals spread throughout the day can control this problem better than eating three larger meals daily.

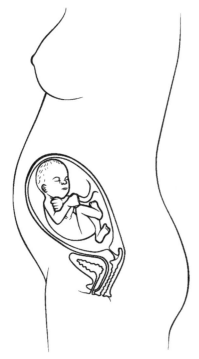

Your changing body: Month six

In your sixth month, you will be more aware of your baby moving inside you, a reminder of the important work your body is doing to nurture and protect your child.

At this point, the TUMS or Maalox you took earlier in your pregnancy may not last long enough to control the pain and other symptoms of your heartburn. You may

I'd heard so much about heartburn that I made my husband raise the head of our bed as a preventative measure. I guess it worked, because I didn't have heartburn once! Like they say, an ounce of prevention is worth a pound of cure! —*Penny, 37, mother of two*

wish to discuss the possibility of taking Zantac or ranitidine with your healthcare provider. It is a Category B drug for use in pregnancy, but no studies of safety in the first and second trimester have been done.

In addition, now would be the time for you or your partner to raise the head-end of your bed with blocks of wood or phone books so that when you sleep, acid is less likely to flow up into the esophagus. You will sleep better as a result.

There is an old wives' tale that says the more heartburn you have, the more hair your baby will have. There is actually a scientific explanation for this possibility. Heartburn is made worse by circulating estrogen, which is higher in some women than in others. High estrogen levels also promote hair growth on the baby—so there may be a good thing coming out of your uncomfortable symptoms!

Sleeping Patterns: Get Your Zzzs

The further along you are in your pregnancy, the harder it is to get a good night's sleep! At this stage, you need to sleep on your side. Many doctors prefer that you sleep on your left rather than on your right side because the uterus can put extra pressure on your descending aorta, the great artery of the

Iron Supplements and Nausea

You should know that taking iron supplements can increase symptoms of nausea, heartburn, and constipation. Different iron pills have different rates of side effects, so you should talk to your healthcare provider or pharmacist about which iron pills to take. The same is true for prenatal vitamins. Take them with food to help with queasiness.

abdomen that supplies blood to the uterus and placenta.

The aorta sits just to the right of the spine, so when you sleep on your left side, your uterus does not compress the aorta and its matching vein, the vena cava. Sleeping on your left side gives the fetus the best chance for healthy oxygenation and flow of blood within the uterus and placenta. Sleeping on your right side is second best. Sleeping on your back is not recommended. Sleeping on your stomach is okay, but it is pretty tough to do at this point!

Sleep can be disturbed due to your hormones, frequent trips to the bathroom, and the inability to sleep in your preferred position. You may find yourself getting up earlier in the morning, particularly if you are depressed or having periods of time during the night where you just cannot sleep. If you wake in the middle of the night and cannot get back to sleep, try getting up out of bed for 30 minutes to an hour to read a book or magazine before going back to bed.

You can now understand what it means to cat nap! Take any opportunity you have during your day to sleep. Allow yourself to go to bed when you get tired and not when the clock tells you it's bedtime. And remember, this is a normal part of pregnancy, and lack of sleep, though a challenge, will not harm your baby.

Sex: Enjoy Yourselves!

A woman's sex drive increases during the second and third trimester but is at its peak around this time in pregnancy. Enjoy these feelings as much as you can! Consider this: The added intimacy you have with your partner may decrease the chance of relational discord as your pregnancy progresses and even after your baby is born.

Remember, no amount of sexual intercourse can harm the fetus unless you have a high-risk pregnancy, such as carrying multiples or having placenta previa (see page 182).

For Dads and Partners: Keep Participating

You have been there through the morning sickness, the crying over commercials, and the cravings! Now is the time to get involved in helping prepare for your baby's arrival by pitching in to set up the nursery. If you have not yet done so, help pick out the theme, color scheme, furniture, or anything else your partner wants input on—even if you really are fine with whatever she wants! Put together the crib, paint the walls, and move the furniture. And if your partner becomes a little irritable at times, be patient. Pregnant women in their second trimester may begin to get more moody again. It is a natural part of the pregnancy journey, so find that support and kindness you have been accessing throughout these first six months and hang in there. Only three months to go!

I got really scared when I started to crave chalk during my pregnancy. I thought I was going crazy! I immediately called my doctor, and she told me that this phenomenon—when you crave inedible things like laundry soap or dirt—is known as pica, and she would help me manage it. I felt so embarrassed but she said not to be upset, and she told me I did the right thing by seeking help right away. Don't ignore any cravings you have for nonedible substances; they are dangerous to both you and your baby and you can get help! —*Deanie, 40, mother of two*

Contractions are possible after a woman has had intercourse and, particularly, if she has an orgasm. This is normal and will not cause the cervix to open at this stage of the pregnancy. These contractions will pass after a few minutes.

This might be the time to experiment with different sexual positions. The uterus is big enough that the usual missionary position during intercourse is uncomfortable or difficult to achieve. This exploration can be fun for both you and your partner and can open up new avenues for sexual experiences.

If you have bleeding after intercourse or if you have an uncomfortable experience during intercourse, you should talk to your health-care provider about your difficulties.

Cravings: Give In or Not, It Is Up to You

Everyone has seen movies or television shows in which pregnant women experience bizarre food cravings. In truth, about half of all pregnant women in the United States

report cravings for at least one food during their pregnancy.

In a survey, pregnant moms said they craved sweet foods about 40 percent of the time. Thirty-three percent of women craved salty foods, and 17 percent had a yen for spicy foods. Only 10 percent of women craved tart foods like citrus fruit or unripe apples. Interestingly, many pregnant women crave ice.

Experts believe that the unusual mix of hormones during pregnancy contributes to cravings, although there is no definitive research on the causes of craving. One study, however, showed that women who had extreme aversions to certain foods while pregnant were twice as likely to experience food cravings as those who did not have any food aversions.

There are some nutrition experts who believe that pregnant women should pay attention to their cravings. For example, cravings for chocolate can be linked to a deficiency of magnesium, which is normally found in beans, nuts, whole grains, green vegetables, and seeds. Similarly, when a woman craves meat, she might be in need of more protein. Other cravings could indicate vitamin, macronutrient, or mineral deficiency. Others disagree with this concept and believe that cravings are just a phenomenon of pregnancy that cannot be explained.

If you crave something healthy, you can indulge the craving as long as the rest of your diet is well balanced. If what you crave is high in fat or sugar, try nonfat and low-sugar alternatives of the same food. For example, if you crave ice cream, try eating low-fat ice cream or frozen yogurt instead (or even better, frozen fruit). Eating small and frequent meals can also cut down on cravings. In addition, skipping breakfast encourages cravings so start your day with a healthy meal.

Bladder Infections: Get Treated

Bladder infections can occur during the first, second, or third trimester and are more common among women who have a history of this problem before becoming pregnant. If you get a bladder infection during pregnancy, you may have no obvious symptoms or you may have many symptoms.

Bladder infections (also called urinary tract infections or UTIs) occur when intestinal bacteria from the skin around the vagina enter the bladder by passing up through the short tube through which urine passes (the urethra). The urine acts like a culture medium in a laboratory and grows many more bacteria, which can stick to the inner wall of the bladder and cause bladder irritability and a bladder infection.

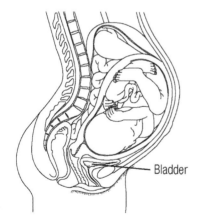

Pregnancy and bladder infections
The fetus pushes on the bladder so bladder infections and irritability are more likely.

Bladder infections in pregnancy are more than just uncomfortable. In the late stages of pregnancy, the infection can trigger pre-

Bladder Infection Symptoms

Some symptoms of a bladder infection (which may not all be present) include the following:

- Increased frequency of urination
- Burning pain on urination
- Lower abdominal pain, which may be steady or crampy in nature
- An increase in uterine cramping pains
- Dark, cloudy, or bloody urine
- Fever

term labor. Because pregnant women do not always have symptoms with a bladder infection, the infection is more likely to travel even further up the urinary tract to the kidneys and to cause a kidney infection, a condition known as pyelonephritis.

Pregnant women with kidney infections often have a high fever and pain on either side of the low to middle back. In addition, they may have the typical symptoms of a bladder infection noted above.

If you think you have a kidney infection, go to the emergency room or contact your healthcare provider. Pregnant women with pyelonephritis often need to be treated with a brief period of intravenous fluids and antibiotics.

Your Emotions: Back on the Rollercoaster

Most pregnant women enjoy a spectacularly energized second trimester. This burst of energy brings the ability to accomplish everything from work projects to setting up house for your new baby. Emotionally, your get-up-and-go makes you feel positive, happy, and excited. Likely you have signed up for your hospital tour and birthing classes and are well on your way to having your nursery organized. As a bonus, your sex drive will be at a peak, providing you with the opportunity to connect more deeply with your partner.

During this month it is normal for you to begin to have emotional ups and downs once again due to hormones. If you have financial concerns, anxiety about parenting, or are concerned about health issues like preterm labor, you may be feeling stressed, which will contribute to a rocky emotional state. Remember, you can help improve your outlook by seeking support from friends and relatives or a therapist, exercising, eating right, and being open and honest with your partner about your feelings. If financial concerns are an issue, it is good to know that many community organizations offer free or low-cost financial

How to Prevent
Bladder Infections

To avoid getting a bladder infection, take the following steps:

- Urinate as soon as you have the urge to void so you do not let urine sit too long in the bladder.
- Drink plenty of water or other beverages. Women who are prone to bladder infections should drink at least 12 eight-ounce glasses of water per day.
- Drink at least eight to ten ounces of water before and after intense exercise.
- Urinate immediately after intercourse to rid yourself of the bacteria that may have been pushed into the urethra during sex.

counseling that can help you to get out of debt and set a realistic budget. Be sure to research these services well, because there are some "financial counseling" agencies that exploit people in debt.

If you have a history of bipolar disorder or any serious psychiatric disorder, you may be on fewer medications and may have an increased chance of episodes of hypomania or depression. For this reason, you should be under the close supervision of a qualified psychiatrist or psychiatric nurse practitioner and continue to seek any additional support you can from family and friends. A psychotherapist can also help you manage your moods.

Your Prenatal Visit: Checking Your "Sugars"

In addition to your usual prenatal visit this month, you may have an extra appointment for a one-hour glucose tolerance test (GTT). This test is often done between weeks 24 and 28 of gestation and screens for gestational diabetes, which is discussed on page 180. Gestational diabetes rarely occurs before week 24. Women who have had gestational diabetes in past pregnancies might be tested with a one-hour GTT as early as 13 weeks. Talk to your healthcare provider about being tested earlier if you have had the disease in the past.

Glucose Tolerance Test (GTT)

The oral GTT measures the ability of your body to process glucose, which is the body's form of sugar. In pregnancy, there can be a disturbance of sugar metabolism, resulting in gestational diabetes. Gestational diabetes must be treated while you are pregnant.

Abuse during Pregnancy

Most women hope for a loving, supportive relationship with their partner during pregnancy. Almost a third of women in the U.S. have experienced intimate partner violence. Sadly, pregnancy is a high-risk time for physical and sexual violence within a relationship, and partner violence is the leading cause of injury-related deaths in pregnancy. If your partner has been violent in the past, or if he or she is controlling and demanding, you may be at substantial risk during your pregnancy. Violence in pregnancy can injure you or your fetus, and living in an abusive relationship creates emotional and biological stress that is not healthy. For many women, fear or a sense of shame or guilt creates a barrier to seeking help. Please know that you are not alone. Community domestic violence and sexual assault agencies offer free, confidential help. Contact the National Domestic Violence Hotline at 1-800-799-SAFE (7233) or RAINN (the sexual assault hotline) at 1-800-656-HOPE for general information or to find out about programs in your community. You may also wish to talk to your healthcare provider or a therapist, and you may decide to contact the police. Your health and life and your baby's are too important to wait until something serious happens.

You do not need to fast for long for your one-hour GTT, but some doctors will require at least some of the following prior to the procedure:

- That you eat a balanced diet that includes at least 150 to 200 grams of carbohydrates during the three days before the test. This helps to avoid false negative test results.
- That you do not eat for one hour prior to the test.
- That you do not smoke, drink a caffeinated beverage, or eat a high-calorie meal for up to eight hours prior to the test.
- That you talk to your healthcare provider about any medications you need to discontinue before the test.

One-hour GTT procedure: At your healthcare provider's office or the hospital, you will drink a small bottle of Glucola. This is a super-sugary beverage that comes in several flavors, including lemon-lime, orange,

I hate sweets so I was dreading the GTT! The week before, I asked the doctor if I could have the Glucola so I could get it as cold as possible. I also got a wide straw to drink it down so I could somewhat bypass my taste buds. When they said "Go!" I sucked down that drink like I'd just crawled out of the desert! It wasn't that bad, but definitely drink it cold and with a straw if you are concerned about the taste or sweetness. —*CeCe, 27, mother of two*

and cola. You will be drinking 50 grams of glucose that will readily be absorbed and processed by your body. The Glucola is usually slightly carbonated and is fairly pleasant to taste—but be forewarned, it is incredibly sweet! You will need to drink the entire beverage within about five minutes. (It helps if the beverage is cold.)

After you drink the Glucola, you will be asked to wait exactly 60 minutes. (Most labs will start a timer in order to properly time the test.) Some clinics will allow you to leave for a period of time during this waiting period; however, you should not engage in heavy physical activity while the timed test is underway. Exactly 60 minutes after you started drinking the Glucola the laboratory personnel will draw your blood and check the glucose levels.

Results of a normal one-hour GTT will show a blood sugar level of less than 130 to 140 mg/dL. Your healthcare provider may select any number within that range as his or her personal professional cutoff. If the cutoff is set at 140 mg/dL, the test misses gestational diabetes 20 percent of the time. If the cutoff is set at 130 mg/dL, the test misses gestational diabetes only 10 percent of the time. Talk to your doctor about his or her rationale for the suggested cutoff.

Are You at Risk for Gestational Diabetes?

Women who are at increased risk of developing diabetes while pregnant include those with the following conditions or situations:

- Previous gestational diabetes
- Having had a baby who weighed more than nine pounds at birth
- Obesity prior to getting pregnant
- Polycystic ovarian disease (POD)
- Strong family history of diabetes

If you are at risk, be sure to get tested at 24 weeks.

I was shocked when I was diagnosed with gestational diabetes. I immediately went to a nutritionist, and she gave me great advice for modifying my diet. I was already exercising but she asked me to add in an evening walk before bedtime. I got my gestational diabetes under control, and the evening walk actually helped me sleep better! —*Jennifer, 37, mother of two*

Three-hour GTT procedure: If the one-hour GTT reveals that your glucose level is higher than 130 to 140 mg/dL, then you will be asked to come back at a later date for what is called a three-hour GTT. You will need to fast prior to your test and have a fasting blood sugar level done before the GTT test begins. After your blood sugar level is tested, you will drink a larger quantity of Glucola (100 grams of glucose). Your blood sugar will be assessed at one-hour intervals until you have a total of four glucose readings over a three-hour period. If two out of the four readings are considered abnormal, you will be diagnosed with gestational diabetes.

Gestational Diabetes

Gestational diabetes is a condition in pregnancy that begins at approximately 24 weeks' gestation and involves having too much sugar (glucose) in your bloodstream. You can get gestational diabetes even if you have never had diabetes before and even if you did not had gestational diabetes in previous pregnancies. It affects approximately 18 percent of all pregnancies.

The cause of gestational diabetes is not known, but it is believed to be related to the increase in pregnancy-related hormones made by the placenta. Such hormones are thought to block the insulin receptors in the body so that, even though the mother's body is making insulin, the cells do not draw the sugar into their interior, leaving more sugar in the bloodstream. This is called insulin resistance.

Risks of Gestational Diabetes

Because the placenta allows glucose to go into the fetus' bloodstream as well, the fetus will experience a higher amount of the sugar in its bloodstream. This will cause the baby's pancreas to go into overdrive and produce more insulin than average in an attempt to bring its own higher levels of sugar down.

Because the elevated blood sugar does not occur until the latter part of the second trimester, when the baby's organs have already been formed, the excess sugar does not affect the baby's organs nor can it cause birth defects.

Gestational diabetes does cause increased levels of glucose and insulin in the fetal body. This combination leads to an increase in the growth and weight of the developing fetus. Babies get more calories than they need, and the insulin produced by the baby causes the extra energy to turn into fat. The result is a baby that may be too big to fit through the birth canal, increasing the risk of birth complications and the need for cesarean sections.

Babies of mothers who have high blood sugar when they give birth also can suffer from neonatal hypoglycemia—a condition where the blood sugar in the baby gets too low. Your baby's blood sugar level will be checked shortly after birth, and the issue will be treated before any serious side effects can occur.

Treatment for Gestational Diabetes

If you are diagnosed with gestational diabetes, you will be treated from now until you deliver in order to avoid the side effects of having too much blood sugar in your system.

Treatment of gestational diabetes involves changing your diet and increasing exercise. You will likely consult a dietician to learn different ways of eating that will improve your blood sugar. You will also be asked to increase your physical activity to burn glucose. You will probably be given a glucose monitor and strips and will be asked to check your own blood sugar at home, often up to four times per day.

Cases of gestational diabetes that cannot be controlled by diet and exercise alone will require the use of insulin. The nurse or

---

Prenatal Testing: Glucose Tolerance Test

Besides the usual hemoglobin and urinalysis testing, you will likely have a one-hour glucose tolerance test (GTT) at around 24 to 28 weeks. The GTT involves drinking a sugary beverage and then testing for the amount of glucose (sugar) in your blood. It is a test to screen for gestational diabetes. We will talk more about gestational diabetes and its implications later in this chapter. At this visit, it is likely that your hemoglobin level will be checked, and you will undergo a repeat of what is called a "type and screen," testing your blood type and screening for antibodies. Some doctors may also test for syphilis or HIV at this point.

---

dietician will teach you how to give insulin to yourself, which involves the use of small needles to inject the medication. You may have to give yourself insulin up to three to four times per day. If it sounds like a lot of pokes, you're right! However, it is necessary to keep your baby healthy and growing properly and to maintain your own health.

Even though your body is making insulin, you will need to take more insulin in order to override the effects of insulin resistance. You will have frequent contact with the dietician, your doctor, or a diabetic instructor in order to change your insulin dosage whenever needed and to make sure your blood sugar numbers are approaching normal. You can usually stop the insulin after you deliver your baby.

Gestational Diabetes: After You Deliver

In most cases, women cease to have gestational diabetes after they deliver their babies. There is about a 66 percent chance that you will get gestational diabetes with subsequent pregnancies. In a few cases, the gestational diabetes turns out not to be gestational after all, but instead, the testing for gestational diabetes has uncovered a hidden case of type I or type II diabetes that will require ongoing management.

In addition, the risk of later developing type II diabetes goes up if you are diagnosed with gestational diabetes. If you have gestational diabetes, you probably should have a fasting blood sugar test every year. Alternatively, you can use the glucose meter you will have from when you were pregnant to monitor your fasting blood sugar every few months. If your fasting readings are above 120 mg/dL of glucose, see your healthcare provider.

Placenta Previa

In placenta previa, the position of the placenta is problematic. The embryo implants near the cervix (the opening of the uterus), and the placenta begins to attach itself to the uterine wall too close to the cervix. There are varying degrees of the problem:

- *Marginal placenta previa* means that the placenta is close to the cervix but does not actually cover it.

- *Partial placenta previa* means that the placenta is only partly covering the cervical opening.

- *Complete placenta previa* means the placenta is lying over the entire cervix.

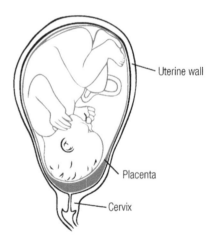

Placenta Previa

Placenta previa occurs when the embryo implants near the cervix, so the placenta overlies the cervix.

The incidence of placenta previa is about 1 out of every 200 pregnancies. You are at greater risk for placenta previa if you

- have an abnormally shaped uterus

- have a very big placenta

- are carrying more than one baby

- have had several children already

- have scarring inside the uterus
- have a history of smoking
- are over 35 years old when you become pregnant

Symptoms of Placenta Previa

If you have placenta previa, you can have increased cramping in the lower abdomen and pelvic region associated with sudden episodes of bleeding from the vagina. The bleeding can begin in the latter part of the first trimester, but usually begins in the second and third trimester. The bleeding, which can be painless, tends to occur when you are having sexual intercourse or are physically active.

The bleeding you experience with placenta previa may stop and start on its own or may continue without stopping. If it does not stop, it can trigger you to deliver your baby prematurely. If you have placenta previa at the time of the baby's birth, you will need a cesarean section because the baby cannot pass through the placenta without excessive bleeding and fetal distress.

Cases of placenta previa can be diagnosed on ultrasound, and, in fact, the healthcare provider may diagnose the problem before you have any symptoms. Fortunately, placenta previa often resolves as the pregnancy continues. This is because the placenta that grows over the cervix will gradually migrate up the wall of the uterus and can rise high enough to be out of the way of the cervix. This is especially true of cases of partial and marginal placenta previa. The doctor will watch the traveling of the placenta by checking ultrasounds on a regular basis, and he or she will tell you if there is a problem.

Managing Placenta Previa

If you have placenta previa, particularly if you are having regular bleeding episodes, your doctor may recommend bed rest or decreased physical activity. You will be advised not to have any sexual intercourse, and, in fact, nothing should be placed inside the vagina, including a tampon or douching

I remember taking a walk one evening by the lake near our home. It was a warm spring night and the sun was just beginning to go down. Birds were chirping, and I was basking in the warm smiles and friendly greetings I was receiving from other walkers—I was so obviously pregnant! I stopped for a moment and gazed out at the lake, and spotted a mother duck with ten fuzzy ducklings paddling near the shore. I burst into happy tears thinking about the circle of life and the little baby I would soon be caring for just like that mother duck!
—*Annie, 38, mother of two*

liquid. Hospital bed rest along with recurrent fetal monitoring may also be advised by your doctor.

Treatment for placenta previa can include the following:

- Prescribed medications to stop preterm labor until at least 36 weeks' gestation.
- Blood transfusions, particularly if you have had heavy bleeding episodes.
- A shot of Rhogam if you are Rh negative (we will discuss Rhogam in Chapter 9).

- One or more injections of steroid medication that will help to mature the baby's lungs, in preparation for a possible early delivery.

Delivery at 36 weeks is ideal; however, if you are having uncontrolled bleeding problems with placenta previa, your doctor may want to do a cesarean section earlier in your pregnancy, provided the baby is mature enough to survive.

Placenta previa can be deadly to both you and the fetus. This means that if you experience heavy vaginal bleeding, particularly if you know you have a placenta previa, you need to contact your doctor or go to the emergency room as soon as possible.

Exploring Childbirth Classes

Childbirth classes are an important part of the prenatal process, even if you have given birth before. Even if you think you do not need them, consider the needs of your partner who may not have done this before or who may need a refresher.

Classes are offered through your healthcare clinic, community education, private programs or educators, and hospital-based programs. Choose one that fits best with your personal thoughts on the birthing process and that is close to home or work. Some labor and delivery classes are free or covered by insurance, but some have fees for workbooks or other materials.

There are several types of classes offered in most areas, so be sure to weigh your options.

Lamaze International Classes

These are certified classes that have been around for many years. Lamaze classes offer about 12 hours of formal and informal education that teaches new parents about the process of normal labor, breathing techniques, what medications can be offered in the delivery process, and how to get through labor and delivery as comfortably as possible.

Teachers of the Lamaze method feel that an informed and confident woman would

> I really loved my birthing class until we got to the part about delivery. We watched videos of women experiencing natural childbirth and a cesarean section. I remember being terrified of both! I turned to my husband and said, "I hope you like the way I look because I'm not having a vaginal delivery or a C-section. This baby is staying put!" And I was serious! Needless to say, our baby girl was delivered a few months later. But I'll always remember that moment of our birthing class! —*Mary Jane, 29, mother of one*

naturally want a natural birth process. They believe that healthcare providers should respect the fact that childbirth is a normal process for both fetus and mother and that she and her baby should not be pressured to take drugs for labor and delivery. The Lamaze class is best for couples who want to learn specific breathing techniques that take them through the labor process without drugs.

I didn't want to admit that I was really apprehensive about the whole giving-birth process. It's so hard to ever see my wife in pain that I didn't know how I'd get through it. Lucky for me, my buddy and I were out for a drink and he mentioned feeling that way himself. He said, "It's just like getting ready to play in a big game—beforehand, you're nervous about the game plan but once you're in the battle you just do what you need to do to win. Just pay attention to what she needs and you'll be fine." He was right. —*Frankie, 40, dad of three*

Bradley Method

This is the method proposed by the American Academy of Husband-Coached Childbirth (AAHCC). The classes stress the importance of having a healthy mom, a healthy baby, and a healthy family. There is emphasis on having a partner learn to coach the pregnant woman through the birthing process. This method also emphasizes natural labor techniques that involve both the partner/coach and the mother. The idea is to be aware of one's body, understand what is happening in the labor process, and to tune into the rhythms of the body's contractions.

Bradley Method childbirth classes are offered once per week for a total of 12 weeks. It is an empowering program for those couples willing to enter the labor process in a natural way. Many of the classes emphasize relaxation and give you a chance to practice relaxation during class time. While the method is called Husband-Coached

Childbirth, your labor and delivery coach can be any individual you trust to help you.

International Childbirth Education Association (ICEA)

This is an association of labor and delivery teachers that number more than 4000 throughout the U.S. Its practices are offered in 42 countries. ICEA classes educate couples on the labor process, ways to comfort a woman during labor, complications that might arise during birth, and the process that goes on in a cesarean section. Medications available during labor are discussed and are not discouraged.

The program respects the fact that women in labor have many choices and that the exploration of these choices before labor actually happens is important. Emphasis is placed on learning different techniques for the labor process, whether you decide to choose an epidural for analgesia or a dose of a narcotic, or decide to take no medication at all.

Nutrition Tip: Extra Calories

You should continue to eat approximately 300 calories above what you would eat if you were not pregnant. Because food cravings can often take up many of these calories, you need to make sure that the rest of the calories you eat are as balanced as possible and that they contain plenty of whole grains, fruits, vegetables, and lean proteins. You should be gaining about a pound a week during this month.

Hospital and Birthing Center Tours

Most babies are born at a hospital that has a maternity ward and a nursery to care for the newborn. Some women choose a midwife to deliver their child and give birth at an independent birthing center. These are stand-alone centers in which midwives deliver babies and help the mother recover and care for her newborn. Some babies are still delivered at home, often with the help of a midwife and possibly a doula. We will talk more about home births and using a doula in Chapter 12.

If you are delivering at a hospital, find out where your healthcare provider has delivery privileges—often they have these privileges at more than one facility. This means you may choose the closest hospital to your home or the hospital that best suits your taste and comfort level.

Hospital tours are usually scheduled in advance. This month is a great time to visit hospitals just in case you have a complica-

> I was so full of energy and gung-ho about childbirth I took my class too early—at 17 weeks! By the time I got to labor and delivery both my husband and I had forgotten everything! No matter how excited you are, don't get educated too soon—wait until after week 20 at least! —*Lorianne, 30, mother of one*

tion that requires you to be hospitalized long before your delivery. Once you have toured your hospital(s), you can formally select the hospital of your choice and register in advance. That way you will not have to go through the admissions process while you are in labor. In addition, your prenatal medical records can be sent to your chosen hospital.

Which Hospital? You Decide

Here are some things to consider when choosing a hospital:

- Do you like the aesthetics of the hospital? Is it warm and inviting? And does it have a comfortable room in which you can labor?

- Do you labor, deliver, and care for the baby after it is born in the same room, or does the hospital require that you move to a different room? Sometimes it is nice not to have to move. On the other hand, you might hear a laboring woman next to your room as you are trying to rest or care for your baby, and this might be upsetting for you. A separate quiet wing for mothers who have already delivered their babies might resolve that problem.

Things to Think About: The Birth Process

This month is the perfect time to begin preparing yourself for the labor and delivery process. This means practicing your Kegel exercises, taking a hospital tour, choosing your hospital or birthing center, preregistering at the hospital or center, and signing up for birthing classes. You also need to begin writing down your birthing wish list and concerns so you can discuss your labor plans with your healthcare provider at one of your upcoming prenatal visits.

- Does the hospital offer a wide range of choices in labor pain management? Is an anesthesiologist on hand at all times for the purposes of inserting an epidural for pain? Most hospitals offer narcotics for pain, but if you really want an epidural for your pain management, an anesthesiologist must be present.
- Does the hospital offer options like laboring in a shower or on a big rubber ball, or bathtub laboring experiences? For women wanting a natural experience, such techniques can make the labor more comfortable.
- How many people does the hospital allow you to have present for the delivery process? Who else is allowed in the delivery room besides the mother and her partner, the nurse, and the doctor or midwife?
- Does the hospital allow videotaping of the big event? Some hospitals are fine with having an individual in the room videotaping the delivery of the baby, while others ban videotaping on legal grounds.
- Does the hospital have its own pediatrician who can see and examine your baby after he or she has been born? If not, you will have to pre-select a pediatrician who will be notified at the time the baby is born.
- Does the hospital have adequate backup for cesarean sections? And is the C-section operating room close to the labor and delivery area? Most of the bigger hospitals have an operating room or two set aside for cesarean deliveries that are near the labor and delivery area should you need an emergency C-section. If your

Remember: When choosing a hospital, you are not choosing a vacation hotel! The quality and reputation of the doctors and nurses, the medical attention available, and the level of emergency services are more important than the comfort of the rocking chair in your recovery room. Be comfortable with your choice, but be practical as well! —*Eliza, 36, mother of two*

doctor is a family practitioner, it is possible but unlikely that he or she may perform cesarean sections. Usually an obstetrician/gynecologist will do the surgery. You will want to know if there is such a doctor available onsite and the average time it takes the surgeon to get to the hospital in case of an emergency.

- Does the hospital have a special-care nursery or a Neonatal Intensive Care Unit (NICU)? These are actually two different places. A special-care nursery—usually located close to the labor and delivery area—is for babies who are only mildly sick or who need extra attention after birth before being able to go to the regular nursery. A NICU is reserved for more seriously ill babies or premature babies who need significant medical care by specialized nurses and a neonatologist (a physician who specializes in newborn care).
- Things do not always go as planned. It is quite possible that even though you have decided on natural childbirth, you may change your mind and want medication or need to have a cesarean section. Having options at your hospital may be important.

Choosing a hospital is a unique process for everyone. All women have their own preferences for how they want the labor and delivery process to go. Take this time to explore what is important to you, and if you are planning a hospital birth, choose a hospital that best meets your own personal expectations.

Choosing a Birthing Center

If you have a low-risk pregnancy and you prefer a delivery with a minimum of medical intervention, a birthing center (or birth center) may be for you. Many of the questions above with regard to choosing a hospital will apply to choosing a birthing center as well. In addition, you should consider the following questions:

- Is the center accredited by a reputable agency?
- Are the practitioners all licensed in their respective professions?
- What birth methods (such as water birth) are available?

Birthing center room
Birthing centers offer a home-like environment and often have amenities such as whirlpool baths and rocking chairs. Medical equipment is available, but it is kept out of sight.

- What are the policies and practices for transferring a woman to a hospital if there are complications?
- What hospitals are nearby?
- Will my insurance cover all the costs involved?
- Would my midwife be able to come with me and help if I had to be transferred to a hospital during labor?
- Who are your staff members, and what is their training?
- What programs and services do you offer?

Cervical Incompetence

Cervical incompetence is a pregnancy condition in which the cervix is not strong enough to remain closed until the normal time of birth. This condition of the cervix can combine with the weight of the uterus to open up and dilate the cervix, which can result in preterm birth or pregnancy loss. Cervical incompetence is the cause of about 25 percent of all pregnancy losses in the second trimester. If you have previously lost a baby in the second trimester and the loss could not be explained in any other way, you may have an incompetent cervix.

Cervical incompetence may occur at any time in the second trimester, but it can show up in the early third trimester as well. It is especially dangerous because it generally leads to fetal loss, and the cervical incompetence causes delivery without the telltale contractions of normal pregnancy.

> I had to have a cervical cerclage with my last child. I was scared to pieces about the entire issue of cervical incompetence, but I followed my doctor's instructions to the letter and delivered a healthy baby boy at 37 weeks! My advice is to be positive and do exactly what your doctor orders! —*Betsy, 33, mother of four*

Causes of Cervical Incompetence

Possible causes of cervical incompetence include having a history of trauma to the cervix such as lacerations from a previous birth, previous cervical surgery such a cone biopsy or Loop electrosurgical excision procedure (LEEP), hormonal issues, and having a prior dilation and curettage (D&C). A D&C is a procedure used to diagnose or treat various uterine conditions or to clean the uterus after a miscarriage or termination of pregnancy. In order to do this, the cervix must be dilated or widened, and then some of the lining of the uterus and/or its contents is surgically removed. Cervical incompetence is also related to abnormal uterine shape or a short cervix that becomes too weak to carry a pregnancy to term.

Diagnosing and Treating the Incompetent Cervix

A doctor can diagnose incompetent cervix by feeling the cervical length or by looking at the length of the cervix with an ultrasound machine. The cervix is normally 2.5 centimeters long, and any shortening may be significant. The cervix first thins out and then it begins to dilate (open out). When this happens, it can be impossible to stop the delivery

of the baby, regardless of its gestational age.

If this is your first pregnancy, you may have no idea you have cervical incompetence until you have an ultrasound showing shortening of the cervix. If you have had prior episodes of cervical incompetence, the treatment of the condition will commence at 14 to 16 weeks of gestation.

The best treatment for cervical incompetence is to put in a stitch that circles the opening of the cervix and, like a purse string, keeps the cervix closed. This is called cervical cerclage. After a 24-hour monitoring period in the hospital, a woman with a cervical cerclage often can resume modified activities that exclude heavy lifting and heavy exercise. When she reaches 37 weeks' gestation or goes into labor somewhat earlier than that, the cerclage is removed and the labor can continue normally. A cervical cerclage cannot be performed if

Risks of Cervical Cerclage

The cervical cerclage is not without its own risks that include the following:

- Premature rupture of the membranes. This can happen in 1 to 9 percent of cases.
- Infection of the birth sac. This can happen in up to 7 percent of cases.
- Laceration or amputation of the cervix. This is rare.
- Preterm contractions or preterm labor, which may be temporary and controlled with medications.
- Injury to the bladder, which is rare.
- Maternal bleeding.
- Rupture of the uterus.

your water has already broken or if you have dilated past four centimeters.

While you have the cervical cerclage in place, you will not be able to have intercourse or put anything in the vagina until after you give birth. You will also need frequent rest periods throughout the day and will have to see the doctor to be checked for cervical dilation every week. You will be asked to be on the lookout for premature contractions. If you experience them, you should contact your healthcare provider immediately.

Cervical cerclage has a high success rate. Eighty to ninety percent of women who have the procedure carry their pregnancy through to the birth of a healthy baby. The earlier a cerclage is performed, the better the probable outcome.

Monthly Monitor

Call your healthcare provider if you experience any of the following:

- Intermittent backache, which may be a sign of premature labor
- A fever greater than 101.5°F
- Contractions that occur more than four or five times per day
- Spotting or bleeding
- Burning or pain on urination
- Blood in the urine

Exercise Idea: Partner Walking

As your belly grows, you may find yourself needing to alter your current exercise regime. A great way to keep moving is walking with someone else! There are added benefits to walking regularly with your spouse or partner. This way, you have built-in time together to enjoy each other's company, talk about your day, and discuss any issues or feelings you have about your pregnancy. It is a great way to get exercise and to improve your relationship at the same time. If you cannot walk with your partner, find a friend or neighbor who would like to exercise with you. But even if you need to go alone, keep moving! (Don't forget your dog, if you have one.)

Notes:

Up until my seventh month I was actually feeling pretty cute in my maternity clothes. I didn't want to spend a lot of money on my wardrobe so I hadn't bought much—and I certainly did not plan to purchase anything ahead. Then one morning, around week 25, I woke up and nothing I owned fit me. It was like I doubled in size overnight! I found a bold necklace to wear with my husband's white work shirt and my black stretch maternity pants, and had to do emergency maternity shopping on my lunch break with the help of three coworkers! This time I bought a few pieces to grow into! —*Ellie, 37, mother of two*

Chapter 9

Month Seven—Weeks 25 through 28

Your second trimester is rapidly coming to a close, and you are beginning the last three and a half months of being pregnant! While you may be continuing to experience the energy and excitement of the past weeks, you are also likely to find it harder to see your feet and bend to tie your shoes. For nearly all women, maternity clothes are a must at this point.

You have been experiencing frequent kicking from your little one and you may even feel the fetus rolling from side to side. These movements can be seen from the outside, and your spouse or partner, friends and family, and even complete strangers will be interested in feeling the thrill of your baby moving. If you have not begun to tackle the preparation of your nursery, this month is the month to do it. As you continue toward the pregnancy finish line, you will have less energy and enthusiasm for decorating and will benefit more from rest than from frantic shopping to get everything in order.

I enjoyed decorating our home but was having trouble deciding on a theme for our baby's room. We were having a boy, but I didn't want any gender-specific theme. Then one sleepless night, it came to me—stars and moons, and the colors of baby blue, navy blue, and butter yellow! I woke up the next morning on a mission. I picked out yellow paint, and for a week after work, painted all the baby furniture, including a dresser, a donated changing table, and a nightstand. My husband thought I was crazy when I wouldn't let him help me, but I was almost possessed with creating my vision just the way I wanted it. I had never sewed anything in my life—not even a hem—but I came up with the idea of sewing three-dimensional felt stars and moons. I made stencils, cut out the felt in baby blue and navy blue, and stitched the moons and stars together with yellow embroidery thread so the stitches popped against the felt. Then I stuffed each moon and star with batting and sewed a yellow string at the top. Honestly, I didn't recognize myself! I hung 29 stars and moons from the ceiling (I did let my husband hold me on the ladder!). I painted one wall sky blue and found my inner Michelangelo and painted clouds across the sky. That room was spectacular when I finished with it, and I was fried. That was my last burst of energy for the rest of my pregnancy—and when I look back, I don't know how I did it. And you'd better believe I still have all those stars and moons!—*Dallas, 41*

You can rest in the knowledge that your baby is now old enough to survive a potential preterm birth. If you experience preterm labor or are having multiples, it is possible that this is the month you will be put on bed rest in an attempt to keep your baby or babies growing inside you for as long as possible.

All in all, you can be proud of how far you have come in your journey. So go ahead and pat yourself on the back for all your efforts to stay healthy, exercise, prepare for baby, and keep up the rest of your regular life at the same time! This is no easy task when your belly is getting big enough to make leaning over to pick up things difficult. In this chapter, we will address the following:

- What's new with my baby's development?
- Why am I short of breath?
- How can I get some sleep?
- How can I handle my fears of birth and financial worries?
- Do I need a birth plan, and how should I prepare one?
- What other preparations should I be making?
- What is Rh sensitization, and should I be concerned?
- What treatments can help with my melasma (facial skin darkening due to pregnancy)?
- Where do I begin with setting up the nursery?
- How can I be sure my baby's crib is safe?

Your Baby's Growth and Development: Make Room!

Your baby will be putting on fat and moving much more this month.

Week 25

By the time your baby is born, he or she will have a very complex spine, with 150 different joints and 1000 separate ligaments. These aspects of the human spine are developing during this week to allow the baby to move and stretch its spine. Blood vessels in the lungs are also developing, enabling your baby to better oxygenate his or her body by the time of birth at about 40 weeks' gestation. If your baby were to be born at 25 weeks of gestation, it would likely need to live on a ventilator because the lungs are not developed enough for the baby to breathe properly on its own.

Up until now, your baby's nostrils have had "plugs" in them. These plugs, which are temporary structures that allow for proper development of the palate, will begin to dissolve this week so that by the time your child is born, its nose-breathing abilities will be in full swing. Babies are habitual nose breathers and cannot normally breathe well through the mouth. In fact, this breathing pattern can be seen on ultrasound, with the fetus breathing in and out of his or her tiny nostrils.

At this point, reproductive organs have completely formed, but your baby's skin is still extremely thin, wrinkled, and fragile. You little bundle of joy is beginning to learn reflexive patterns of movement that serve as practice for the intentional movement that occurs after birth. Toes and fingers wiggle reflexively.

Your baby weighs about 1.5 pounds and is about 13.5 inches from head to heel. This month, your baby is about the size of an eggplant or a small loaf of bread.

Week 26

This week, the tiny air sacs in the lungs, which are responsible for the exchange of oxygen and carbon dioxide after birth, begin to grow and develop. But instead of containing air, they are either collapsed or filled with amniotic fluid. The lungs are beginning to make and secrete surfactant, a type of lubricant that helps the air sacs expand. Should you deliver early, this process increases the chance your baby will survive outside the womb.

The visual and auditory portions of the brain continue to develop. By the time your baby is born, his or her hearing is acute. Visual systems lag somewhat, so when your baby is born, he or she will only be able to see things in about a 20-inch range from the face. Even so, your baby's eyes open and close in the darkness of the uterus. Your child is continuing to develop fat deposits (a good thing at this point in life!) as it grows in weight at a rapid pace.

This week your baby weighs about 1.7 pounds and has a crown-to-heel length of about 14 inches.

Week 27

This week, the lungs and brain continue to grow both in size and in development. The retinas begin to form so that your baby will be able to see the breast nipple or the bottle nipple by the time of birth. Fat layers grow so that your child develops the ability to regulate its body temperature. The chance of out-of-the-womb survival increases this week by leaps and bounds.

Fetus at 28 weeks of development
A 28-week-old fetus is rapidly gaining fat but still has skinny arms and legs. Approximately almost 15 inches long and weighing 2 to 2.5 pounds, the fetus kicks and stretches, can make grasping motions, responds to sound, and can open and close its eyes and sense changes in light. The lanugo (downy body hair) begins to disappear.

Your baby will be moving regularly at a rate of about 10 movements per hour. Your healthcare provider may have you count fetal movements once a day during a period when you can relax and the baby is moving. If the baby is not moving at least 10 times an hour over a period of two hours, contact your healthcare provider for further advice.

Your baby is an incredible 14.4 inches long, compared to the 18 to 22 inches long it will be at the time of birth. In addition, your baby now weighs nearly two pounds!

Week 28

Your baby's growth will continue at a rapid pace, not slowing down until the third trimester. The hair on his or her head is growing steadily, and the eyes are completely formed, even though good vision will not occur until about three to four months of age.

Your baby has about 2 to 3 percent body fat, compared to roughly 20 percent body fat for the average adult. The lungs now have the ability to breathe air, but babies born at this point still have difficulty getting enough oxygen. Your baby can hear you well, so now is the time to talk, sing, and even read books to your baby. Your baby has the ability to recognize your voice as distinctive from other voices!

The lanugo (the fine hair covering your developing fetus) might have disappeared from your baby's body, and the top of his or her head will be flush with hair if the baby will be born with head hair. But remember: Not every baby is born with hair on his or her head!

During this week of pregnancy, your baby weighs about 2.2 pounds and is about 14.8 inches in length from crown to heel.

a soccer ball in a while, go to your sporting goods store and check one out—it is big! So big, in fact, that it is now probably difficult for you to bend over to pick something up off the floor, tie your shoes, or carry a bulky object. If it becomes too difficult to do these things yourself, ask your partner or someone else who is available to help.

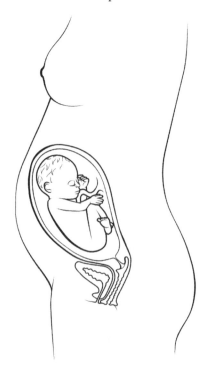

Your Changing Body: Things Are Changing Fast!

For most women, the second trimester is the happiest and most energetic of their entire pregnancy. Your body changes dramatically in mid-pregnancy. Let's look at what's happening this month.

Increased Uterine Size: Soccer Anyone?

Your uterus is now about the size of a soccer ball. If you have not taken a look at

Your changing body: Month seven
Your partner may be able to see the baby kick! The pregnancy hormones that prepare your pelvis for birth by relaxing the ligaments may also make walking a bit more challenging.

Because bending to reach your feet is becoming increasingly difficult, adequate foot care may become an issue. You know you are loved when your spouse or partner offers to cut your toenails for you! Even better, get yourself a professional pedicure every few weeks. Not only do you deserve the pam-

Don't hesitate to pamper yourself while you can! A pedicure, like shoes, always fits and feels good—even when your maternity wear doesn't! —Bethany, 40, mother of three

pering, but you can boost your self-esteem and mood with pretty feet. Though you may have trouble reaching them, you should still be able to see your toes and can enjoy your pedicure as much as anyone else who sees it.

Back and Leg Pains

Because your uterus has expanded and may press on nerves in your lower to middle back, you may begin to feel shooting pains in your back or down the back of your legs. When a nerve is pinched, it responds by sending pain signals down your back and into your legs. Walking or lying on your back when sleeping usually makes the pain worse. Such pains can come at irregular intervals or can occur on a regular basis.

In order to prevent or ease these pains, consider requesting that your employer provide an ergonomically correct chair for you at work or buy one for working on the computer at home. A good chair will take the excess pressure off your spine and will lessen the pain. You may make yourself more comfortable simply by putting a pillow behind your back for support. If you walk for long periods of time, wear good supportive shoes and take frequent breaks if you experience pain. These pains are more annoying than they are dangerous and do not mean you have a back or nerve problem. The pains should go away after you deliver your baby.

Shortness of Breath

Your uterus is beginning to impinge on your lungs' ability to fully expand, and the added weight of the fetus and uterus can make you feel shortness of breath that may worsen when you sit or exercise. This shortness of breath does not mean that you and/or your baby are getting less oxygen or that something harmful is happening. It is just one more normal annoyance of pregnancy! Continue to exercise as best you can, knowing that exercise with some shortness of breath is better than not exercising at all.

Sleep Problems

There are several reasons why you may be finding it hard to catch your zzzs!

The size of your uterus: Your uterus is now big enough that finding a comfortable

---

Nutrition Tip:
Don't Throw In the Towel

It is around this time, when you begin to feel large and heavy, that you may have the urge to give up your good eating habits and just go wild! But now more than ever, you and your baby need good nutrition. Eating well will help provide you with energy and a sense of well-being. Paying attention to your diet will help you avoid overeating, which can lead to heartburn and unnecessary weight gain. Certainly it's okay to give into cravings and treat yourself once in a while, but at the same time keep up with the great work you've been doing for the past six months. You are almost at the finish line, and like any athlete in a big event, you deserve to finish strong!

I'm a lawyer, and I remember one day meeting with a client. All I did was walk from my office to the meeting room, and I was completely out of breath. I was handling a high-profile case and was so embarrassed when I couldn't get my sentences out properly. Luckily, my client was a mom herself and said she remembered being out of breath just like I was. Her kindness put me at ease. And I learned to get to my meetings early to catch my breath before I had to speak!

—Darla, 35, mother of two

sleep position is getting harder. According to the American Pregnancy Association, you should try to sleep on your side (preferably the left side) rather than on your back, and try to avoid sleeping on your stomach. Get several more pillows to put behind your back or between your legs. Hugging a pillow on your side will also improve your side-sleeping ability.

Changes to your breathing patterns: You may feel as though your breathing is getting shallower. Your uterus expands and encroaches on your lungs—causing you to breathe faster. This breathing pattern may keep you from normal sleep. To remedy this, try some meditative deep breathing for five to ten minutes before bedtime. Breathe slowly in through your nose and exhale slowly out through your mouth. Focus only on your breath, letting go of any thoughts that arise. This type of breathing will relax your body and help you fall asleep more easily.

Increased need to urinate: You may be going to the bathroom more often during the night because your uterus is putting pressure on your bladder. It is important to respond to your urges to urinate during the night so you can avoid getting bladder infections. Try putting nightlights along the path to the bathroom so you do not have to illuminate your entire bedroom. Bright lights can awaken you to the point that it is hard to go back to sleep after you go to the bathroom.

Heartburn and indigestion: Heartburn and indigestion can keep you from solid sleep. As mentioned in Chapter 4, you can take TUMS, Maalox, or ranitidine (Zantac) before going to bed in order to reduce the incidence of nighttime heartburn and indigestion. Remember, too, that you can avoid heartburn by putting blocks of wood or phone books under the frame of your bed so the head is slightly elevated. These simple adjustments to the incline to your bed will keep stomach acid from flowing back into your esophagus.

Stress: Stress can also affect sleep patterns. You may be feeling worries you have not had before about the upcoming birth of your child or may have troublesome concerns about your relationship or finances. As mentioned above, several minutes of meditation and deep breathing exercises before bedtime can reduce stress and promote sleep. You might also try writing your worries in a journal (a notebook or a private online journal) earlier in the day. When your thoughts turn to worries, remind yourself that they are written down and you can address them more effectively in the daytime.

Heightened dreaming: You dream more often during pregnancy, and your dreams may seem more real and vivid than before you were pregnant. It is not known why this occurs, but some experts suggest that because you awaken more frequently you remember more dreams than you normally would.

Body Aches and Pains

Aside from possible pain in your back and legs, you may have more body aches and joint pains due to the increased weight your body is now carrying—about 14 pounds by the beginning of your seventh month, on average. Your frame is not used to this weight, and you may be walking and sitting differently than you normally do.

Consider doing gentle yoga stretches to ease your aches, or have a professional massage performed by a massage therapist trained in treating pregnant women. You can also ask your partner to give you a massage using scented massage oils. A massage will increase your well-being both emotionally and physically. If you and your partner are not up to sex for whatever reason, a massage is another way to increase your intimacy and help you both feel closer. When you feel up to it, return the favor, perhaps with just a quick foot massage. This will help your partner to feel that caring attention is still a two-way street.

Your Emotions: What? Me Worry?

Most pregnant women are busier than ever during this month, getting ready for the upcoming birth, caring for their household, and perhaps putting in a full day's work. This is also the time, however, when many women become overwhelmed by all the demands of their daily life and begin to think about cutting back on their work week, household duties, and social calendar to de-stress and have time to rest and prepare for baby.

Fears about Giving Birth

This is the time in pregnancy when the idea of actually giving birth becomes more real and perhaps a little terrifying! Your baby is moving around so much that the reality of bringing your child into the world can come to the forefront for you and be overwhelming. If this is your first child, fear of the unknown—like what the birthing process is really like or the amount of pain you might experience—can begin to overtake your thoughts and even nighttime dreams. Know that this is completely normal. You can ease your fears by visiting your hospital or birthing

For Dads and Partners:
Shoulder the Housework

If you feel as though you are doing the lion's share of the work around the house, know that you probably are. And your pregnant partner is grateful for your efforts! Your partner cannot be exposed to strong cleaning solutions, and she can't do the kind of lifting she used to do. Her belly is in the way of many tasks, and it takes much more effort for her to do the things she used to easily accomplish. This is the time to let her rest and relax. You have been an amazing help throughout the pregnancy with your emotional support and understanding, and now your practical help is needed as well. Keep up the good work. Your reward—a new little person!—has almost arrived.

center, taking childbirth classes, talking with friends and relatives about their birth experiences, confiding in your healthcare provider, or developing a good birth plan. (For more details on creating a birth plan, see page 203 of this chapter.)

Financial Worries

You may also have worries about finances that can lead to distraction, depressive feelings, and lack of sleep. You may be concerned about medical costs that are not covered by insurance. The cost of baby supplies, baby clothes, and food for your baby can add up. You may also be concerned about the potential reduction to your household income if either your partner or you have decided to be a stay-at-home parent. And even if you are returning to work, daycare expenses can put a huge dent in your budget.

Now is a good time to sit down with your partner and set up an "after-baby budget." You can also do this with the help of a financial planner. If you are already on an extremely tight budget, you may be able to receive financial guidance from a nonprofit organization at little or no cost. List your current income and expenses, including mortgage or rent, utilities, food, transportation, and other items. Then list your after-baby income and new expenses. From there, you can decide where you can cut items or save on costs if need be. Some of the key items you will need in your "after-baby budget" are listed below.

The cost of baby clothes and baby gear: Purchasing things at consignment sales or yard sales or getting hand-me-downs will help keep these costs down considerably.

My wife was frustrated with me because every time she mentioned something else we needed for the baby, I got quiet and sullen. She thought I wasn't happy about the baby. Finally, one night when she burst into tears over the fact I didn't do backflips over the rocking chair she had purchased, I admitted my fears about money. She was actually relieved and we went ahead and made a budget together. We both felt better. Guys, communication really is key. Talk about your fears before things get out of hand and this worry interferes with your joy about the baby. —*Joshua, 35, dad of two*

The cost of feeding your baby: Breast-feeding is obviously a money saver! The FDA regulates all formula, so there is no harm in purchasing store brands of formula (such as Walmart) instead of name-brand formula. If your household income is extremely limited, you may be eligible for supplemental food through the government Women, Infants, and Children (WIC) program, which provides food and nutrition information for pregnant women, those who breast-feed, and children up to age five.

The cost of diapers: Go to your local store or check online sites with free shipping and price the brand of diaper you are planning to use. Also know that you may have to change brands once you have your baby, due to fit or comfort. If you are going to use a diaper service or reusable diapers, estimate that cost as well.

The cost of daycare and babysitters: If you need daycare, you should already be registered or close to being registered for the facility of your choice. If you are not, be sure to do this right away, as many daycare centers have long waiting lists. Knowing your daycare arrangements in advance will also allow you to have an accurate idea of the cost.

Remember: To ensure an accurate budget, you should actually go to the stores where you plan to make these purchases and price out the items.

The idea behind this exercise is not to worry you further but to give you a realistic view of what to expect financially after your baby is born. Try to put your worries and fears into common-sense action. There are always ways to cut costs and save money. For example, a diaper changing table is not a necessity. Most parents find themselves changing their baby on the floor or bed anyway, and the floor is safer once your baby begins to move and roll. Both open communication with your partner and preparation will help to ease your financial concerns and worries.

Your Prenatal Visit: Talk about Your Wishes

Until you reach week 28, you will continue to see your healthcare provider once every four weeks. After week 28, you will begin to see the doctor or midwife every two to three weeks. The frequency increases to address possible issues that can arise after week 28, which include gestational diabetes, preterm labor, and hypertensive problems of pregnancy. Be prepared for medical visits more often from this month onward.

Your doctor will listen to the fetal heart tones and measure the length between your pubic symphysis and the top of your uterus—typically this will measure about 25 to 28 centimeters. This is quite a change from just a month or two ago!

You will have a urinalysis and possibly a hemoglobin check. If you are Rh negative, the doctor will perform an Rh sensitization test between weeks 24 and 28, even if you have no symptoms. If the test is positive for antibodies against the Rh receptor on red blood cells, your doctor will talk to you about treatment. We will talk more about Rh sensitivity later in this chapter on page 205.

If you did not have a one-hour glucose tolerance test (1-hour GTT) in week 24, you will most likely have the test during this month. Remember that this is a nonfasting blood test that measures your blood sugar

Prenatal Testing:

Urine and Glucose Tolerance Testing

Your healthcare provider will continue to check your urine for sugar or infection. If there is a question regarding infection, your urine will be cultured. If you have an infection, you will be encouraged to drink extra water and to take antibiotics for up to a week in order to clear the infection. Fortunately, there are several completely safe antibiotics to take in pregnancy. Your hemoglobin level may also be checked sometime this month for your iron stores. If you did not have a one-hour glucose tolerance test (GTT) during week 24, you will likely be tested this month. (Details on this testing for gestational diabetes are discussed in Chapter 8.)

> My girlfriend had warned me that strangers might come up to me and touch my belly—something she'd hated! But I remember being in the grocery store one day and my little boy was literally doing flips. I stopped shopping and laughed at my belly. The woman next to me asked if she could feel him, and I let her. Before I knew it, the produce man, an old woman, and three other mothers were gathered around chatting and touching my belly. I loved sharing the moment with someone—even though they were strangers.—*Janice, 28, mother of one*

level after drinking a dose of sugary liquid. If the test indicates you might have gestational diabetes, your doctor will confirm the diagnosis with a fasting three-hour glucose tolerance test (3-hour GTT).

This month, talk to your healthcare provider about labor preferences regarding pain control, cesarean sections, and other aspects of labor and delivery. While your birthing wish list is completely up to you, it helps to have your provider's opinion of how a normal labor and delivery should go. You may wish to ask for more detailed information about what you should do if complications of later pregnancy develop or you believe you are in labor.

Logistics for Getting to the Hospital

It is a good idea to have a simple plan for the logistics of getting to the hospital or birthing center once you are in labor and for taking care of household concerns while you are having your baby.

Child and Pet Care while You Are Away

If you have other children, of course you will want to make arrangements for their care while you are giving birth and away from home. Counting on an out-of-town grandparent to be present can be a bit tricky, so if this is your plan, you will want to have an alternative caregiver in case your baby comes sooner than expected. Let your child pack a small bag, and, depending on the child's age, consider telling a little story about where he or she will stay so that it won't be a disturbing surprise if you have to bring your child to the neighbor's without warning at 3:00 a.m.

Don't forget to make arrangements for pet care. Your partner may be at the hospital with you for a couple of days and you don't want to be worried about Fido using the living room rug as a restroom while you are both gone. You probably won't want to detour to a kennel on your way to the hospital, so in-home care makes the most sense.

Preparing for the Hospital Trip

If you are not very familiar with the route to the hospital or birthing center, be sure to have a map or a preprogrammed GPS handy. Under stress, your partner may lose all sense of direction! It's also a good idea to be sure your partner or labor support person has a list of the people to notify when you have had the baby and has entered their phone numbers into his or her cell phone. Again, this is the kind of information that may be easily forgotten in a crunch.

Backup Transportation Plans

While in most cases you will want your partner or labor support person to transport you to the hospital, it is wise to have a backup plan—or actually, a couple of backup plans. If the baby comes early and your partner is out of town, who will take you to the hospital or birthing center? What if that person is not available? Don't forget to keep your own copy of the directions to the hospital so you can share them with the backup person if necessary.

Developing a Birth Plan

A birth plan is simply a wish list of how you want your labor and delivery to go if everything goes just as you imagine it. In the not-too-distant past, labor and delivery procedures were often determined solely by the medical community, and women were expected to simply cooperate. Now, there are many more options within the labor and delivery process, and (unless there are urgent medical or safety concerns) decisions about the setting and medical interventions can often be made collaboratively with your healthcare provider.

While creating a plan is important to many women, remember that labor is an innately unpredictable event. What you want and what actually ends up happening may be completely different. Nonetheless, creating a plan can diminish anxiety by helping you anticipate, step by step, some of the decisions you will have the opportunity to make. A birth plan may be of particular help to women who are survivors of trauma such as sexual abuse or assault, because it can specify ways in which your partner, your doctor or midwife, and your doula (if you have one) can assist you to manage aspects of the birth process that may trigger emotions from past experiences.

Some women prefer to make a simple list of their preferences, while a detailed birth plan is valuable for others. However, life certainly is what happens while we are making

I'm a planner by nature, so I came into my labor and delivery process with a 10-page booklet that was my birth plan. As life would have it, nothing went as I'd described in my document! I ended up having all the things I didn't want: induction, an epidural, and eventually an emergency C-section. Make a birth plan, but also plan for things not to go your way!
—Trish, 33, mother of two

other plans! Use your birth plan as a means to communicate your preferences to your healthcare provider in a clear manner and as a way to help you think through what will make you feel comfortable. Ultimately, it is crucial to be flexible and open minded. Know that in the end, what is most important is that you and your baby are safe and healthy.

Once you and your partner have created your birth plan, share this information with your healthcare provider during your third trimester, preferably about a month before your expected due date. This gives you and your doctor or midwife time to discuss your options and for you to change your choices depending on what your provider recommends.

The next pages detail options to consider when creating your birth plan.

Birth Plan Checklist

People I Would Like to Have Present

❏ Partner

❏ Nonpartner labor coach

❏ Friend. *Know that some hospitals have limits on the number of people allowed in the room. Decide on the people you would like to have with you, and plan to ask them well in advance.*

❏ Relative

❏ Child or children. *Find out if this is possible and what ages of children are allowed. Your children are unlikely to be able to be present at a hospital delivery, but some birthing centers welcome children. Of course, you will want to prepare your children carefully and to have an adult present who can support them and take them out of the room if the experience becomes overwhelming or you would prefer to have them leave.*

❏ Doula

Preferences for Surroundings

❏ I would like to be able to play music during labor.

❏ I would like to have aromatherapy during labor.

❏ I would prefer low-level lighting during labor and/or delivery. *This may not be available.*

❏ I want someone to take pictures or video during the labor and delivery process. *The hospital might not allow the videotaping of births.*

Labor Preferences

❏ I would like to stay in my own clothes as long as possible. *Check hospital or birthing center policy on this.*

❏ I would like to be able to walk around.

❏ I do not want my labor induced unless there is a strong medical reason to do so.

❏ I want my water to be broken if it does not break on its own. *Labors during which the water is broken by the doctor or midwife tend to go faster than labors where the water remains unbroken for a longer period of time.*

❏ I do not want an IV catheter in place during labor. *There are pros and cons to both choices. While an IV catheter can be annoying, it can also be lifesaving if you need an emergency cesarean section.*

❏ I would like to be able to eat and drink during labor. *Keep in mind that nausea and vomiting are common in the later stages of labor, and that eating may be a risk factor if you need general anesthesia in an emergency.*

❏ I would like to be able to use a shower, bath, or whirlpool bath. *Not all hospitals have this option.*

❏ I prefer to have intermittent monitoring of the fetal heart rate and contractions. *The policy of some hospitals is to have continuous monitoring.*

Pain Management

❏ I would like to have massage.

❏ I would like to use additional pain control methods (such as acupressure, hot/cold therapy, hypnosis, or self-hypnosis). Specify methods:

_____

❏ I want to try to have an unmedicated labor (with the right to change my mind if labor becomes intense).

❏ I prefer not to be offered pain medication; I will ask if I need it.

❏ I want to have systemic medications for pain during labor.

❏ I want an epidural anesthetic during labor. *More on epidural anesthesia in Chapter 13.*

Delivery

❏ I want to try squatting on the bed for delivery. *Try out the positions at home to see what feels most comfortable to you.*

❏ I want to try lying on my side.

❏ I want to try being in a semi-sitting position.

- ❏ I would like to use a birthing stool, birthing chair, squatting bar, or birthing pool or tub. *Ask whether these are available or whether you can bring your own equipment. Be sure to check what is allowed.*
- ❏ I want my partner to cut the umbilical cord or help in the bathing and measuring of our baby. *Find out whether this is possible according to policy.*
- ❏ If possible, I want my baby on my chest immediately after birth.
- ❏ I want to nurse my baby while still in the delivery room and shortly after it is born.

Cesarean Birth

- ❏ If I need to have a C-section, I would like my partner to be present.
- ❏ I would like my partner to be able to hold the baby as soon as possible.
- ❏ I would like to breast-feed in the recovery room if possible.

Postpartum

- ❏ I want rooming-in, and I want the baby with me at all times, if possible.
- ❏ I want rooming-in, but I'd like the baby to be in the nursery at night.
- ❏ I would prefer to have my baby stay in the nursery except for visitation and feeding times.

- ❏ I would like a private room. *Check your insurance coverage.*
- ❏ I would like my partner to be able to stay in my room on a cot.
- ❏ I would like my children to be able to see the baby as soon as possible.

Feeding

- ❏ I do not want my baby to have a pacifier, sugar water, or formula in the nursery unless there is a medical reason to do so and I am informed in advance.
- ❏ I would like an appointment with a lactation consultant.
- ❏ I plan to breast-feed.
- ❏ I plan to bottle-feed.
- ❏ I have a formula preference. *Some hospitals have their own formula choices. Find out what options you have, and if they do not have your choice, be prepared to bring your own formula to the hospital.*

Circumcision

- ❏ If I have a boy, I want him to be circumcised in the hospital.
- ❏ This is the individual who will perform the circumcision procedure:

_____

Rh Sensitization

The Rh factor (or Rhesus factor) is a specific protein found on the surface of red blood cells. Those who lack the factor are called Rh negative. About 15 percent of Caucasian women are Rh negative, while only 7 percent of African American women and 1 to 2 percent of women of Asian descent are Rh negative.

Rh-positive mothers and their children are not at risk of complications from this blood factor, even if the baby is Rh negative. If you are Rh negative, however, steps need to be taken during your pregnancy to prevent the occurrence of Rh sensitization.

How Does Rh Sensitization Occur?

Rh sensitization occurs when bits of blood from an Rh-positive fetus mix with the mother's Rh-negative blood during pregnancy or delivery. Experts believe that this is relatively uncommon during the pregnancy itself. If the two blood types mix, however, the mother's immune system turns on, making antibodies that can cause complications, usually in future pregnancies.

Besides during delivery, you can be sensitized to the Rh factor during a past miscarriage, an elective abortion, an ectopic pregnancy, placental abruption, abdominal injury in pregnancy, or by having an amniocentesis or chorionic villus sampling (CVS) during this or a previous pregnancy.

Preventing Rh Sensitization

Rh sensitization, which happens about once in 1000 pregnancies, can be more safely and easily prevented than treated once it occurs. When you have your first prenatal visit, your doctor will determine whether your blood is Rh positive or Rh negative. If your blood is Rh negative and if you are certain that the father of your baby is also Rh negative, you have nothing to worry about

If you have melasma like I did, definitely try some kind of treatment. I'd had a challenging pregnancy, and that's where I drew the line and got myself laser treatments. It's worth every penny to feel better! —*Helena, 30, mother of one*

because your baby's Rh status will most definitely be Rh negative as well (two negatives cannot make a positive). However, even if you feel certain of the parentage of your baby, your doctor may not wish to take any chances and will treat you as though you are at risk for Rh sensitization anyway.

The good news is that Rh sensitivity and its complications can be prevented. Rhogam is a good preventative (99 percent effective) against Rh sensitization. You should get a Rhogam shot if you have bleeding during your pregnancy, a miscarriage, or an ectopic pregnancy; after a chorionic villus sampling (CVS) or an amniocentesis; at around 28 weeks; and after the delivery of the baby. The baby's blood type will be checked, and if the baby is Rh positive, you will get another shot. If the baby is Rh negative, you will not need anything. Unfortunately, if you are already sensitized, Rhogam cannot help you.

Treating Rh Sensitization

If you are known to be Rh sensitized, your healthcare provider will measure the level of Rh antibodies at various intervals during the pregnancy. You will have regular Doppler ultrasounds, which can measure the degree of anemia your fetus has. An amniocentesis

Things to Think About:

Count Fetal Movements

Now that your baby is moving regularly, the best way to determine its health status is to count fetal movements. Lie down for half an hour every day and count fetal movements, whether small or large movements. If you can count five fetal movements per half hour, the fetus is probably doing fine. To better promote fetal movements, drink an eight-ounce cup of juice before you do your "test." You might have to lie there another half hour to get five fetal movements because fetuses do sleep. If you do not feel fetal movement after an hour, call your healthcare provider for advice.

might be done at around 15 weeks to see what the baby's blood type really is. The treatment of Rh incompatibility (sensitization) is mostly a watch-and-wait situation. Your healthcare provider will monitor the fetus and provide treatment.

Melasma Treatment

As you may recall from Chapter 7, melasma is a condition of pregnancy that primarily affects the face. Hormonal changes affect the melanin content of the skin, causing a mask-like darkness to spread across the face. It is not at all harmful, and you will gradually lose the discoloration after you deliver your baby. But if the melasma is making you uncomfortable or unhappy, there are a few things you can do about it.

Melasma
Melasma usually does go away after pregnancy, but not always.

Chemical Peel

You can see a dermatologist for a chemical peel. This involves the use of mild acids on the face to remove a part of the top layer of pigmented skin. The use of chemical peels is considered safe in pregnancy, but be sure your pregnancy healthcare provider okays your

Stress and Melasma?

What NOW?

While some doctors seem to believe that stress makes melasma worse, there is no strong research evidence for this connection, and the American Academy of Dermatology does not list stress among the triggers for melasma.

The known triggers of melasma are genetics and sun exposure. You can't choose your ancestors, but you can wear sunscreen every day and find a wide-brimmed hat that you like!

visit to the dermatologist and tell the dermatologist you are pregnant before scheduling your chemical peel. One treatment should last the duration of your pregnancy.

Skin-Lightening Cream

There are natural lightening creams and creams containing hydroquinone that can gradually lighten your skin if used regularly. Hydroquinone has the tendency to make you look a bit ashen, so be aware of this possibility when you get the cream. You can also use a natural product such as SkinBright, which is a combination of natural skin-lightening substances and moisturizers. These natural substances inhibit melanin production and are best used early in the course of melasma. For these creams, it takes three to four weeks in order to see an effect. Products similar to SkinBright include Makari and Revitol.

Laser Treatment

A dermatologist who specializes in laser treatments can also help with melasma. There are several types of laser treatment, and your dermatologist will tell you the pros and cons of each type of treatment. Laser treatments are the most effective and fastest way to treat melasma, but they are also the most expensive, and insurance is unlikely to cover these treatments.

Setting Up Baby's Nursery: Common-Sense Planning

Setting up your baby's nursery should be a pleasurable experience, not an overwhelming task. The following are some things to consider as you plan this project.

Exercise Idea: Swimming

At this juncture you probably feel large and somewhat awkward in your body. While a 30-minute brisk walk is always beneficial and an easily accessible form of exercise, you may also enjoy swimming at this point in your pregnancy. Swimming offers you a full-body workout, gently stretches your muscles, and provides isometric toning. All this while allowing you to feel weightless—and no need to worry about your balance in the water, either! If you are not an accomplished swimmer, get a pair of water shoes and simply walk in the area of the pool where the water is less than chest-high. There are plenty of options out there in maternity swimwear. (Try online stores for the most variety.) As always, any exercise—even walking indoors at a mall during inclement weather—improves your circulation and can help prevent deep vein thromboses (blood clots) of the lower leg. So whatever you choose to do, just keep doing it!

Cramped for Space?

If you do not currently have a specific room for your nursery, no worries! A newborn needs very little at the start of his or her life, and there are really only three essentials: diapers, snap-crotch t-shirts, and a bassinette or co-sleeper, which can be placed in your room. When the baby first comes home, most couples do this whether or not they have a nursery room set aside. This allows new parents to be close to their baby, and it makes night feedings easier.

How Much Is Too Much?

There is a lot of stuff out there for babies, so it is easy to get carried away in a baby superstore. Before you buy, research what you really, truly need; make a list, and stick to it. Ask other new parents what was most useful for them and what they bought but really did not need. Learn from someone else's mistakes when you can! Don't fall into the trap of thinking that what you buy for your baby reflects your level of caring. Overspending is not a sign of love—something you will be discussing with your child when he or she becomes a teenager!

Everything Does Not Have to Be New!

Many new parents become tied to the idea of purchasing everything brand spanking factory fresh. There are items—like a car seat, crib, and perhaps stroller—that you may want to buy new for safety reasons, but most everything else can be used, including clothing. Wash used baby clothes in a gentle detergent and clean used gear and plastic toys with a solution of bleach and warm water. Your baby really won't care if he or she has the newest and most expensive gear, and you will be far less stressed if you stay within your budget.

With these thoughts in mind, the following information will help you organize a safe, healthy, and adorable space for your baby!

You can create a functional nursery in the corner of your bedroom.

Choose a Theme: Rosebuds or Planets or Trains? Oh My!

Choosing a theme for your nursery will give you direction and structure when decorating and purchasing items. If you know you are having a girl or boy, you can choose a gender-specific theme like pink roses or airplanes. Or gender-neutral décor like stars and moons, animals, or the alphabet may be your preference. Look online, in baby catalogues, and in stores for fabrics or decoration ideas that catch your eye. Once you choose a theme, it is much easier to decorate!

If you can, find a picture of a baby room you love and use that as your guide to building your own nursery. You do not have to purchase the items in the picture but can use the visual image to show to salespeople, friends, and family when looking for less-expensive alternatives to create the same effect in your own nursery. It will also help keep your theme

on track so you do not end up with airplanes on the wall and circus sheets in the crib!

Sometimes you can find a single item—like a stuffed lion, a model train, or an adorable doll—that you use as the inspiration for your nursery theme. Other times, you may fall in love with crib bedding or a color scheme in a fabric! Whatever inspires you, bring that item with you as you shop, and use it to keep your theme on track and build your room.

Painting the Nursery

Your theme, once chosen, should provide guidance for room color. Paint is one of the

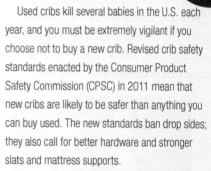

Warning about Used Cribs

Used cribs kill several babies in the U.S. each year, and you must be extremely vigilant if you choose not to buy a new crib. Revised crib safety standards enacted by the Consumer Product Safety Commission (CPSC) in 2011 mean that new cribs are likely to be safer than anything you can buy used. The new standards ban drop sides; they also call for better hardware and stronger slats and mattress supports.

If you must purchase or borrow a used crib, inspect it beforehand for any protruding parts, sharp edges, splinters, peeling paint, and slat width before you use it. Be sure it does not have drop sides, and refer to all the crib safety specifications above. The CPSC requires that all cribs sold, new or used, meet the 2011 safety standards, but you can only be sure of this with a certified new crib.

Remember to check any cribs used by babysitters, childcare centers, or grandparents who are caring for your baby as well.

most inexpensive ways to make a huge impact when decorating a room. Changing those white walls to a butter yellow, rosy pink, honey orange, or baby blue will instantly transform your room. And if you do not like the color once it is on the wall, it is easy to pick a new color and paint over it!

Choose your wall color as soon as possible and get the painting done early. If you can, leave the actual work to your partner, friends and family, or a professional. Regardless of who paints, be sure you choose paint that is safe to use while you are pregnant and safe for baby to live with as well. The best choice is a good-quality latex-based paint. Latex-based paints give off little odor and are safe for you to use during pregnancy—even if you have to do all the painting and cleaning up yourself. There are also numerous eco-friendly and low-VOC (volatile organic compound) paints available that reduce fumes and use fewer chemicals than traditional latex paints.

A baby monitor consists of a base unit that transmits from the nursery and a portable unit that allows you to keep tabs on your baby while you move around the house or yard. Most monitors simply transmit sound, but you can get a video monitor that allows you to see your child. There are even advanced monitors that let you check your baby from your smartphone or computer at work!

What about Lead Paint?

Lead-based paint was banned in the U.S. for household use in 1978, but it can still be present in homes painted before that time. Your child could get exposed to lead by ingesting pieces of peeling lead-based paint. If you do not know when the nursery was last painted or if your home was built before 1978, you can have your home tested for lead through a private company. You can also paint over the possibly contaminated paint, but *only* after scraping the walls and corners for loose paint chips first.

Choosing a Crib: Safety First!

When you buy a crib, you can choose to buy one new or used, although there are serious safety considerations with used cribs (see above). Regardless of the crib you select, make certain it is safe for baby's use. Look for the Juvenile Products Manufacturing Association (JPMA) certification stamp somewhere on the crib. This means that the crib has been tested for both safety and quality. Regardless, use the following guide to double-check the safety of your crib.

Slats: The slats can be no further apart than 2⅜ inches. Bring along a tape measure to be sure. This maximum distance between slats protects your baby from getting his or her head caught between the slats.

Posts: If the crib has posts, they should not extend more than 1/16 of an inch above the crib, so the baby's clothing will not get caught, causing a strangulation hazard. If you have a crib with a canopy, the poles holding up the

If you can, take a moment and write a letter to your baby telling him or her exactly what you're feeling about the upcoming birth and what it has been like to be pregnant. Include any wisdom or thoughts about life, family, love, and your anticipation of your child's arrival. Seal it up, and one day, after your baby is born, open it and read the letter. Then save it for when your child is old enough to read it by himself or herself. You'll be amazed at what you had to say, and so will your child! —*Misty, 34, mother of two*

corners of the canopy must be at least 16 inches in height. The mattress support ideally should be adjustable so that, as your baby gets taller, you can lower the height of the mattress so the baby does not jump or fall out.

Interior and mattress: The interior part of the crib should be approximately 51¾ inches in length by 27¾ inches in width. Buy the mattress and the crib together so you know the mattress fits snugly within the confines of the crib. If you can fit two fingers anywhere between the mattress and the crib itself, the mattress is too small and you'll want to get a bigger one.

Convertible cribs: If you want a crib that will convert to a toddler bed, make sure it is relatively simple to make the switch from crib to bed.

No bumper pad or pillows! Crib sets are often sold with a sheet, blanket, ruffled

skirt, and bumper padding. The American Academy of Pediatrics recommends that you leave the bumper pad off the crib. While bumper pads are pretty, experts believe they pose a threat to your baby and can contribute to the incidence of SIDS (sudden infant death syndrome). Babies can get trapped, suffocated, or strangled by bumper pads. Also, bumpers prevent you from seeing your baby in the crib unless you are peering over the side. Don't let the appeal of a fancy crib set blind you to the very real hazards of using the bumper pads. Pillows and other soft bedding are also a hazard for infants.

Dangers of decorative cutouts: If either the headboard or footboard on the crib has decorative cutouts, know that many of those cutouts are too big and can entrap your baby's head or limbs. The headboard and footboard should be made of slats like the sides (no greater than 2⅜ inches apart) or should be solid wood without cutouts.

Monthly Monitor

Call your healthcare provider if you experience any of the following:

- Fever greater than 101.5°F
- Bleeding
- Constant abdominal pain
- Uterine cramps or back pains that occur at 5-to-10-minute intervals, especially if the cramps become painful
- A sudden gush of fluid from the vagina
- Absent fetal movement or less than five fetal movements within half an hour after you have consumed a sweet beverage such as juice

I totally made the mistake of not planning a theme for the baby's room. One day my husband went into the nursery to see what I had purchased. He came out saying, "Do you know you have airplanes, zoo animals, toy soldiers, and trains in there? It looks like an explosion in a baby store." Blame the hormones, but I burst into tears and wailed that I couldn't make up my mind. My husband hugged me and said he would help. We settled on a completely new theme my husband chose—monkeys (because he called me his "Little Monkey"). And we took everything else back to the stores.
—*Kelsey, 33, mother of one*

Placement of crib: Do not place your crib near any windows where drapery cords or cords for blinds are within reach of the baby and could cause a strangulation risk. Keep windows locked at all times. Make sure all picture frames and dresser top items are not reachable from the crib so that when your baby is old enough to stand up, he or she cannot reach those items.

Notes:

I drove myself and everyone around me crazy with my worries about possible preterm birth. There was no logical or physical reason to be worried, but the idea was stuck in my head. Finally, my husband called my doctor, and at our next prenatal visit, she told me that the stress I was causing myself was unhealthy for me and my baby and could actually contribute to a preterm birth. Well, I stopped stressing right then and there! Sometimes you need a neutral party to set you straight. Don't worry when there isn't anything to worry about! —*Josephine, 32, mother of one*

Chapter 10

Month Eight—Weeks 29 through 32

Whew! You have made it to your third trimester! You are officially in the home stretch of your pregnancy—though you still have a way to go. Your baby has a way to go, too. He or she still needs to grow and gain weight. And, if you deliver this month, your baby risks breathing problems and other issues related to premature birth. You will need to pay close attention this month to any signs of preterm labor.

This chapter covers a variety of important topics as you draw nearer to your delivery date:

- What is going on with my baby's development in late pregnancy?

- How can I cope with body changes?

- What will help me ride through my emotions and keep fears at bay?

- How can I maintain a vital sex life and closeness with my partner?

- Are these contractions just Braxton-Hicks, or is it preterm labor?

- What if I go into labor early or give birth prematurely?

- How do I choose a pediatrician or family doctor to care for my baby?

- What is cord blood banking, and how does a person go about it?

As your uterus continues to expand and you feel more awkward and uncomfortable, you may also begin to feel a little irritable or edgy.

I love fashion and vowed my pregnancy would follow suit with my usual flare for dressing. I certainly got a lot of compliments on my creative attempts to be fashionable and pregnant at the same time! My wardrobe was working great and making me feel good until I hit my third trimester. I suddenly felt huge and frumpy! When I looked at my body in the mirror, I felt like an alien—especially because of the size of my breasts. I was irritable and resentful of how hard it was getting to dress myself and feel good. I was so unhappy with my appearance I wanted to give up all my healthy eating and careful wardrobe choices and throw in the towel. Thankfully my best friend came to the rescue with encouragement and three shopping trips! With her help, I found maternity clothes I liked and that didn't add volume to my increasingly large size. Those clothes and my friend gave me the "oomph" I needed to get me through until I gave birth! Whatever you do, ladies, don't give up now!
—Ebony, 30

You may also have mixed feelings about your upcoming birth process. Thoughts about the unknown are always a challenge—and the mystery behind how your labor and delivery will go is no exception! You may be wondering about the extent of pain you will experience while giving birth and whether or not you will be strong enough to handle it. You might ponder what you will do if you have a serious complication or your baby is born with a health problem. Your physical and emotional state may be in flux again, and you will need to take good care of yourself with rest and relaxation and by surrounding yourself with positive, supportive friends and family.

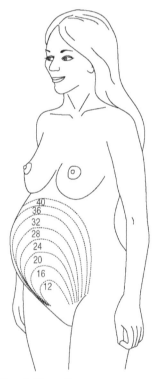

Gestational silhouette
Your uterus grows to accommodate the growing fetus, and the top of the uterus is higher in your abdomen each month. The lines represent the number of weeks you have been pregnant.

This is a good month to tie up loose ends: Visit your birthing center or hospital if you have not already, complete your birthing classes, finish your birth plan, complete your nursery, and wash all new (and used) baby clothes, sheets, and blankets. As your pregnancy continues, you will have less energy to get things done!

Your Baby's Growth and Development: Growing and Maturing

Your little bundle of joy is continuing to grow, put on weight, and develop the capacity to live outside the womb on his or her own. Let's look at what's happening this month:

Week 29
Your baby's head is now in the same proportion to the body as it will be at birth. In fact, your baby's head will make up about one-quarter to one-third of his or her total body. Growth is your baby's primary function now as fat is distributed throughout his or her body, so that at birth, your baby will be able to regulate his or her own body temperature. Your baby can see, touch, taste, and smell even though he or she will not need those senses for about three more months. Your baby's eyes are sensitive to light, and he or she can distinguish vague shapes but cannot see anything clearly.

Your baby's growth is not as fast as it was in the second trimester; however, the baby still needs to gain about four to five pounds before birth. Your baby will make irregular but increasingly frequent breathing movements in preparation for eventual birth. A baby born at 29 weeks would likely need a brief period on a respirator to breathe effectively.

Your baby weighs 2.5 pounds and is about 15 inches from its head to its feet. This month, the baby will resemble the size of an acorn squash when folded up and the length of a large zucchini when stretched out.

Week 30

The baby's lanugo (fine body hair) has almost disappeared by this week, and the baby's skin is becoming less wrinkled as more fat is deposited beneath it. The skin is also becoming less translucent than it was during your second trimester. The baby's bone marrow is now making all of his or her own red blood cells.

Your baby's face now looks almost as it will at birth; however, its chubby cheeks will not fill out until later. Your baby is able to turn its head from side to side and from back to front. The nostrils breathe amniotic fluid into and out of the airless lungs. A baby born at this time in gestation has an excellent chance for normal survival, growth, and development as long as it is born in a facility that is prepared to attend to preterm infants.

Your baby now is about 15.7 inches long and weighs almost 3 pounds!

Week 31

Your baby's growth is even slower than in week 30 as he or she expends energy to put on more fat. The brain and the lungs are the only major organs left to mature. The lungs will mature in another six to seven weeks, while the brain will continue to mature into childhood and beyond.

Your baby can recognize your voice and your partner's voice. Singing, talking, and

reading to your baby now can bolster infant bonding later on. Your baby's fingernails and toenails have grown out to nearly the tips of the fingers and toes. If your baby is born on your due date or later, you may even have to clip the toenails and fingernails after birth so your baby does not accidentally scratch him or herself.

Your baby weighs about 3.3 pounds and is about 16.2 inches long!

Week 32

There would be a very positive outlook for survival if your baby were to be born during this week. As a preterm baby, he or she might not even need a ventilator to breathe. Weight gain slows even further. Still, the baby will have gained more than half of his or her total birth weight at this point!

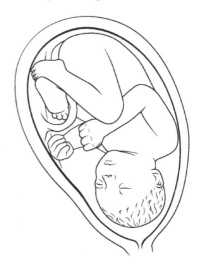

Fetus at 32 weeks of development

A 32-week-old fetus is nearly 17 inches long and 4 pounds! With its major development finished, the fetus gains weight quickly. Bones harden, but the skull remains soft and flexible for delivery; the different regions of the brain are forming; taste buds develop, and the fetus can taste sweet and sour.

If you are having multiples, their growth will begin to lag behind that of a singleton baby because they are "roommates" in the tight confines of the uterus. At this point in gestation, babies will begin to establish regular patterns of sleep and activity. This "routine" will most likely persist after the baby is born; so if you notice a lot of nighttime activity, you might expect that your newborn will be a night owl!

Your baby weighs about 3.75 pounds and is about 16.7 inches long!

Your Changing Body: You Are Carrying a Bundle!

Now that you are in your third trimester, there is a whole new set of physical changes and symptoms you may experience. Let's look at a few things you might notice this month:

Swelling

Swelling is at its worst in the third trimester, especially if you are on your feet a lot or if your third trimester is during the heat of summer. Water retention affects the feet and legs the most, but you can have swelling in your face and arms as well. You may also find that your wrists are swollen. Fluid retention causes a narrowing of part of the wrist called the carpal tunnel. The median nerve that runs through the carpal tunnel gets pinched, resulting in numbness and shooting pains in the hands. It is worse if you do a lot of typing or if you have a manufacturing or cashier's job. See your healthcare provider if you have any of these symptoms. He or she can fit you with wrist braces to wear until the symptoms subside.

As for your feet, they can become visibly swollen. You might even have to purchase shoes that are a half or whole size bigger than your normal size. Stay off your feet as much as you can, and elevate your legs when possible. This will help draw the fluid away from your feet and back to your circulatory system.

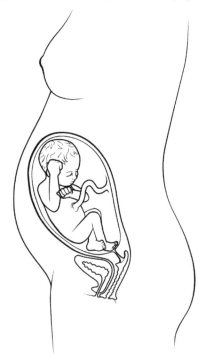

Your changing body: Month eight
The baby growing inside pushes your uterus up so that by week 36, it's pressing under your rib cage.

Believe it or not, the best thing to do to combat swelling is to drink more fluids. Pushing the fluid intake helps flush more fluid through the kidneys. If you are able to sit back and relax for a while, you should change positions often so that your circulation doesn't slow down.

Every day after my wife got home from work, I made her sit on the couch and put up her feet. I prepared dinner and then, after we ate, I gave her a foot rub. I wanted her to know I appreciated all she was going through carrying our son. It meant a lot to her, I know. It kept our sex life going great, too. Because I was helping her she had more energy for us! —*Steven, 32, father of one*

Dizziness

Many women in the third trimester experience dizziness, especially if they sit too long and then stand up abruptly. This phenomenon is due to the pressure of the uterus on the vena cava—the large vein that runs from the pelvis to the chest. Lying down on your back or even sitting can cause the uterus to press on the vena cava so that the blood return to the heart is temporarily diminished. This leads to orthostatic hypotension, which is the same as saying "low blood pressure when you get up from a sitting or lying position." This experience can lead to dizziness and nausea. You should call your healthcare provider if these symptoms occur regularly or if you actually pass out.

To avoid feeling dizzy, sit upright rather than in a reclined position. Lie on your left side when you lie down or go to bed and move around frequently so your circulation can flow. When getting up from a lying down position, sit at the edge of the couch or bed for several seconds to get your circulation moving before you slowly rise to a standing position.

Dizziness can also be caused by anemia of pregnancy, low blood sugar, tiredness, high blood pressure, and becoming too hot. Pay attention to your body and be aware of your surroundings. Stay out of hot, stuffy places, and eat several small meals per day to maintain a more constant blood pressure.

Itching

Itching is a common problem in later pregnancy. Often your belly is irritated from stretching and dryness caused by your skin being overstretched as your uterus grows. Usually the itching is unaccompanied by a rash. You may get relief by using moisturizers or oils on the itchy, dry areas. In very rare circumstances, itching (along with dark-colored urine, lighter-colored stools, extreme fatigue, depression, and appetite loss) can indicate a gallbladder problem. If you experience these symptoms or just have severe itching of your skin that you cannot explain, talk to your healthcare provider as soon as possible.

Shortness of Breath

In this month, shortness of breath will become more noticeable as you go about your daily activities. This will also be noticeable when you are sitting down because the uterus pushes up onto the lungs, interfering with breathing. Your uterus will be about four and a half to five inches above your belly button—large enough to be taking up a great deal of room inside your pelvis, abdomen, and just beneath your chest.

You should still continue to exercise as best you can. Take extra breaks if you need to. When you get short of breath while sitting, you can sit up straighter and take a few deep

> Every morning after my shower, my partner rubbed lotion on my itchy belly. Not only did it help with the dry, stretchy feeling I had on my skin, it gave her time to talk to our baby. It was a real bonding time for all of us, and those mornings were the favorite times of my pregnancy. —*Molly, 34, mother of one*

breaths to feel as though you are getting more air.

Leg Cramps

Leg cramps are common in pregnancy and can happen day or night. During the day, cramps are painful and a nuisance; but when they happen at night they can interfere with the amount and quality of sleep you get.

Experts are not sure why leg cramps occur, but they speculate that cramping may happen because of the pressure the uterus puts on the veins of the abdomen and pelvis, causing a backup of blood in the legs. Pinched nerves in the pelvis might also lead to recurrent cramps.

If you can, relax and gently stretch your cramping muscles. Better yet, ask your partner to massage your legs whenever possible!

Trouble Sleeping

Sleeping on your left side is best for your baby's health. When you sleep on your left side, blood flow to the uterus is maximized, and your placenta gets all the nutrients and oxygen it needs from your blood in order to feed and oxygenate your baby.

You are likely to have trouble sleeping during your third trimester. You are bigger, physically more uncomfortable, and may have aches, cramps, pains, and heartburn. You may also dream more than normal and have to make frequent trips to the bathroom. This doesn't sound like a fun night, does it?

Do whatever you can to make yourself as comfortable as possible at night. Make use of pillows, including full-body pillows, so you can find a relaxed position. Many pregnant women like a regular-sized pillow between their knees. Try putting one pillow behind your back, one between your legs, and have a body pillow for hugging and for resting your large belly on. Also take every opportunity to nap and relax during daytime hours. Rest is vital to good health, especially in your final stages of pregnancy!

Sleep position
Use all the pillows you need to have a comfortable night's sleep!

Aches and Pains

At this point, expect that a day's shopping will cause your feet to ache miserably and that standing for long periods of time will cause your back to feel sore. In your third trimester, you may experience what's called lumbar lordosis. This is your body's way of counteracting the extra weight you are carrying on the front of your body. Your body automatically leans back in order to compensate for the weight differential, and your back muscles suffer as a result.

A seated back massage or a good foot rub will come in handy as your uterus further expands during this trimester. Indulge yourself in some massage oils for a sensual experience with your partner or seek out a trained massage therapist to rub those aches and pains away. You can also take up to 1000 mg of Tylenol (acetaminophen) every four to six hours during pregnancy to ease any pain you have, especially when you need a good night's rest.

Your Emotions: Am I Done Yet?

The sense of well-being and explosion of energy you may have felt during your second trimester is beginning to wane this month. Fatigue and even irritability can set in as you begin to have more trouble sleeping and your body continues to expand. It becomes increasingly difficult to feel attractive in your maternity wear, and the body aches and pains you may have only add to your frustration. Some women begin to feel a strong sense that they are simply "finished" being pregnant, yet there are two months left to go!

When you add these things together, you may find yourself losing control of your PMA (positive mental attitude). This is the time to take a deep breath and relax. What you are experiencing is completely normal. Use some of the following suggestions to cheer yourself on to the finish line:

- Reward yourself for all the healthy habits you have maintained. Get a massage, facial, or that cute but pricey maternity outfit you've been eyeing; have your partner take you out for a special dinner. If money is tight, find some low-cost entertainment such as a free concert or time with a special friend.

- When you look in the mirror do not criticize your beautiful, pregnant body. Instead, repeat three times: "My body is healthy and beautiful." Your mood will lift immediately.

- When you find yourself in negative thinking, immediately change your negative thought to a positive one. For example, if you are thinking, "I'll never get through this pregnancy!" change that thought to, "I'm doing a great job getting through my pregnancy in a healthy, happy manner." It really will make a difference!

- Schedule nap time! Turn off the phone and ask your partner not to disturb you for an allotted amount of time.

For Dads and Partners: Be Encouraging

Your pregnant partner is in the home stretch, but from now until the end of her pregnancy she will be more tired and more uncomfortable. She may even feel somewhat down about her appearance or irritable due to aches and pains. One of the most important things you can do this month is to be supportive and encouraging. Compliment your partner often about how she looks or about what a great job she is doing in spite of all she is enduring. Pitch in with chores without being asked, make dinner, even take your partner shopping. Anything you can do to make life easier and more enjoyable for your partner will go a long way in helping her through the most challenging part of her pregnancy!

- Spend time with friends or family members who are supportive and positive.

- Remind yourself that you will not be pregnant forever and once your baby is born you will be able to get your body back to normal.

- If you can't talk yourself into a better frame of mind, and your low mood is interfering with everyday life, consider seeing a therapist.

Sex Drive

Many women continue to have a strong sex drive during their third trimester, while others may experience a slight decrease in sexual desire until the end of their pregnancy. Either way, you and your partner will need to be creative at this point, which can enhance your intimacy and emotional closeness!

Either you or your partner (or both of you) may be adjusting to your ever-expanding body. Some partners feel turned off by changes in Mom-to-be's appearance, which can lead to sexual frustration, sadness, or even feelings of isolation. Your sexual relationship is an important part of being a couple and sharing your lives together. If you are having difficulties in your sexual relationship, try talking together about your feelings. Often a simple, open conversation can clear the path to deeper intimacy and an enhanced sexual relationship. Remember that having fun together is an important component of a good sex life. If you need more focused help, seek a therapist who can support you and your partner as you navigate through this bump in your sexual journey. Remember, listening is a key component to a productive conversation. Try to hear what

your partner is truly saying and respond with love and kindness.

Labor and Delivery Fears

As your due date draws closer, it is natural to have fears about labor and delivery—especially if this is your first child. Fears can manifest as feelings of anxiety, increased nighttime dreams, and even ruminating on worries throughout your day.

> I felt so much better once I stopped beating myself up for cutting down my running from five miles to only two. I reminded myself that I was still doing great things for my body and my health, and therefore taking great care of my baby. Instead of focusing on what you aren't able to do, focus on what good things you are doing! —Catherine, 40, mother of two

While labor and delivery are unpredictable and your experience will be different from every other woman's experience (and even your own past experiences if this is not your first pregnancy), chances are that everything will be completely fine! Statistically, the incidence of neonatal death—which is the chance that a baby will die around the time of birth—is far less than 1 percent, and tends to occur only in situations where there are preexisting complications, poor hygiene, poor nutrition, lack of newborn care, harmful neonatal practices (such as those that occur in developing countries), and extreme prematurity.

This means that, instead of worrying and being fearful about your baby's health or about the pain of labor, be proactive by having a good birth plan in place and by making sure you are taking care of yourself while watching for any signs of preterm labor. Turn your fear into positive action and enjoy the rest of your pregnancy, safe in the knowledge that you are being the best pregnant mother you can be!

Your Prenatal Visit: Is Baby Right Side Up?

You should now be seeing your healthcare provider every two weeks as long as you are having a normal pregnancy. If your pregnancy is complicated by high blood pressure, high blood sugar levels, preterm labor risk, or other preexisting conditions, you will likely see your doctor once per week or more often.

At your prenatal visits, you will have a urinalysis done. You will be weighed, and the expectation is that you will have gained about 20 to 25 pounds so far. If you have gained more or less than that, talk to your healthcare provider to see if this is a source of concern.

Your healthcare provider will measure your uterine size at each visit. Your abdomen should measure between 29 and 33 centimeters from the pubic bone to the top of your uterus. The doctor will also listen to heart tones. In the third trimester, the fetal heart tones should be around 140 beats per minute, but can be as low as 110 if the baby is sleeping or as high as 160 if the baby is very active. Heart tones lower than 110 or higher than 160 might indicate a fetal heart abnormality, fetal distress, or an infection in the uterus, and your healthcare provider may wish to investigate the situation more carefully.

One way of checking the health of the baby, which is actually better than an ultrasound, is by performing a nonstress test. A nonstress test is a noninvasive monitoring of the fetal heart rate over a 20-to-30-minute period. We will discuss nonstress testing in Chapter 11.

Your healthcare provider may check your cervix during at least one of your prenatal visits this month. This is to see if your cervix is starting to become prematurely thinned out or is dilating. While some cervical changes might be present in a woman who has had children before, new moms should have a closed and thick cervix during this time in pregnancy.

If your healthcare provider detects the possibility of preterm labor because of changes in the cervix, you may be evaluated further or be asked to rest more often. Some women are put on modified bed rest or total bed rest in order to keep their baby in the uterus for as long as possible. Details of bed rest are discussed in Chapter 11.

Prenatal Testing: **Urinalysis and Dealing with Any Complications**

You will be seeing your healthcare provider more often now and will have a urinalysis at each visit. Other tests done during this month are only ordered if there are concerns about your baby's growth or if you have a complication of pregnancy such as preterm labor or hypertension. These tests might include extra ultrasounds or a nonstress test. We will talk about nonstress tests and contraction stimulation tests in Chapter 11.

This month, your healthcare provider will also do what are called Leopold's maneuvers, which involve pressing firmly through your abdomen to check the baby's position, including the position of the back and the head. This will tell your healthcare provider if your baby is head down, which is the preferred position for labor and delivery. Sometimes the firm pressure of the provider's hands during these maneuvers may be uncomfortable. You can help yourself by being sure to empty your bladder first and by asking the doctor or midwife to warm his or her hands!

If your baby is breech—meaning its feet or buttocks are at the lowest position in the uterus—you need not worry yet. There is still plenty of time for the baby to flip around prior to birth so you can have a normal delivery. If the baby is breech near the delivery time, your healthcare provider may be able to turn it around so the head enters the pelvis first during birth (see "Breech Babies" in Chapter 11).

Complete breech
Breech presentation, with the baby upright at the time of delivery, happens in 3 to 4 percent of pregnancies. This picture shows a baby in the complete breech position, sitting cross-legged. A more common presentation is frank breech, with the baby's bottom directly over the cervix and the legs pointing upward. The least common type is footling breech, with the feet or knees closest to the cervix.

Braxton-Hicks Contractions

As early as the second trimester, you may notice an increase in intermittent tightening of the uterus that lasts for varying lengths of time. These tightening episodes come and go like labor, but the contractions are irregular. These episodes are called Braxton-Hicks contractions and are generally a normal, usually painless part of later pregnancy. They tend to increase as the pregnancy progresses. They are your body's way of practicing for delivery.

While some women have no pain whatsoever with Braxton-Hicks contractions, other women will experience a mild cramping pain that is easy to live with. These contractions are basically "practice contractions" or uterine irritability that is preparing the uterus for real labor. Even so, it can be hard to tell the difference between Braxton-Hicks contractions, which do not generally cause the cervix to open and thin, and real labor contractions, which result in cervical thinning and dilation.

The Braxton-Hicks contractions you experience become more and more uncomfortable as you get closer to real labor. If you are near term, the Braxton-Hicks contractions can feel exactly like real labor, and then are called false labor.

Preterm Labor, False Labor, and True Labor

These three terms—and their symptoms—can be confusing. While you are in the throes of your last trimester, it can be difficult to sort out which symptoms mean you are in labor and which symptoms mean your body is just practicing for birth. We hope the

The third time I went to the hospital with Braxton-Hicks contractions, my doctor photocopied a page like this one out of a pregnancy book and asked me to post it on the fridge and follow the contractions for at least 30 minutes to see if they were regular. So every time the Braxton-Hicks contractions began, my partner and I remained calm. And once the real contractions set in, there was no comparison! Live and learn. —*Francis, 27, mother of one*

following information will keep you from any unnecessary trips to the hospital!

Preterm Labor

Preterm labor is defined as any contractions that change the effacement and dilation of the cervix, and that occur prior to 37 weeks. Preterm labor is a form of true labor—with back pains that come and go, pressure sensations on your vaginal or pelvic area, and tightening of the uterus that comes in a regular pattern. The only difference is that preterm labor comes at the wrong time, and your healthcare provider would prefer that the baby stay in the uterus for another few weeks.

If you think you are having preterm labor, call your healthcare provider immediately. You will likely be asked to go to the hospital and have your cervix checked. If you are indeed having regular contractions, medications such as magnesium sulfate might be given in order to stop the contractions. If the labor can be stopped, you will probably go home on bed rest.

False Labor (or Braxton-Hicks Contractions)

False labor usually happens when you are close to your due date. It is defined as contractions that have a somewhat regular pattern, are somewhat uncomfortable, but do not change the effacement or dilation of the cervix. While you have probably been experiencing Braxton-Hicks contractions for some time, they may become more intense toward the end of pregnancy, thus becoming false labor. If you happen to be in the last trimester of pregnancy, and especially if you are in the last few weeks of pregnancy, it is easy to confuse false labor with real labor.

Some ways you can tell the difference between false labor and true labor are that the contractions of false labor are unpredictable, with contractions coming at different intervals and at different strengths; false labor contractions are mostly felt in the lower portion of your abdomen, while in true labor, the contraction often starts in the back and travels around your sides to the entire abdo-

Nutrition Tip:

Now Is Not the Time to Diet

By now you may be worrying about gaining too much weight, especially if the visit to the doctor showed you have already gained 25 pounds or more. Even if you gain more than the recommended 25 to 35 pounds during this pregnancy, now is not the time to diet. You should eat the recommended amount of calories per day and know that you will gain less weight if you increase your exercise level.

While they might feel the same, here are some of the telltale differences between Braxton-Hicks contractions (sometimes known as false labor) and true labor:

Braxton-Hicks Contractions (False Labor)	True Labor
• Contractions are painless or relatively pain free initially, but may become uncomfortable as pregnancy progresses. • Contractions occur at very irregular intervals. • Contractions can be stopped by drinking water, breathing exercises, a warm bath, changing your physical position, or rest. • Contractions are generally felt in the abdomen only.	• True labor persists no matter what you do. • Contractions increase in frequency, and you may be able to time them at about 10 to 15 minutes apart in the beginning. • Contractions may begin in the back. • Real labor is more painful.

men; false labor contractions often stop when you change what you're doing or change the position you are in.

If this is your first baby it really is hard to know when a contraction is false! Don't hesitate to call your doctor or even go to the hospital if you aren't sure. And don't be hard on yourself for false alarms—it's all part of the journey! —*Tish, 40, mother of four*

True Labor

You know you are experiencing true labor if you have a gush or trickle of clear fluid come out of your vagina (meaning "your water broke"). In early true labor, you will often have diarrhea or a bit of nausea as the cervix dilates. The baby will feel low in the pelvis as though it has "dropped."

The contractions of true labor gradually become closer together and increase in intensity over time. The pain will gradually get worse as your labor progresses. Call your healthcare provider if you think you are in labor.

Preterm Birth

Preterm or premature birth, defined as birth before 37 weeks' gestation, occurs in 12.8 percent of pregnancies. The rate of preterm birth has risen significantly over the past 30 years in the United States, indicating that not enough is being done to prevent the problem, which has an identifiable cause about 50 percent of the time. Preterm babies often have health issues that may or may not be overcome by modern technology.

Babies born early carry an increased risk of intellectual disability, cerebral palsy, breathing problems, loss of vision, hearing loss, and

Preterm Labor: Are You at Risk?

There are several factors that increase the risk of preterm labor:

- Carrying multiple babies
- Previous preterm delivery
- Uterine or cervical abnormalities
- Lack of adequate prenatal care
- A history of smoking
- Alcohol consumption during pregnancy
- Illicit drug use during pregnancy
- A lack of appropriate social support
- High levels of stress
- Physical, sexual, or emotional abuse
- Standing for long periods of time on the job
- Diabetes
- High blood pressure or preeclampsia
- Obesity or underweight
- Infections, including STDs and urinary tract infections
- Rapid repeat pregnancy (18 months or less between births)
- Conception via in vitro fertilization
- Clotting problems
- Vaginal bleeding
- Being African American
- A birth defect in the fetus
- Mothers who are younger than 17 years or older than 35 years

babies that are more premature. About 12 percent of preterm babies are born between 32 and 33 weeks of gestation, with another 10 percent being born between 28 and 31 weeks. Babies born before 28 weeks make up only 6 percent of all preterm deliveries.

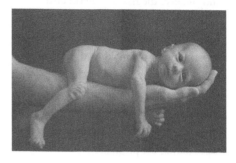

A preterm baby can have many complications after birth.

What Causes Preterm Birth?

Prematurity can be caused by many factors, and the cause of about half of preterm births is unknown. Most commonly, labor simply starts too early, sometimes after the premature rupture of the membranes (breaking of the "bag of waters"). Often infections and inflammation are the cause of premature labor. But most often (about 25 percent of the time) a baby is delivered prematurely in order to treat serious health problems in the baby or the mother.

Reducing the Risks of Preterm Labor

While many risk factors for preterm labor are beyond your control, you need to be aware of anything you can do to reduce the risks of premature birth and learn how to recognize preterm labor in its early stages. For example, if you have diabetes, high blood pressure, or another risk for preterm labor, you need to have your medical conditions under the best

learning or behavioral problems. Preterm babies are also at higher risk for autism, and babies who are very preterm (less than 28 weeks) can be at greater risk of heart disease, hypertension, and diabetes.

The good news is that most premature babies are born after 33 weeks of gestation, which puts them at a great advantage over possible control. You need adequate prenatal care that caters to your special needs and health conditions. For future pregnancies, it is good to know that there is some research that indicates taking folic acid supplements for a year prior to getting pregnant significantly reduces the risk of preterm birth.

Get healthy and stay healthy: Ideally, you will have addressed smoking, drug abuse, and alcohol consumption *before* the pregnancy. You are at less risk of preterm labor if you were at a healthy weight at the time of conception and you are gaining the proper amount of weight during the pregnancy.

Progesterone supplements: Progesterone supplements have been shown in some studies to stop the process of prematurity when given to women who already have had a preterm birth. While this may be effective in a singleton pregnancy, it does not work well in treating women who are pregnant with multiples.

Exercise Idea: Keep It Moving!
Women who are physically fit at the time of labor and delivery do better than women who are less so. Continue to do whatever exercise you can to stay healthy and strong. If you are lifting weights, use machines if possible rather than free weights so you do not accidentally drop a weight on your belly—or any other body part! Be sure to ask if you should modify your exercise routine as your pregnancy progresses toward the finish line. It is not a good time to try a new exercise, so remember that walking is almost always a great option. Just keep moving!

Recognize the Signs of Preterm Labor

Be aware of the following signs of imminent birth:

- Contractions of the uterus that are regular and no more than 15 minutes apart, possibly associated with a low backache
- Losing your mucus plug before 37 weeks' gestation (The mucus plug serves to block infection from entering the cervix during pregnancy and is released as a thick, not watery, vaginal discharge when labor is nearing. It sometimes is tinged with blood.)
- Increasing pressure in the lower pelvic region
- Sudden loss of amniotic fluid

Call your healthcare provider as soon as possible if you have any of these signs!

If Preterm Birth Is Inevitable
If you are under 34 weeks and are showing signs of preterm labor, your doctor might give you corticosteroids to try to stop your labor for at least 24 hours. These corticosteroids help mature the fetus' lungs. Medications called tocolytics—like magnesium sulfate or terbutaline—can be given to slow down or stop your labor. Your doctor will also make arrangements for your baby to be placed in the hospital neonatal intensive care unit (NICU). If your baby is very preterm and the progress of labor cannot be stopped (or if membranes have already ruptured), your doctor may deliver the baby by cesarean section. In certain circumstances, delivery by this method is less harmful to a premature baby than a natural delivery process.

Choosing a Doctor for Your Baby: Pediatrician or Family Practice Physician?

As soon as your baby is born, he or she will need to be examined by a qualified pediatrician or family doctor. If you have used a family practice doctor throughout your pregnancy, he or she can become your baby's doctor as well. If, on the other hand, you are seeing an obstetrician or a midwife, you will need to find a doctor for your baby. Both family practice physicians and pediatricians are medical doctors who have trained for a minimum of three years in their field after attending four years of medical school. Family practice doctors receive extra training in treating patients ranging in age from newborn to elderly, while pediatricians receive specialized training in the diseases and developmental issues of patients from birth through age 21.

Some pediatricians have additional specialized training in neonatology, which is the care of newborns. Your baby will need to see a neonatologist if he or she has a significant illness at birth, has problems with breathing or circulation after birth, is born prematurely, or has a congenital anomaly or birth defect. However, if your baby is born at term and is healthy, he or she is in good hands in the care of either a pediatrician or a family practice physician.

You should research and choose your child's doctor this month if you have not already done so. You do not want to go hunting for a pediatrician after you deliver!

Things to Consider when Choosing Your Baby's Doctor

Your pediatrician or family doctor should be someone you trust implicitly with your baby. So, take the time to research your options by considering the following:

• You can choose a pediatrician who is hospital based and manages the care of newborns and sick children in a hospital. This physician can examine your baby after birth but will *not* be the doctor the child sees after he or she leaves the hospital.

• You can also select a pediatrician who will be your baby's doctor as he or she grows and needs checkups and vaccinations. This doctor will come from the office to see the baby in the hospital after birth.

• Your pediatrician should evaluate your child for growth and development issues and can provide education about how to raise your child in a healthy manner.

• A pediatrician will order the recommended immunizations.

• Your pediatrician will also see your child for common and uncommon childhood illnesses and will be able to prescribe any medications needed.

• Look for a board-certified pediatrician or family practice doctor who has privileges at the hospital of your choice and an office within a reasonable distance from your home.

• Check your insurance coverage to be sure that the physician you prefer is in network.

• Ask friends and relatives about the doctor they use to treat their children. Find out if they feel that their appointments are rushed and if they have problems communicating with their doctor. Ask if their pediatrician is good with children and answers their questions satisfactorily.

- Find out which emergency room your pediatrician uses, since problems can develop on the weekends or during the night.
- Find out if the doctor or a nurse in the office is available by phone to answer questions.
- Before you deliver, see the pediatrician or family practice physician for an interview visit. Remember, you are the consumer, and it is important that you feel comfortable with your child's doctor.

Bear in mind that you may also be able to receive most pediatric medical care from a pediatric nurse practitioner (PNP). Pediatric nurse practitioners earn basic credentials in nursing and then must complete a master's degree with specialization in treating children. A PNP can perform well-child checks, give immunizations, and provide routine pediatric care.

We found that word of mouth was the best way to find a great pediatrician. Ask your friends and family, but don't be shy about hanging around the playground and asking other moms who they use or would recommend. —*Janice, 40, mother of three*

If there is nothing significantly wrong with your child at birth, seeing a family doctor or a PNP is perfectly acceptable. If your child is born with a congenital defect or there is an issue with growth and development, however, you might want to select a board-certified pediatrician instead. If your child has a condition that will require periodic hospitalization, you may want to choose a pediatrician with privileges at a children's hospital, if there is one in your area.

It is critical that your child's healthcare provider is not only knowledgeable but is also a good communicator, both with parents and with children. You want to feel free to ask questions and receive all the information you need to ensure your child's health, and you want to know that the doctor cares deeply about children. If you find yourself uncomfortable with the healthcare provider you have chosen for your child, feel free to change.

Cord Blood Banking

You may have heard or read about cord blood banking. Before making a decision about whether or not to bank your baby's cord blood it will be helpful to understand the reasons to do so as well as the process.

Things to Think About:
Tie Up Loose Ends
What do you have left to purchase for your baby's arrival or to finish setting up your nursery? Now is the time tie up all those loose ends. Look over the list provided in Chapter 9 to make sure you have what you need. In a few weeks, you will have less energy for shopping, and if a complication arises that requires bed rest you will want to be prepared. If your friends have given you a baby shower, don't delay your thank-you notes. You will be somewhat distracted in the near future!

What's So Important about Cord Blood? Stem Cells

The blood in the placenta or umbilical cord is the same as your baby's blood and is rich in immature cells called stem cells. These stem cells exactly match your baby's cells. In addition, they may be a match for the red blood cells and bone marrow cells found in other family members, such as parents or siblings. Stem cells may be used in the treatment of more than 75 diseases, including various types of leukemia and lymphoma. Their effectiveness in treating type 1 diabetes and other conditions is being studied.

Your baby's stem cells have a 75 percent chance of being matched to other siblings' cells and a 50 percent chance of being matched to yours and those of his or her biological father.

Stem cells have the ability to become any type of cell that is missing in the body. The stem cells given by a matched cord blood sample will mature into normal blood and bone marrow cells, and the process can be life-saving if given to a sick but blood-matched recipient.

In short, if your baby has a serious disease, the stem cells in the cord blood you have banked could potentially cure the disease and save the child's life.

How Does Cord Blood Banking Work?

You have two choices: banking cord blood with a private company in a fee-based procedure or donating cord blood to a public bank free of charge.

We decided to donate our baby's cord blood to a public bank. We hoped never to need it but felt it was an easy way to give something back in thanks for our little baby. It felt good to know that even if we never needed it, the blood might help save some other child's life. —*Bernadette, 29, mother of one*

Public or private? Private companies charge a fee to process and store your cord blood. Your health-care provider should be able to provide you with information about cord blood banking and what companies you may wish to contact. When you bank cord blood privately, you pay for the service and it is maintained for the sole use of your family. There is some controversy over whether it is ethical to maintain cord blood in this manner, since the odds of it being needed by your child or another family member are very slight (about 1 in 217 for any individual, up to the age of 70).

You should also be aware that there are public cord blood banks that will take your donation for free, just as if you were donating blood. The idea is to build a cord blood bank that can be used to match any person in need of stem cells. In a public blood bank, you do not retain ownership of the cord blood. Unless there is a family member who is potentially in need of the cord blood, donating it is an excellent option.

Procedure for private banking: If you decide to bank your baby's cord blood privately, you will need to sign up with a reputable cord blood bank and let your healthcare provider know your intentions. The bank will then send you the materials you need for collection of your baby's cord blood. Approximately 75 milliliters of blood will be collected within ten minutes of your baby's birth by "milking" the umbilical cord for blood and Wharton's jelly, a gelatinous substance in the umbilical cord.

Doctors can also remove stem cells from the placenta by drawing blood from the placenta. These are called placental stem cells. The placenta itself can be sent immediately to the laboratory to extract as many stem cells as possible. Find out exactly what the company wants you to do and let your healthcare provider know.

The company you sign up with will ask for a fee to super-freeze the cells of the umbilical cord and placenta and then will charge you "rent" to keep the sample frozen until you might need it.

When you send the blood cells to your chosen company, they may or may not separate out the red blood cells. They will test the stem cells for HLA type, which is a series of identification markers that allow the cells to be matched to a specific individual. Then the cells are frozen in liquid nitrogen, where it is believed they can be viable indefinitely.

There are uses for stem cells that have yet to be determined, but what doctors know for sure is that stem cells are very important and may someday be used to treat an even larger variety of serious illnesses. Your decision to store your baby's stem cells privately depends partly on your belief that they may be potentially useful at some point in your baby's life or that of another family member. There is only one chance to save the contents of the umbilical cord, so it is essential to make the decision well before you deliver.

Procedure for public donation: If you decide to donate cord blood to a public bank, procedures will be somewhat different. Some hospitals participate in public cord blood donation programs, so the first step is to ask whether your chosen hospital does so. If the

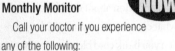

Monthly Monitor

Call your doctor if you experience any of the following:

- A significant decrease in fetal activity that persists for 12 hours or more
- A sudden increase in the amount of fluid you have in your ankles
- A severe backache, whether it is continuous or intermittent
- Uterine contractions that are regular and approximately 1 every 10 minutes
- Weight gain of greater than three pounds in a single week
- Vaginal bleeding
- Fever greater than 101.5°F
- A sudden gush of fluid from your vagina
- Constant abdominal pain
- Shortness of breath, especially if associated with anxiety and chest pain
- Burning on urination or blood in your urine
- Painful, hard veins in your legs
- Pain in the back of your calf
- The onset of a rash, especially if associated with flu-like symptoms

Starting in my third trimester, once a week I gave myself a "baby-break." I'd spend two hours by myself doing absolutely anything I wanted to that did not have to do with being pregnant or with my baby. It was a time just for me to try and be me. It didn't matter if I just napped or took myself to the movies or a bookstore. The idea was to find a mini-respite from all I was going through and feeling. I can't tell you how much those few hours helped me get to the finish line! —*Jill, 38, mother of two*

hospital does participate, they should be able to provide you information about how to proceed. The National Blood Marrow Donor Program (marrow.org) and the National Cord Blood Program (nationalcordbloodprogram .org), among others, offer detailed information about public donation, including what to do if your hospital does not participate in a donation program. Your healthcare provider may also have information about public cord blood donation.

Surprise! There are 10 months of pregnancy!
Pregnant women are prepared for everything
under the sun except that fact! Now I tell all my
pregnant friends right from the beginning, and I
have a campaign going on Facebook!
—*Zena, 31, mother of two*

Chapter 11

Month Nine—Weeks 33 through 36

Yes, it is true—there actually are 10 months of pregnancy. So, although you are in the home stretch, you may feel as if you have a million miles to go! Month nine can be challenging. At this point, it is likely impossible to see your feet or bend to put on your shoes or socks. Some women even have a hard time fitting behind the steering wheel of their car. You may begin to walk with a waddle as you manage the ever-increasing size of your belly.

(Remember: Your baby is now gaining nearly half a pound weekly!) Even if you do not have any fears or concerns about your pregnancy, you may very well feel that you have had enough of being pregnant.

But there is good news, too! Babies born in weeks 33 through 36 have an excellent chance of thriving on their own. They may need a bit of time in a heated incubator with oxygen, a feeding tube in their nose, or a few days

Shoes were the way I kept my maternity wear looking fashionably up to date. I especially loved boots and my platform dress shoes and wedges. They were easy to walk in (I wore lower heels as time went on) and cute! And they always fit, even when my clothes didn't. But when I entered my ninth month, I couldn't bend forward to buckle straps or pull on my boots. Nor could I get them off at the end of the day. At first my husband tried to help me, but we argued nearly every morning because I was so frustrated and annoyed at him—for no reason other than hormones! I didn't like how he pulled this boot too hard or that strap too tight. And I hated how he kept saying, "Just get some shoes you can slip on!" I knew I was tired of being pregnant, but I had never worn flats or slip-on shoes, and I didn't want to start now! One morning I woke up and found a card next to my pillow. On the front was a series of silly cartoons of a pregnant woman trying to tie her shoes—inside my husband had written: "Slip-On Shoes—Just Do It!" He included a gift card to a shoe superstore and the name of a sales clerk whom he had asked to help me when I went in. I laughed so hard I thought I would go into labor. Well, the sales clerk was extremely kind and she did help me find some fashionable shoes I could put on and take off by myself (although I did buy a new pair of boots for after the baby was born). Looking back now, the whole thing was ridiculously funny, and it was hard to believe how stubborn I'd been. But at nine months pregnant, your belly makes it hard to see past everything—even simple solutions to everyday problems! —*Morgan, 35* of monitoring; all in all, however, the odds of survival are greatly increased. Braxton-Hicks contractions are probably the biggest annoyance you will experience, beyond your expanding belly and trouble sleeping!

Many pregnant women find themselves in the throes of "nesting" this month! This is a common phenomenon that compels you to get everything in order for your baby's arrival. From organizing the nursery to frenzied cleaning out of closets, you may find yourself on a mission to systematize and arrange everything in your path!

Keep your chin up, keep exercising, keep eating well to provide your baby with the nutrition he or she still needs, and be positive! You are almost there. In this chapter, we will take a closer look at the following questions:

- How is my baby getting ready for life outside the womb?
- What do I need to know about my cervix and how it will change?
- What is "nesting," and will I experience this?
- What if my baby is in the breech (bottom down) position?
- What is group B strep, and why will I be tested for it? Are nonstress and contraction tests important?
- What happens if I am put on bed rest?
- What is placental abruption?
- What are the dangers of hypertension and preeclampsia?
- How can I prepare for breast-feeding my baby?
- What is superficial phlebitis, and what can I do if I develop this condition?

Your Baby's Development: Growing Strong!

Expect your baby to be energetic this month until the last week, when your baby may simply run out of space to really kick.

Week 33

At this point in your pregnancy, the amniotic fluid is at its greatest volume, so your baby has the maximum amount of fluid to roll around in. The fluid level will stay the same or will gradually decrease until birth. As your baby's brain grows rapidly, its head size increases about ⅜ of an inch in circumference. Finally, your baby's skin will become pink instead of red, due to the fat deposits beneath the skin's surface.

Your baby's sensory system is well developed at this point and your little one can hear, taste, touch, see, and smell. Vision is still cloudy, so instead of sight, your baby is focused on sound—the sounds of your voice, nearby music, your heartbeat, and your stomach gurgling. Your baby is storing iron in his or her liver for use in making red blood cells after birth.

Your baby weighs 4.25 pounds and is about 17.2 inches long from crown to heel. During this month, your baby is about the weight of a large honeydew melon.

Week 34

Your baby has complete newborn reflexes and responses. When he or she is awake, the eyes are open, and when your baby is asleep, the eyes are closed, just as with newborns. There is a gradual acceptance of immune molecules (antibodies) from the mother to the fetus, and immune cells are being made to help the baby get ready for life outside the uterus.

Your infant's muscles are maturing so that your baby's kicks and punches take on new strength. Some kicks may even be painful. The lanugo, or downy hair on your baby's body, is nearly gone, and instead, the vernix—a thick, cheesy, protective substance—is deposited on your baby's skin. This substance makes it appear as though the baby is covered in lard!

Your baby is 17.7 inches long and weighs about 4.75 pounds.

Week 35

According to the March of Dimes, a baby born now would be considered late preterm. It is preferable for a baby to stay in the womb at least another two weeks. While your baby has developed everything it needs for feeding, the suck reflex is not as strong and predictable as it will be at full term. A baby born at week 35 could encounter feeding problems.

Fat continues to be deposited in your baby's body in order for him or her to regulate the body temperature outside the womb. Fat will continue to be deposited until after your baby is born. If you have a 3D ultrasound this week, you will see fat cheeks and fat legs on the monitor.

Your baby continues to have a regular sleep-wake cycle. If your fetus kicks a lot during the night, you could be in for some for some long nights with an active baby!

Your baby weighs 5.25 pounds and is about 18.2 inches long during this week.

Week 36

This week your baby will begin to descend into the birth canal, becoming engaged and putting pressure on the cervix with every Braxton-Hicks contraction. The baby's fat now dimples at the elbows and knees and creases are easily visible around the wrists and neck. The baby's gums are now hard to the touch.

Your baby has certain body positions that he or she favors in the uterus. Fetuses like hanging upside down in most cases, and will prefer to lie on their left or right side. Movement is somewhat diminished this week since there is less room for the baby to be active, but you should still feel regular fetal movements.

Your baby weighs 5.8 pounds and is about 18.7 inches in crown to heel length. It's almost time for your little honeydew melon to be born!

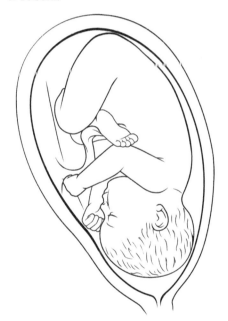

Fetus at 36 weeks of development
At approximately 19 inches and 6 pounds, most 36-week-old fetuses can survive nicely out of the womb. The fetus usually turns into a head-down position for birth; the skin is less wrinkled; the lungs mature and are ready to function on their own; and sleeping patterns develop. The fetus will gain about one-half pound per week this month.

Your Changing Body: It Won't Be Long Now!

Both your uterus and your breasts may start to go into production mode, producing contractions and colostrum, respectively.

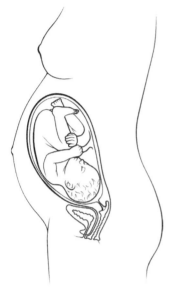

Your changing body: Month nine
It's hard to believe, but your tummy continues to grow! Your breasts may be leaking colostrum, and you may feel enormous and puffy. Remember, you are still beautiful!

More Braxton-Hicks Contractions

Because of the enlarged size and increased sensitivity of the uterus this month, you may experience many more Braxton-Hicks contractions. You may even wonder whether or not you are in labor and could find yourself making a few false labor runs to the hospital or birthing center. (See Chapter 10 for an introduction to Braxton-Hicks contractions and how to distinguish them from true labor.)

Braxton-Hicks contractions do not harm either you or your baby. In fact, they may be

the body's way of softening and thinning out the cervix so that labor, when it happens, will not be as long.

Cervix 101: Understanding Cervical Changes

Your healthcare provider will usually check your cervix this month. Your cervix is a part of your body you probably never thought about prior to pregnancy, but you will become an expert on this body part between now and your baby's birth! To help you understand what your doctor or midwife is telling you about your cervix during your prenatal visits, think of the inside part of the cervix as a tunnel from the vagina to the uterus. This tunnel is about 4 centimeters (a little more than an inch and a half) in depth before

> At the end of my ninth month, I remember starting to have a pain under my right rib. Sometimes it felt like a painful poke and sometimes it was a constant pressure or a jolt. My doctor said it was just the position the baby was in. The sensation was consistent and so annoying, and it lasted the rest of my pregnancy. When my little boy was born, it was obvious what had caused the pain—his feet were huge! (And they still are!) Those feet had been stuck up behind my ribs all that time!
> —*Laura, 35, mother of one*

pregnancy. By the time your baby's head pushes down on the cervix during labor, the "tunnel" will be only a few millimeters thick or what is sometimes called "paper thin" or "completely effaced." All of this effacement

I'd never gotten help from a salesperson to choose my bras. But during my third trimester, my breasts became so large and heavy—and foreign to me!—that I was at a loss. I sheepishly found an older woman at a lingerie shop and asked for help, and am I glad I did! She measured me and knew exactly what I needed. I left in ten minutes with a half dozen of the most comfortable, supportive bras I've ever owned. Some I could use for breast-feeding as well! Ladies, don't be afraid to ask the experts for help! —*Casandra, 34, mother of two*

can happen during labor. In most cases, however, the Braxton-Hicks contractions and the weight of the baby's head will partially efface or thin out the cervix before labor actually occurs. The gradual process of the cervix softening in preparation for the passage of the baby is called ripening of the cervix. Your healthcare provider checks your cervix to see whether you are anywhere near going into labor.

Breast Changes

Believe it or not, your breasts will become even bigger and heavier—so much so you may be more comfortable wearing a bra to bed. This is because your milk glands are expanding in preparation for the possibility that you will be breast-feeding your baby by the end of the next month. There are some soft bras that offer support but are more comfortable than a regular bra for sleeping. Look for "leisure bras" in catalogs or stores.

If you are buying new larger bras for daytime use at this point in pregnancy, you may wish to purchase nursing bras if you plan to breast-feed. They are supportive and will do double-duty after the baby is born. Most types of nursing bras have a clip that opens to allow each cup to drop down. Be sure the clip is easy to open with one hand, since you will be holding your baby, who may be hungry and squirming! The wrong size bra can be uncomfortable or can even cause plugged milk ducts and inflammation, so it may be worth going to a department store where you can be fitted properly.

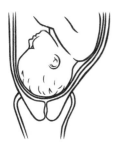

Cervix is not effaced
or dilated yet

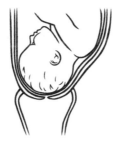

Cervix is fully effaced
and beginning to dilate

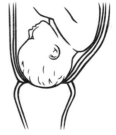

Cervix is completely
effaced and dilated

Cervical effacement and dilation
The cervix becomes shorter and thinner as it effaces, which can begin to happen at this stage of pregnancy. During labor and delivery, the cervix will also dilate (open up) to allow the baby to emerge.

You may notice a feeling of wetness on your bra or shirt from the leakage of a substance called colostrum from your nipples. Colostrum is early breast milk that is yellow in color instead of white like regular breast milk. It is a special type of milk that is high in carbohydrates, protein, and important immune-building antibodies, and low in fat. It is easily digestible and may be the first food your baby takes in after birth. There are only a few tablespoons of colostrum available, but even that little bit helps your baby push stool through its digestive tract and helps his or her body get rid of bilirubin so your baby will be less likely to become jaundiced.

Even if you do not plan to breast-feed, now is the time to think about whether or not you want to try to feed the baby colostrum in the first three to four days of life. Colostrum provides your baby with potentially lifesaving immunoglobulin A, which effectively "vaccinates" your infant from external pathogens that can cause infectious diseases. It also seals up the "holes" in your baby's digestive tract so that he or she is less likely to have allergic reactions to foreign foods and substances.

For Dads and Partners:
Be Attentive
Now is the time to be as attentive to your pregnant partner's needs and moods as you can. Be gentle, helpful, and affirming, and respond to whatever it is she is asking for. This way you can enter the labor and delivery process on the same page and with the same amount of excitement and anticipation. It is all about to be worth it—your baby is almost here!

If you are having issues with colostrum leaking from your breasts, you can purchase breast-feeding pads, which are absorbent circular disks you wear inside your bra. You can find both disposable and washable pads. The pads will soak up any colostrum that leaks and will be useful after your baby is born as well.

Your Emotions: Feathering Your Nest

Any feelings of anxiety or fear you may have been experiencing may be giving way to immense excitement and the anticipation of meeting your child! Your baby is almost at his or her due date, and you have done an amazing job caring for yourself and your little one all these nine months! You can congratulate yourself and relax. Nature will be taking her course soon!

Nesting

Get ready for one last burst of energy! Many pregnant women at the end of their third trimester begin to feel an intense urge to "nest." Nesting is believed to be an innate instinct common to many higher animals. In humans, it involves the urge to clean and organize your house, perfect the nursery, and buy anything you think you will need for your home or baby by the time the birth occurs.

Nesting instincts can be mild or intense but always result in a very productive and creative period of time. Nesting also provides a distraction from any feelings of apprehension you may have about giving birth and keeps you busy these last weeks of pregnancy when there is not much left to do but wait! You

My wife and I both read about nesting, but I thought it was a bunch of hooey until I came home from work one night and she was on her hands and knees cleaning every cabinet in the kitchen. Everything we owned was on the floor and she was scrubbing, reorganizing, and tossing things out. I didn't think she should be exerting herself like that, but she bit my head off when I mentioned it. For the next two weeks, I only got involved when she asked me to move something or throw something out. When it was all over, our house had never been so clean and organized. My advice to all those husbands and partners: Nesting is no joke! Stay out of the way and let it happen! —*Alexander, 33, dad of two*

might find yourself cleaning your home from top to bottom, sterilizing floors, reorganizing closets, and throwing out old items you no longer use. You might empty and scrub your refrigerator, then restock it by turning into the Magic Chef, cooking and freezing things in large quantities. You may have an unstoppable urge to do all the laundry in the house, pre-address your baby announcements, or sew curtains, quilts, or new baby clothes!

Whatever form nesting takes for you, you will probably have some urge to clean, organize, or create during this month. Know that these are normal instincts that will help you feel more confident and prepared for the upcoming birth of your baby. If you don't experience nesting, don't worry. Every woman is different.

Your Prenatal Visit: Meet the Whole Team

By now, you are familiar with your healthcare provider and you probably feel reassured that your familiar doctor or midwife will deliver your baby. But if your healthcare provider works in a group practice, someone else may be on call when you are in labor, and another professional in the practice may deliver your baby. Often these types of practices have "meet the doctors" evenings where all doctors in the practice gather to meet moms-to-be and their partners and tell everyone a little about themselves. This way, each pregnant woman will be somewhat familiar with the doctor they may encounter at the hospital. Find out your clinic's practices so you know for sure.

At your prenatal visits this month, your healthcare provider will obtain a urinalysis to check for sugar or infection in the urine. You will also have the routine measurement of your uterus, which should measure 33 to 36 centimeters from your pubic symphysis (pubic bone) to the top of your uterus. The doctor or midwife will check the fetal heart tones. Your cervix will be checked for the possibility of early effacement (thinning out) or dilation (opening up), signs of possible preterm labor.

Breech Babies

About 25 percent of all fetuses are in the breech position at 28 weeks' gestation. This percentage falls rapidly over the next 12 weeks so that by 40 weeks, only about 3 to 4 percent of all babies are breech. The incidence of breech babies is greater if you are

I was determined to have a natural birth, so when my doctor said my baby was breech I was devastated. She recommended a C-section but I wanted to try to have the baby turned. Well, I should have listened to her because the procedure caused me to go into labor and I had an emergency C-section that day! My advice would be to know what you want but be flexible as circumstances arise.

—Sandra, 43, mother of two

carrying multiples. Breech births are also more common if there is too much or too little fluid in the uterus, if a baby has a physical birth defect, if the uterus is misshapen or there is a placenta previa, or if the mother has had a previous cesarean section.

If your baby gets entrapped in a breech presentation, your healthcare provider will generally advise you to have a cesarean section. This is because vaginal breech deliveries are more complicated. The head becomes the last part to exit the woman's vagina, and because it is the largest part of the baby, the baby's head can become stuck. If there is a delay in the emergence of the head, the baby will be without adequate oxygenation and can suffer from birth asphyxia. The umbilical cord may also be pinched when the baby is in the birth canal, which can also lead to oxygen deprivation of the fetus. Most doctors feel that a cesarean section is preferable. The American Congress of Obstetricians and Gynecologists states that the decision about how to deliver a baby in the breech position may depend on the experience of the healthcare provider,

hospital protocols, and the mother's decision after being informed of the increased risks to the baby.

External Cephalic Version (ECV)

Some doctors and midwives can perform a manual maneuver that can turn a breech baby around. This is called an external cephalic version (ECV) or simply external version. It is recommended that this be tried in most situations where the baby is not head down in late pregnancy. ECV is more successful when performed earlier in pregnancy (at about 36 weeks), but the baby may turn around again. ECV can then be tried another time. ECV is successful more than half of the time, so it is definitely worth trying unless there is some condition or complication that would make it unsafe.

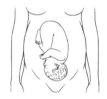

External cephalic version
During external cephalic version, an attempt is made to turn the baby head down to be in the best position for delivery.

An ECV is usually done at 36 to 37 weeks, though it has been used in some cases during labor as long as there has been no rupture of membranes. A doctor or midwife must perform ECV in a hospital where an emergency cesarean section can be performed if fetal distress develops.

How ECV works: A technician does an ultrasound to show the position of the fetus before and after a version takes place. During the procedure, the fetus is continually monitored for heart rate, and you will be given an IV or subcutaneous medication such as terbutaline that allows the uterus to relax and prevents contractions. Sometimes epidural anesthesia is used to block the sensation of pain.

When the uterus has relaxed, the healthcare provider uses both hands externally to turn the baby from a breech position into a cephalic or head-down position. You will be mildly to moderately uncomfortable during the procedure. The presence and assistance of a doula during ECV may help the mother to tolerate the procedure with less discomfort. The procedure is stopped when the baby is in the correct position or if fetal distress occurs. After the ECV, both you and your baby will be monitored for a few hours and then allowed to go home.

Risks of ECV: External cephalic versions work about 58 percent of the time. Risks associated with an ECV are low. Possible risks include: an abruption or tearing of the placenta, damage to the umbilical cord, excess squeezing of the umbilical cord, rupture of membranes, and the onset of labor. In addition, if you are Rh negative, you will need a shot of Rhogam after the ECV attempt.

Other Methods of Turning a Breech Baby

There are some additional methods to attempt to coax a fetus to turn head down in time for delivery. There is research that suggests the chiropractic technique called the Webster technique may help to turn the baby. In addition, doulas and midwives may suggest certain positions that a woman can use at home to encourage the baby to change position.

When ECV Can Be Performed and When It Cannot

Your healthcare provider will consider ECV for a fetus in the breech position as long as there are no factors that would contraindicate this procedure. The decision to perform or forego an ECV is based largely on the following factors:

Requirements for an ECV

- You must be at least 36 weeks along. Any earlier and the fetus has a high likelihood of turning back around to the breech position.
- Only one fetus can be present.
- The fetus has not engaged a part of its body into the pelvis. It is too difficult to get the buttocks up and out of the lower pelvis.
- There must be enough amniotic fluid present in which to move the baby.
- Version works most successfully on women who have been pregnant before. A previous pregnancy makes the abdomen more flexible.
- The baby can be in the frank breech position (buttocks down, legs straight up), the complete breech position (buttocks down, legs folded at knee near the buttock), or the footling breech position (both feet down).

Why an ECV Cannot Be Attempted

- A cesarean delivery is needed for some other reason.
- The bag of waters has already ruptured.
- The mother has a heart condition that prevents the use of terbutaline.
- The baby has a known birth defect.
- There are two or more babies in the uterus.
- There is an abnormal uterine shape.
- The fetus' head is hyperextended.
- There is too little fluid around the baby.
- The umbilical cord is noted to be around the fetus' neck.

Group B Streptococcus (GBS)

Group B streptococcus (GBS) is a bacterial infection that can live in a woman's rectum and vagina. It is found in 25 percent of all women but rarely causes any symptoms. During pregnancy, your baby is protected from getting GBS because of the mucus plug in the cervix and the amniotic sac surrounding the fetus. However, during the birth process, a woman with GBS in her body may pass this infection onto her newborn, leading to the possibility of potentially serious consequences for the baby.

Do not be too worried if you do have GBS. It is easily treatable with intravenous antibiotics given to you during the labor and delivery process. It does not need to be treated before labor. Having the antibiotics during labor will temporarily kill off the GBS in your system, and your baby will have less risk of contracting the bacteria while passing through the birth canal. The strep bacteria then usually come back after you deliver, but they do not harm you or your baby after birth.

Prenatal Testing: Group B Strep Test

You will likely have two and possibly three prenatal visits this month. You will have a urinalysis. Many women also have a group B strep test this month. If you have not had this test by week 36, ask your healthcare provider to perform one. In addition, women with third trimester complications may have extra ultrasounds this month as well as nonstress tests.

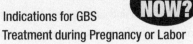

Indications for GBS Treatment during Pregnancy or Labor

The following conditions may be associated with GBS infection, and therefore you will be given antibiotics as a precaution:

- Rupture of membranes 18 hours or more before delivery
- Onset of labor or rupture of membranes before 37 weeks' gestation
- A bladder infection with a urine culture that is positive for GBS
- Having a baby in the past who had a GBS infection
- Fever during labor

The GBS Test

About 1 in every 2000 babies in the U.S. get GBS per year. Even though this neonatal infection isn't very common, the Centers for Disease Control and Prevention recommend routine screening of all pregnant women within five weeks of delivery (usually between weeks 35 and 36 of gestation). The results usually become available within 24 to 36 hours.

For a group B strep test, your doctor will take a swab of both the vagina and the rectum in order to pick up possible traces of the bacterium. The swab is then taken to the laboratory and attempts are made to culture out the group B streptococcus bacterium.

Fetal Tests

This month, your healthcare provider may schedule tests to monitor fetal health if you have a complicated pregnancy or the provider wants to determine how well your baby might be able to handle a preterm delivery.

Fetal Nonstress Tests

If you have a complication of pregnancy or if your healthcare provider wants to check the status of your baby, you may be given a fetal nonstress test. A nonstress test measures your baby's heart rate, heart reactivity, and movement. Nonstress tests are often done at least once per week in high-risk pregnancies.

The test itself is simple and noninvasive. Your healthcare provider may first order an ultrasound to check for the presence of small and large fetal movements and breathing movements of your baby and to check the amount of amniotic fluid. The umbilical cord blood flow may be measured as well.

Next you may be asked to drink fruit juice, which temporarily increases your blood sugar and that of your baby and encourages fetal movements. A technician will strap a contraction monitor and a fetal heart tone monitor around your belly. These are attached to a machine that records the baby's heart rate and your contractions over time. You will also be given a device to press every time you feel a fetal movement. The device makes marks that show up on the strip that comes out of the machine.

Ideally, when your baby moves, his or her heart rate goes up. The line on the strip that measures the heart rate should match up with marks you make indicating that the baby moved. The test goes on this way, measuring movements, heart rate, and any contractions you might have, for about 20 to 30 minutes. If the test shows a normal rise in heart rate with the baby's movements, your healthcare provider will call this test reassuring, and you can probably go home.

Contraction Stress Tests

In some situations, such as when the healthcare provider is not sure that the fetus will tolerate labor, a contraction stress test is ordered. This is similar to the nonstress test, except that you will have several contractions stimulated (by medication or by nipple stimulation) to see how the fetus tolerates the few contractions created during the test.

Ideally, you want to have a negative test. This means that there were no reductions in the fetal heart rate with the contractions and indicates the fetus should tolerate labor well. A positive result means that your baby may not tolerate contractions during actual labor. There is a high rate (up to 30 percent) of false positives, which create concern even though the baby is actually okay. Therefore, this test is not commonly performed.

Nutrition Tip:

Now You're Eating for Two

We said earlier in this book that you are not eating for two—but at this point, you actually are! Your baby now weighs five to six pounds, and nutrition is as important as it ever was. You may find it difficult to eat a full meal at this point, as your baby-filled uterus is taking up so much space and encroaching on your stomach. A good strategy is to eat small meals throughout the day that include plenty of fruits, vegetables, whole grains, and lean meats or fish. Also, keep taking your prenatal vitamins. You should continue taking vitamins if you decide to breast-feed, so stock up now!

Bed Rest

If you have a medical condition like hypertension or diabetes, or if you have a pregnancy-related condition like multiples, placenta previa (see Chapter 8), or partial abruption of the placenta (to be discussed later in this chapter), you might be placed on bed rest. Bed rest can be at home or in the hospital, and may last from a few weeks to a month or more—until the baby is considered developed enough to be delivered.

Your doctor may prescribe bed rest for some of the following reasons:

- Takes pressure off your cervix, reducing the chance of premature contractions, preterm labor, and miscarriage
- Increases blood flow to the placenta to enhance nutrients and oxygen getting to your baby
- Helps your heart and kidneys function more efficiently, improving symptoms of high blood pressure
- Slows the progression of preeclampsia
- Reduces further complications from a high-risk pregnancy

At first, the idea of bed rest (and being waited on hand and foot) may sound like just what the doctor ordered, but after a few days of literally not moving, the reality of what the doctor actually ordered will set in—it is a tremendous challenge to live your normal life when you are not able to move around. But remember your PMA (positive mental attitude)! There are ways to make your time on bed rest both productive and enjoyable.

First, let's take a look at the types of bed rest your doctor might prescribe, then we will talk about things you can do to make the best of your bed rest.

Modified Bed Rest

Bed rest at home is usually considered modified bed rest. This means you must be in bed or lying on the couch for most of the day with brief breaks for going to the bathroom, making a quick meal, or going to the doctor's office. If it takes a lot of effort to go to the doctor's office, such as having to take a bus, you should make other arrangements for getting to the doctor's visits, even if it

I'm the epitome of a type A personality. So when my doctor said I had to go on strict bed rest, I burst into tears. And then I got organized! I literally scheduled my entire day, including 30 minutes at 5:30 p.m. to plan the next day. I included work time, computer shopping time, meal times, pedicures and manicures, lunch with my friends, movie time, reading time, nap time, phone calls, even date night—you name it! And I followed that schedule to the letter! Even though I couldn't move, I still felt like my productive, organized, type A self—and it really helped! —*Anastasia, 34, mother of twins*

means taking a cab. You cannot go to work, do household chores, or pick up kids from school. Use of stairs should be limited.

Strict Bed Rest

This usually means you will have to stay horizontal for the entire day, except for trips to the bathroom or for taking a brief shower.

You will have to get your spouse, partner, friend, or relative (or hire someone) to help you with meals, cleaning, and child-related responsibilities if you have kids. If you have a two-story home, you will have to choose which floor to stay on and then stay there! You will have to keep everything you need (like food, reading material, beverages, and your laptop) within arm's reach.

Hospital Bed Rest

If you or your baby needs constant monitoring, or if you need IV medication because preterm labor has already set in, your doctor may put you on total bed rest in a hospital. The nursing staff may allow you to go to the restroom or you may have to use a bedside commode or bedpan. This type of bed rest may be most challenging, since you do not

Making the Most of Bed Rest

Here are some ways to help you feel productive, comfortable, and happy during your bed rest:

- Make use of the Internet for grocery shopping and home delivery, purchasing items for your baby and your nursery, and accessing DVDs, books, and magazines.
- Have meals delivered from your favorite local eateries, if the budget will allow.
- Take up a new hobby like knitting, scrapbooking, or crocheting.
- Read books and magazines you do not normally read.
- Entertain by having friends or family come over to hang out with you in your chosen room! Pick a theme—like movie night or taco night—and ask them to bring over corresponding food and beverages.
- Be sure to get dressed every day, do your makeup, and keep your hair pretty. Looking good always makes you feel good! Do not give up just because you are on bed rest.
- Ask your partner to give you a pedicure or manicure, or splurge and have a professional come to you!
- Make a schedule for your day. Having a routine is a sure way to keep your day moving and have things to look forward to.
- Eat well and avoid eating too much or too little. You and your baby still need nutritious food, but overeating will simply add unwanted pounds.
- Ask your doctor what exercises you can do while lying down—stretching and using light weights for arm exercises can keep your blood circulating and lessen loss of strength.
- Stay connected to family, friends, and work through email, texting, and phone calls. Keep your computer and phone—and related chargers—at hand.
- There are now online bed rest support groups. Connecting with other women in the same situation can really boost your mood, and you may get practical tips from those who have been there.
- When friends and family offer to help, let them. Make a list of chores that need to be done, and when someone says, "What can I do to help?" find out how much time they are willing to devote and then make a specific suggestion.

Remember: Like everything else you have done during your pregnancy, bed rest is another way you are taking excellent care of yourself and your infant. This too shall pass, and you can rest easy knowing you have done everything possible to ensure the best for your baby!

have access to anything in your home unless it is brought to you.

Placental Abruption

A placental abruption is the premature separation of the placenta from the wall of the uterus. It can happen in the second or third trimester but is more common in the third trimester. It can be caused by a fall, an accident, a strike to the abdomen, or from a sudden loss of volume of the uterus, such as when the first of two twins is born. Placental abruption can also be caused by high blood pressure, smoking, or drugs such as cocaine. It can also happen spontaneously. A woman who has had a previous placental abruption is more likely to have another one.

Placental abruption, which can be total or partial, is very dangerous for the fetus and mother alike. Placental abruption occurs in approximately 6.5 per 1000 births.

Things to Think About:
Organize Your Diaper Bag
While you are in the throes of nesting, it is a great time to organize your diaper bag for when baby comes home. First, purchase a light, functional (and attractive!) diaper bag and fill it with diapers, bags for soiled diapers, wipes, a sleeper, two snap-crotch t-shirts, pacifiers, an extra baby bottle, an individual sterilized bottle (or two) of baby formula or water, nursing pads, bulb syringe, bibs, and a receiving blanket. You may want to add a thin folding pad to serve as a clean place to change your baby when you are out. Your diaper bag will go with you (or your partner) everywhere for many months, and you want to stock and restock it properly.

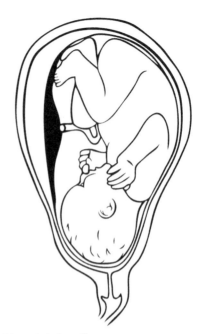

Placental abruption
A placental abruption, in which the placenta separates from the uterine wall, can endanger the fetus and the mother.

Risks Factors for Placental Abruption
You are more likely to have a placental abruption if you

- have a bleeding disorder
- smoke cigarettes
- use caffeine
- drink more than 14 alcoholic beverages during your entire pregnancy
- have high blood pressure
- are older than 35 years of age
- have fibroids in the uterus
- are pregnant with multiples
- have a history of placental abruption

Symptoms of Placental Abruption
Symptoms of placental abruption include

- severe pain in the abdomen
- frequent contractions

- a severe backache
- vaginal bleeding
- constant contraction

If you are experiencing any of these symptoms, regardless of your risk factors, seek medical attention right away. Even if you are wrong, it is always best to err on the side of caution. If you are bleeding heavily, call an ambulance.

Care for Placental Abruption

Once at the emergency room or with your healthcare provider, the fetal heart rate will be monitored for any signs of distress, and you will be given blood transfusions and/or intravenous fluids in order to restore your circulation. If there is any sign of maternal or fetal distress, the baby will be delivered by cesarean section. The likelihood of maternal and fetal complications increases with situations involving a closed cervix, a delay in diagnosis, excessive blood loss, hidden bleeding within the uterus, and the absence of labor.

Hypertension Related to Pregnancy

Hypertension, or high blood pressure, that occurs during pregnancy is a relatively common condition, usually occurring in the latter half of the second trimester and in the third trimester of pregnancy. It can restrict the fetus' blood circulation and prevent the fetus from receiving enough oxygen. Hypertension may present in different ways. The first is simply high blood pressure as noted by your healthcare provider.

A normal blood pressure is below 140/90; however, most pregnant women have blood pressure readings much lower than that, in the range of 100/60 to 120/80. Blood pressures that are technically within the normal range but are at least 20 points higher than those in the first trimester are considered too high, and the healthcare provider may consider that to be hypertension related to pregnancy.

Forms of Hypertension in Pregnancy

Hypertension or high blood pressure during pregnancy may or may not be part of preeclampsia, a serious condition that includes both high blood pressure and protein in the urine (see below). Here are some of the ways hypertension can manifest during pregnancy:

Gestational hypertension: This is a condition in which you have high blood pressure in pregnancy; however, you have no evidence of excessive amounts of protein in the urine. Gestational hypertension can turn into preeclampsia over time if left untreated.

Chronic high blood pressure: This is high blood pressure that occurs during the first 20 weeks of pregnancy and lasts more than three months after the delivery of the baby. Chronic hypertension usually existed before pregnancy but may have gone undetected.

Preeclampsia: You have high blood pressure and protein in your urine, associated with increased swelling and other symptoms (noted below).

Preeclampsia superimposed on chronic hypertension: This is when you have preexisting high blood pressure that is worsened over the pregnancy and is associated with protein in the urine.

Preeclampsia

You will be diagnosed with preeclampsia if you have both high blood pressure and protein in your urine (another reason why a urinalysis is conducted at prenatal visits). Preeclampsia occurs in about 2 to 6 percent of all pregnancies. Untreated preeclampsia can be dangerous or even fatal to the mother and fetus. It can damage the mother's liver, kidneys, and brain.

The only real cure for preeclampsia is to deliver the baby. If your baby is too under-developed to be born, your doctor will manage your condition until your baby reaches a reasonable level of maturity or your condition worsens.

Signs and Symptoms of Preeclampsia

The following are key symptoms of preeclampsia:

- An elevated blood pressure reading that persists after resting for a period of time
- Too much protein in the urine
- Severe headache
- Visual changes such as a brief loss of vision, sensitivity to light, and blurry vision
- Upper abdominal pain, usually in the right upper portion of the abdomen
- An increase in nausea or vomiting
- Dizziness
- Low urine output
- Weight gain of more than two pounds in a single week
- Swelling in the hands and face (but this happens in normal pregnancy as well, so it is not an indication of preeclampsia in the absence of other symptoms)

Risk Factors for Preeclampsia

Risk factors for preeclampsia include the following:

- This is your first pregnancy.
- You or a family member has had pre-eclampsia in the past.
- You are you are younger than 20 or older than 40 during the pregnancy.
- You were considered obese prior to getting pregnant.
- You have more than one baby in your uterus at the same time (twins or triplets).
- Your baby was conceived with a different father than previous pregnancies.
- There has been a long time between pregnancies.
- You have gestational diabetes or you had diabetes prior to pregnancy.
- You have a chronic medical condition, such as migraine headaches, hypertension prior to pregnancy, diabetes, rheumatoid arthritis, lupus, or kidney problems.

Potential Complications of Preeclampsia

Most women with preeclampsia have normal babies without health problems, but if your preeclampsia is particularly severe, it can carry a risk to both you and the fetus.

Preterm delivery: You may have to deliver your baby early, leading to a preterm birth.

Placental abruption: Any form of hyper-tension can lead to placental abruption, or separation of the placenta from the uterus, as discussed earlier in this chapter. This can lead to serious complications that threaten your life and the life of your unborn baby.

HELLP syndrome: Preeclampsia may be associated with a condition called HELLP syndrome, which stands for hemolysis (H), or the breakdown of red blood cells; elevated liver protein (EL); and low platelet count (LP). When you have preeclampsia, your doctor will order a complete blood count (including a platelet count) and check liver enzymes. If you have pain in the right upper portion of your abdomen, nausea, vomiting, and a headache, you could have HELLP syndrome.

Risk of heart disease: Women who have preeclampsia are at a significantly elevated risk for heart disease, stroke, and blood clots in later life. Researchers believe that these conditions are not caused by preeclampsia, but are the result of underlying factors that make preeclampsia more likely. If you have preeclampsia, you have additional reasons to be sure that you adhere to a healthy lifestyle after pregnancy and have regular monitoring of your blood pressure and other risk factors for heart attack and stroke.

Eclampsia: Preeclampsia can lead to a much more severe condition called eclampsia. Eclampsia usually only occurs when preeclampsia is left untreated. The symptoms of eclampsia include severe headache, visual changes, a change in mental status, seizures, coma, and brain damage—all of which can affect both you and your baby. This is an important reason for regular prenatal visits, because preeclampsia that is caught and treated early will usually not harm you or your baby and will not develop into eclampsia.

Treatment for Preeclampsia

The best treatment for preeclampsia is to deliver the baby. If this is not possible because it is too early in pregnancy, and your medical condition is stable enough, you may need to be treated with bed rest, frequent blood pressure readings at home, and medications to lower your blood pressure. You should see the doctor every two weeks beginning at 20 weeks instead of 28 weeks if you have had preeclampsia in the past.

Exercise Idea:
Break Exercise into Smaller Increments

It may be harder to do, but keep moving! As your due date approaches, your physical fitness is as important as ever. Being as strong and healthy as possible for labor and delivery can only help you have a smoother experience. You still need to get in 30 minutes of exercise a day at least four times a week. You do not have to do the 30 minutes all in one go—divide your time into 10- or 15-minute increments if it is easier or more convenient. Walking is still a great option if other forms of exercise have become too cumbersome. Keep up what you are doing and congratulate yourself for getting this far! Regular exercise is a challenge for many people—let alone pregnant women. Great job—you are almost there!

Breast-feeding Preparedness

According to a recent study by the Centers for Disease Control (CDC), 75 percent of American infants were breast-fed at birth. By six months, only 45 percent were still being breast-fed, and 22 percent were breast-fed at 12 months. A national health goal is to increase these numbers, which the CDC states are low because of a variety of factors, from hospital policies to lack of state legislation supporting breast-feeding.

If you are interested in breast-feeding, advance preparation will increase your chance of being successful.

During pregnancy, the breasts prepare themselves by increasing in size. They begin to secrete colostrum (the very first milk), which may be noticed "leaking" between the fifth and sixth month of your pregnancy. This month of pregnancy is a good time to consider whether you want to breast-feed your infant.

Benefits of Breast-feeding

Your decision to breast-feed depends on your beliefs about the health benefits to your baby and your own personal comfort. Breast-

What You Will Need for Breast-feeding

You should consider having these items available by the time you deliver if you are choosing to breast-feed:

- An electric or manual breast pump
- Lanolin cream (to soothe sore nipples)
- Storage bags for breast milk
- Bottles for expressed breast milk
- Several good nursing bras
- Nursing pads
- A breast-feeding lap pillow, usually shaped like a half-circle (you place the pillow around your middle and it helps you hold your baby comfortably for breast-feeding).

feeding is certainly easier if you are able to be at home with your infant, at least for a while. If you are going back to work soon after the birth, you can still breast-feed by pumping breast milk at regular intervals during your day and refrigerating the milk. Breast-feeding is an excellent way to help keep your baby healthy throughout his or her first year.

The following are some benefits of breast-feeding:

- Breast milk contains valuable antibodies that help protect your baby from disease.
- Breast milk provides the perfect blend of proteins and fat for your baby, with a greatly reduced risk of allergic reaction.
- Babies digest breast milk relatively easily.
- Breast-feeding releases the hormone oxytocin, which helps the uterus contract and decreases the amount of bleeding you will have after your baby's birth.
- Breast-feeding is considered a good way to bond with your infant. As the sole provider of your baby's food, you can begin to feel the importance of your presence in the baby's life.
- Breast-feeding delivers some of the calories you eat to your baby, so it is easier to get back to your pre-pregnancy weight.
- Breast-feeding is convenient! You will not have to get up in the middle of the night to mix bottles of formula.

How to Prepare for Breast-feeding

First, take a look at your breasts in the mirror. Notice how the skin of the nipples has darkened. Are your nipples flat, inverted (sucked into the breast), or sticking out above the rest of the breast? If your nipples stick out, you are in good shape for breast-feeding as the baby can latch onto the nipple and areola (the

Be sure to use lanolin cream as soon as you begin breast-feeding. Don't wait for soreness to occur. I didn't know any better and my nipples were so cracked and dry that I was in tears when my baby breast-fed. The cream worked, but it took a few weeks for my nipples to heal and adjust to their new purpose. Stock up on some lanolin before you give birth—an ounce of prevention really is worth a pound of cure!

—*Tiffany, 39, mother of two*

pigmented area around the nipple) without difficulty. If your nipples are flat, do they push out or suck in when you pinch the nipple? Can you get your inverted nipple to push outward?

If you have a flat or inverted nipple, you can attempt to get it out by means of a process called "rolling the nipple." Basically, you encourage the nipple to stick out and then roll it between your thumb and forefinger for a few minutes several times a day. This can train your nipple to protrude so your baby can latch on.

The La Leche League is an international organization to promote breast-feeding. Local chapters hold meetings, and pregnant women are welcome. These meetings usually include a number of nursing moms, so they provide an opportunity to learn about breast-feeding from women who are doing it.

Lactation consultants can also help you prepare to breast-feed. You can find a lactation consultant through your hospital, health insurance, healthcare provider, or the La Leche League. Your lactation consultant will look at your breasts and will make recom-

mendations about what you can do now to be prepared for breast-feeding. She may offer you a special shield that fits over the nipple and areola so that the nipple is sticking out more when you breast-feed for the first few times. After a while, though, you will not need the shield.

If you are living on a restricted income, you may be eligible for breast-feeding supplies such as breast pumps and shields, as well as supplemental food packages and breast-feeding support from peer counselors, from the Women, Infants, and Children (WIC) program. You do not have to be destitute to qualify for WIC, so if your finances are limited,

Monthly Monitor

Call your doctor if you experience any of the following:

- Fever greater than 101.5°F
- Contractions that are regular, increasing in intensity, and that are 10 minutes apart or less
- A lack of fetal movement over a half hour (drink juice or eat something sugary to promote fetal activity if you are concerned)
- Diminished fetal movement over a 24-hour period
- Vaginal bleeding
- Intermittent back pain that occurs every 10 minutes or less
- Steady and significant uterine or abdominal pain
- A hard, painful, and red lump beneath the skin of your legs
- Shortness of breath that comes on suddenly
- Excessive swelling or weight gain
- Changes in vision

it is worth checking to see if you are eligible. Your county health department should be able to provide you with more information about WIC.

Some survivors of sexual abuse have concerns about breast-feeding because they are worried it may trigger traumatic memories. Working with a lactation consultant or a doula who is knowledgeable about trauma-informed care can help you to feel more confident and less worried about breast-feeding.

Remember: A woman of any breast size can successfully nurse her infant! Even if you have small breasts, you should be able to breast-feed without difficulty or with help those first few weeks from a lactation consultant.

Superficial Phlebitis

Superficial phlebitis is a blood clot that forms in the superficial veins of the legs. It is a common pregnancy-related condition, although you can get it when you are not pregnant. If you have had superficial phlebitis in the past (before you got pregnant), there is a higher likelihood that you will get it during pregnancy.

Causes of Superficial Phlebitis

The following can cause superficial phlebitis in pregnancy:

- Low blood flow in the veins of the legs from the weight of the uterus on the vena cava (the large abdominal vein)
- Standing for long hours
- Increased levels of estrogen associated with pregnancy
- Hereditary clotting disorders

In your body and in particular your legs, you have both deep veins and superficial

Extending Pregnancy for Optimal Outcomes: Weeks 33 through 38

Although you do not have complete control over when your baby is born, the following is a general guideline for the delivery of healthy babies. If you are having triplets, your doctor will want you to get to at least 32 to 33 weeks before delivering them by cesarean section. If you are having twins, doctors would like you to get to approximately 37 to 38 weeks before delivery. Ideally all babies would remain in the uterus until 37 to 38 weeks of gestation. At 38 weeks, babies can normally survive birth and be expected to breathe on their own, eat from the breast or bottle, and maintain their own body temperature. Be aware of any signs of preterm labor this month (see Chapter 10 for details) and call your healthcare provider immediately if you are at all concerned. If the labor cannot be stopped during this month, the healthcare provider will likely go ahead and deliver the baby, relying on the skill of the pediatrician or neonatologist to care for the late preterm baby you will be having.

veins. The deep veins generally cannot be seen. Superficial veins can usually be seen and felt. For example, the superficial veins in your arms and hands are the ones technicians draw blood from.

A blood clot in the deep vein is called deep vein thrombosis (DVT), which was discussed in Chapter 7, under "Traveling while Pregnant." DVT is dangerous because a piece of clot can break off and travel to the lungs, causing severe complications.

I was three weeks from my due date when I went for a walk one afternoon alone. A new mother walked by with her sleeping infant in the stroller. She looked at me said, "It's so much more wonderful than you can even imagine!" and she walked on. My baby kicked and I felt a surge of joy I cannot even describe. My final weeks of pregnancy were filled with sweet anticipation. And now I know just how right that new mom had been! —*Jessica, 30, mother of one*

Superficial phlebitis is uncomfortable but unlikely to cause severe problems. While superficial phlebitis is not inherently dangerous, it could signal that you have a clotting problem or that you have a hidden DVT at the same time. Superficial phlebitis can also lead to infection in the vein, which requires additional treatment.

Signs You Have Superficial Phlebitis

Superficial phlebitis looks like a red or purple hard vein that can be felt beneath the skin. Even if the phlebitis is not infected, it will be red, warm, and painful due to inflammation in the area. The pain may come on suddenly or develop gradually.

The likelihood of getting superficial phlebitis increases throughout pregnancy and persists until about six weeks after the baby is born. During pregnancy and in the weeks beyond, the estrogen in the body makes it more likely that clots will form in places where blood flow is poor.

Treatment for Superficial Phlebitis

If you think you might have superficial phlebitis, see your healthcare provider as soon as possible so he or she can confirm the diagnosis. After examining you, the provider may perform blood tests to see if there is an infection within or around the clot. If the doctor suspects an infection, you will be given antibiotics. You will be encouraged to put heat on the affected area, and you may also be given a nonsteroidal, anti-inflammatory medication if your healthcare provider feels that the benefits outweigh the risks.

As you recover, it is also recommended that you walk as much as you can and that you avoid sitting for long periods of time with your legs down, such as on a long airplane flight. You should use heat for about half an hour and then get up and walk around as much as you can for another 30 to 60 minutes before applying heat again. Keep your feet up as much as you are able.

Hemorrhoids

Hemorrhoids are nothing more than superficial veins, and they can develop superficial phlebitis as well. If you have little lumps around your anus during pregnancy, those are likely external hemorrhoids. If you experience pain and a feeling of hardness in one or more of those lumps, see the doctor or go to the emergency room. The doctor might lance the clotted hemorrhoid to remove the clot. You will need to take warm baths on a regular basis to allow this type of superficial phlebitis to heal.

By the time I hit my due date, I felt like I'd been pregnant for 40 months instead of 40 weeks! I think nature designed it that way so women could care less how painful labor was—they'll go through anything just to have that baby out! —*Gail, 37, mother of two*

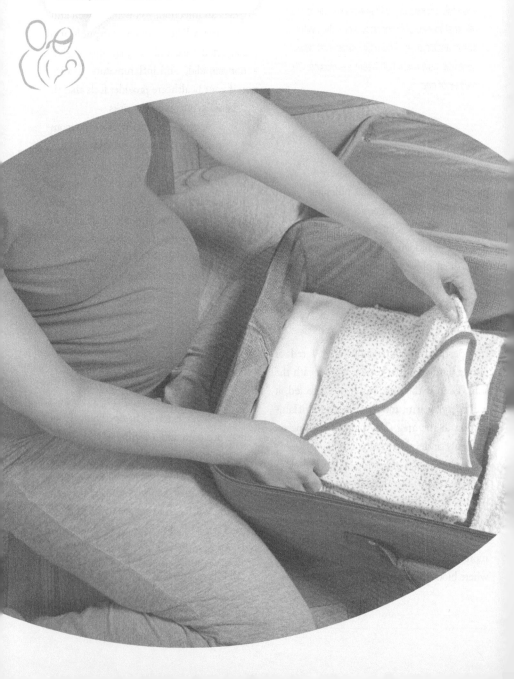

Chapter 12

Month 10—Weeks 37 through 40

Yes, it is month 10! (We mentioned it last chapter so you would not be so shocked to find yourself still pregnant while reading this one!) The average length of human gestation is about 259 to 294 days. If a month is about 30 days long, then average gestation is 8.6 to 9.8 months. Add the two weeks at the beginning when your body is just getting ready for conception, and you have a 10-month pregnancy.

The good news is that your baby is considered full term at this point and can thrive outside the womb on his or her own. You have probably completed your labor and delivery classes and have your birth plan in place. If you have not completed your birth plan, refer back to Chapter 9 for guidance in creating one. Be sure to share your plan with your healthcare provider so you can make any changes necessary based on his or her advice and the rules at your chosen hospital or birthing center.

You may have been on bed rest for conditions related to your pregnancy or preexisting medical conditions. In some cases, if your baby is doing well inside the uterus,

I vividly remember the moment I felt completely "done" with being pregnant! I was in the shower and my belly felt so heavy I was leaning forward resting my head on the shower wall. I looked down and couldn't see my feet or the drain, nor could I reach the soap I had just dropped. No one was home and all I remember feeling was "Ugh! I've had enough!" I got out of the shower—having used shampoo as soap—and pouted on the couch with a bowl of ice cream. When my husband came home from the grocery store, he asked what was wrong, and I shouted, "You try being pregnant for 40 weeks of your life!" Then I huffed off and slammed the bedroom door. I married a wise man; he left me alone. I came out only because I was hungry, and I could smell something delicious from the kitchen. I walked into the dining room and the table was set with my favorite china, candles, and flowers! My husband had made my favorite dinner and when I started to tear up he put his arms around me and said, "Wow, you really are huge, aren't you?" I burst out laughing—I was used to his teasing!—and he said, "I have been pregnant for 40 weeks—just from the outside. We're almost there, Babe. For now, let's eat!" It was one of the most memorable moments of my pregnancy and, for that matter, my life. I love the man I married, and we both love our son to pieces! —Nina, 34 your healthcare provider will continue bed rest for an additional two to four weeks and will then induce your labor or perform a cesarean section, depending on the situation. Either way, delivery is right around the corner. If you are on bed rest due to preterm labor, you will likely be allowed to get up by week 37 or 38. You can discontinue medications designed to stop labor and move about any way you wish. If you go into labor now, your baby will be full term, so preterm birth is no longer a concern.

You may still be nesting, getting everything ready for the arrival of your newborn. Be sure to complete the tasks on your to-do list as soon as possible. Use the list provided in Chapter 7 to make certain you have everything you need for your baby's first weeks at home!

These final days of pregnancy can seem like the longest days of your life. As each day becomes one day closer to your due date, you may find yourself thinking, "Could today be the day?" Just in case it is, have your bags packed, your healthcare provider's phone number handy (and numbers for anyone else you might need to call), and know the best route to the hospital—both during the middle of the night and in rush hour.

Congratulations! You have nearly made it to the end, and your reward is close at hand! Here are some questions we will address in this chapter:

- How is my baby doing during the home stretch?
- How will I know that I am ready to give birth?
- What happens if I have pain from my pelvic ligaments?
- How can I cope if the baby is late?
- What are the pros and cons of a planned home delivery?
- What is a doula, and should I hire one?
- How are problems with the placenta diagnosed and treated?
- What is a cesarean section like, and can I prepare for it?
- Can I have a vaginal delivery if I have had a C-section before?
- What should I pack for the hospital?

Your Baby's Growth and Development: Ready for the Outside World!

What a journey it has been! Here is what your baby will be up to for this final month of your pregnancy.

Week 37

A baby at 37 weeks is technically full term; however, some babies, especially boys, still have a bit of lung maturation to do. This is why it is not recommended to induce labor before 39 weeks. The baby's grasp will become stronger by this week. Babies born at 37 weeks' gestation are able to turn toward a light source.

The lungs are filled with amniotic fluid, which will be squeezed out during the baby's passage through the birth canal or absorbed into the body when the baby takes his or her first breaths. The eyelids are fully formed and open and close frequently while your baby is awake but remain closed when he or she is asleep.

Your fetus weighs 6.3 pounds and is about 19.3 inches long from crown to heel, and this month, he or she is the size of a medium watermelon.

Week 38

While the baby's growth is much slower than in the second trimester, he or she is still gaining an ounce per day, or about half a pound a week. The baby's head is about the same distance around as the abdomen, so the baby is well proportioned to leave the birth canal safely. The intestines are now producing meconium, which will become the baby's first bowel movement. The meconium is dark green in color.

Your baby has little room in which to move its arms and legs, so you will feel your baby rolling back and forth as it tries to settle into a good position.

Your baby weighs 6.8 pounds and is about 19.6 inches long from crown to heel.

Week 39

The baby's downy lanugo has long disappeared. Beginning in week 39, the vernix (the waxy white skin coating) begins to disappear. By 40 weeks, only a small amount of vernix remains. The lungs become more mature as the amount of lifesaving surfactant is continuing to increase, so the alveoli or air sacs of the lungs can expand and contract with ease as your baby takes its first breaths.

Most babies are in the head-down position, curled up with legs folded and buttocks near your ribs. This is the time that babies drop into the birth canal and begin to put more pressure on the cervix. If you are having a breech baby, this is the week that many doctors choose to do a cesarean section.

Your baby weighs 7.25 pounds and is about 20 inches long from crown to heel.

Week 40

In this final week of pregnancy, the vernix covering the baby is almost gone, and 15 percent of the baby's weight is due to body fat. The chest is bigger than the abdomen since the lungs are fully formed. Your baby is perfectly ready to live outside the womb!

Your baby is 7.6 pounds and is about 20.2 inches long.

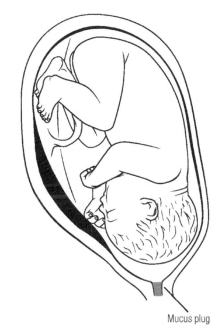

Mucus plug

Fetus at 40 weeks of development
A 40-week-old fetus is ready to meet the world.

Weeks 41 and 42

Overdue babies live in an environment with increasingly less room to move due to decreasing amniotic fluid levels. The baby has no vernix in most cases, and its skin is becoming a bit more dried out. Your baby may have a meconium bowel movement inside the uterus, which can be seen when your membranes rupture. Your healthcare provider will take extra care to make sure your baby does not inhale meconium at the time of birth.

At 41 weeks, the fetus weighs 7.9 pounds and is about 20.3 inches long. At 42 weeks' gestation, the fetus is about 8.1 pounds and approximately the same length as the previous week.

Your Changing Body: Getting Ready for the Big Day!

You are nearing the completion of your long and fascinating journey, yet there are still changes taking place inside your body. While there may still be a few weeks to go, know that your body remains fully focused on growing and preparing to deliver your child. Let's take a look at some body changes you can expect to experience this month.

Energy Level

Your energy level will not be as intense as in weeks prior to this month. While you may still have some nesting feelings, most women are settling down to rest and wait for labor and delivery. You may find yourself unable to do the exercise routine you have been maintaining throughout your pregnancy, and you may need to simply walk at this point. While walking is excellent exercise, it can bring on Braxton-Hicks contractions. But, keep in mind, walking will not send you into labor if your body is not already ready for labor and delivery.

You may be feeling sleep deprived since it is has become so difficult to find a comfortable position in bed. Loss of sleep can certainly zap your energy. Take naps when you can, and

think about slowing down at work or reducing your work hours and any other duties or chores you can in order to get extra rest.

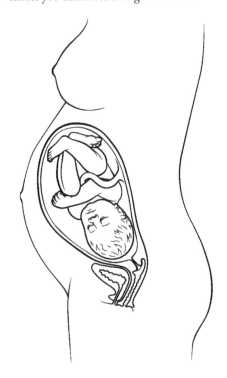

Your changing body: Month ten
You and your baby are ready to go! Your body is preparing for delivery.

Weight Gain

Your weight gain will begin to slow so that you are no longer gaining a pound a week. An exception is if you are experiencing a great deal of water-weight gain, but this will dissipate once you deliver your baby. Water-weight gain happens when the weather is extremely hot or if you are still on your feet or sitting with your legs dangling during the bulk of the day. Because of swelling in your legs and feet, you might experience your shoes becoming too tight and thickening of your ankles by the end of the day. If you have sudden or extreme swelling, contact your healthcare provider.

At this point, your total weight gain ideally should be about 25 to 35 pounds. Let's look at where that weight came from:

- The baby itself will weigh about 7.5 pounds.
- The placenta will weigh about 1.5 pounds.
- There is about 2 pounds of amniotic fluid inside the uterus.
- The extra breast weight is about 2 pounds total.
- You will have gained about 4 pounds of body fluid.
- The extra blood inside you will weigh about 4 pounds.
- Extra maternal stores of fat and nutrients for the fetus weigh about 7 pounds.

That is about a total of 30 pounds. If your baby is bigger or smaller than 7.5 pounds, your weight gain will be slightly different. If you gained 35 pounds or more during the pregnancy, the excess is due to fat that you will need to lose later. If you breast-feed, the weight will come off faster and more easily!

Lightening: Your Baby's Head Dropping into Position for Delivery

Up until this point in your pregnancy, you have carried your baby high inside your body, near your abdomen, which has sometimes caused shortness of breath and the sensation that the baby was right up under your ribs. One to two weeks before your baby is born, however, the baby's head will drop into the circular pelvic bones and the head will be positioned in your pelvis.

This dropping of the baby (also called lightening) causes the head to be directly on the inside of the cervix so when you have contractions, it pushes directly on the cervix. The cervix is normally about 4 centimeters long (a little more than an inch and a half). During the last part of pregnancy, the cervix starts to soften and thin out, a process called effacement. Effacement is described as a percentage. A normal cervix before thinning is zero percent effaced. At 50 percent effacement, the cervix is about two centimeters long. At the time of a vaginal birth, the cervix has thinned out completely, and is considered to be 100 percent effaced.

If your cervix is thinning out, it does not necessarily mean that you are in labor or that labor is imminent. It can still take a couple of

Nutritional Tip:

Keep Up Your Strength and Your Spirits

No doubt your uterus is encroaching on your stomach, making it harder to eat large meals. But do not let this deter you from continuing to eat healthy and nutritious foods. Just do so in smaller portions. You and your baby still need as many nutrients as possible, so do not give up all your good habits in the home stretch! Drink nutritious smoothies with fruit and yogurt in them; try small bowls of whole-grain pasta or brown rice with vegetables and lean fish or meat. Protein bars are also a good option, but be sure to check for high protein and low fat content. Stocking your refrigerator and pantry with healthy food items that you and your partner can share after the baby is born is also a good idea. You will appreciate your own efforts when neither of you has to run to the grocery store with a crying baby on your hands!

I knew I'd chosen the right doctor after I began calling her every time I had a Braxton-Hicks contraction! I must have called 10 different times, and every time she was patient and reassuring, never annoyed. I remember so vividly her words the last time I called: "Well, Grace, guess what? I'll see you at the hospital!"
—*Grace, 26, mother of one*

weeks before you give birth. In the meantime, dropping of the baby can mean that you will have an easier time breathing and will feel more pressure in your pelvic area. It also means that labor and delivery will probably happen within the next two weeks.

For Dads and Partners:

Decide on Your Role during Labor

Now is a great time to discuss with your partner what your role will be during labor and delivery. Will you be the coach at your pregnant partner's head, telling her to breathe, counting breaths for her, and encouraging her to relax or to push the baby out? Or do you want to see everything happening from the perspective of the perineum—watching the baby actually come out—or both? Decide if you want to cut the umbilical cord or not, and make sure the doctor or midwife knows your wishes. Whatever you decide, be prepared for the possibility that while in the throes of delivery, your partner may send you in a completely different direction. No one knows what will happen during the delivery process, and your partner may need something neither of you even thought about!

False Labor as You Approach Delivery

While you have experienced Braxton-Hicks contractions for some time, when they become stronger and closer together as your delivery approaches they are known as false labor. These contractions, while seeming strong, do not usually significantly change the cervical opening, although they can cause some thinning or effacement of the cervix.

Many couples find themselves in the hospital during this month with the belief that they are in labor, only to be told that it is not time yet and to head back home! False labor is a common occurrence in weeks 37 through 40 and can even occur in women who have had babies before. If it happens to you, do not stress about it. It can happen to anyone!

Feel free to refer back to Chapter 10 to review the differences between false and true labor. But keep in mind that if your contractions stop when you change positions, sit, or walk around, they are Braxton-Hicks contractions (false labor). True labor pains are regular and increase in intensity. Changes in position do not make them disappear. False labor pains tend to stay the same over time and do not have a regular pattern, nor do they get closer and closer together. When in doubt, call your healthcare provider and get advice on how to proceed.

Loss of the Mucus Plug

The mucus plug sits in the cervix during pregnancy. Not every woman loses her mucus plug in an obvious way. You may simply experience an increase in thick, clear, cervical mucus or a light spotting when you wipe yourself, or you may find it on your under-

I knew my doctor was going to induce me in one week if I did not deliver on my own, so I decided to go ahead and leave work to have a week "off" before the big event. Well, that was a mistake! I was too tired and too uncomfortable to do anything but sit around the house. My husband continued to work, and all my friends were either working or busy with their own children! I was bored to pieces and constantly worried about the labor process and being induced. My advice is stay as busy as you can for as long as you can! —*Wendy, 28, mother of one*

wear. If you lose your mucus plug all at once, it looks like a thick glob of mucus tinged with blood that can be as big as the size of a ping-pong ball.

Losing your mucus plug means that the cervix is starting to open and thin. Loss of the plug could mean that you will go into labor within 24 hours. In some cases, however, it does not signal imminent labor, and you may still have a week or so to go. In general, it is a good indicator that labor will soon start, but it could still be days away. Follow your contraction pattern as an indication of labor rather than just the loss of the mucus plug.

Separation of the Pubic Symphysis

The pubic symphysis is the joint between the two pelvic bones on the front of your body. It consists of a fibrocartilage disc and two ligaments. Your healthcare provider has used this place at the bottom of your abdominal wall as the starting point to measure your uterine height. Because your body produces the hormone relaxin during pregnancy, the ligaments become looser and more elastic. This allows the baby's head to squeeze through the birth canal more easily. In fact, a normal woman's pubic symphysis is about 5 millimeters wide, while a pregnant woman's pubic symphysis may normally stretch to 9 millimeters.

In some women, however, the ligaments of the pubic symphysis stretch beyond their capacity, leading to a separation called pubic symphysis dysfunction. This is more common when the fetus is large or has a larger-than-average head. About one in four women experience some level of discomfort from the pubic symphysis area during pregnancy, but a much smaller number experience more extreme and debilitating symptoms.

Separation of the pubic symphysis can occur late in the third trimester or during the delivery itself. If it happens, you will experience pain in the area of the pubic symphysis and will have difficulty walking. You will feel as though you have to waddle and you may feel a grinding sensation in the area of the ruptured ligament.

Exercise Idea: Do What You Can!

If you have separation of the pubic symphysis or moderate to severe pain with walking, you get a pass this month when it comes to exercise— resting should be your priority. The same is true for those on bed rest for complications. If you can still walk comfortably, even if you waddle, try to walk on a treadmill, around the neighborhood, or at your local mall so you can remain physically fit in these last few weeks of pregnancy.

> My partner was overdue, and every night she ranted to me saying, "This baby is never going to come out—I'll be like this forever!" Frankly, she was driving me crazy, but I tried to comfort her anyway. But all that did was make her more angry and riled up. So one night after she had been ranting I turned to her and said, "Listen, if you stay like this forever at least we'll save a ton of money on college tuition." She laughed until she cried. And I don't know if the events were related, but thankfully that night she went into labor! —*Jodi, 40, mom of two*

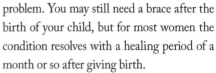

Walking may be painful. Medical supply companies make braces that are worn around the hips to hold the pelvis together so you can walk more comfortably. If you are at term and are experiencing a great deal of pain, you can ask your doctor about inducing your labor in order to relieve the problem. You may still need a brace after the birth of your child, but for most women the condition resolves with a healing period of a month or so after giving birth.

If you feel pain in the pelvic area, the low back, the hips, or the legs, see your healthcare provider as soon as possible. Early diagnosis and treatment can prevent pubic symphysis dysfunction from becoming more severe. A physical or occupational therapist can recommend gentle exercise and help you to modify your movements during daily activities to minimize discomfort. If you have severe pubic symphysis dysfunction, you will need to modify your position while giving birth to prevent pain from this condition. Be sure to discuss this with your healthcare provider and add any needed position changes to your birth plan.

Your Emotions: Relax and Wait

Emotionally, these last four weeks can be a time of apprehension, joyful anticipation, and frustration. Your baby is full term but still nestled safe and sound inside you. Any fears you have about the labor and delivery process may intensify this month as your due date draws closer. On the other hand, you may care less what you have to go through as long as your baby comes out! Due to lack of sleep and feeling so uncomfortable, you are likely to be more irritable and may find yourself arguing more with your partner or having no patience for the slow service in the bank.

Your days may feel long and your nights— if you are having trouble sleeping—may feel

Prenatal Testing:
Weekly Visits to Your Doctor or Midwife
During weeks 37 through 40, you will see your obstetrical doctor or midwife every week. You will have a urinalysis to check for infection, protein, and sugar. If you did not have a group B strep test last month, remind your healthcare provider to do it at about week 37. This can be a lifesaving test, since it can prevent infection in the baby. You will have your blood pressure checked at each visit, and, if you have a high-risk pregnancy, nonstress tests and ultrasounds may be done each week.

even longer. Waiting is difficult under most circumstances, and you have been waiting for your baby for 10 months! You have a right to a little frustration. Do not be hard on yourself. But do take these last weeks to continue to be good to yourself and your baby. Eat well, exercise when you are able, and keep yourself busy. Go out with friends, relax in front of the television, or go to the movies. Anything you can do to stay relaxed and positive will help you enter the labor and delivery process with a light and confident heart.

Your Prenatal Visit: Keeping Close Tabs

You will now see your healthcare provider at least once a week—more often if you have complications. Your doctor or midwife will continue to perform a urinalysis at every visit and will measure your uterus. Your uterine size may actually appear to shrink during this month because your baby's head drops into the pelvis and no longer pushes the uterus up as far. If your baby is head down, the head is now hidden behind the pubic bone.

Your healthcare provider will also listen to fetal heart tones and will make sure your baby is still head down. If the head is down at this point, it is likely to stay down. If your baby is not head down, the chance of a spontaneous turn-about is very low. If your baby is breech (buttocks down), you may need to consider an external cephalic version (see Chapter 11) or a cesarean section (see page 271 of this chapter), which can be scheduled to happen around 39 weeks' gestation. Finally, the healthcare provider will check your cervix each visit to see if it is changing in dilation (opening) and/or

effacement (thinning). This can help both you and your healthcare provider know if delivery is imminent or not.

If your pregnancy is higher risk, your doctor might perform ultrasounds at each visit to check fetal breathing movements, small and large motor movements, and the amount of amniotic fluid. Ultrasounds can demonstrate that your baby is doing fine inside the uterus. Nonstress tests (see Chapter 11) can be done along with an ultrasound to measure how the fetus' heart rate changes as it moves and with any contractions you are experiencing. When these tests become less reassuring, arrangements are made for immediate delivery.

Coping when the Baby Is Late

The only thing harder than waiting for your due date to arrive is waiting *past* your due date! After 10 months, that magic date has been like a beacon in a dark tunnel signaling the end of a long journey. When that date comes and goes and your baby is still inside you, life can become more than just frustrating. You may feel downright angry!

Risk Factors for Postterm Birth

There is no set reason why some women go past their due date and some do not, but the following suggests some reasons why you might be at a higher risk for a postterm baby:

- The exact date of your last menstrual period was not clear or was misunderstood.
- You are having your first baby.
- You have had overdue babies in the past.
- You are obese.
- Your baby is going to be a boy.

You can always talk to your healthcare provider about when induction of labor might be a good idea. If your cervix still is not favorable for induction or if your provider believes that you will go into labor soon enough, he or she may opt for a later, more natural delivery process. Many doctors will wait until at least a week has gone by before having you induced unless some kind of complication has arisen.

Your doctor or midwife might choose to see you twice a week after your due date and may do nonstress tests and ultrasounds to check for fetal well-being during the days or weeks following your due date. These tests can be repeated every few days.

Labor Induction

If your healthcare provider believes your labor needs to be induced, he or she has several options. Your doctor or midwife can "strip your membranes" if the amniotic sac is intact. This involves separating the amniotic sac from the lower uterine segment and feels like you are having a very rough cervical exam. This can release prostaglandins in the area of the cervix and can bring labor on. Prostaglandin medications can be given inside the cervix or orally to further ripen the cervix and to initiate labor.

In the meantime, try to accept the emotions of frustration and disappointment you are likely having. Sleep as much as you can and do what you can to keep yourself busy. A really absorbing novel can be a lifesaver at this point! Make no travel arrangements beyond an hour from your home and spend as much time as you can surrounded by friends and family who support what you're going through. Be cautious about home remedies that are advertised to jumpstart labor.

Consult your healthcare provider, and follow medical advice about when you should consider an induction of labor.

Home Births

Women have been having home births for millennia. With the advances in modern medicine in the 1900s, however, home births began to give way to hospital births based on doctor recommendations. Today, fewer than 1 percent of births are planned to occur in the home setting, even though the option exists. Whether this is your first pregnancy or your fifth, you may be thinking about having a home birth. In order to be successful, you need to weigh the risks and benefits of having your baby at home.

Reasons to Consider a Home Birth

Some women decide to have a home birth with the help of a certified midwife or a nurse-midwife. Home births should only be considered in low-risk, singleton pregnancies in which the mother and fetus have been entirely healthy. Home births also require a great deal of preparation. Those women who have a midwife and have prepared in advance might want to have a home birth if all the following conditions exist:

• You have had a low-risk pregnancy and are otherwise completely healthy.

• A vaginal birth is expected and indicated.

• The baby is in the head-down position.

• You want to avoid an epidural, a cesarean section, or an episiotomy, if possible.

• You want the help and support of several family members and/or friends to deliver your baby.

- You want personal freedom to be able to move about your house, try different positions for labor and delivery, and to be able to eat or drink anything you want during labor.
- You want a shower or bath during labor or you are interested in a tub or pool birth (although some birthing centers will accommodate these preferences).
- You do not want to give birth in a sterile hospital setting and want your child to be born in your own surroundings.

Reasons *Not* to Consider a Home Birth

You should *not* consider a home birth if you have any of the following conditions:

- Chronic high blood pressure
- Preeclampsia
- Gestational diabetes
- Any other complication of pregnancy
- Any serious chronic medical condition
- Current preterm labor or preterm labor with previous pregnancies
- Lack of agreement by your partner

The high likelihood (about 37 percent) that you will need to be transported to the hospital during labor or delivery is another reason that many women decide a home birth is not for them. For many couples, a birthing center offers most of the same freedom and flexibility found in a home birth, with an added measure of safety and comfort.

Preparing for a Home Birth

If you are planning a home birth, you will likely see a midwife who will have a doctor to supervise her. You will see the midwife for your prenatal visits but may see the doctor at least once during the pregnancy. You and the

Why Your Doctor May or May Not Induce Labor

In years past, induction of labor was recommended only if you had reached the 42-week mark; however, more recent evidence indicates that babies born at this time have greater problems fitting through the birth canal due to increased size, have more meconium stooling in the amniotic fluid, and have an increased risk of fetal distress in labor. For this reason, many healthcare providers have as their policy to induce labor at 41 weeks rather than 42 weeks. Ask your doctor or midwife what his or her policy is about postterm vaginal deliveries and induction of labor. Labor should never be induced for convenience only.

midwife will consult about the appropriate time for her to come to your home.

When to Go to the Hospital During Home Birth

In most cases, you will be able to labor and deliver at home with the help of a midwife. There are certain situations, however, that might send you to the hospital to deliver your baby instead of having a home birth. About 40 percent of first-time mothers trying to have a home birth end up going to the hospital, and 10 percent of women who have previously delivered a baby at home must be transported to the hospital.

The following are reasons why you might be transferred by car or ambulance to the hospital:

- Premature rupture of the membranes
- Exhaustion, with the feeling of being unable to continue a home birth

- Maternal high blood pressure
- Lack of progression of labor for several hours
- Evidence of fetal distress
- Hemorrhaging before or after the delivery
- Emergence of the cord from the vagina before the baby comes out (called cord prolapse)
- Maternal fever
- Meconium-stained amniotic fluid
- Deterioration in the mother's health

Risks and Benefits of Home Birth

The American Congress of Obstetricians and Gynecologists says: "Although the Committee on Obstetric Practice believes that hospitals and birthing centers are the safest setting for birth, it respects the right of a woman to make a medically informed decision about delivery.... although the absolute risk may be low, planned home birth is associated with a twofold to threefold increased risk of neonatal [newborn] death when compared with planned hospital birth."

A successful home birth requires a serious commitment to go through labor naturally. You will also need support from your partner, friends, and relatives; a well-trained midwife with obstetrician backup; a "Plan B" in place in case you need to go to a hospital; and a pediatrician or family practice doctor willing to see the baby at home within 24 hours after birth.

Benefits: The benefits of home births need to be weighed against the risks. There are many benefits to home births, including greatly reduced cost when compared to a hospital birth. Some studies suggest that a home birth costs 60 percent less than a hospital birth. Home births may increase infant/parent bonding. You can nurse your baby right away, although many hospitals and birthing centers now allow breast-feeding nearly immediately after birth as well. For many women, the primary benefit of home birth is the lower rate of medical interventions in the labor and delivery process.

While we still need more research on the different outcomes of hospital versus home births, studies indicate that women who give birth at home have fewer severe lacerations (tears) of the vagina, fewer infections, and similar rates of other complications.

In addition, you can be surrounded by those who love you, including your children, your partner, and any of your relatives and friends you wish to include during or after labor.

Risks: The major risk of home birth is an increased rate of death of the newborn, which is estimated to be two to three times higher than for hospital births. Although neonatal death is highly uncommon in any birth setting in the United States, research suggests that the risk is higher in a home birth. If the mother or baby experiences a dangerous complication during birth, there is the risk of not being able to be transported to the hospital in time.

If you are considering a home birth, contact a midwife who does home births and share your wishes with your partner.

Hiring a Doula

A doula is a trained birthing coach who helps you through the labor and delivery process. Along with your partner, she can provide emotional and practical support. Doulas also help with pain management, relaxation, and the creation of a birth plan. The cost of a doula varies depending on your location and the services she provides. Insurance rarely pays for a doula's services. However, in some areas low-cost (or even free) or sliding-scale doula services are available. If you are interested in a doula but concerned about cost, do some research and call several doulas or agencies. A doula can be a big help.

How a Doula Can Help

- In the final weeks of pregnancy, a doula can help you prepare and overcome fears about pregnancy or birth.
- She can explain the various procedures in your chosen birth setting and assist you in developing an individualized birth plan.
- She can help during the labor and delivery process so that your delivery will go smoothly and with a minimum of anxiety.
- A doula can come to your house after you give birth to help you get organized and comfortable with having a newborn in the home.
- A doula is also able to help you prepare for what you'll need when the baby comes home.
- A doula is your constant companion during labor and delivery. During labor, she can assist you in changing positions, help with your breathing exercises, and offer a welcome massage that can help you to relax.
- A good doula will connect with you emotionally so you have someone who understands what you're going through as you labor toward the inevitable goal of having your baby. Labor is unpredictable,

and a doula has usually seen everything when it comes to having babies.

- If you do not have a partner, your partner will be away during the birth, or you feel you will not get enough support from your partner during labor, a doula can fill this void in a way your doctor or even your midwife or nurse cannot.
- If you have had a negative birth experience in the past, or if you are a survivor of

All of my immediate family lived on the other side of the country, so I knew I wouldn't have family support during delivery. My husband has a fear of hospitals, so I wasn't sure if I could count on him or not. So I hired a doula and she was wonderful—coaching me, supporting me, and caring for me all through labor and delivery, and for that first week home. Her help was worth every single penny! —*Roz, 33, mother of one*

any form of abuse, a doula who has special training in trauma-informed care can help you navigate your medical care and the labor and delivery process to minimize re-traumatizing experiences.

A trained doula can increase your satisfaction in the birthing experience. Mothers who have this kind of continuous support release fewer stress hormones during their labor when compared to women who were coached by someone who is untrained. Having a midwife might decrease your need for a doula, but a busy midwife may not be able to provide you with the continuous support you need.

How to Find a Doula

Ask your midwife or doctor to recommend a doula. You can also contact the Doulas of North America (DONA), which can help you locate a nearby professional. The Association of Labor Assistants and Childbirth Educators (ALACE) and the Childbirth and Postpartum Professional Association (CAPPA) also maintain referral information. Contacts for these organizations can be found easily online or through directory information. If you have financial concerns, try searching online for "low-cost doula."

Placental Insufficiency

If your pregnancy progresses from due to overdue, your placenta can start to develop calcium deposits and can become "too old" to properly supply nutrients and oxygen to your baby. Your baby may stop gaining weight, or you might have a fetus that actually loses weight over time. Placental insufficiency is often associated with low amniotic fluid levels (a condition called oligohydramnios), which can restrict fetal movements.

Placental insufficiency occurs more often in women who have

- diabetes of any kind
- medical diseases that increase blood clotting
- high blood pressure
- a history of smoking
- taken a medication that can result in placental insufficiency

- a placenta that is too small or not correctly shaped
- a poor connection between placenta and uterus
- a partial placental abruption previously in the pregnancy

Diagnosing Placental Insufficiency

In general, you cannot recognize any signs of placental insufficiency yourself. Your healthcare provider may suspect that you have the condition if the measurement of uterine size decreases. Your healthcare provider can confirm the presence of placental insufficiency by looking at fetal growth and the structure of the placenta using ultrasound technology. A lack of amniotic fluid can often be seen on ultrasound as well.

Your doctor may also be able to tell that you have placental insufficiency by doing regular nonstress tests. If your fetus is not getting enough oxygen he or she will not sustain an increase in heart rate with movements or will move far less than normal. You might notice a decrease in fetal movement yourself.

Treatment for Placental Insufficiency

The first treatment for placental insufficiency is to manage any underlying health conditions you may have to the extent possible. Bed rest will also help placental insufficiency if it is not yet time to deliver. If your fetus is full term, your doctor may do a contraction stress test to determine if your baby will tolerate labor. Your doctor may also decide to start labor induction, being careful to watch the fetal heart rate and to be prepared for a cesarean section if your baby does not do well during labor and delivery.

Some cases of placental insufficiency result in a condition called intrauterine growth restriction (IUGR). This is when a baby is small in size compared to other babies of the same gestational age. An IUGR baby has an increased risk of complications during labor and delivery, including an increased risk of stillbirth.

Information on Cesarean Sections

A cesarean section (C-section) is a surgical procedure that doctors use to deliver an infant by making an incision in both the mother's lower stomach and in the uterus to allow passage of the baby into the outside world. The procedure takes about an hour; however, the part involving the delivery of the baby only takes about 5 to 10 minutes. In some cases, having a C-section is safer for both you and your baby than a vaginal delivery.

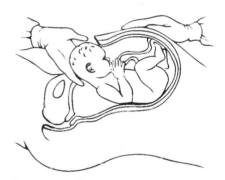

Cesarean section
In a cesarean section, the baby is delivered through an incision in the abdomen.

Whether you already know you are having a C-section or expect to have a vaginal delivery, it is worth reading about this procedure in order to be prepared. Many women have gone

Things To Think About:
Pack Your Bags!
If you have not done so already, now is the time to pack your bag for the hospital! Buy travel-size shampoo and creams and a small make-up bag just for the hospital. Include what your baby will need as well as your personal items. Do not forget to pack a few things for your partner! Remember: If you wait until you go into labor, you will not be thinking clearly as you pack. For a detailed list of what to bring, see page 277 of this chapter.

into the hospital expecting a vaginal delivery and have needed to have a C-section.

Indications for a Cesarean Section

Reasons why you might need a C-section include the following:

Stalled or stopped labor: You are in labor and your labor has stalled or stopped. This is one of the most common reasons C-sections are performed. Your baby's head may be too big or the cervix may have stopped opening in spite of your contractions.

Breech baby: Your baby is breech with either the feet or the buttocks facing the birth canal. Babies in transverse or sideways positions may require a C-section as well. In rare circumstances, your baby's face may be the presenting body part in the birth canal. It is often not possible or advisable to deliver a face presentation baby vaginally.

Fetal distress: Your baby's heart tones suggest a lowered oxygen supply. If your baby's heart rate and contraction monitor are showing fetal distress, an emergency cesarean section might be necessary.

Multiples: If you are carrying twins that are both in the head-down position, you have the option of delivering both babies vaginally. If one or both of the babies is transverse or breech, you will need a cesarean section. Triplets are generally delivered by cesarean section.

Placental abruption and/or placenta previa: Your placenta has detached from the uterus, called a placental abruption (see Chapter 11), and there are signs of maternal or fetal distress. In addition, if your cervix is covered by the placenta (placenta previa—see Chapter 8), you will need to have a cesarean section for your and your baby's safety.

Umbilical cord prolapse: If the umbilical cord comes out before the baby's head emerges, this is called umbilical cord prolapse. It is an obstetrical emergency because if the umbili-

cal cord is compressed and blood cannot flow through it, the fetus cannot get enough oxygen. You will need an emergency cesarean section.

Your baby is too big! Sometimes a trial of labor is done to attempt to deliver a large baby vaginally, but if this doesn't work and the baby is stuck, you'll need to have a cesarean section.

Medical conditions: You have a medical condition that precludes vaginal birth such as unstable heart disease, high blood pressure, or an active herpes infection in the genital area. These conditions might make labor and delivery too difficult or harmful to either you or the baby.

Previous C-section: If you have had a previous cesarean section in which the incisions in the abdomen and uterus were horizontal, not vertical, you may be offered the chance to have a vaginal birth after cesarean section (VBAC). (See page 276.)

Hydrocephalus: Your baby has hydrocephalus, which is excess fluid on the brain, or your baby has another structural problem that would prevent a normal vaginal delivery.

Requesting a C-section

What NOW?

Some women simply request a C-section in order to avoid the pain of labor. Most doctors (and health insurance plans) will not allow you to do this. Unless there is a medical reason for a C-section or you have an emergency situation during labor, you will have to reconcile yourself to having a vaginal birth, which is ultimately less of a health risk barring complications. If you have this level of fear about vaginal birth, seek help from a doula and/or a therapist to reduce your apprehension. You may also benefit from hypnosis.

Risks of a C-section

While cesarean sections are generally considered to be safe, you should know about the following risks:

• *An increase in breathing problems for the baby.* Because a C-section baby is not squeezed through the birth canal, excess fluid can remain in the lungs and the baby can have a temporary increase in breathing rate. Your newborn may need oxygen for a few days after birth.

- *Endometritis or an infection of the inner lining of the uterus.* This can lead to your developing fever and chills, back pain, bad-smelling discharge from the vagina, and pain in the uterine area.
- *Increased bleeding.*
- *An allergic or other reaction to the anesthesia.* This can occur even if you have regional anesthesia with an epidural or spinal anesthetic.
- *Development of deep vein thrombosis (DVT) or a pulmonary embolism (PE) during the recovery from a C-section.* This is why nurses have you get up frequently after your surgery.
- *A wound infection after surgery.*
- *Accidental injury of the bowels or bladder during the surgery.* This might require additional surgery in the near future.
- *Risk to future pregnancies because of having had a C-section.* You are at higher risk for bleeding problems, uterine rupture, or placenta previa in a subsequent pregnancy.

Planning Ahead for Your Cesarean Section

If you know you are having a C-section delivery, your doctor will guide you through the steps to prepare for your surgery. First, a date will be set. Your blood will be drawn and analyzed once again to assess your pre-surgery condition. (The hospital will make sure your blood type is available in the blood bank as well.) You should talk with your doctor and one of the hospital's anesthesiologists in advance, to discuss the types of anesthesia available to you as well as their risks and benefits. Read our discussion of the C-section procedure but also ask your doctor to explain (to both you and your partner) what will happen during the surgery so you can ask questions and be prepared. If you know you are going to have a C-section, plan ahead for extra help when you bring the baby home.

Even if you are not planning for a C-section, you should talk to your healthcare provider about the possibility of having one if there are labor complications. Find out where and under what circumstances a cesarean birth may be necessary and find out who will be performing the surgery. You may want to discuss your preferences, such as having your partner hold the baby as soon as possible after birth and being given the opportunity for you to initiate breast-feeding and have skin-to-skin contact with your baby at the earliest possible time.

The C-section Procedure

Your partner will ordinarily be allowed to attend the C-section birth of your child, but check with your hospital if you want others to be present as well. Most doctors will not allow others to attend the procedure in case an emergency occurs. A curtain will be placed at your chest to block you from seeing the procedure. Your partner will usually be asked to leave while preparations are made for the surgery, but then will be invited in to sit at your head. If your partner is squeamish about being present during surgery, reassure him or her that it is possible to be present for the birth without seeing the actual surgery occur, by proper positioning.

Anesthesia: Once it has been determined that you will have a C-section (or you have arrived for your scheduled surgery), a nurse will give you an IV for fluids and medication. You may receive an oral antacid to settle your stomach before and during the procedure to lessen any

I was glad I'd kept up my exercise routine during my pregnancy. I was strong and healthy, and it made the recovery from my surprise C-section go quicker. Also, it's really important to eat well and drink a lot of water during that first month home after the birth. I was so busy with the baby I wasn't eating, and I felt awful. It took my husband to point it out to me. Take care of yourself so you can care for your baby!
—*Becca, 31, mother of one*

potential damage to the lungs if you were to vomit from anesthesia. You will talk to the anesthesiologist and anesthetist who will administer your anesthetic and will take care of you during the procedure. If you know in advance that you will be having a C-section, you should not eat or drink anything for about eight hours prior to the scheduled procedure.

Depending on what you, your doctor, and your anesthesiologist decide, you will likely receive an epidural anesthetic. In this case, medicine is inserted via a catheter (thin tube) placed in the area outside your spinal cord in your lower back. Less commonly, you may receive a spinal block, in which the pain medication is injected into the spinal fluid. (See Chapter 13 for more information about epidural and spinal anesthesia.) With either of these methods, you will be awake for the cesarean birth of your infant. In an emergency, however, you might be placed under general anesthesia and will not be awake for the birth.

After you are given the anesthetic, you will have a catheter placed into the bladder. This tube draws urine out of your bladder and into a bag in order to keep your bladder empty.

Incision and delivery: The vast majority of C-section incisions made in the abdomen and uterus are transverse, or horizontal. This allows for a normal cesarean delivery with the least-noticeable scar after you heal. (Yes, bikinis will still work!) However, in dire emergencies, a vertical incision will be made because it is faster and your doctor can more quickly pull your baby out. Fortunately, this is rarely necessary.

As your baby is removed, you will feel pressure on your abdomen. Your doctor will push on your upper uterus to get the baby out through the tight lower incision. You will hear the sound of mucus being sucked out of the baby's nose and mouth, and the pronouncement that the baby is a boy or girl. Sometimes the doctor will show you a brief glimpse of the baby over the curtain that separates your head and chest from the surgical area.

After nurses have cleaned off and examined your baby (see information on the Apgar score in Chapter 13), they may let your partner hold the baby for a few minutes so you can all begin to bond. You will still be on the operating table, but you may also be able to snuggle your baby while doctors continue your surgery. When you have finished having your surgery (it takes about 50 minutes to put everything back in order), you will go to the recovery room, where holding and seeing the baby may be allowed and encouraged. The World Health Organization outlines hospital policies that promote successful breast-feeding, and they recommend allowing mothers who have had a C-section to have skin-to-skin contact with their babies within half an hour after they are able to do so.

Hospital recovery: Your postoperative stay will last about three to four days. You will receive pain medications for your operative discomfort and will be allowed to take care of your baby and breast-feed your baby as if you had a vaginal delivery. Walking will be encouraged in order to prevent blood clot formation. Your diet will gradually be advanced, which means you will progress from liquids and jello to soft foods and then to a normal diet. When you go home, you will need to take it easy and follow your doctor's restrictions and recommendations for recovery. It takes four to six weeks to heal from C-section surgery.

Recovering at home: Although you will finally have your bundle of joy in your arms, you will still need to rest as much as you can while you are healing from surgery. Most doctors recommend that you not lift anything heavier than your infant. Use good posture when sitting, standing, and walking and hold your abdomen near the incision if you are sneezing, laughing, or coughing. Place your baby on a pillow when breast-feeding or giving a bottle so you will not have to use your abdominal muscles as much. Drink extra fluids and eat a nutritious diet to promote quicker healing and the production of breast milk. Keep taking your prenatal vitamins! Do not have sex until your doctor says it is OK—generally four to six weeks after surgery.

Take Tylenol for discomfort or pain as this medication is safe to take when you are breast-feeding. Call your doctor if you have a fever greater than 101.5°F. Watch your incision for pus or other drainage, increased pain, or redness, which may signify an infection at the wound site. If your doctor used staples to close your wound, you will have to see the doctor to have them removed, approximately four to seven days after delivery.

Because you are recovering from major surgery while caring for your newborn, you really need additional help and support at home after a C-section. If your partner is able to take time from work when the baby comes home, this can be a lovely time to be together as a family and to have the help you need. If not, having practical support from friends and relatives can be most helpful, especially if you have other children who need care at home. Don't hesitate to ask for what you need. If you are breast-feeding, your partner can bring the baby to you for nursing, especially at night. Someone other than you should be doing most of the household chores for some time after your surgery. If you don't have the support system you would like, consider hiring whatever help you can afford. Even a young teen who can wash the dishes or safely entertain your two-year-old while you and the baby nap can be a lifesaver!

Emotional Recovery from a Cesarean Section

In addition to the normal hormonally driven ups and downs women have after giving birth, you may have some emotional challenges as a result of your cesarean birth. If you had your heart set on natural childbirth, you may feel that you have somehow failed or that your body has betrayed you. The pain medications you are given in the hospital can also exacerbate your emotions. When you get home, you may have extra difficulty getting sufficient sleep because of your postoperative discomfort.

You also need more help after a C-section, and if it is not forthcoming from your partner or somebody else, you may feel let down and angry. Your partner may not understand the need to do the lion's share of household work or may not be supportive enough for your needs. Your job is to communicate your needs as clearly and firmly as possible and to seek help from a friend or relative if your partner doesn't respond appropriately. You can't expect your partner to read your mind, so you do have to speak up. If your partner really doesn't seem to hear your explanation of what is needed, suggest that he or she accompany you to a medical visit and ask the healthcare provider to explain what you need to make a full recovery.

If you feel terribly disappointed in yourself because of the cesarean birth, remind yourself that your body has created a true miracle in supporting the growth of a new human being throughout pregnancy. You have also been through a substantial physical ordeal, so be kind to yourself. Give yourself adequate time to recover while you enjoy your newborn. You will feel better, emotionally and physically, in the next few weeks. Talking to other moms who have had cesareans may help. Consult your healthcare provider if your mood remains depressed. Remember that the entire parenting journey will be unpredictable—your unpredictable journey just started a bit early!

Vaginal Birth after Cesarean Section (VBAC)

If you have had a cesarean section in the past and the C-section involved a low transverse incision across your lower uterus (as opposed to a vertical incision), you may be offered the opportunity to have what is called a vaginal birth after cesarean section, or VBAC (pronounced "V-Back").

In most cases, your doctor will agree to this unless you had a stalled labor because of the size of the baby and it is believed that you are currently pregnant with an even bigger baby. About 40 percent of women who attempt a VBAC will fail to have a successful vaginal birth and will need a C-section for the second time. On the positive side, you have a 60 percent chance that a trial of labor will lead to a vaginal birth.

Risks of a VBAC

The major risk of a VBAC is rupture of the lower uterine segment, requiring an emergency C-section. The risk of uterine rupture goes up if you have had more than one C-section in the past. Some doctors limit VBAC delivery to women who have had only one previous C-section.

You will need to be monitored more closely during your VBAC labor, and the provisions for an emergency cesarean section will need to be in place so that it can be done immediately if there is evidence of uterine rupture.

Benefits of a VBAC

There are several benefits to having a VBAC rather than a C-section:

- You will not have to have an additional uterine scar, which could mean that future vaginal births would be out of the question altogether.

- A vaginal delivery is less painful than the major surgery of a cesarean birth.
- The risk of infection is less than with a repeat C-section.
- Your recovery time will be much less with a vaginal birth.
- Your labor and delivery experience will be less "sterile" with greater opportunity for infant bonding after birth.

What to Pack for the Hospital

Pack your bags—your journey is nearly over! Be prepared for your hospital stay by packing now. Don't try to pack as you go into labor—you are likely to forget just about everything. If you are a procrastinator, use the lists below and ask your partner to pack for you.

For Labor

For labor, pack the following:

- A picture ID
- Your insurance card
- A copy of your birth plan
- Eyeglasses, if you need them. Try not to wear contacts.
- Toothbrush and toothpaste
- Lip gloss or lip balm
- Hair brush or comb
- Makeup
- Hair items like clips or hair bands
- Deodorant
- Snacks for your partner
- Money for the cafeteria or vending machines for your partner

When to Call Your Doctor

Call your doctor if you are experiencing any of the following:

- Fever greater than 101.5° F.
- You do not feel the baby move at all a half hour after drinking a cup of juice.
- You feel you might be in labor—contractions that are increasing in intensity, do not go away with a change in position, and are 5 to 10 minutes apart.
- You have vaginal bleeding.
- You have steady abdominal pain that cannot be explained.

- Bathing items if you are having a water birth
- A CD player or your MP3 player with soothing music
- Massage oils
- Your own pillow and pillowcase
- Something to read
- A list of medications you normally take at home, including dosages and timing

For after Delivery

You may need these items after the delivery and for the remainder of your hospital stay:

- A clean nightgown and robe, cute pajamas, or comfortable gym clothes (if you are breast-feeding, you might like a nursing nightgown, which has discreet but convenient openings)
- Your cell phone and charger or a prepaid phone card for making calls, texting, and emails
- A list of the phone numbers of your friends and relatives
- Snacks for after the delivery

I hate packing! So as one last hurrah before my baby was born, I threw myself a packing party! I invited my closest friends over and divided them into teams. I made a game of reading an item off my packing list and watching the teams run wild, crashing into each other trying to be the first to find the item and pack it! It was hysterical! Afterwards, the losing team cooked a great meal and we put on a movie. As life would have it, before the movie was over, I went into labor! Lucky for me, I was all packed!

—Claudette, 32, mother of one, with another on the way

- Comfortable bras for nursing
- Breast-feeding/nursing pads
- Underpants you can live without later as they will likely become soiled
- Gifts for older siblings
- A journal or notepad so you can jot things down
- An outfit to go home in—knowing you will still look as though you are five to six months pregnant
- Shoes, socks, slippers

For Your Newborn

Finally, you can see those cute purchases in action!

- An outfit for wearing in the hospital and an outfit for going home (bring a spare in case of spit-up or a leaky diaper)
- A hat for the baby, especially if it is cold outside
- An infant receiving blanket
- A heavier blanket or snowsuit if the weather is cold
- A properly installed car seat

Try not to bring valuables, including cash and jewelry (send these home with your partner if you forget to leave them there). If you need medication, the hospital will provide it. The hospital will also provide you with diapers for your baby, a snap-crotch t-shirt if you didn't bring an outfit for the baby to wear while in the hospital, and receiving blankets for in-hospital use. Breast pumps, if necessary, can be provided by the hospital as well.

Notes:

For a pregnant woman at her due date, finding patience is like trying to touch a rainbow—you can see it in the distance, but the more you try and grasp it, the more elusive it becomes. —*Hillary, 35, mother of two*

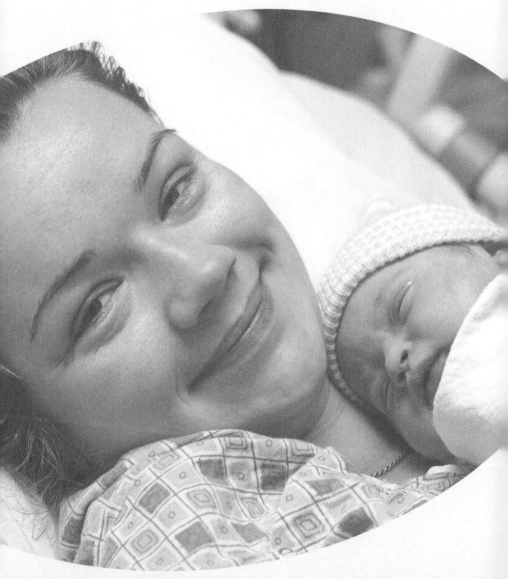

Chapter 13

Labor and Delivery

Ta Da! The big day (or night) is about to arrive! Any day now, you will be in labor and your baby will literally be on the way. And that is a good thing, because by week 40 and beyond you are oh-so-ready to have your baby in your arms instead of in your uterus! At this point, your birth plan is in place (see page 203 in Chapter 9 for help in creating your birth plan), your hospital bags are packed, your doula is on call, the camera is ready, and your friends and relatives are checking in every day to see how you are feeling. Your emotions can range from utter impatience and frustration to excitement and apprehension.

By reading this chapter, speaking with your healthcare provider, and talking with

I was two weeks past my due date, and I was sure I was going to be the first woman to stay pregnant her entire life. At my prenatal visit, my doctor said that if I did not deliver in the next 24 hours she would induce me. I went home feeling dejected because I was so set on having a natural delivery. My husband made dinner that night and tried to cheer me up, but I sullenly and silently just picked at my food. The phone rang. I could hear my husband saying no to his friend who was offering him a ticket to an NBA playoff game that night. I interrupted my husband and begged him to go. I knew I wasn't going into labor and I felt better knowing he could enjoy himself before I was induced the next night. He was reluctant to leave me, but I could see the glimmer in his eyes about the opportunity to go. I cleaned up and went to bed early. Astonishingly, around 9:30 p.m., I woke up because my water had broken! I frantically called my husband, but he wasn't answering his phone. I tried his friend's phone, and he didn't answer either. I was panicked because my contractions were coming close together. I called my mom and she said just get to the hospital and she would find my husband. She actually went down to the stadium and spoke with several ticket takers, ushers, and finally two police officers. The officers were able to have my husband paged during a television timeout. The stadium announcer said: "Will Mr. Kyle Bradford please meet his wife at the hospital— she is about to give birth to your first child!" The entire stadium erupted in applause and cheers, and my husband was high-fived all the way up the aisle. The officers who had had him paged drove him to the hospital, and I gave birth only 30 minutes after he arrived! We named our little boy Benjamin Michael after those two amazing policemen who stayed to see the baby! In fact, they have become two of our best friends! —*Mary Barbara, 36* other moms, you can prepare yourself to some degree for giving birth. It is a good idea to inform yourself about cesarean sections by reviewing this topic in Chapter 12, even if you plan on having a vaginal birth. Remember, no two women have the same birthing experience, and many women have a delivery that's completely different from what they had hoped for. As you enter the delivery process, remain flexible and go with the flow!

When it comes to labor, you can expect the unexpected. Anything is possible—an induced labor, a prolonged labor, a fast labor, a painful labor, or a smooth labor. You cannot even rely on past labor experiences to predict when and how you will go into the hospital or call the midwife this time! Nature will take her course no matter what plans you have.

You may have heard the saying, "They don't call it labor for nothing!" For the majority of women, even if you have good pain control during the process, labor involves endurance, patience, and often a lot of hard, physical work. This is when all your efforts to eat well, tone your body, and strengthen your pelvic floor with Kegel exercises will pay off.

Regardless of how you deliver your infant, this is the day your ultrasound images will become a reality as you finally hold your child in your arms. All you have endured will be worth it! In this chapter, we will answer the following questions and more:

- How is my body preparing for the onset of labor?
- Can I do anything to get my labor started?
- What is natural childbirth?
- What are my choices in pain management during labor and delivery?
- How do I know I'm in labor?

- What happens if my labor must be induced?
- What are labor and delivery really like?
- What does my partner/coach need to know about how to support me?
- What will happen after my baby is born?
- What will it be like to meet my baby for the first time?
- When do I begin breast-feeding my baby, and what will that be like?

How Your Body Is Preparing for Labor

Prior to labor, most women experience "dropping" or "lightening" (see Chapter 12), which involves the lowering of the baby's presenting part, usually the head, into the pelvis. As a result, you will be carrying your baby lower and can see this change from the outside. Inside, there is now more space for your lungs and ribs to expand and you will find it easier to breathe again!

If your baby's head does not drop or engage in the pelvis, your contractions will not dilate the cervix adequately, and it is likely your labor will stall at two to three centimeters. When the head is engaged, your contractions press the head down in order to thin out and open the cervix to its maximum of 10 centimeters.

You may also notice an increase in the production of colostrum, the early milk, and more breast leakage, to the point where you might already have to wear nursing pads. The quantity of colostrum will further increase from the time your baby is born until about three to five days later, when your milk will begin to mature into regular breast milk.

Your doctor or midwife might notice an increase in effacement (thinning) of your cervix and possibly some dilation (from one to three centimeters) before you actually go into labor. Your cervix will change from being about as firm as your chin or nose to a softer consistency, like that of your cheek. A softer, riper cervix is more likely to dilate than a cervix that is harder. These changes are what your healthcare provider is looking for when determining how close you are to going into labor.

Your estrogen level rises at this point and your progesterone level drops in response to a bodily signal that has yet to be completely understood. This combination of hormones, in conjunction with a hormone called oxytocin, results in an increase in contractions. Oxytocin is the natural equivalent of Pitocin, which is a medication given by doctors to induce labor.

Waiting for the Big Event

Like most major events in a person's life, it is increasingly difficult to wait as the occasion approaches. Stay busy if you can, and look for these signs that things are progressing:

- Contractions that increase in painfulness, length, and intensity
- Contractions that are about three to seven minutes apart and getting closer together
- Contractions that begin in the back and wrap around to engulf the entire abdomen
- Contractions that begin with or start after spontaneous rupture of membranes (breaking of the water)
- Intermittent low back pain that is moderate to severe in intensity (back labor)

Your Mucus Plug and Labor

Losing your mucus plug usually means that you can expect to go into labor within the next one to seven days—but it is *not* considered a sign of being in labor.

Can You Induce Your Own Labor?

Some women actively try to get their labor going. Methods to bring on labor at home can only work if your body and uterus are already completely prepared for the labor and delivery process. Some mechanisms to bring on labor at home are considered folk remedies, while others have a solid basis in science.

Ask your healthcare provider if you can do any of these things in order to bring on labor. Most (but not all) are completely harmless, and some can trigger stronger contractions than you may have bargained for! The following are some natural ways to bring on labor:

Acupressure: There are specific pressure points in the area of the shoulder, the web between the thumb and forefinger, the heel, and the small of the back that, when firmly pressed, can begin labor contractions. For best results, see a person who specializes in acupressure who can teach you the pressure points.

Acupuncture: Acupuncture, which involves the insertion of very slender needles by a trained practitioner, has been used as a traditional method to begin labor for many years in Asia. Some recent research suggests it may be effective.

Sex and orgasm: Vaginal sex seems to release chemicals that soften the cervix, and orgasm increases uterine contractions. If your membranes have not ruptured yet, sex at the end of a full-term pregnancy might bring on labor. Semen contains prostaglandins, which are similar to labor-inducing hormones.

Herbal remedies: Approach herbal remedies with care, and be sure to consult your health-care provider. Some herbal remedies include balsamic vinegar, basil, black cohosh, blue cohosh, borage seed oil, Clary sage oil, eggplant, evening primrose oil, goldenseal, natural licorice, motherwort tea or pills, oregano, fresh pineapple, raspberry tea, quinine, spicy food, thyme tea, and squaw wine. For best results, contact a reputable herbalist.

Physical activity: Taking a bumpy car ride, swinging on a swing, bouncing on an exercise or birthing ball, dancing, doing squats, swimming, walking, climbing stairs, yoga, and horseback riding can bring on contractions, and, if your body is ready, you may go into labor. Be cautious about overexerting—you don't want to be exhausted before labor even starts.

Castor oil: There is no reputable research confirming that this works, and castor oil brings on nasty diarrhea and vomiting. Only take castor oil if you are prepared for the side effects, which may include dehydration from vomiting.

Nipple stimulation: You (or your partner) can manually stimulate your nipples, which releases oxytocin to cause contractions, or you can use your breast pump. In some cases, this can bring on contractions that are too strong and frequent. Ask your doctor if nipple stimulation is advisable in your situation.

There is no guarantee, but any of the above may help you bring on labor if your body is ready and receptive.

How Does Labor Start?

No one knows exactly why labor begins, but doctors have found that labor depends on the number of active chemical receptors on the uterus. When the number of chemical receptors is high enough to start the contraction process, labor begins.

Some research indicates that, at least in mice, a protein given off by the fetus' lungs triggers the initiation of labor. This insures that labor only happens when the fetus is prepared to enter the outside world. This research has been repeated in humans and indicates that when the substance, known as surfactant, reaches a critical level, it triggers labor. Surfactant is necessary for adequate fetal lung function. What these findings do not explain is why some infants are born before the lungs are mature, as in the case of preterm birth.

Women with preterm labor often have subtle infections of the membranes surrounding the fetus. This infection increases the number of infection-fighting cells within the uterine wall that trigger labor. This is believed to be why some women have problems with preterm labor.

Other scientists believe that the levels of progesterone and estrogen in the bodies of pregnant women control whether or not they go into labor. Progesterone is known to stop contractions and is generally at high levels during the latter part of pregnancy. When it is time for labor, the estrogen level goes way up and is dominant over the progesterone.

In addition, the placenta releases a hormone called corticotrophin-releasing hormone (CRH), which causes the fetal brain to release ACTH (adenocorticoprophic hormone), which in turn causes the fetal adrenal gland to release cortisol (a steroid) and DHEA, a hormone that brings up the estrogen level in the body. The estrogen releases prostaglandins, which are found in the cervix as well as in the blood stream. Prostaglandin release softens and ripens the cervix so that contractions and the pressure of the baby's head can begin to efface or thin out the cervix.

My doctor said it was just a coincidence, but with both my babies I went into labor after eating super-spicy Mexican food! I'm waiting to give birth to my third, so we'll have to see if the theory holds up! —*Victoria Ann, 38, mother of two, with another on the way*

In the meantime, your uterus is busy releasing oxytocin. When oxytocin levels are high and there are enough oxytocin receptors on the uterus, labor can happen. In addition, the more the cervix dilates, the more oxytocin is released, strengthening contractions.

Much of life is a mystery, and going into labor and giving birth is no exception. Although scientists have some idea of the "why" of labor, what really matters is that your miraculous body knows just what to do and when to do it!

Exploring Pain Management in Labor

Whether you choose to have a natural childbirth or use medication for pain control during labor and delivery, remember to remain flexible and be prepared to alter your plans if need be.

Natural Childbirth

If you choose to approach childbirth without medication, you will need to make careful preparations and create the right mindset to have a positive labor experience. It is crucial to have a supportive healthcare practitioner and an appropriate environment, such as a birthing center, a hospital with practices that support natural childbirth, or a midwife-assisted home delivery. Women who commit to natural childbirth often believe in the wisdom of the body and want to participate fully in their birth experiences. Variations on natural childbirth include water births (using a tub or pool in which to give birth) and "gentle" birth practices that emphasize a quiet, peaceful environment for the birth.

The most critical thing to remember when planning for natural childbirth is that labor and delivery are unpredictable experiences. Educate yourself and plan for the best, but be flexible enough to do whatever is necessary for your comfort and safety and that of your baby. Some women are harshly self-critical if they plan a natural childbirth and are unable to have this experience. The most important outcome is the birth of your baby. Natural childbirth practices can be helpful even if you ultimately choose to use pain medication, because they can ease your anxiety and make you feel more comfortable throughout labor.

Here are some tips for preparing for a natural childbirth:

Breathing technique: Through your childbirth class, find a breathing technique that works for you and practice it daily. When you are in the throes of labor pain it will be easier to rely on your breathing technique if it has become a practiced habit.

> I was definitely planning to take meds during labor for my first child. As soon as I started having contractions, we headed to the hospital because it was one and a half hours away. Lucky we did, because by the time we got to the hospital I was ready to push! My labor lasted only three and a half hours from start to finish, so I did not have any meds. Both my other two children were born just as quickly—so you never know. Plan for the worst, but maybe like me, you'll end up with the best!
> —*Yola, 36, mother of three*

Labor coach: Find a good labor coach (or practice with your partner). The person you choose to coach you through labor should be supportive, knowledgeable in how to manage contractions with a variety of methods (such as breathing, massage, and movement), and able to encourage you to resist the pain. It is important that your labor coach accompanies you to childbirth preparation classes.

Doula: See Chapter 12 for information about doulas, who provide nonmedical

support through pregnancy, delivery, and the postpartum period. A doula will stay with you throughout your labor and delivery and can offer comfort measures and support to encourage natural childbirth. (They can also support you through other forms of childbirth.)

Distracted, calmed, and soothed: Create an arsenal of ways to distract and calm yourself during contractions. Choose soothing music, visual imagery, meditative breathing—whatever you think will work for you—but be sure to have several options. It is hard to know exactly what labor will be like for you, and having a variety of coping options is key to remaining committed to a natural childbirth during actual labor.

Hypnosis: Hypnosis is a method of harnessing the power of the mind to focus and relax. It may be used successfully to reduce fear and anxiety about labor and delivery and to control pain. There are many methods of learning hypnosis, including classes that teach "hypnobirthing" and online self-tutorials. Contrary to some of the myths about hypnosis, you remain in control of yourself and it works best for people who are intelligent.

Strong mindset: Your commitment to natural childbirth must be strong, positive, and unwavering. Be sure whoever is attending your child's birth is on board with your wishes so that everyone in the room can support your efforts to have a natural childbirth. Remind yourself that contractions are episodic, no matter how intense they are. You will have periods of relative comfort after each contraction to relax and prepare for the next one.

Finish line: Remind yourself that the labor process will end. On average, labor lasts between 12 to 18 hours from start to finish for women who are having their first vaginal birth, and about 7 to 8 hours for women who have had a previous vaginal delivery. Not all of those hours will be intensely painful, and it may only be significantly painful for one-third to half that time.

Options for Pain Control with Medication

Many women know they want to control labor pain with medication and choose their method of pain control even before they go into labor. Others who plan for a natural vaginal delivery may change their minds in the middle of labor and need to make a quick decision on pain control. Even if you are planning a natural childbirth, it is a good idea to familiarize yourself with pain control options just in case.

Intravenous (IV) pain management: You can receive systemic (whole body) pain medications through an intravenous (IV) line. This requires that you have the nurse or anesthetist place an IV line that is connected to a plug through which the medication is delivered. Some hospitals routinely use an IV bag filled with sugar or saline solution that can provide you with fluids during labor and can be an access point for giving intravenous medications. IV bags with fluid are helpful if you are vomiting during labor and think you might become dehydrated.

Intravenous medications are usually narcotics such as Nubain, Demerol, or mor-

phine. These are all strong painkillers that will make you feel drowsy and will take the edge off the pain for one to two hours so you can rest a bit more comfortably.

Some hospitals will only allow one injection of pain medications during labor unless your labor is very long. They reserve the injection of narcotic until you are far into your labor but not so close that the medication will still be in the baby's bloodstream at the time of delivery, which could result in a drowsy baby who may struggle to breathe properly. For this medication, timing is crucial and you will want to think about when in labor you most want to have it.

The IV narcotic medication can be mixed with relaxants such as benzodiazepines or Vistaril, also called hydroxyzine. This medication can help relieve nausea and vomiting in labor, but it will also make you drowsy.

While intravenous medications do work during labor, they are effective for only a short period of time and can make you so drowsy that you become unable to focus on your contractions. In addition, if the baby is affected by the medication, he or she may need extra breathing support or a shot of Narcan—a medication that reverses the effects of narcotic medication.

Epidural anesthesia: Epidural anesthesia has been available for the last 40 years or so and is an anesthetic technique that is generally performed by an anesthesiologist (a medical doctor with specialized training). The epidural involves placing a catheter in your lower back that enters the space outside the sac that surrounds your spinal cord, called the epidural space. A needle is used to place the catheter, and then the needle is withdrawn.

The catheter is attached to tubing that is in turn attached to a bag of fluid that contains a quantity of a narcotic medication (such as fentanyl or morphine) combined with a local anesthetic.

The combination of drugs works to block sensations of pain, movement, temperature, and touch from about your waist to the tips of your toes. Some women experience total anesthesia of their belly and legs so they can't move them without help. Others will just experience pain relief but will retain the ability to move their legs, even if they are clumsy. Still others will experience little pain relief, either because the catheter was placed in the wrong position or migrated to the wrong position. Every woman's experience with epidural anesthesia is different.

Epidurals are usually placed when your cervix is dilated to between four and seven centimeters; however, the epidural can be placed earlier or later than that, depending on your circumstances and the practices of the obstetrical doctor and the anesthesiologist.

On the whole, most women are happy with their epidural experience as it offers a way for you to have a relatively pain-free labor and delivery without making you or the baby drowsy. The pain in putting in the catheter is minimal when compared to labor contractions and takes only about 5 to 10 minutes to complete. Once placed, it takes a few minutes to kick in, so be patient.

After you have delivered, the epidural medication is stopped, and you can expect sensation and function to return to your legs and abdominal area within about half an hour. Then you can get up and use the rest-room. While you have the epidural in place, you will not be able to get up out of bed, so you will have to use a bedpan or a urinary catheter will be placed inside your bladder in order to drain your bladder throughout the rest of labor.

I won't even take Tylenol for a headache, so when it came to the question of taking meds for childbirth pain I was completely against it. Even when I had to be induced and my nurse explained that labor would likely be more intense, I didn't change my mind. Determined, I managed through my horribly intense contractions for hours, but they started to come so close together I did not have enough time to recover in between. My doctor examined me and said that the contractions were putting too much pressure on my cervix and I would have to have an epidural to allow my cervical ripening and dilation to catch up with each other. I was so disappointed! But after the epidural took effect, I was amazed at the miracle and secretly thrilled at the relief! I still don't take Tylenol for headaches, but I've had an epidural for all my deliveries!
—Angela, 43, mother of four

Spinal block: A spinal block delivers medication directly into the spinal fluid and inside the sac that surrounds the spinal cord. Unlike an epidural, which works until it is shut off, the spinal block involves a single injection of medication. It lasts for varying amounts of time but usually is effective for about two to four hours. After that, it will wear off and your pain will return. Neither a spinal block nor an epidural will do anything harmful to the baby, so you can feel confident that your baby's health will not be affected if you make the decision to use either of these two methods. Spinal blocks might be preferred if you are late in your labor process and want quick pain relief. The results are extremely fast—faster than with an epidural anesthetic.

Combined epidural and spinal anesthesia (CSE): Some hospitals offer a newer technique that involves giving morphine in ways that are as fast as a spinal but last as long as is necessary—like with a traditional epidural. Medication is injected into the spinal fluid and a catheter is left in the epidural space. You get immediate relief from the spinal and a longer-lasting effect from the epidural. It can be given anywhere from 4 to 10 centimeters of dilation, but is usually given when you are about 4 to 5 centimeters dilated. The CSE is sometimes called a "walking epidural" because it allows somewhat more freedom to move about.

Am I in Labor?

Knowing when you are in labor and when it is time to go into the hospital or call the midwife can be difficult, even for those who've been in labor before. Even when labor is induced, it does not just suddenly "turn on."

The one true signal that labor has begun is the sudden rupture of membranes (your water breaking). It can be felt as a gush of fluid that drips down your legs and onto the floor or it can be a slight trickle that feels like

I was sent home three times from the hospital with false labor! So when the real thing started I ignored it for hours and did not tell anyone—including my husband, who was at work. Talking to my friend on the phone, a strong contraction came and I said, "Ooh, wait a minute..." and had to stop talking. After it passed, she asked me what was wrong. "Oh just false labor," I answered. "Wait there," she said, and the next thing I knew she was at the door to take me to the hospital! She'd even called my husband to tell him to meet us there! Lucky for me, I gave birth only three hours after I got there! —*Patsy, 37, mother of one*

you have urinated, except that the trickle persists and the fluid is clear and odorless.

If you are not sure whether you have had rupture of membranes or not, you can go to the hospital or see your healthcare provider to be checked. A sterile speculum will be introduced into your vagina, and a small paper test strip will be used to tell if the fluid is amniotic fluid. If the strip is equivocal, the doctor can have a fern test done, in which some of the fluid in your vagina is smeared onto a microscope slide and dried quickly. Under the microscope, amniotic fluid, when dried, looks like it has a crystallized fern pattern, whereas fluid from the vagina alone will appear differently when viewed with the microscope.

For most women, labor comes on with intact membranes and with irregular contractions that feel nearly identical to false labor or Braxton-Hicks contractions. The only real differences between Braxton-Hicks contractions and the onset of labor is that the contractions of labor will progress from being further apart to being closer together, will be felt higher in the uterus and in the back, and will be rather regular in their pattern regardless of whether you change positions, rest, or move around (see Chapter 10 for more information about distinguishing false labor from true labor).

Some women want to go to the hospital or birthing center as soon as they feel they are in labor. They do not want to miss the opportunity to have pain medications, or they may simply feel more comfortable being in the hospital. Going to the hospital as soon as you believe you are in labor is a good idea for any woman with a history of very fast deliveries or if you are insecure about laboring at home.

Others want to go to the hospital or birthing center when they are absolutely sure they are in labor and are experiencing regular, moderately intense contractions. A good guideline is this: Talk to your partner or to your healthcare provider for five minutes straight. If you have to stop talking at some point to handle the pain of a contraction, then you are likely in labor and will deliver with the next several hours. This is the time when many women feel a strong urge to be in the capable hands of a nurse, midwife, or hospital staff.

Of course, if your hospital or birthing center is very far away or if you have had one or more prior labors that were very short, you may wish to go to the hospital when you believe you are in early labor, or you may choose to talk to your healthcare provider

about having an elective induction of labor near your due date.

Labor Induction

Some women go into the labor process knowing exactly when it will happen. This is because they are having an induction. Labor induction is a scheduled jumpstart of labor using medication.

When Is Labor Induced?

The reasons for inducing labor are varied and can include

- the baby's health
- the mother's health
- a history of precipitous (fast) deliveries that may put you at risk for delivering at home or on the way to the hospital
- placental insufficiency
- oligohydramnios (low fluid volume in the uterus)
- being extremely overdue (as mentioned in Chapter 12, some doctors will induce labor at 41 weeks in order to avoid late postterm complications)
- maternal high blood pressure
- gestational diabetes (with gestational diabetes, an induction might be done prior to 40 weeks in order to avoid having a baby that is too big to fit through the birth canal)
- preeclampsia
- labor that starts but stalls or does not progress (your doctor may give Pitocin to increase both the strength and intensity of contractions in the hope of progressing labor)
- ruptured membranes without the start of labor

Methods for Inducing Labor

Once your doctor or midwife determines that your labor needs to be induced, there are a few options to choose from.

Stripping the membranes: A healthcare provider can attempt to stimulate labor in the office or hospital by stripping the membranes. This involves inserting one or two fingers into the vagina, locating the cervix, and separating the membranes from the lower uterine wall. It can only be done if the cervix is at least two to three centimeters in diameter. This procedure feels like having a really rough vaginal exam, and it carries the risk that it could break the amniotic sac or bag of waters. Stripping the membranes may do nothing at all, or it may trigger labor to happen within a few days.

Ripening the cervix: Sometimes oxytocin does not work to dilate the cervix. (See next page for more information.) Good cervical dilation depends on having a soft and pliable cervix that is easily able to open from pressure during contractions. Some women go into the labor process with what is called an unfavorable cervix, meaning the cervix is not ready to dilate.

Doctors use a measure of cervical ripening called the Bishop score to determine whether or not a cervix is ripe enough for dilation. The Bishop score looks like this:

The highest score possible is 13. The parameters include whether the cervix is toward the back of the body (posterior) or toward the front of the body (anterior), how soft the cervix is, how thin the cervix is (effacement), how far dilated the cervix is (from 0 to 10 centimeters), and where the top of the baby's head is in comparison to the pubic bone, from −3 (high) to +2 (low) centimeters. A Bishop score of less than five means the cervix is not very favorable for induction and cervical ripening is needed.

Methods for Ripening the Cervix

The cervical status can be changed in several ways:

Medication: Two medications, Prepidil and Cervidil, contain prostaglandin-like ingredients that increase the ripening of the cervix when placed inside the cervix. Cervidil is imbedded in mesh and placed behind the cervix for a 12-hour release of medication, while Prepidil is a gel that is placed inside the cervix itself. After the cervix is ripe, oxytocin can be used intravenously to dilate the cervix.

An antiulcer medication called Cytotec is sometimes used for cervical dilation. Either a 25 mg tablet is crushed and placed on the cervix or it is taken by mouth every four hours. The risk of Cytotec and the other

Bishop Score				
Parameter	0	1	2	3
Cervical Position	Posterior	Intermediate	Anterior	−
Consistency	Firm	Intermediate	Soft	−
Effacement	0–30 percent	31–50 percent	51–80 percent	>80 percent
Dilation	0 cm	1–2 cm	3–4 cm	>5 cm
Fetal Station	−3 cm	−2 cm	−1, 0 cm	+1, +2 cm

prostaglandin medications is that the uterus can go into overdrive and the medication will have to be washed out of the cervix.

Foley catheter treatment: Another technique used to help ripen the cervix is called a balloon catheter or Foley bulb treatment. A Foley catheter (a tube) is placed in the cervix, and the balloon at the end of the catheter is filled with 30 to 50 milliliters of saline solution. It is kept in the cervix until it falls out or until about 12 hours have gone by. It is often used as an overnight technique in the hospital.

Absorptive devices or hygroscopic dilators: Devices such as Dilapan and Lamicel are also used to ripen the cervix. These are absorbent devices that contain hygroscopic material (material that holds fluid). They are small when placed in the cervix and enlarge as cervical moisture expands the device. Within several hours following insertion, the cervix becomes more dilated. These are called hygroscopic dilators and are in use at some hospitals. While they dilate the cervix, they also facilitate ripening by stimulating the release of prostaglandins.

Dilating the Cervix

While the above products and medications will ripen the cervix, they will not dilate the cervix much, although in some cases they will trigger labor. If you do not have adequate contractions and it is necessary for you to deliver, you will likely receive Pitocin or oxytocin intravenously. This is the same as the hormone produced by the body that causes natural labor.

The medication is started slowly and is increased until you get a steady labor pattern of about one contraction every three minutes.

> I renamed the three stages of labor as follows: Miserable, Excruciating, and Ecstasy! The third one is so worth the previous two!
> —*Annmarie, 35, mother of two*

If the contractions are too weak and the cervix is not dilating, more Pitocin is given to promote contractions. If your contractions are coming too fast for you to catch your breath between them, the Pitocin can be dialed down.

Pitocin almost always works to dilate the cervix. If the Pitocin is causing effective contractions as measured by an internal pressure monitor (a pressure-sensitive catheter placed inside the uterus during labor) and cervical dilation still fails to progress, something else is likely amiss, such as your baby's head being too big to for the pelvic bone or having an abnormal presentation, and a cesarean section will need to be performed.

Apps to Keep Track of Labor Contractions

What NOW?

Many couples enjoy using cellphone apps that help keep track of labor contractions. There are different versions for various phones. Most will allow you to enter the start and stop time of a contraction and will then automatically calculate the duration and frequency of contractions.

Effacement and Dilation of the Cervix

In order to deliver a baby vaginally, your cervix needs to thin out in a process called effacement. If your cervix is 0 percent effaced, it is thick and unable to dilate, and a baby cannot be delivered. You need to reach a level of 95 to 100 percent effacement before you can push your baby out into the world. When your cervix is 100 percent effaced it is termed "paper thin." This indicates the opening to the cervix has shortened from four centimeters to only a few millimeters. In addition to effacement, your cervix must also dilate from 0 centimeters (or closed) to 10 centimeters so your baby can pass through the vagina, or birth canal. After you have reached 10 centimeters dilation, you can push the baby out. Following your baby's birth, your placenta must also pass through the birth canal and out of your body. Once this happens, your labor and delivery process is complete.

Three Stages of Labor and Birth

Doctors refer to the labor and delivery process as occurring in three stages: labor, delivery of your baby, and delivery of the placenta. The first stage—labor—is divided into three parts: early labor, active labor, and transition.

First Stage of Labor and Birth: Labor

Early labor: In early labor, which is about zero to four centimeters of cervical dilation, you experience a gradual increase in the intensity of contractions and the cervix becomes more effaced.

Early labor will begin at home (or in the shopping mall!) and may last for hours before you actually need to go to the hospital. In a first pregnancy, the first stage of labor can last 20 hours. Your contractions (which vary greatly from woman to woman) generally last from 30 to 60 seconds and may occur at irregular or regular intervals, anywhere from 5 to 20 minutes apart. As you try to relax and distract yourself at home, be aware of when your contractions become more intense and closer together, signaling that it is time to head to the hospital.

When the first stage of labor begins, your cervix may be completely thinned out (100 percent effaced) but still tightly closed (zero centimeters dilated). This means you probably have a long way to go before you can push the baby out. Most women, however, begin early labor at least one to three centimeters dilated and 30 to 50 percent effaced. This is due to the previous work of Braxton-Hicks contractions and the natural pressure of the baby's head on the cervix.

Early first-stage labor lasts up to eight hours or more, although individual labor patterns can greatly deviate from this, especially if this is not your first delivery. While in early first-stage labor, you can generally talk through your contractions and walk around. It can still be stressful and exhausting.

If you are definitely in early labor, take the time to nap when you can, eat a light snack, and find relaxing ways to distract yourself. If you feel you want to focus on timing your contractions, do so for only 15 minutes every hour and then rest. Drink plenty of fluids in early-stage labor so that you do not get dehydrated later in labor, when you will not feel like eating or drinking because of possible nausea and vomiting.

As early labor progresses, your contractions become about five minutes apart and last about 45 seconds. Real labor, as we have discussed, will gradually increase in intensity, and the contractions will become closer together. The cervix will be thinning out and dilating as your baby's head descends from the lower uterine segment into the pelvis. When you have increasing contractions that become closer together and increase in intensity, that's when it is time to go to the hospital or birthing center. (Remember: Call your doctor or midwife if you have any questions or concerns about your labor and when to head to the hospital.)

Active labor: In active labor, your contractions will become quite intense and sometimes excruciating. (This is the time to use the breathing and relaxation techniques you learned in your childbirth education classes.) At the beginning of this portion of labor,

My partner was not very attentive during active labor—he was having a hard time seeing me in so much pain. Luckily, my nurse was like an angel and she massaged my back through every contraction. I can't tell you how much she helped me until I was able to get my epidural. —*Allie, 31, mother of one*

your will be about four centimeters dilated; when you begin Part III (transition) after active labor, you will be at about eight centimeters. Your contractions are often two to three minutes apart and last for up to a full minute. The bright side of active labor is that your body is moving your baby through your pelvis as your cervix continues to soften and dilate. Active labor can last anywhere from three to eight hours.

During active labor, your vital signs will be checked, you will have occasional pelvic exams to assess how your cervix is dilating, and you may need more help from

Labor positions
Changing positions during labor can help alleviate discomfort and encourage progress.

Lean over an exercise ball or chair. Use pillows or a folded towel under your knees if this is more comfortable.

Walking can really help, especially in early labor.

Place one foot on a chair, and slowly lean toward the chair, then back to your original position.

your partner, nurse, doula, or labor coach as you move through your contractions. Alternatively, this is the point at which many women have a change in focus. Your excitement and joy may transform into an inward and single-minded focus on your body and your contractions. Many women resist help and words of encouragement at this stage and prefer to stay in control by themselves through quiet focus. It is important to communicate your desire for active support or freedom from distraction during this time, so those who are helping you know what to do.

The last two to three centimeters of cervical dilation signal the end of the first stage of labor. This is called "being in transition."

Transition: By the time you reach transition, you will definitely want to be in the hospital or birthing center, or you may run the risk of delivering your baby at home or en route! Although transition is the shortest part of the first stage of labor and delivery (lasting from one to two hours), it is also extremely intense. Your contractions will be closer together and longer in duration. Unless you receive pain medication by IV or via an epidural or spinal block, this is the time you will need to have the deepest concentration and focus intently on your breathing. Nausea and vomiting are common during transition and mean that your cervix is changing rapidly and releasing hormones that make you nauseated. There will also be some increase in bloody discharge.

The descent of your baby's head can occur throughout active labor or may happen just near the end of transition. During the transition phase, you may feel tremulous and be visibly shaking. This is a natural part of the labor and delivery process and can happen

after the baby is born as well. It is just your body's way of making the transition from being pregnant to not being pregnant. Late in transition, you might also feel pressure on

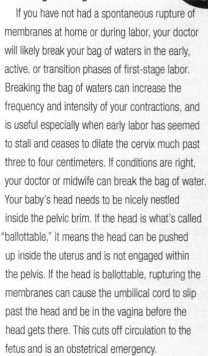

Breaking the Bag of Waters

If you have not had a spontaneous rupture of membranes at home or during labor, your doctor will likely break your bag of waters in the early, active, or transition phases of first-stage labor. Breaking the bag of waters can increase the frequency and intensity of your contractions, and is useful especially when early labor has seemed to stall and ceases to dilate the cervix much past three to four centimeters. If conditions are right, your doctor or midwife can break the bag of water. Your baby's head needs to be nicely nestled inside the pelvic brim. If the head is what's called "ballottable," it means the head can be pushed up inside the uterus and is not engaged within the pelvis. If the head is ballottable, rupturing the membranes can cause the umbilical cord to slip past the head and be in the vagina before the head gets there. This cuts off circulation to the fetus and is an obstetrical emergency.

A vaginal exam is done to confirm the fetal station (how low the fetus is) and dilation status. Then a long plastic rod with a hook (like a crochet hook) is inserted in the vagina. The doctor locates the bag of waters and breaks it with the hook.

For you, it feels just like having a vaginal exam. You will feel a gush of warm fluid between your legs or a slight trickle of fluid coming out. Your baby will generally be unaffected, although the rare baby will end up with a tiny scratch on its head from the device used to break the bag of waters. Your contractions and cervical dilation will move faster after this procedure.

Dads, don't eat in front of your wife or partner during labor. My wife was in labor for 20 hours, and when I broke out a bag of chips in front of her during hour 14, she screamed: "You eat that now and you'll never have sex with me again!" If she could have gotten up, I'm pretty sure she would have walked across the room and dumped those chips over my head. No matter how long labor seems to you, remember just how much longer it is for her. If you need to eat, pretend you are taking a bathroom break and eat in the hall. —*Chase, 30, dad of two*

your rectum as though you want to have a bowel movement. This is due to the pressure of the descending head on the rectal wall. If you feel the urge to push, tell the nurse or midwife so

he or she can check your cervix and see if it is actually time to do so.

Second Stage of Labor and Birth: Delivering Your Baby!

The second stage of labor is often referred to as the pushing phase. It begins when you are 10 centimeters in cervical dilation and ends with the actual—and long awaited!—delivery of your baby. During the pushing phase, your contractions tend to space out a bit so you have time to catch your breath before the next contraction occurs.

Your focus and concentration at this stage is intense. It requires all the strength you can muster to push your baby out. Your baby's head will descend to the outer part of the vagina by fitting through the pelvis and moving through the pelvic tissue that must get out

Birth positions

The delivery position of lying on your back with your feet in the air is convenient for the doctor, but other positions are often more comfortable for women giving birth. These alternate positions may result in less serious tearing for the mother and enhance the delivery process.

All fours position: This can help to alleviate back pain.

Side-lying: You can use this position during labor or delivery, even if you have had an epidural.

Squatting: You can squat on the floor or bed, with or without the support of another person. Birthing centers often have bars or supports to hold onto, or chairs or stools that will help you maintain an upright position to facilitate delivery.

How Long Will You Have to Push?

The second stage of labor (pushing and birth) may only be a few minutes long or as long as three hours. For moms who have not had a baby before, the average length of time for the second stage is one to two hours. For moms who have had babies before, the average length of time for this stage is about 20 minutes. An epidural can make this stage a bit longer because you do not feel the same urge to push as with a natural delivery.

of the way in order for you to have the baby. Each push will lower the head (if you push correctly). Between pushes, your baby's head will suck back into the pelvis with only millimeters of progress made each time. Once the head has passed the pelvic bone (the pubic symphysis), the head tends to stay down more readily and will not retreat into your body as much between contractions.

If you have an epidural, you will not feel the baby descending nor will you feel the baby's head pushing on the rectum. Sometimes doctors will turn your epidural medications down or off during this stage so you can feel and respond to the pushing process more easily. When you feel the pressure on the rectum and are having a contraction, this is the time to push. Pushing without a contraction tends not to be very productive.

Eventually, your baby's head will become visible. If this is your first baby, reaching this stage will take an average of one to two hours of pushing. Often, nurses will hold a mirror so you can see the first glimpse of your newborn baby. The head is considered to be "crowning" when it is visible at all times, even

when you are not pushing. At this time, it is okay to reach between your legs and touch your baby's head for the first time. With your baby's birth so close, you will be spurred on through the next contractions to really focus on pushing.

At this point, you will want to push more carefully in order to gradually deliver the head. Your doctor or midwife may use a lubricant in order to ease the passage of the head through the birth canal, and he or she may stretch out the perineum (the area between the vaginal opening and the anus) so that the baby's head can pass through the outer part of the birth canal without tearing the tissue.

Episiotomy—yes or no? In the past, many doctors performed episiotomies (a surgical cut to enlarge the vaginal opening) during vaginal deliveries. It was thought that an episiotomy would be easier on the mother than having

Soothing the Episiotomy Following the Birth

If you have an episiotomy and it is properly repaired by the doctor with local anesthetic and sutures, you should feel free to soothe the area with witch hazel and ice. Witch hazel can be found in hemorrhoid pads. Use a squirt bottle in the first few days to wash off the wound after using the restroom. Keep a clean pad over the incision when you have a bowel movement and continue to do your Kegel exercises to strengthen the area again. If pain is worse with sitting, sit on a doughnut-shaped cushion. Take pain medication and call your doctor if you see signs of infection like pus, discharge, increased pain, or redness of the area.

the vaginal opening tear during delivery. However, medical research has shown that most women do better without an episiotomy, and that the minor tears they may experience can heal or be repaired more easily than the episiotomy incision. Presently, episiotomies are done only to expedite a difficult delivery or if a very large laceration (tear) would otherwise be expected.

It is possible to tear if you have an episiotomy, but you usually tear in such a way that it extends the episiotomy incision. There are several degrees of episiotomy tears that are better or worse, depending on the degree of the tear:

- A first-degree tear involves extension of the episiotomy just through fat, skin, and connective tissue.
- A second-degree tear involves a laceration into the muscle between the vagina and rectum.
- A third-degree tear involves a rip through the skin, muscle, and the rectal sphincter that controls the passage of stool through the anus.
- A fourth-degree tear extends into the rectal lining and is the most difficult to repair because now there is a connection between the vagina and the rectum.

Fetal position: Even though your baby is probably in the head-down position as a vaginal delivery approaches, variations in this position will affect how long it takes for the second stage of labor to reach its completion.

- Fetal position only really applies to the head-down or vertex presentation.

- Most babies are born with their face facing the floor. This is called the occiput anterior position because the occiput, or the back of the baby's head, is facing upward. Babies can be right occiput anterior (ROA) or left occiput anterior (LOA), depending on whether the rest of the baby's body is oriented to the right or left side of your body.

- Babies born occiput posterior are also known as being born "sunny-side up" or face up. These babies do not fit as well within the contours of the pelvis, so the second stage of labor can be several times longer than for face-down births. However, this position is not harmful to the baby or to you. As in occiput anterior, a baby can be born right occiput posterior (ROP) or left occiput posterior (LOP).

- Your doctor may be able to tell if the baby is occiput posterior or occiput anterior just by doing a vaginal exam.

I was nearing the end of a three-hour push phase and 22 hours of labor. I was exhausted and practically delirious, and only focused on getting my baby out. I remember the nurse actually screaming at me to open my eyes so I could see my baby being born. Thankfully she did or I would have missed the single moment I'd waited 10 months to see! —*Carla, 33, mother of one*

Your baby is born! Eventually the head will ease its way through the birth canal and those watching will usually see the back of the baby's head, although the face can sometimes be seen. The doctor or midwife will ask you not to push while he or she checks for the presence of the cord around the neck. If there are one or more loops of cord around the neck, the doctor or midwife simply slips these cords over the baby's head so they are not wrapped around the baby's neck and will perform a maneuver to get the baby's shoulders and body out.

The healthcare provider may clean out the baby's nose and mouth before getting the rest of the baby's body out and may repeat that procedure once the baby is delivered. If the baby appears healthy, he or she will be placed upon your now-empty belly so you can see and touch your baby for the first time. This signals the end of the second stage of labor. Congratulations!

Third Stage of Labor and Birth: Delivering the Placenta

By the time you reach the third stage of labor, you are holding your beautiful new baby and are likely oblivious to what is still happening in your body. The third stage of labor begins after your baby is born and ends when the placenta is delivered. The placenta, which has been nourishing your baby for the last 40 weeks, has done its job, and it is time for it to separate from the uterus and exit the vagina.

The third stage is very short, only five to ten minutes in length. Your doctor or midwife may put gentle traction on the umbilical cord while attempting to contract the uterus by squeezing it in the lower to mid-abdomen. Eventually the uterus contracts and the now pancake-like placenta slips out of the vagina. You may not even feel or notice that it has

> My mother had told me that, as soon as the baby is born, the pain you experience immediately stops—and she was right. The nice thing for me was that I delivered the placenta only a few minutes after my baby, and if the nurse hadn't been so excited about it, I would never have even noticed. —*Constance, 29, mother of one*

happened. If the placenta does not come out after 15 to 20 minutes, or if you are bleeding heavily, the doctor or midwife may reach in and pull the placenta out in a procedure called a manual extraction. This procedure may be somewhat painful but does not last longer than a couple of minutes.

If you have decided to bank the cord blood for stem cells (see Chapter 10), this is also the point in delivery that umbilical cord blood is collected because the cord blood is still being pumped by the umbilical cord.

Advice for the Labor Coach

As the labor coach and/or partner, it is your job to be as attentive, supportive, and calm as possible during labor and delivery. Your commitment to Mom-to-be is essential to making her experience go as smoothly as possible. So read the following and use these tips as a guide to help you be the best coach you can be!

- Resolve yourself to the fact that this is going to be a long process and be prepared to get bored, hungry, tired, and told what and what not to do by Mom-to-be.

- Prepare for labor and delivery by reading about what to expect and attending childbirth classes.
- Take care of yourself by packing snacks and beverages to keep up your energy, but don't eat or drink in front of the laboring woman if it bothers her.
- Remember that Mom-to-be is the focus of this entire process, so all your attention needs to go toward helping her for the duration of labor and delivery. Time her contractions and record them; help her decide when to go to the hospital or birthing center.
- In the hospital or birthing center, help her through contractions by breathing with her, encouraging her with enthusiasm, and complimenting how she is doing.
- Help distract her by telling stories, joking, asking her to tell a story, watching television, reading to her, or going for a brief walk. Be sure to stop if this activity is annoying her.
- Give her a massage whenever she wants one.
- Ask her what she needs often and listen to her response. If you want to give her a back massage and she says "no," then do not do it! She is in control and knows what she wants, so pay attention to what she says.
- During active labor, keep yourself and the room as calm as possible; ask Mom-to-be if she would like relaxing music on, the lights dim, or the door shut.
- Help her through her contractions—her uterus will tighten as they begin, enabling you to alert her to what is coming. Be encouraging and ask if massage or other techniques you have practiced will help her.
- Support her through the hundredth contraction in the same way you supported her for the first few contractions—with love, compliments, and encouragement.
- Many women become intensely focused during active labor and do not want to be touched, talked to, or told what to do at this point. Be sure to check in to see what will work for her—and then do as she asks!
- Advocate for Mom-to-be by asking doctors questions about how things are progressing, when medication can be given, and any explanations that you think she (and you) may want about a particular procedure.
- Continue to give encouragement and positive feedback as long as Mom-to-be has not told you to stop—sometimes talking of any kind can be distracting and annoying during painful contractions.

Hey dads, if you are coaching your wife or partner, take this advice: Think of yourself as a basketball coach. You have to be there for the team from warm-ups through to the final buzzer. You would never leave your team in the middle of the game or simply quit coaching because you got tired. Your best player can't leave the court for a break, and she can't quit! She needs you from start to finish—be there for the whole game! —Tony, 40, father of four

- Do not take anything Mom-to-be says personally! Many women become irritable and frustrated during active labor—hours of contractions are painful and exhausting. Remind yourself it is only stress relief and let it go.
- Be sure to put her needs first at all times. Keep the focus on her instead of texting, calling friends and family, watching TV, or taking photographs. She needs you now, so everyone and everything else can wait.
- Know that labor is unpredictable and requires the utmost amount of flexibility on your part. Be the rock she needs during her labor and delivery process.

What Happens after the Baby Comes Out?

When a healthy baby comes out, he or she will be placed on your chest or abdomen almost immediately. Through your relief and your partner's excitement and your shared joy, you will hear your baby's first cries, feel his or her slippery body, and finally have a chance to look directly into his or her beautiful face. While you are doing this, a nurse will be drying off your baby and continuing to stimulate cries, which will clear the fluid out of your baby's lungs, increasing the depth of breaths and the strength of the cry.

The Apgar Score

Your baby may then be placed in the infant warmer, further dried, and assessed by the nursing staff. Babies are scored after birth using a system called the Apgar score named after Dr. Virginia Apgar who devised it in 1952. It is a measurement of your baby's heart rate, skin color, muscle tone, reflexes, and breathing at one minute and five minutes after birth.

A total Apgar score can be between 0 and 10, although few babies score at the extremes. Most pediatricians do not give scores of 10, usually because most babies have some blue on their extremities. Common Apgar scores are between six and nine points. The Apgar score at one minute usually reflects how well your baby did during the last several minutes of labor. If the baby suffered some distress at the end of labor, he or she might have a low score after a minute. With further stimulation, the Apgar score should improve.

In almost all cases, the Apgar score is better at five minutes than at one minute. If the Apgar score is less than five at five minutes, it is repeated at 10 minutes to look for further improvements. While a low five-minute score may mean nothing over the long haul, it could indicate that a baby will suffer some type of developmental delay during infancy. Talk to your pediatrician if you believe your

Apgar Score			
Criterion	0	1	2
Appearance	Blue All Over	Pink with Blue Extremities	Pink All Over
Pulse Rate	None	Less than 100	Greater than 100
Reflex Irritability	No Response	Weakly Irritable	Strongly Pulls Back with Stimulation
Muscle Tone	Floppy	Some Muscle Flexion	Strong Muscle Tone
Respirations	No Respirations	Weak Cry	Cries Lustily

baby had a low Apgar score 5 to 10 minutes post-birth.

After the Apgar

If all is well and the Apgar scoring is completed, the nurse will weigh and measure your baby, announce the results, get infant footprints, and give the baby to you for some private time with your partner. You can continue bonding with your newborn and may find yourself counting fingers and toes and marveling at your baby's appearance. You can breast-feed if you want to. If you want to breast-feed but are uncertain about how to proceed, ask a nurse for help. Skin-to-skin contact with your baby is a natural way to begin your lives together.

I joined a new moms' group when my baby was four weeks old. I remember all the other moms with four-week-old infants comparing Apgar scores like they were talking about where their kids got into college, trying to one-up each other. The woman next to me turned and whispered, "I don't even remember my kid's Apgar score. Do you?" I didn't. We both laughed, joined another moms' group, and became best friends! —Joy, 32, mother of two

As you are doing this, your epidural will wear off (if you had one, of course) and the urinary catheter will be removed. You will be cleaned off and be able to sit up in a regular position. The nurse will periodically knead your stomach to try to get it to contract and expel any blood clots that

have collected. When you are deemed stable, relatives can come in and see the baby if you feel ready. If this is the room you will be in for the rest of your hospital stay, the room will be cleaned out of all the supplies needed for the delivery, making more room for you and your friends and relatives to celebrate.

In the hospital setting, if you will be moved to a postpartum room, this may happen as your baby gets his or her first bath. Partners can participate in the bath if they wish; just ask the baby's nurse. You will then go into the room that will be your home with your baby for the next one to three days.

Meeting Your Baby for the First Time

When your baby is placed in your arms for the first time, you may notice that he or she is still blue around his or her hands and feet. This is because circulation opens up from head to toe and from the center of the body to the extremities, so the hands and feet get the best circulation last. This phenomenon lasts a few minutes to a few hours.

Your baby will most likely also be covered in vernix (a white, cheese-like protective coating), especially if the baby is a bit early. The vernix coats and moisturizes the fetus in the uterus. If your baby has some vernix on his or her skin, rub it gently into the baby's skin and save some for the back of your hands or other dry areas. It is the best moisturizer in the world!

Other babies will have dry skin and no vernix at all. This is especially true if your baby is overdue. The skin tends to look cracked, especially after that first bath. Areas most affected are the fingers, wrists, ankles, feet,

I will always remember when the nurse handed me my little boy all swaddled up in a blanket. He was lying next to me and I turned and looked into his eyes for the first time and he looked into mine, and in that moment we were bonded forever in love. —*Bernadette, 36, mother of one*

and around the neck folds. An overdue baby will also have long fingernails and moderately long toenails. You or the nurse may have to give the baby his or her first manicure and pedicure in the hospital!

You will find that your baby has flexed knees and arms. This best mimics the environment of the womb and will be your baby's preferred position for several months to come, especially when tired or irritable. Young infants often seem to be most content when swaddled tightly into a receiving blanket.

Your baby's head may be a bit cone-shaped when you first meet him or her if you have not had a cesarean section. This is because the head molds itself in order to fit through the birth canal. A newborn's skull is not just one solid bone as it appears to be in adults. The lines that mark the end of one bone and the beginning of another will not be solid, so one bone will temporarily override the other, leaving the infant more room to pass through the birth canal. The molding and cone-head appearance will disappear within a day or two.

Your baby's face will reveal that he or she has all the appropriate parts: from eyebrows, eyelashes, and eyes that open and close to

a slightly squashed nose and a squalling or partly open mouth. The eyes of white babies will usually be blue, while babies of color will ordinarily have black or brown eyes. Your baby will be a nose breather for a long time, so use the bulb syringe they will give you at the hospital to clean out the baby's nose, especially before the baby feeds.

Touch your infant's cheek. You will notice a classic reflex called the rooting reflex. This reflex allows the infant to turn toward the nipple whenever its lip or cheek is touched. The rooting reflex is innate in infants so they can find the nipple and begin to suckle.

If you are breast-feeding your infant and the infant stops sucking, stroke his or her cheek. This will elicit the sucking reflex. It helps the baby continue to suck and get the nutrition he or she needs.

Your First Breast-feeding Experience

If you have never breast-fed before, your first attempts may be clumsy and unsure. Not to worry! There are nurses and lactation consultants in the hospital to help you, and if you gave birth in a birthing center, your midwife or a doula will help. You may have problems with your baby latching on to your nipple, or your baby may fall asleep before he or she really gets going. Such problems can be overcome with practice and aid from your nurses or lactation consultant.

A lactation consultant, nurse, midwife, or doula will show you the different ways to hold your baby. The traditional position involves cradling your baby's head in the crook of your arm, with the baby's body across your abdomen. The "football hold," where you support the baby's head with your hand, while the body goes under your arm (baby's feet behind you), may be helpful if you have had a cesarean and want to avoid pressure on your abdomen. Take the time to practice with each of the various holds the nurse or consultant teaches you, and be prepared to change holds as your infant grows. While the football hold works well for newborns, older babies are often more easily fed using the traditional hold.

Be sure to settle yourself into a comfortable position for nursing your baby, using whatever cushions you need. Many mothers use the semicircular support cushions made especially for nursing.

Initially, your baby will get only colostrum from your breasts. Know that this is what

It's amazing how, in a single moment, your entire life changes. Giving birth is like crossing a bridge from one world into another. And that new world is filled with a love you cannot imagine or understand until you hold your minute-old baby in your arms. Life and love are more boundless than we know! *—Donna, 39, mother of three*

nature intended, and trust that it is going to be sufficient for the first few days until your milk supply comes in. Nurse your baby as often as you can to promote your milk coming in, and your baby will begin to get the nutrition and immunity he or she needs to start the first year of life.

Notes:

You need a license to drive a car, you take tests to get into college, and you even have to pass a test to be a postal worker, police officer, or firefighter! So when you simply leave the hospital with a brand new human being and no one checks to see if you know what you are doing, it is bizarre. There is no stranger feeling than walking into a hospital pregnant and walking out with a tiny person who wasn't there before and now belongs to you! —*Allison, 31, mother of one*

Chapter 14

Caring for Your Newborn:
A Quick Guide

Welcome to the new and wonderful world of parenthood! You and your partner (if you have one) survived pregnancy and now have a delightful newborn in your care. You leave the hospital or birthing center, drive home, walk in the front door, and now what? If you have a lot of experience with babies, then you may know what to expect and can transition more comfortably into your new role as mom or dad. But if this is your first child and your experience with babies is limited, you may be wondering where to go from here.

If you had a hospital delivery, your baby's pediatrician will have arrived within 24 hours of the birth to examine your baby. Hopefully, you were able to ask him or her about any concerns you had, and you have received answers to any pressing questions. Your baby will have received his or her first vaccines and have been given the first bath. Hospital doctors and nurses will be monitoring your baby for evidence of things like neonatal jaundice, feeding problems, and neonatal infection, as well as hypothermia.

The average hospital stay for an uncomplicated delivery is only two days, and for a cesarean birth, only three days or so. Women often leave birthing centers even earlier. In

We moved to a new apartment only two months before our son was born—which, by the way, I don't recommend doing! I was still working and so exhausted at night that I'd had no time to meet the neighbors. Our first day home from the hospital I was exhausted, overwhelmed, and hungry all day. My husband didn't cook, and I remember sitting down around 7:00 p.m. just after I'd nursed our son to sleep. I was starving! I knew I needed to eat but I didn't have the energy to cook anything and didn't want take-out either. I didn't know what I was going to do. At that exact moment, our doorbell rang. It was our neighbor from across the hall. She had roasted a chicken with potatoes and carrots and brought it over for me. She said she'd love to see the baby when I was up to it and to let her know if I needed anything at all. And she meant it! That meal was a miracle and made with so much love that I wept the entire time I ate. To this day, I've never had a meal as soul satisfying or delicious as that one. And every time I tell someone this story, I tear up. My neighbor and I are now the best of friends. She is like family to me and always will be! —Sara D., 37 addition to recovering physically, your role those few days in the hospital is to absorb as much information as you can, ask questions, and get help with anything from how to bathe or burp your baby to assistance with breast-feeding. Nursery nurses and doctors in the hospital as well as your pediatrician have a wealth of experience and knowledge when it comes to babies and any issues you may encounter. Use your time in the hospital or birthing center not only to bond with your baby but also to get expert help with anything you can think of.

Once home, you will need to allow yourself time to adjust to your new role and the new person living in your household. Friends and family may offer help, or you may be going it alone. Whatever your circumstances, this chapter will help you with some of the basics.

- Should I worry about my baby's breathing?
- What happens at our first pediatrician's visit?
- What reflexes do newborns have?
- What shots or vaccines will my baby receive?
- What about circumcision?
- What are the basics of infant care?
- When should I worry about jaundice?
- What are some common conditions seen in newborns?
- How long will expressed breast milk keep in the fridge or freezer?
- How do I choose bottles, nipples, and formula?
- How can I help my baby develop good sleep habits?
- What do I need to know about baby poop?
- How can I comfort my baby?
- What's involved in giving a baby a bath?

Baby Breathing

If you are like many inexperienced new parents, you may not be able to rest even when your baby is sleeping. You might find yourself watching and listening to your baby breathe, frightened or concerned that he or she will somehow stop breathing. This is a common occurrence among new parents!

Here are some facts about babies' breathing while asleep that may help ease your worrying:

- "Baby breathing" is fast for a minute or so, and then it slows or stops for up to about 10 seconds. Do not panic. This is normal.
- Apnea (lack of breathing) in newborns can happen, especially in preterm babies. If the apnea spells last longer than 15 seconds or occur consistently over a long period of time, call a nurse or doctor after giving your baby a gentle shake to get the breathing going.
- If your baby seems to breathe normally while sleeping (with breath stoppage of 10 seconds or less), break yourself of the habit of watching the infant sleep by giving yourself a set interval—say three minutes—to watch, and then take a break. Each day, force yourself to watch less and less until you can allow your baby to sleep without watching at all.

Baby's First Pediatric Visit

Your little one's first pediatric exam comes within 24 hours of birth and can be done by the pediatrician of your choice or the pediatrician who works for the hospital. Often the pediatrician that works for the hospital will see your baby within the first hour or two of birth to make sure he or she is healthy

Cephalhematoma vs. Caput (or Conehead)

Babies often have swelling, bruising, and a slight malformation of the head after a vaginal delivery because of the physical trauma of the head going through the birth canal. This common condition is called a caput or "conehead," and is present at birth. It can sometimes look alarming because the swelling on your baby's head can vary from the size of an egg to a larger area, but it will resolve in a couple of days.

A cephalhematoma is different in that it is not present at birth but develops 24 to 48 hours later. The swelling is not necessarily on the part of the baby's head that went first through the birth canal, as with the caput. A cephalhematoma has distinctive edges at the suture lines of the skull. It takes much longer (sometimes months) for this blood clot to be absorbed. The pediatrician will sometimes order an ultrasound to check for a skull fracture in the presence of a cephalhematoma.

Neither scalp issue is dangerous to your baby. Both will go away.

enough to room in with you on the postpartum floor.

Components of the First Exam

During the first visit, the doctor's exam of your baby will be thorough, from head to toe. The exam will make more sense to you if you know what the pediatrician is looking for and why.

- He or she will examine the sutures on the baby's head. These are joints made of strong tissue that hold the bones of the skull together. The doctor will also look for a cephalhematoma. A cephalhematoma is a collection of blood with an overlying

bruise. It is inside the outer flexible layer of bone, so it does not cross suture lines. It lasts for several weeks as the blood clot that makes up the cephalhematoma breaks down.

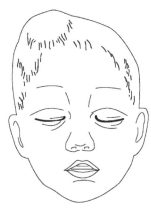

Cephalhematoma
A cephalhematoma will go down in several weeks.

- The pediatrician will also examine your baby's face for evidence of facial features indicating Down syndrome or other congenital birth defects. The ears will be examined to see that the external canals are open and that the eardrum is intact and normal in appearance. The doctor will examine your baby's eyes, including checking for a retinal light reflex.

- The nose is checked to make sure there is no membrane blocking the nasal opening and that the baby is nose-breathing normally. The doctor examines the mouth to make sure there is no cleft palate, that there is normal sucking strength, that the gums are normal and without premature teeth (it can happen!), and that the throat is normal.

- The doctor examines the neck for abnormal masses and listens to the lungs for evidence of residual fluid or a lack of breath sounds in any area of the lungs. Then he or she will listen carefully to the heart for the presence of a normal heart rate (110 to 150 beats per minute) and normal heart sounds without murmurs or extra sounds.

- The pediatrician examines the baby's abdomen to make sure the attachment of the remaining umbilical cord is normal. At this time, the baby will still have a clamp on the cord to keep it from bleeding. The abdominal wall is checked for hernias, and the liver and spleen will be examined to see if they are enlarged. The doctor will evaluate the baby's genitalia for evidence of undescended testicles in boys or for ambiguous genitalia in both boys and girls. Ambiguous genitalia are those that don't look like typical newborn male or female genitals.

- The doctor will examine the baby's back for normal infant curvature and to make sure there is no evidence of a hidden condition called spina bifida occulta. Spina bifida is failure of the spinal cord to close during its early development, resulting in neurological problems. Spina bifida occulta is smaller and less significant and often is no reason for concern. Sometimes it can cause pain or numbness in the lower extremities or changes in bowel or bladder function. It can be seen as a tuft of hair just above the cheeks of the buttocks or a dimple present in that area.

- The doctor looks at the extremities to be sure the baby has all his or her fingers and toes and to check for normal muscle tone and reflexes.

- The doctor checks to see if the hip joint is properly formed. The examiner will listen for a click upon moving the hip, which might indicate the joint is not formed properly.

Infant Reflexes

Newborn infants have their own distinctive set of reflexes. These should be present in all normal full-term newborns. If reflexes are absent, this may reveal a neurological difficulty; if they persist beyond the time they are supposed to disappear, this may indicate a developmental problem. Your pediatrician will check for infant reflexes at your baby's first visit. You may want to watch and learn about these interesting reflexes during your baby's examination.

Here's something I wish my pediatrician would have told me. One night around 10:00 p.m. after a feeding, I changed my son's diaper. When I opened it, he was covered in what looked like large salt granules. I became hysterical and shouted to my husband, "Call the doctor! Jay is peeing salt!" The doctor called back immediately and graciously tried to stifle her giggles as she told me that the granules were simply the pellets inside the diaper that soak up urine. There must have been a tear in the diaper and they leaked out. It was so ridiculous that I broke out in hysterical laughter and so did the doctor! —*Ellie, 43, mother of three*

The Moro reflex: Testing this reflex involves picking the baby up and dropping him or her a few millimeters onto a soft surface. Startled, the infant will spread his or her arms out wide and then pull them back in, often crying in the process. It is sometimes called the startle reaction and usually disappears by the age of two months. It can happen with a sudden noise, if the baby's head changes position abruptly, or if the ambient temperature suddenly changes.

Moro reflex

The newborn Moro reflex, also called the startle reaction, causes a baby that suddenly feels as if it's dropping to spread its arms. A loud noise or even a change in temperature can also trigger the reaction.

The stepping reflex: This is unique to babies younger than about two months of age. If the doctor picks the baby up into an upright position and touches the baby's feet to a horizontal surface, the baby makes walking movements with his or her feet. One foot is placed in front of the other for a few steps. This is really fun to watch!

The rooting reflex: When an infant's cheek is stroked or touched with the breast, the infant automatically turns toward the stroked side and makes sucking motions in an attempt to latch onto the breast. You can also use this

What NOW?

Intersex Babies

The first question most people ask about a baby is, "Is it a boy or a girl?" In about one-tenth to two-tenths of one percent of births, the answer to that question is not clear, because the baby is born with ambiguous genitals that don't look exactly like either a boy's or a girl's genitals. These babies are called intersex individuals, and there are a number of causes and many variations in the condition, some of which are not immediately apparent at birth. In the past, when a baby was born with atypical genitals, doctors usually made a decision about the baby's sex and often performed surgery as soon as possible to try to make the genitals look like those of a boy or a girl. Because "maleness" or "femaleness" is a reflection of many things—genetics, hormones, anatomy, and social expectations—babies who are assigned a gender at birth may feel, when they grow up, that they have been assigned to the wrong gender. The medical, psychological, and social treatment of intersex children is controversial, and parents who have intersex babies will want to educate themselves thoroughly and make thoughtful decisions on behalf of their children.

reflex to stimulate sucking in an infant who is eating sluggishly. It disappears at about four months of age.

The sucking reflex: This reflex is connected to the rooting reflex. When anything touches the roof of the infant's mouth, he or she begins to suck vigorously as if sucking on a nipple. Sucking has two stages, that of expressing the milk from the breast and that of swallowing the milk. Preterm infants may not have fully developed this reflex, which sometimes results in a weak sucking movement. Babies lose this reflex and develop intentional sucking behavior at about two months of age.

The tonic neck reflex or asymmetrical tonic neck reflex: This interesting reflex is sometimes called the fencing position, because

> I thought our four-week-old baby was a genius when I held him up and touched his feet to the floor and he made walking motions! I was so excited when I called the pediatrician, my babbling hardly made sense. After she explained that it was just a reflex, I was mortified! She assured me it happened all the time, but it took me a while to get over my humiliation. —*Marianna, 30, mother of one*

the baby looks like a little sword fighter! When the baby's head is turned to one side, the arm and leg on that side extend, while the arm and leg on the opposite side bend. This reflex should disappear by six months of age.

The palmar grasp reflex: If the baby's palm is stroked with an object or finger, the baby responds by closing his or her fist tightly and strongly. While the grasp is strong enough to support the baby's weight, it can be released spontaneously and unpredictably, so do not try this one at home unless the baby is safely supported. This reflex is present even in preterm babies born at 27 weeks' gestation, and it lasts until five or six months of age.

The plantar reflex: If you stroke the sole of the baby's foot, its toes curl or flex as if they are grasping something. This reflex disappears in approximately one year.

The Galant reflex: When the infant has one side of his or her back stroked, the back will swing toward the side of the stroking. This reflex is present at birth and normally disappears by six months of age. If it lasts past six months, a neurological problem might exist.

The swimming reflex: When a baby is placed face down in a pool of water, he or she responds by involuntarily paddling and kicking. This reflex is lost at around six months of age.

The Babkin reflex: Newborns respond in several ways to the application of moderate pressure to both palms. The baby may flex his or her head, rotate the head, and/or open the mouth. This reflex is seen in preterm infants as early as 26 weeks' gestation as well as in full-term infants and persists until about three to four months of age.

Early Vaccinations and Shots

Your baby's vaccination schedule usually begins while your baby is in the hospital and will last through adulthood.

- **Vitamin K shot:** Your baby will get a vitamin K shot shortly after birth, usually while still in the labor and delivery room. This injection is designed to prevent the possibility of excess bleeding due to vitamin K deficiency. You might be too busy to see that it happened, but trust that your baby will be given this brief shot. There is no harm in getting the shot.

> Vaccines are one of the most beneficial advances of modern medicine and have done miraculous things in terms of disease control. Be sure to keep up your baby's vaccinations. Some people have concerns, so if you do, talk to your pediatrician. But I believe it is essential to do everything I can to keep my baby healthy.
> —*Laurie, 33, mother of one*

- **Hepatitis B vaccine:** Unless you specify otherwise, your baby will receive a hepatitis B vaccination in the first day or so of life. Hepatitis B is a viral infection that is passed through blood exchange or sexual activity with an infected individual. The virus causes acute and chronic liver problems, and in some people, it can last for the rest of their lives, leading to possible liver cancer. If you do not want your baby to be vaccinated against hepatitis B, tell the nurse your wishes.

  The hepatitis B vaccination is usually given at birth, at one to two months, and then again between six and eighteen months. It is given during routine infant checkups during these time periods.

- **Hemophilus influenza type B vaccine:** The Hemophilus influenza type B vaccination fights against infections that can lead to infant death or meningitis (a brain infection). It is given at two months, four

months, six months, and between twelve and fifteen months of age.

- **Polio vaccine:** The polio vaccine fights against the polio virus, which caused paralysis and death in many children before routine polio vaccination began about 50 years ago. It used to be given orally, but current recommendations are for intramuscular injection at two months, four months, between six and eighteen months, and finally between four and six years of age.

- **DTaP vaccine:** The abbreviated name stands for the combination of diphtheria, tetanus, and pertussis (whooping cough). This vaccine protects against several serious diseases. It is given at the two-month visit, at four months, five months, between fifteen and eighteen months, between four and six years, and again at eleven years of age.

- **Pneumococcus vaccine:** There is a relatively new vaccine against Pneumococcus that prevents the most common type of pneumonia. The Pneumococcal vaccine is given at two months, four months, six months, and between twelve and eighteen months of age.

- **Rotavirus vaccine:** Another newer vaccine is the rotavirus vaccine, which protects infants against an intestinal virus that can lead to nausea, vomiting, severe diarrhea, and dehydration. It is given at two months, at four months, and at six months of age.

- **Hepatitis A vaccine:** The hepatitis A vaccination protects the infant from the foodborne hepatitis A virus. It is given twice: at twelve months and at eighteen months of age.

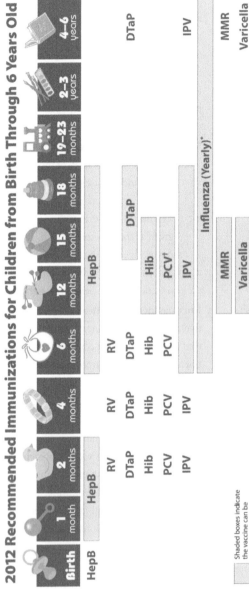

2012 Recommended Immunizations for Children from Birth Through 6 Years Old

	Birth	1 month	2 months	4 months	6 months	12 months	15 months	18 months	19–23 months	2–3 years	4–6 years
HepB	HepB	HepB			HepB						
			RV	RV	RV						
			DTaP	DTaP	DTaP		DTaP				DTaP
			Hib	Hib	Hib	Hib					
			PCV	PCV	PCV	PCV†					
			IPV	IPV		IPV					IPV
						MMR					MMR
						Varicella					Varicella
					Influenza (Yearly)*						
					HepA§						

Shaded boxes indicate the vaccine can be given during shown age range.

NOTE: If your child misses a shot, you don't need to start over, just go back to your child's doctor for the next shot. The doctor will keep your child up-to-date on vaccinations. Talk with your doctor if you have questions.

FOOTNOTES

† Children 2 years old and older with certain medical conditions may need a dose of pneumococcal vaccine (PPSV) and meningococcal vaccine (MCV4). See vaccine-specific recommendations at http://www.cdc.gov/vaccines/pubs/ACIP-list.htm.

* Two doses given at least four weeks apart are recommended for children aged 6 months through 8 years of age who are getting a flu vaccine for the first time.

§ Two doses of HepA vaccine are needed for lasting protection. The first dose of HepA vaccine should be given between 12 months and 23 months of age. The second dose should be given 6 to 18 months later. HepA vaccination may be given to any child 12 months and older to protect against HepA. Children and adolescents who did not receive the HepA vaccine and are at high-risk, should be vaccinated against HepA.

SEE BACK PAGE FOR MORE INFORMATION ON VACCINE-PREVENTABLE DISEASES AND THE VACCINES THAT PREVENT THEM.

For more information, call toll free
1-800-CDC-INFO (1-800-232-4636)
or visit
http://www.cdc.gov/vaccines

Vaccine-Preventable Diseases and the Vaccines that Prevent Them

Disease	Vaccine	Disease spread by	Disease symptoms	Disease complications
Chickenpox	Varicella vaccine protects against chickenpox.	Air, direct contact	Rash, tiredness, headache, fever	Infected blisters, bleeding disorders, encephalitis (brain swelling), pneumonia (infection in the lungs)
Diphtheria	DTaP* vaccine protects against diphtheria.	Air, direct contact	Sore throat, mild fever, weakness, swollen glands in neck	Swelling of the heart muscle, heart failure, coma, paralysis, death
Hib	Hib vaccine protects against *Haemophilus influenzae* type b.	Air, direct contact	May be no symptoms unless bacteria enter the blood	Meningitis (infection of the covering around the brain and spinal cord), mental retardation, epiglottis (life-threatening infection that can block the windpipe and lead to serious breathing problems) and pneumonia (infection in the lungs), death
HepA	HepA vaccine protects against hepatitis A.	Personal contact, contaminated food or water	May be no symptoms, fever, stomach pain, loss of appetite, fatigue, vomiting, jaundice (yellowing of skin and eyes), dark urine	Liver failure
HepB	HepB vaccine protects against hepatitis B.	Contact with blood or body fluids	May be no symptoms, fever, headache, weakness, vomiting, jaundice (yellowing of skin and eyes), joint pain	Chronic liver infection, liver failure, liver cancer
Flu	Flu vaccine protects against influenza.	Air, direct contact	Fever, muscle pain, sore throat, cough, extreme fatigue	Pneumonia (infection in the lungs)
Measles	MMR** vaccine protects against measles.	Air, direct contact	Rash, fever, cough, runny nose, pinkeye	Encephalitis (brain swelling), pneumonia (infection in the lungs), death
Mumps	MMR**vaccine protects against mumps.	Air, direct contact	Swollen salivary glands (under the jaw), fever, headache, tiredness, muscle pain	Meningitis (infection of the covering around the brain and spinal cord), encephalitis (brain swelling), inflammation of testicles or ovaries, deafness
Pertussis	DTaP* vaccine protects against pertussis (whooping cough).	Air, direct contact	Severe cough, runny nose, apnea (a pause in breathing in infants)	Pneumonia (infection in the lungs), death
Polio	IPV vaccine protects against polio.	Through the mouth	May be no symptoms, sore throat, fever, nausea, headache	Paralysis, death
Pneumococcal	PCV vaccine protects against pneumococcus.	Air, direct contact	May be no symptoms, pneumonia (infection in the lungs)	Bacteremia (blood infection), meningitis (infection of the covering around the brain and spinal cord), death
Rotavirus	RV vaccine protects against rotavirus.	Through the mouth	Diarrhea, fever, vomiting	Severe diarrhea, dehydration
Rubella	MMR** vaccine protects against rubella.	Air, direct contact	Children infected with rubella virus sometimes have a rash, fever, and swollen lymph nodes.	Very serious in pregnant women—can lead to miscarriage, stillbirth, premature delivery, and birth defects
Tetanus	DTaP* vaccine protects against tetanus.	Exposure through cuts in skin	Stiffness in neck and abdominal muscles, difficulty swallowing, muscle spasms, fever	Broken bones, breathing difficulty, death

* DTaP is a combination vaccine that protects against diphtheria, tetanus, and pertussis.
** MMR is a combination vaccine that protects against measles, mumps, and rubella.

Last updated on 02/01/2012 · CS2099Y2.8

- **Flu shot:** The flu shot, or influenza vaccine, is given yearly starting at six months of age. After the first shot only, another shot is given at least four weeks later (usually at seven months of age). After that, it is given every year during flu season, and it is recommended throughout childhood and adulthood.

- **MMR vaccine:** The measles, mumps and rubella (MMR) vaccine provides protection against these commonly known yet potentially very serious viruses. The first dose is given between twelve and eighteen months, and another dose is given between four and six years of age.

- **Chicken pox vaccine:** The varicella, or chicken pox, vaccine provides protection against the common chicken pox virus, which also causes a painful condition called varicella zoster (or shingles) in adulthood. Even common childhood illnesses can have serious complications, which is the reason for vaccination. It is given between twelve and fifteen months of age and is repeated between four and six years of age.

Circumcision

A circumcision involves removal of excess skin from the glans, or tip of the penis. It is a procedure that takes about 5 to 10 minutes and is relatively pain-free if local anesthetic is used. Various devices are used to trim off the foreskin and stop the bleeding. Even so, the tip of the exposed glans is raw, red, and a bit bloody for a few hours. The glans creates its own skin protection over about one week or so, and the penis looks like a normal circumcised penis.

If you choose not to have the circumcision done, the penis comes to a point at the end with foreskin covering the glans, and this usually only retracts during an erection. The foreskin retracts in only about 1 in every 20 newborns and in about 50 percent of one-year-olds. By age three, the foreskin is able to retract in about 80 to 90 percent of boys who have not been circumcised.

Circumcision
A circumcision (right image) heals over several days.

Pros and Cons of Circumcision

Of course, as with most things, there are pros and cons to circumcision. While some parents have religious beliefs that affect their decision, other parents make the decision based on medical information and personal preferences.

Benefits of circumcision

- *No complications related to the foreskin.* Sometimes the opening of the foreskin narrows so it cannot retract properly. The foreskin can also become infected or inflamed.

- *Easier hygiene.* In general, circumcised penises are easier to keep clean. In the hidden recesses beneath the foreskin, there can be a buildup of a substance called smegma that can irritate the glans of the penis. If the foreskin can be retracted, it should be done so that the glans can be

Medical Recommendations about Circumcision

What NOW?

Until recently, the American Academy of Pediatrics (AAP) and the American Congress of Obstetricians and Gynecologists (ACOG) stated that there were no medical indications to perform a circumcision on a newborn. These medical associations released a new policy statement in August 2012, however, saying that the medical benefits of circumcision outweigh the medical risks and that circumcision should be available for families who wish their infants to have this procedure. They stopped short of recommending routine circumcision for all male infants, because both the benefits and the risks are modest, but encouraged parents to review the evidence and consider their personal preferences in making this decision. These new recommendations may reverse the trend to not circumcise newborn males in the United States.

cleaned in its entirety. Young boys should be taught how to retract their foreskin and clean their own penis once it is retractable.

- *Lower risk of HIV.* There is a well-studied connection between circumcision and lower rates of HIV. The Centers for Disease Control state that the relative risk for HIV infection is 44 percent lower in circumcised men. The World Health Organization has suggested that male circumcision be promoted as a means of HIV reduction, but this recommendation is still under study in the United States.

- *Lower risk of other sexually transmitted infections (STIs).* Some studies have suggested that uncircumcised men have a higher risk of other STIs, including genital herpes, syphilis, and human papilloma virus (HPV). The foreskin may trap small bits of infectious particles, leading later to full-blown infections. Uncircumcised men are more likely to pass on HPV to their female partners, causing a higher risk of cervical cancer.

- *Reduced risk of penile cancer.* Penile cancer is very rare, but it is more common in uncircumcised men.

- *Lower rate of urinary tract infections.* While baby boys do not get many urinary tract infections, those who are not circumcised do have higher rates of infection.

Risks of circumcision

- *Risk of bleeding or infection.* As with any surgical procedure, there is a small risk of bleeding complications or postsurgical infection. About 1 in 500 boys experiences significant bleeding.

- *Possible loss of sexual sensation.* This possibility has not been well researched, but some people believe that circumcision makes the glans of the penis less sensitive, thus decreasing sexual pleasure.

- *Meatitis.* Meatitis is an inflammation of the opening (or meatus) through which urine comes out at the tip of the penis. If unprotected by the foreskin, the meatus is exposed to chafing and can become inflamed or narrowed, possibly needing surgical correction.

When making your decision regarding circumcision, weigh the pros and cons carefully while considering the medical data, your personal preferences, your religious background, and the practices of your family and friends. (And no, you do not have to watch it being done if you decide to have the procedure performed!)

My husband and I are an interfaith couple—
I'm Jewish and he's Christian—though neither
of us practice. Not only did we hit the jackpot
with the blessing of our son, but it turned
out the doctor who delivered him was also a
mohel [a person who performs Jewish ritual
circumcision]. So my family was pleased that
she could perform the circumcision in the
hospital. —*Ruth, 30, mother of two*

Circumcision Care

If your baby boy is circumcised,
you will need to take special care
of his penis for about one to two weeks.
During this time, the tip of the penis will be
red and easily irritated.

Your doctor may want you to wrap a
piece of gauze slathered with petroleum jelly
around the area that was cut near the glans
of the penis or to put the petroleum jelly
directly on and around the glans to keep it
from being exposed to stool or bacteria. After
a couple of days, you can simply pat the penis
dry or wash it off if to keep it clean. When it
is healed, your baby's penis will look like it is
formed completely from normal skin.

If the circumcised penis becomes increasingly red, bloody, or swollen over time, see
the doctor to make sure there is no infection
of the area. Fortunately, infections are not
that common.

Umbilical Cord Care

After delivery, a piece of umbilical cord is
left attached to the baby. While your newborn is in the infant warmer, a clamp will be
placed to tie off the cord near the abdomen
and the excess is trimmed off so there will
be an umbilical stub. The clamp is removed
after about 24 to 48 hours, and your baby is
left with a small piece of umbilical cord that
will dry up and fall off within one to three
weeks after birth.

To keep the cord stub clean, some hospitals put a purple antiseptic on the cord. Other
hospitals have you apply a small amount of
isopropyl alcohol to the tip of the cord with
a Q-tip or cotton ball after every diaper change. Still others will ask you
to do nothing but keep the diaper
from rubbing up against the cord
until it falls off by itself.

All approaches to keeping the cord
stub clean work just fine. Just be careful with
manipulating the cord or rubbing the diaper against it, and call the doctor if the skin
around the umbilical cord becomes reddened
or inflamed. This could mean a cord infection, and it needs immediate treatment.

Neonatal Jaundice

Neonatal jaundice occurs in about half of
all newborns from two to three days old, and
it causes your baby's skin and eyes to become
yellowish in color. Jaundice occurs when
excess bilirubin (produced by the breakdown
of red blood cells) accumulates more rapidly
than your baby's liver can break it down and
pass it out of his or her body. In most cases,
your baby's bilirubin level rises for two to four
days, and then the level drops as your infant's
liver catches up and processes the bilirubin
out of his or her system. Bilirubin turns
your baby's stool dark green to black and is
exactly why a baby's first stools are that color!
Generally, jaundice clears on its own in one

week and does not cause any discomfort or harm to your baby.

Situations that lead to increased jaundice in the baby include drug use by the mother, a delay in clamping the cord (with too many red blood cells pumped into the infant), birth trauma that causes bruising (such as a cephalhematoma—see description earlier in this chapter), breast-feeding exclusively, and some infant metabolic diseases or low thyroid conditions. Other causes include hypoxia (low oxygen levels), severe newborn infections or sepsis, cystic fibrosis or hepatitis, and certain genetic or hereditary disorders.

If the buildup of bilirubin becomes too great, a condition called kernicterus develops, which can cause permanent damage to a baby's brain cells. Kernicterus doesn't usually occur until bilirubin levels are between 20 and 25 mg/dL or greater. This is why it is important to monitor jaundice.

A blood bilirubin level of 12 mg/dL is considered safe. Levels greater than 12 mg/dL or levels that rise more than 5 mg/dL before your infant reaches one day of age (24 hours) will warrant further evaluation and management. The doctor will attempt to look for the cause of the problem and will likely begin some form of treatment.

If your infant has bilirubin levels between 12 and 17 mg/dL and is otherwise healthy, you can simply increase breast-feeding to 8 to 12 times per day and can augment the feedings with water to flush the urine and stool out of your baby's system. There is no chance of kernicterus at these bilirubin levels.

If the bilirubin is 17 to 25 mg/dL, the doctor will also add phototherapy to the treatment plan. Phototherapy involves placing your

It was hard for me to leave my little naked baby under those lights instead of holding her all day while in the hospital. But when the nurse explained to me in detail about jaundice, I knew I was doing what was truly best for her in the moment. I realized then and there that parenting is truly a process of letting go, right from the start. —*Tracie, 35, mother of two*

baby in an incubator equipped with special lights that reduce the amount of unconjugated bilirubin (bilirubin that has not been fully processed by the liver) in the system. Your baby is kept blindfolded to preserve his or her vision and is usually naked in the light box to expose as much of the skin to the light as possible.

Babies need to be well hydrated to overcome high bilirubin levels. If you are breast-feeding, you can continue, but the baby may need additional formula or even intravenous fluids.

If your baby has an elevated bilirubin and appears jaundiced, follow your doctor's directions carefully and follow through with treatment recommendations. *Early detection and treatment of jaundice can prevent serious complications later on, including possible brain damage.*

Hearing Tests

About 1 to 2 percent of newborns will show some sign of having a hearing deficit. This is why all newborns in the United States undergo routine hearing screening. For hospital births, about 95 percent of hearing tests are conducted while the mom and baby are still in the hospital. A nurse or nursing assistant will perform one of two types of hearing test. Both are noninvasive and require no response from your baby.

Types of Hearing Tests

Auditory brainstem response (ABR) test: This test is performed by putting tiny earphones on your baby and placing five electrodes on the baby's head. A clicking sound, given at different intensities, is presented through the earphones; the electrodes pick up your baby's brainwave activity, which is displayed on a computer screen. The brainwaves indicate at what levels your baby is hearing sound. The test takes about 15 minutes.

Otoacoustic emission test (OAE): The inner ear contains a structure called the cochlea, which is spiral shaped. When

Causes of Hearing Loss **What NOW?**

Hearing loss can be caused by certain conditions, but nearly 50 percent of the time the cause for a child's hearing loss remains unknown. Some possible causes for hearing loss include

- hereditary conditions
- neonatal jaundice (high bilirubin levels)
- exposure to certain drugs in the uterus
- having to be on a ventilator for long periods of time
- meningitis (brain infection)
- preterm birth and/or low birth weight
- in utero infections, such as cytomegalovirus, rubella, syphilis, herpes simplex virus, or toxoplasmosis
- craniofacial abnormalities (abnormalities in the development of the skull or face)

the cochlea is stimulated by a sound, hair cells vibrate, creating a very soft sound in response. This sound from the cochlea, called an otoacoustic emission, reverberates in the ear canal. In this test, a tiny microphone with a speaker in it is placed inside your infant's ear. When sounds are generated, the resulting otoacoustic emission from the cochlea is picked up by the microphone and shows up on a computer screen. If there is normal emission in response to sounds that are in the range of human speech, the infant is considered to have passed the test.

Evaluating Hearing Test Results

While these hearing tests are valuable, babies who have normal hearing may not pass them the first time around. Both tests may have false positive results, which indicate a hearing impairment that isn't really there. If conducted in the first three days of life, the ABR test has a 4 percent false positive rate, and the OAE has between 5 and 21 percent false positives. This higher rate for the OAE is said to reflect its increased sensitivity to amniotic fluid and vernix that might be in the newborn's ear canal. A child may also fail a hearing test because he or she is moving around, there is a lot of noise around the baby, or the baby is crying. It may be helpful to feed your baby just before the tests so he or she is more settled during this new experience.

If your baby fails the hearing test, have your child retested in a week or two. Almost always, the child will past the rescreening test. If baby does not pass the retest, he or she will be referred to an audiologist for a complete evaluation. Hearing specialists can identify the nature and degree of hearing loss in most cases.

Infants with hearing impairments whose hearing loss is identified by the age of six months are more likely to develop the skills they need to catch up to the developmental level of their peers by the time they need to go to school. If they are not diagnosed with hearing impairment until two to three years of age, children tend to have more difficulty adjusting to being deaf and have more problems with their peers and with school in general.

Taking Care of Your Baby: The First Few Days

Whether you breast-feed or bottle-feed your baby in his or her first few days of life, you will be kept busy! Most bottle-fed newborn infants consume about two ounces of formula every two to three hours around the clock, with the possibility of going a bit longer during the night. If your baby was active in the womb during the night, he or she may continue to be something of a night owl. It will take some time to get your baby on a more regular schedule of nighttime sleeping and daytime wakefulness.

Remember that whether you are bottle-feeding or breast-feeding, feeding times should be special moments to enjoy your infant. Don't get distracted with the television or start texting with one hand; take the time to cuddle your newborn and take in the wonder of it all. This emotional connection is as important to your baby's development as the nutrition of the milk or formula you supply.

Breast-feeding

Breast milk is considered the best way to feed your baby, providing the baby with essential nutrients as well as immune-boosting antibodies. It is a ready source of infant nutrition, usually giving the baby exactly the right amount of milk whenever he or she needs it. The more you breast-feed, the more milk you will produce. While you cannot measure the amount of food consumed in

> I felt really left out when my wife began breast-feeding, but I didn't want to interfere either. One day, while she was nursing, my wife noticed my mood. She asked me what was wrong and I said, "Well, I wish I could feed the baby, but you're doing great." The next day she handed me a bottle of breast milk for the morning feeding and said, "I want you to be involved. It helps me too!" Even if you're not a communicator, tell your partner what your needs are—don't make her guess!
> —*Robert, 34, dad of two*

each nursing session, if the baby is satisfied after eating and does not need to feed for another two to three hours, he or she is getting enough!

Technique: How-To's for You and Baby

Babies do not just suck on the end of the nipple when they breast-feed. Your baby needs to take as much of the surrounding tissue—the areola or colored part of the breast—as possible into his or her mouth.

The baby expresses milk by squeezing the areola between the upper and lower jaw in order to pump milk out of the breast. Simply sucking on the nipple does not really get out the breast milk, so it is helpful to ensure that the areola is in the baby's mouth as well.

Breast-fed babies usually eat a bit more frequently than those who are bottle fed. The number of feedings will space out and be more like those of bottle-fed babies within a month or two. One or the greatest benefits of breast-feeding is that your milk is always ready and you never have to take time to prepare a bottle of formula!

There is a wealth of help and information available to you if you are having trouble breast-feeding. You can contact your hospital's lactation consultant or your local La Leche League organization in order to get some personalized advice about how to breast-feed your baby. You can also go online, read books and articles, and ask other moms who have breast-fed for their advice.

Obtain and use a breast pump. Most women prefer electric pumps, which can be pricey. However, you can rent an electric breast pump from a hospital or maternity store, and you may be able to participate in a "rent to own" program. If you are receiving help through the WIC (Women, Infants, and Children) supplemental nutrition program, be aware that they can supply breast pumps as well. Begin using the breast pump when your milk comes in and your baby is not drinking that much. Later on, you will use your breast pump between feedings or if you go back to work and want to keep providing breast milk for your baby.

Two Different Points of View

I didn't love breast-feeding like so many of my friends seemed to. It was convenient and good for the baby, but that's really the only reason I did it. Don't feel bad if you don't experience breast-feeding as an intense bonding experience—it is still important that your baby is getting the nutrition and immune boost he or she needs. —*Aria, 32, mother of two*

Breast-feeding was an incredible experience for me. I loved the special time together, the physical closeness with my baby, and the sense of wonder that my body was actually able to provide nourishment for another human being! I had a friend who was nursing her own baby at the same time, and it helped to have someone to talk to about the rewards and challenges. We would go out for lunch together and both be nursing our babies under blankets as we talked and ate! —*Ashley, 35, mother of two*

Storing Breast Milk

Here are some tips for storing breast milk safely, according to the Centers for Disease Control:

- Breast milk left out at room temperature is considered safe for up to six hours, provided it is freshly expressed, but four hours is considered even safer by some experts.

- You can freeze breast milk if you will not need it in the near future. Breast milk should be frozen if it may not be used within five days.

- You can safely refrigerate breast milk at 32 to 39°F (in a cold refrigerator) for up to five days. It would be a good idea to buy a refrigerator thermometer so you can ensure the temperature is appropriate.

- Breast milk will remain usable for three to six months if stored in a freezer with a separate door or six to twelve months in a chest or upright freezer (not part of a refrigerator). If you are storing the milk in the freezer compartment inside your refrigerator (without a separate exterior door), it should be used within one to two weeks.

- Do not store breast milk within the door of the refrigerator or freezer because the temperature fluctuates too much in these areas. It is best to put the milk toward the back of a main shelf.

- Plastic breast milk storage bags are convenient, disposable, and can be dated with a permanent marker. However, when pouring milk from the bag to a bottle, some of the breast milk will collect on the sides of the bag, wasting some of your precious milk! Glass jars are preferable, but you run the risk of breakage, and many daycare facilities will not accept glass containers. You can try Bisphenol-A (BPA)-free plastic bottles for storage or just go with the plastic bags.

- If you are traveling or on the go, you can keep breast milk for up to 24 hours in an insulated cooler bag. The milk containers should be in contact with frozen ice packs at all times, and you should open the cooler as little as possible.

Bottle-feeding

There are a variety of reasons women choose to feed their babies formula instead of breast-feed. Babies have been successfully bottle fed for many decades. Some couples prefer it because both the mother and the

partner can routinely feed the baby, thus dividing the work of taking care of the baby and offering dad or partner additional bonding time. It is also a more convenient choice if you are returning to work and your baby will be in daycare or with another caretaker during the day, especially if you do not have the time or privacy to pump breast milk while at work. In addition, baby formula has improved significantly over the years, and many formulas now closely mimic the powerful nutrients of breast milk. In rare cases, a mother's illness or medication needs may make her breast milk unsuitable for her baby. If a breast-fed baby is weaned early, parents will need to provide formula until the baby is one year old.

If you choose to bottle-feed—or if it is a necessity—there are a few things you will need to consider.

Choosing Nipples and Bottles

All you have to do is take one glance at the shelves of a baby superstore to get an idea of the variety of choices in nipples and bottles for a baby. You will likely have to make some changes until you find the combination that works best for your baby, so purchase only a few nipples and bottles to start until you are sure what works best for you and your baby.

Nipples: Nipples come in rubber, latex, or silicone. They come in different shapes, including flat-topped nipples, traditional nipples, and orthodontic nipples. Orthodontic nipples were invented in order to best match the baby's palate and gums, but are slightly more expensive than traditional nipples. Flat-topped nipples are designed to simulate the shape of a woman's breast. Traditional nipples are longer and smooth all the way around.

Nipples also come in different sizes and allow for the flow of liquid at different rates. Toddler nipples have an increased flow rate and aren't intended for use by small infants. To be on the safe side, buy nipples of different types to make sure you have a nipple that your baby can tolerate. Once you find the right nipple, discard the other ones and buy a batch of bottles and nipples of the type your baby prefers.

If your baby is exclusively bottle fed, the nipples will not last forever! The hole eventually widens so that the milk comes out in a steady stream or the nipple cracks. This is the time to buy new nipples to replace the old ones. Check nipples at every feeding to ensure they are intact. You do not want to run the risk of a piece of nipple breaking off and choking your child.

For newborns, purchase the smallest size nipple and only purchase larger nipples as

Bottles and Bisphenol-A (BPA)

In 2012, the federal government outlawed the sale of baby bottles and sippy cups that contain BPA. Scientists are concerned that BPA in plastic containers is leached into their contents and may have adverse health effects, especially for infants. You can be confident that new bottles do not contain BPA (check the packaging information just to be sure). You may not wish to use older plastic bottles or cups unless you are sure they are BPA-free. Glass bottles do not contain BPA.

your child grows into the toddler stage. Check packaging for age recommendations from the manufacturer.

Bottles: The bottle type you choose must match the nipple, so it sometimes pays to

  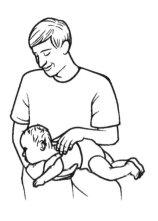

Burping positions

No matter how you feed your baby, you will need to burp him or her. Hold the baby sitting on your lap, over your shoulder, or tummy down on your thighs, and gently pat the back until you hear a satisfying burp! Don't forget to use a towel or diaper to protect your clothes.

select a bottle and nipple combination. There are disposable bottles, traditional bottles, bottles that are set at an angle in the middle so the infant gets less air when feeding, and wider-mouthed bottles. Bottles come in glass and plastic varieties. While glass bottles are breakable, plastic ones can deteriorate over time.

Never use a microwave to warm baby formula. The microwave can leave hot spots you will be unaware of that can burn your baby's mouth.

Buy four-ounce bottles for newborns, and the bigger eight- or nine-ounce bottles when your baby reaches about four or five months old.

Baby Formula: The Basics

Infant formulas come in three types: ready-made, powdered, and liquid concentrate forms.

Ready-made formula: While ready-made formulas are convenient, once you open the sterilized contents, the rest of the formula is only considered good for 24 to 48 hours. After that time, you must discard the rest of the formula. Ready-to-use formula takes up a great deal of storage space and costs approximately 25 percent more than powdered formula. This can be costly if you find yourself throwing out unused formula. Often, ready-made is a good choice for limited use, as when you are on vacation or long outings away from home.

Powdered formula: Powdered formula is the least expensive and the most environmentally friendly formula you can purchase. You can take it anywhere at room temperature and use what you need whenever you need it. Most powdered varieties come with a measuring scoop so you can easily mix the designated amount of water with a scoop of formula. You can make up a bottle in just a minute or two. Because you need to add water, you will want to be sure your tap water is safe, use bottled water, or purchase a water purifying system. If you use bottled water, be sure that the water bottles are BPA-free.

Liquid concentrate formula: Liquid concentrate formula is expensive, albeit convenient. You mix equal parts of water and the liquid formula to make the right concentrate. Do not feed your baby concentrated formula without diluting it 50:50 with water. As with powdered formula, you need to be assured that your tap water is safe. Use bottled water or a purifying system if you are concerned. You can also boil tap water and let it cool down before using it to make baby formula.

Selecting a Formula for Bottle-feeding

As you will find with most products for baby, there are numerous choices when it comes to baby formula. The only limits you have on your selection may be if you are on a federally funded program like the WIC (Women, Infants, and Children) program, which provides infant formula to bottle-fed infants, or if your baby is allergic or colicky on a formula you choose. Read through the information on baby formulas presented in this book carefully, and be sure to consult with your pediatrician if your baby is having any issues with formula.

> We went through 10 different formulas before finding one that didn't make our baby gassy, colicky, or have a rash. If you're having a problem, don't panic! Listen to your pediatrician and keep trying. You'll find one that works!
> —*Takai, 35, mother of two*

What Exactly Is in Formula?

Formulas are based on cow's milk, soy milk, or lactose-free milk and are designed to mimic breast milk as closely as possible. All formulas contain fat, carbohydrates, protein, vitamins, minerals, and some additional rare nutrients in different combinations depending on a baby's needs and tolerance.

Breast milk's main source of carbohydrate is lactose. This is also the main source of carbohydrate in formulas derived from cow's milk. Some formulas also contain corn maltodextrin. Special formulas that are not derived from cow's milk, such as lactose-free formula, soy formula, and specially made formulas, are made with sucrose, corn maltodextrin, corn syrup solids, or modified cornstarch.

The protein content of breast milk is about 60 percent whey protein and 40 percent casein protein. Formulas made for infants usually copy this pattern although some contain all whey protein. Formulas with all whey protein are good for infants who have gastroesophageal reflux disease, also called GERD.

Soy formulas contain soy protein, which is sometimes broken down to be more easily digested by the infant. Partially broken-down proteins can reduce the incidence of protein allergies and allergic skin rashes.

Breast milk contains essential fat for your baby in the form of monounsaturated, saturated, and polyunsaturated fats. Formulas use a combination of coconut oil, palm olein oil, regular palm oil, sunflower oil, corn oil, and soy oil in varying amounts to try to mimic breast milk. Both palm oil and palm olein oil are used extensively in baby formulas, but research has shown that these types of oils can diminish the baby's fat and calcium absorption. Special formulas make use of medium-chain triglycerides, which are easily digested and absorbed by the infant gastrointestinal tract.

DHA (docosahexaenoic acid) and ARA (arachidonic acid) are also found in breast milk and are now approved for use in infant formula. Both these fatty acids promote your baby's brain and visual growth and development. Look for a formula that includes DHA and ARA as part of its formulation.

When reading the label on formulas, you may find it hard to decipher what some of the long, technical names actually are—especially when it comes to vitamins. For example, if the packaging says it contains ferrous sulfate, it means that it contains iron. Similar long and technical names are given for other types of vitamins. The vitamins are important in the development of a healthy blood supply and to make cells that have the right nutrients in them. Iron-fortified formula is recommended for all babies, especially premature infants. They should receive this formula up to one year of age. If you are unsure if your formula of choice contains all

Things to Consider when Choosing a Formula

- If your baby has serious digestive problems, you may need infant formulas that treat protein sensitivity. You should get your pediatrician's recommendation before purchasing these formula types.

- Preterm infants need more calories and higher nutrient levels than full-term babies. Your pediatrician will recommend a specialty formula if necessary.

- There are formulas recommended for infants who suffer from excessive spitting up or reflux. Sometimes a doctor will ask parents to put a bit of rice cereal in their baby's formula to cut down on reflux symptoms. One formula contains rice starch for this reason.

- There are formulas for infants older than six months, which can be used to treat watery diarrhea. The formula is soy-based and can be used intermittently for diarrhea.

- In addition, some babies with rare bowel problems need a special formula. Ask your pediatrician before starting such a formula.

- Low-iron formulas do exist; however, because infants need iron, they should not be used unless your pediatrician recommends it. They were initially designed because it was believed that iron in the formula caused constipation. This has since been refuted, so in the vast majority of cases, you should use iron-enriched baby formulas.

- There are two infant formulas that contain particular fatty acids that are usually only found in breast milk. These tend to be pricier choices but are excellent choices if you want to provide your baby with the closest possible formula to breast milk. They include Enfamil Lipil and Similac Advance.

the necessary nutrients and vitamins for your baby, ask your pediatrician.

In addition, some formulas contain ingredients like nucleotides (to build immunity and make DNA), rice starch (to reduce regurgitation), fiber (usually added to soy formula for the management of diarrhea), and amino acids (to make protein). Special "designer formulas" are available that have the same protein ratios as breast milk, but the proteins are broken down so they are easier to digest than regular formula.

If your baby has specific needs or issues, there is a formula for that as well. There are formulas for premature infants that have more calories per scoop as well as formulas designed for colicky babies that have their proteins broken down extensively. If your child has special nutritional needs, you can obtain a human milk fortifier designed to be mixed with breast milk. In rare cases, an infant may need a metabolic formula that provides specialized nutrition for that particular baby.

Types of Formula

Starter formulas: These commonly found formulas are a good choice to begin with. All are based on cow's milk. They include brands like Enfamil with Iron, Similac with Iron, Nestle Carnation Good Start, and Parent's Choice Milk-Based Formula (sold at Walmart stores).

Soy formulas: These can be used when a baby is allergic to cow's milk or when an infant has digestive problems. Vegetarian parents often choose this type of formula for their infants as well. Such formulas include Isomil, ProSobee, Nestle Carnation Alsoy, and Parent's Choice Soy-Based Formula.

Lactose-free infant formulas: These are used when a baby is colicky or has a rash or diarrhea from other formulas. They are still based on cow's milk but have the lactose removed. Choices include Similac Lactose Free and Enfamil LactoFree.

Baby's Sleeping Habits— or Lack Thereof!

There are books upon books written about and solely dedicated to babies and sleep! Every parent will make their own choices about what they feel is best for their baby when it comes to things like co-sleeping versus sleeping in a crib, scheduled naps versus spontaneous napping, and putting your baby to sleep awake versus rocking or nursing him or her to sleep first and then putting your baby in the crib. The following are just a few thoughts to consider when it comes to your baby's sleeping habits:

- Newborns will sleep up to 80 percent of the day! Typically they will eat, have a diaper change, play with you a bit, and then go to sleep for one to two hours.
- Babies generally do not sleep solidly through the night until they have reached about 12 or 13 pounds and are at least three months of age.
- Infants have small stomachs and cannot go more than four hours without feeling

hungry. Although some experts say that in the first five to six weeks you should awaken a newborn baby if he or she has slept more than five hours straight, check with your healthcare provider for recommendations about waking your baby. Some might suggest waking the baby to feed during the day but not at night.

- Babies often demonstrate sleepiness by rubbing their eyes, yawning, fussing, or looking away from you. Over time, you will get to know what signs your baby uses to signal sleepiness.
- Babies can get to sleep by being rocked, driven in a car, or by being breast-fed in your arms. While this may work, your

> When my son was about two months old, I realized I wasn't taking advantage of his nap time to rest. One day while he was sleeping, I stopped dusting the shelves to look through our baby photos. There were at least 15 photos of my husband and our baby sleeping together, and not a single one of me sleeping with the baby. A picture sure does paint a thousand words. I threw down my duster right then and there, and lay down on the couch for a nap! —Dina, 37, mother of one

baby may get used to falling asleep in your arms and won't fall asleep in his or her bassinette or crib. Consider feeding your baby first and then putting the child in the crib just before he or she falls asleep.

- It is a good idea to get your baby as tired and as full of milk as possible, bundle him or her up, and place the bundled baby in a crib or bassinette in order to sleep.

- When your baby is awake but sleepy, playing soft music may help your little one to drift off to dozeland.

- Because of the risk of SIDS (Sudden Infant Death Syndrome), which has been linked to putting babies to sleep on their stomachs, babies should always be placed on their backs when being put down to sleep at any time of the day or night. The incidence of SIDS has dropped dramatically since this "Back to Sleep" recommendation has been made to parents.

- It is hard advice to follow, but do try to nap when your newborn is sleeping! It is easy to use this time to clean, read email, wash clothes, or shop online, but you will be sleep deprived in those early weeks, and baby's naptime is your opportunity to get some needed rest.

Your Baby's Bodily Functions: Potty Talk!

Among other things, you are about to become an expert on poop! Consistency, color, frequency and, yes, scent! Poop can tell you a lot about how your baby's digestive tract is working, so be prepared to answer questions when you see your pediatrician!

- Breast milk has a natural laxative effect, so your baby may have a bowel movement with almost every diaper. (Don't panic, you will get used to it.)

- Baby's first stools are generally dark green, thick, and sticky. Within a week, the baby will have transitional stools, which are yellow in color, not as sticky, and look like they have tiny seeds in them. After another few days to a week, the stools will be brown in color and vary in consistency depending on what the baby has eaten.

- Bottle-fed babies have more malodorous (stinky) stools than breast-fed babies; and when the baby eats solid foods at around six months of age, he or she will have stools that vary with the type and quantity of food eaten.

- You should have newborn diapers available for when you get home from the hospital. But do not stock up on this small size because most babies grow out of those tiny diapers in just a few weeks (unless they are born premature).

- Expect to go through eight to ten wet or soiled diapers every day!

- Purchase a diaper pail that can store used diapers odor-free until you can get them out to the garbage can or reuse plastic grocery bags by wrapping diapers in those.

- Make sure you purchase baby wipes or expect to go through a lot of washcloths to handle your baby's several bowel movements per day.

- Over the first few months of a baby's life, the stooling frequency will decrease to one to three times per day.

- With today's disposable diapers, it is often difficult to tell if the child has wet his or her diaper. For this reason, you can purchase diapers that have a color-changing strip that turns blue when the diaper is wet, so you only have to check the strip to see if you need to change the baby's diaper.

- There are still diaper services available if you want to use cloth diapers, and you can always wash diapers in the washing machine. If you choose this route, look up safe washing methods before starting.
- Cloth diapers are now made with Velcro closures and waterproof covers so you will not have to use the old-fashioned diaper pins, rubber pants, and diapers you have to fold.
- If you know you're going to use cloth diapers, purchase them before you take the baby home from the hospital and be

> I remember the moment I realized I was really living a new life. Three new moms and I had met for coffee, and we were suddenly engrossed in a conversation about poop. It's no joke when they say everything changes after you have a baby! —*Jean, 34, mother of two*

aware that when your baby grows out of the smallest diapers, you will have to purchase a whole new set of bigger diapers.

- While no one enjoys dealing with smelly diapers, remember that the time spent changing your baby offers an opportunity for positive interaction with your little one. Be aware of your own reactions and try not to show disgust, because as your baby gets older, he or she will think you are reacting negatively to him or her, not the icky diaper. Smile and talk to your baby while you are changing diapers.

- Remember that no one except your partner (and perhaps your mother) wants to discuss your baby's poop. Restrain yourself when talking to friends without children in particular!

Comforting Your Baby: Skin-to-Skin Contact and Swaddling

Newborn babies come from a quiet, warm, tight-fitting, snuggly environment and are born into a relatively loud, wide-open, and cool environment. As you can imagine, this is a bit of a shock to their little systems! There are some things you can do for your new baby to help his or her transition into this new world.

Skin-to-skin contact is an enjoyable experience for both you and your baby. You can explore skin-to-skin contact by having your baby, clad in nothing but a diaper, lie on your belly. Your baby will hear your stomach rumble and your heart beating just as he or she did in the womb.

Women who have the opportunity to breast-feed with skin-to-skin contact are often rewarded with a happier and soothed baby. While breast-feeding, your baby can take in your unique smell and the soft warmth of your chest and abdomen. Crabby babies can often be soothed with skin-to-skin contact—and partners can do it, too! This allows your partner to experience some of the sweet nearness you enjoy while breast-feeding.

Skin-to-skin cuddling, sometimes known as "kangaroo care," can even make a difference in the survival rates of preterm babies.

It helps create a powerful emotional and biological connection for the baby, and research now suggests that full-term infants can benefit as well. If you are not breast-feeding, consider skin-to-skin contact as your baby takes the bottle.

Swaddling with a blanket can soothe even the fussiest of babies, often lulling them to sleep. Swaddling blankets can be purchased at infant supply stores. These special blankets contain a pouch for the feet and have Velcro closures for the upper part of the body to keep the arms and hands snuggled tightly within the confines of the blanket. You can also use a regular large, thin baby blanket and fold it in such a way as to keep the arms and legs tightly in place. If you do not know how to swaddle a baby with a blanket, be sure to ask a nurse at the hospital or birthing center to show you! Some dads and partners pride themselves on championship swaddling, which offers another way for them to feel involved and competent with their newborns.

As babies get older, they need to be swaddled less and less, but fussy babies up to six months old can benefit from being swaddled, especially when it is time to sleep or if they need help calming down.

Swaddling your baby

Place baby on a large, lightweight blanket with the top corner folded down.

Fold one corner over the baby.

Tuck the end under the baby.

Bring the bottom corner up and over the baby's shoulder.

Fold the other side corner over the baby.

Tuck the end under the baby.

Rubber Ducky Time: Bathing Your Baby

If you are like many parents, the idea of bathing your newborn for the first time can be intimidating, if not outright frightening. But like everything else you have tackled and achieved so far (such as the first poopy diaper and possibly breast-feeding), you will be a pro at it in no time.

First, you should give your newborn sponge baths rather than tub baths until his or her umbilical cord falls off. Sponge bathing involves using a warm, wet washcloth or sponge and gentle, baby-friendly liquid soap to wash your baby. There is no need to immerse the baby in water at this point. In the first few weeks of life, you don't need to sponge bathe your baby more often than every three to four days or even longer.

Remember, babies do not really get dirty except in their diaper area. So if you are thorough about cleaning the baby off during every diaper change, you do not need to wash your baby's hair or the rest of your baby's body more than once or twice a week. Also, babies need to keep moisture in their

I was petrified the first time my wife and I bathed our little girl. She was so small, and I didn't want her to slip. I didn't know how to hold her and she cried the whole time! I'm six foot, four inches tall and can lift 300 pounds without a thought, but that tiny baby scared me completely for a while! —Jerome, 33, dad of two

skin, and bathing can be drying if done too often.

After a sponge bath or regular bath, you can hydrate your baby's skin with baby lotion. If your infant has very dry skin, bathe him or her less often, do not use soap, and try using hypoallergenic Eucerin cream on his or her skin right after a bath.

When you are ready to actually put your baby in bath water, you may be a little frightened if you have not done it before. The best way to bathe your baby at this point is in a special baby bath that can be used from the newborn stage to the toddler stage. As always, you will find many varieties to choose from, but most have inclined slings that can hold a newborn's head up out of the water while you bathe their body and then wash their hair. The sling can be removed for older babies who are able to sit up well.

Never take your hands off your baby or leave him or her alone in a bath, even for a second. Infants and toddlers can drown quickly in surprisingly little amounts of water! If you put your baby's bathtub on a kitchen or bathroom counter, be aware of safety hazards (such as the hot water faucet) nearby.

Newborn Monitor

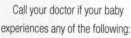

Call your doctor if your baby experiences any of the following:

- Several episodes of projectile vomiting
- Spitting up frequently for several days in a row
- Watery diarrhea lasting a day or so
- Redness around the umbilical cord area
- Fever of greater than 100.5°F (rectally)
- Persistent crying despite soothing measures

Cradle Cap Treatment

Cradle cap—also referred to as seborrheic dermatitis—is a very common skin condition for children, from newborns up to age three. Cradle cap occurs on the scalp because the scalp tends to be oilier than the rest of your baby's body. It looks like dandruff in some ways because there are scaly patches on the skin. The skin underneath may be red and irritated or it may be normal.

While cradle cap is not dangerous or even uncomfortable for your baby, it is not pretty—especially if the scales are thick and yellowish. The best treatment for cradle cap is to coat your baby's scalp with baby oil and leave it on for several minutes. Then use a fine comb to comb out the scales. When all the scales have been sufficiently removed, wash the baby oil out of your baby's hair with baby shampoo and water. You may have to repeat this treatment; however, one treatment is often effective.

I hadn't realized how much weight I'd gained while pregnant until a few days after being home from the hospital, when I sat in our rocking chair and my hips touched the armrests on both sides. I remember feeling so depressed thinking about how far away I was from my normal size 4 body, and I started to cry. I think I was finally allowing myself to realize all I'd been through in the last 10 months, and after that cry I felt a whole lot better. —*Lola, 36, mother of two*

Chapter 15

Postpartum Issues

You finally have your beautiful baby in your arms and you are home. Now the real work of caring for both yourself and your baby begins. You have the dual task of meeting your baby's needs as well as your own, and this can be a challenge for many new mothers.

During the first few weeks of your baby's life, your body must make major adjustments, hormonal and otherwise. Consider what your body has gone through with pregnancy, labor, and delivery. Now your body may be producing breast milk. No wonder it takes a while for the body to return to its normal ways of functioning. Whether you had a C-section or a vaginal delivery, your body will be sore and tired and needs time to heal. Emotionally, you have had an intense, life-altering experience, and need time to process your feelings and adjust to your new life and your new role as mother.

Many women, regardless of how ready they were to give birth, miss having their baby inside of them, kicking and close at all times. They miss the intense experience of being one with their child. Sometimes women even resent the fact that others have as much

I remember lamenting to my mom that I seemed to have no time to do anything but care for my baby. The house was a mess, I had no clothes to wear that looked good on my postpartum body, and I was too tired to cook a decent meal. I hadn't gone anywhere with the baby yet, my husband was back at work, and I felt lonely and isolated. I told her how I felt like a bad mother, and the baby was only three weeks old! She assured me that everything I was feeling was normal and that I was being way too hard on myself. She reminded me that I was doing a spectacular job taking care of the baby, and now I needed to spend a little time taking care of myself. She told me to relax and do the following: (1) Go for a walk with the baby in the baby carrier once a day right after a feeding; (2) Go online and buy a few things to fit my body for now, knowing that the weight will come off eventually; (3) Order healthy take-out until I felt more organized and energized; and (4) Find a new-mother's group to attend to feel supported and less alone. I started crying. My mom asked why and I told her I didn't have time to brush my teeth and shower every day—I could only make time for one or the other, so how could I go to a moms' group! She said, "Don't sweat the small stuff—just brush your teeth in the shower!" All her advice really worked, but brushing my teeth in the shower really helped me turn the corner and feel better! —*Daphne, 28, mother of one* access to their baby as they do and that others can help meet their baby's needs. These are normal feelings that will gradually pass, but they can be a challenge to cope with in the early weeks of motherhood.

Many of you will begin parenting with a partner. You will have to adjust to your partner's way of parenting and his or her ideas about how to best meet your baby's needs. Your partner may be extremely helpful or perhaps nervous and less involved, and you will find yourselves negotiating through a whole new set of circumstances while sleep deprived and unsettled. This can cause a great deal of tension. In addition, your sex life may need some repair as well. Every new mother has her own timing for wanting to participate in normal sexual activities again. Your body has a new function in producing breast milk and you may be having trouble adjusting to your postpartum body. This also takes emotional and physical energy, and your body and your perceptions will take some time to normalize again.

This can be a joyous yet exhausting time in your life as you, your body, and your partner adjust to having a new little person in your life, someone who is completely dependent on you for everything. To the extent possible, taking care of yourself as much as you take care of your baby and your partner will get you through this postpartum period much more smoothly. This chapter will help you by discussing several postpartum topics including the following:

- How can I more easily adjust to the exhaustion I feel?
- Will it take a long time to heal from my episiotomy or vaginal tear?
- If I am breast-feeding, how can I make it more comfortable?
- What about pumping milk at work?
- What can I do about stretch marks now that the baby is born?
- How long will it take to get my body back in shape?
- How do I know if I have postpartum depression or just the baby blues?
- What can help me to feel better during this time?
- What about sex and contraception after the baby?
- How can my partner and I bond with our baby?
- What if my baby has special needs?
- What are some questions frequently asked by new parents?

How Are You Feeling?

Once you return home from the hospital with your newborn, you will have a new set of physical challenges.

Exhaustion

The first few days after you get home from the hospital are exhilarating yet exhausting. Between visitors coming to see the baby; dressing, diapering, and feeding the baby; and taking care of your own needs as well as those of your partner and perhaps other children, you may wish you had 10 arms or 10 helpers! It is normal to feel exhausted and overwhelmed when you are adjusting to a completely new life.

The best way to combat exhaustion is to give in to your urge to rest and let go of some things—like keeping a perfect house. If you have a partner living with you, he or she can clean and cook; you can hire help or enlist friends and family; or you may simply need to let go of nonessential tasks for a while. Your baby will be sleeping a lot in those first few weeks. Take the opportunity to have as many naps as you can to combat the effects of interrupted sleep and emotional exhaustion.

If you have had a cesarean section, remember that you are recovering from major surgery as well as from many months of pregnancy. You really need to rest and recuperate, and if at all possible, someone should stay with you and the baby for a few days.

If you do have help (other than your partner), be sure to speak up if your helper wants to care for the baby, leaving other chores to you. It is easier to negotiate this issue if you are breast-feeding, but in any case, your baby's care is your pleasure as well as your responsibility, and your helper can be of more use by doing the laundry and preparing meals.

Even if you are breast-feeding, your partner or other helper can bring the baby to you, change diapers, and pamper you a bit. You need to eat especially well, drink plenty of fluids, and rest in order to successfully produce breast milk.

Soreness

You will have soreness in your muscles and in your perineal or vaginal area following birth. Whether you are breast-feeding or not, you can take Tylenol for pain; and if you are not breast-feeding, you can take Aleve or Motrin as well (as long as you do not have other medical conditions that preclude taking these medications). Soak in a hot tub to

A sitz bath was like a miracle for me and helped me heal so much more quickly from my episiotomy. I also took advantage of my time in the bath by turning the sitz bath into a bubble bath. It became my time to relax and take a mini-break for myself! —Dalia, 37, mother of three

ease your muscle pain and make a sitz bath to ease the perineal pain or the pain from an episiotomy or vaginal tear.

To make a sitz bath, fill the bathtub with a few inches of warm water and put several tablespoons of table salt or Epsom salts in the water (you can buy Epsom salts at any pharmacy). Sit back in the tub with your legs spread apart. Splash the water on your vulvar and perineal area, allowing the warm, salty water to soothe the area. Do this at least once per day for about 15 minutes at a time. Within a couple of weeks, the perineal area will feel nearly normal.

Sitz baths and cleansing your perineal area with water after a bowel movement or after urination can also help prevent vaginal infections. You were probably given a squirt bottle at the hospital, which you can fill with water and use so that you don't have to rub the area you are cleaning. It is possible to get a bacterial infection in any cut or stitched areas of the vagina, and the change in your hormones can lead to a yeast infection. If you get an infection of the perineal area or the vagina, see your healthcare provider as soon as possible to determine what type of infection it is

> Be sure your partner is getting the nutrition she needs once you are home with the baby and things are going a million miles an hour. Even if you don't cook, ask what your partner wants for take-out, and if you are back at work, call at meal times and remind her to eat. It's healthy for everyone! —*Chuck, 32, dad of one*

and to get the recommended treatment. Keep your wound clean and dry and use a sitz bath as often as possible to soothe the area and promote faster healing.

Besides sitz baths and Tylenol, you may need to take a stool softener. Ask your healthcare provider about what kind of stool softener to use. Docusate sodium is one of the better stool softeners available. It will allow you to have a softer stool that will not be as painful as it would be if you had constipated stools. Even hard stools will be unlikely to open up a well-sutured tear, but the pain could be substantial. See your doctor if you are having problems with bowel movements even with a stool softener or if you think your tear has opened up.

Hormonal Changes

Your levels of estrogen and progesterone, as well as the level of hCG (human chorionic gonadotropin), will plummet as soon as you deliver. This leaves just about every woman with a feeling of low mood shortly after delivery. Add to that the changes in your life and the increase in psychosocial stressors, and this can lead to anything from "baby blues" to postpartum depression. We will talk in more detail about postpartum depression later in this chapter; but know that it is perfectly normal to have some periods of low mood during this time.

Your Appetite and Diet

Your appetite may be completely normal after the baby is born or somewhat increased, but you will find there is certainly less time to prepare healthy foods. This is when you enlist your partner, friends, family, or local take-out restaurant in making sure your meals are as healthy as possible, especially if you are breast-feeding. Stick to meals with whole grains, fruits and vegetables, and lean protein. Keep taking your prenatal vitamins and be sure you are getting enough calcium and drinking plenty of fluids.

If you find yourself unable to sit down for a full meal because of the demands placed on you, make sure you have plenty of quick, healthy snacks available to you. If you are breast-feeding, be sure you take in the extra 300 to 500 calories that your body needs to produce breast milk. It is a good idea to get yourself a nutritious snack and a glass of water before you sit down to feed your baby.

You also need to drink plenty of water, especially if you are breast-feeding. Your body needs fluids to produce adequate amounts of breast milk, replenish fluids your baby takes from your body when breast-feeding, and to rid your body of extra fluid in your tissues. Liquids also stimulate the kidneys to get rid of all the fluid in your system.

Eating a healthy diet rich in fiber along with drinking plenty of liquids will also help prevent constipation, which is especially important during the first few weeks after delivery. Constipation will make bowel movements extremely painful, especially if you are recovering from a C-section. Keep up with the good eating habits you had while pregnant, and you and your baby will both continue to benefit!

Breast Care for the Breast-feeding Mom

Breast-feeding has numerous known health benefits for your baby and is therefore highly recommended. The longer you breast-feed, the more benefits your baby is likely to receive, and those benefits will be more enduring. The American Academy of Pediatrics (AAP) reaffirms its recommendation of exclusive breast-feeding for about the first six months of a baby's life, followed by breast-feeding in combination with the introduction of complementary foods until at least 12 months of age, and continuation of breast-feeding for as long as mutually desired by mother and baby. You will begin breast-feeding right after your baby is born and continue up to 12 times per day in the beginning. Right after birth, your baby will reap the benefits of protein-rich colostrum for the first few days. Your milk production will gradually increase between three and five days after birth.

At this point, your breasts will look and feel full and may be tender. After a few days, your milk will "come in," and your milk supply will increase. After about a week, the extreme fullness you felt after the baby was born should begin to normalize. While your breasts will still feel larger than before you got pregnant, the amount of milk within your breasts should better match the amount your

Our pediatrician gave us some great advice before our son was born. She recommended that we have no help and no visitors for the first two weeks of our baby's life. She felt it was a vital time for bonding with our baby and for establishing our own routines and methods for caring for the baby without interference (although well meaning) from family and friends. We took her advice and by the time our family and friends were visiting and telling us what to do, we had already become comfortable with our own way of doing things and felt like competent, confident parents. Now we recommend our friends do the same thing! —*Heather, 31, mother of one*

baby needs. The newborn baby will consume one to two ounces of milk from your breasts each time he or she feeds.

After about 10 days, you will begin to make only mature milk and experience a let-down reflex or a surge of milk flowing into the breast when the baby cries or when your baby suckles. The breast will feel full before breast-feeding and emptier after your baby breast-feeds. This is normal.

Caring for Your Breasts

If you decide to breast-feed, you need to take good care of your breasts and learn to recognize any signs of trouble with them.

Nipple soreness: Nipple soreness is one of the most common problems caused by breast-feeding, and the hormonal changes you will be experiencing make it worse. Try putting the areola (the darker-colored part of the

When Not to Breast-feed

Even if you want to breast-feed, there are some circumstances that can prevent you from doing so. You should not breast-feed under the following conditions:

- You have active tuberculosis.
- You are HIV positive.
- You are being treated with cancer-fighting drugs or radiation therapy for cancer.
- You drink alcohol either too much at one time or too often.
- You use illegal drugs.
- You have active chicken pox.
- You have herpes infections affecting your breasts.

feeding your baby often or by pumping your breasts for breast milk and storing it for later use. You can also express breast milk by hand to ease the pressure. Do this under a warm shower for a soothing effect on tender and engorged breasts.

If your breasts are engorged, it may be difficult for your little one to latch on to the breast. Express a small amount of milk from the area beneath the areola so the areola can best conform to your baby's mouth. Then your baby can latch on and breast-feed as normal. Cool packs on the breast can also ease engorgement after a feeding if your baby isn't as hungry as you expected. As your body gets used to the baby's needs, engorgement will improve somewhat.

breast) into your baby's mouth along with the nipple when you feed. Nipple sucking alone will not dispense as much milk as when your baby is sucking the nipple and areola. Nipple sucking also causes sore, cracked nipples.

If you do have cracked or sore nipples, moisturize them generously with lanolin cream throughout the day and night. You do not need to wipe the cream away before breast-feeding. Other remedies for sore, cracked nipples include placing warm, wet compresses on your nipples (use a washcloth or even a tea bag) or expressing a bit of breast milk, rubbing it on the cracked areas, and letting the milk dry. The milk will leave a protective coating on your nipple.

Breast engorgement: Breast engorgement refers to the heavy, sore feeling you may have in your breasts when they are very full. Engorgement can be easily remedied by

Plugged milk ducts: Plugged milk ducts appear as lumps on your breasts that are painful or tender to the touch. They are caused by not completely emptying your breasts of milk after feedings. Plugged ducts can be treated by pumping your breasts so they are empty or by breast-feeding enough to empty the breasts of milk. You can massage a plugged duct from the edge of the breast toward the nipple until the lump goes down.

Plugged ducts can lead to a breast infection called mastitis. Mastitis involves having a sore, red area on your breast along with flu-like symptoms, including body aches, chills, and fever. If you have these symptoms, see your healthcare provider or head to your emergency room to get an antibiotic to kill the infection. Be sure to let the doctor know you are breast-feeding so you can get an antibiotic that is safe for your baby. You can still breast-feed from an infected breast.

Discomfort Associated with Breast-feeding

If you are breast-feeding, you will likely experience uterine cramping, which can be mildly to moderately painful. This is because the infant's suckling releases oxytocin, which contracts the uterus, especially during the first week or so. In addition, you may feel some pain when your baby first starts to nurse. Breast pain can be reduced by ensuring that your baby is latched onto the nipple properly or by changing the baby's position.

You are likely to experience cracked or dry nipples in the first weeks of breast-feeding. Purchase some lanolin before your baby is born and begin using it right away to try to avoid painful cracked nipples. Lanolin is the perfect healing moisturizer and does not have to be washed off before your baby nurses.

Breast pain may also be caused by mastitis, an infection (see the previous page).

A board-certified lactation consultant can be extremely helpful in assisting you to find comfortable, effective ways to nurse your baby. If breast pain persists, be sure to consult your healthcare provider and seek help from a lactation consultant if appropriate.

An Ounce of Prevention Is Worth a Pound of Cure: Latching On

The best way to prevent breast-feeding issues is to practice a good latching-on position for you and your baby. This way your baby will get enough milk and you will avoid most of the problems associated with breast-feeding your baby. Initially, feed your baby eight to twelve times per day. Space out breast-feeding so that it occurs at regular intervals throughout the day and night, especially in these first few weeks. If you pump after each feeding, you will increase your milk supply and can have some frozen breast milk stored for later use.

Getting your baby to latch on

Learning how to help your baby latch on to the breast will make it easier for your baby to nurse and minimize sore nipples. From WomensHealth.gov.

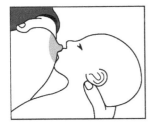

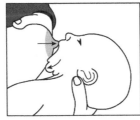

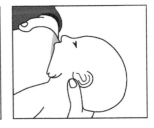

Tickle the baby's lips to encourage her to open wide.

Pull your baby close so that the chin and lower jaw moves into your breast first.

Watch the lower lip and aim it as far from the base of nipple as possible, so the baby takes a large mouthful of breast.

Making Breast-feeding Easier and More Pleasant

Your physical comfort during breast-feeding will make a big difference. Choose the most comfortable chair or couch and experiment with pillows to support your arms while you are holding the baby. Many moms use special semicircular breast-feeding pillows such as the Boppy brand.

Before you sit down to nurse your baby, take a moment to use the bathroom if necessary and to get yourself a tall glass of water. You will be sitting in one position for a long time, and you want to be comfy and take care of your own needs as well as your baby's.

Some mothers use a small safety pin on their blouse to remind themselves which breast the baby nursed from last so they can start with that breast the next time. This helps prevent breast engorgement and ensures the baby has a full meal if he or she falls asleep before nursing on both sides.

Nursing holds

Find the position that is most comfortable for you to breast-feed your baby.

Cradle hold: You may wish to use a nursing pillow to support the baby.

Side-lying hold: Moms who have had cesareans may find this position most comfortable.

Cross cradle hold: This position helps the baby to latch on.

Football hold: This hold is helpful for moms with large breasts or to protect a cesarean incision.

Being around other breast-feeding moms will help you to feel less self-conscious while you nurse. You can easily feed discreetly with a light blanket to throw over your torso and the baby. You will discover which items in

> With my first child, I made the mistake of buying a manual breast pump. The electric ones were so expensive! But after the ridiculous effort and energy it took to use it, I got my husband to go out and buy the electric pump. It is worth every penny if you plan to breast-feed and need to pump breast milk! —*Elisa, 42, mother of two*

your wardrobe lend themselves to easy access for nursing, such as loose-fitting t-shirts that you can lift and night-gowns with nursing slits or front openings. Be sure your nursing bras fit you properly, since your breast size can change during different phases of breast-feeding.

Pumping at Work

If you return to work while you are breast-feeding, you will most likely need to pump during the workday. As a result of a healthcare bill passed by Congress in 2010, a woman has both the right to take reasonable breaks to express milk until her baby is a year old and the right to have a private place (not a bathroom) in which to pump. Employers with fewer than 50 employees are exempt from this law. Check your employer's policies and talk to any other staff members who

have pumped at your workplace. You will also need a safe place to store expressed milk, which may need to be an insulated cooler bag with ice packs (see Chapter 14) if there is a shared or unsanitary refrigerator. Plan your work wardrobe to minimize the need to disrobe when you pump. Talk to other moms and seek out online information to help you handle the inevitable challenges of expressing milk at work.

Postpartum Stretch Mark Treatments

Stretch marks bother some women more than others. Some women wear them with pride as the "battle scars" of having a baby. Other women are distressed by stretch marks and want to get rid of them if possible. The following treatments are for use on stretch marks only *after* you have given birth to your baby.

Vitamin A and Other Retinoids

These products contain ingredients that increase the amount of collagen and elastin in the skin. This treatment appears to work best when the stretch marks are in their earliest stage. Creams are preferable to gels, which may dry out your skin. You can get a prescription for the product from a respected dermatologist. One particular treatment involves the use of vitamin A products and glycolic acid together.

Laser Treatment

This is a great treatment that has been tested and is used by many dermatologists. It can be used on white stretch marks but is most effective at correcting purple or red marks. Laser treatments work by increasing the growth of collagen within the skin. They increase skin cell production as well. Treatments with laser often take three to six separate sessions spread over several months. The cost of the treatment is prohibitive for some women since it will not be covered by insurance.

A special type of laser, fractionated laser, is able to treat older stretch marks. It smudges the stretch marks so they become less perceptible to the eye. This treatment takes about three to four months before you can see a positive effect.

Glycolic Acid

This product—a derivative of sugar cane—is an alpha hydroxy acid that appears to work by increasing the levels of skin collagen in the body so that the skin can "knit" itself together. While glycolic acid is available without a prescription, a qualified dermatologist can administer it in high enough doses to have a better effect. It often takes three to four visits to the doctor for adequate treatment.

Getting Back into Shape: Be Kind to Yourself

Ladies, you just grew and housed a baby for 10 months and then gave birth. Your body just performed the greatest miracle on Earth, and now it needs time to adjust, just as you do. This is a time to be loving and kind to yourself, no matter how you think you look after you have given birth. While you may be happy about the instant weight loss you had when you delivered your newborn, like most women you likely have some additional weight to lose before getting back to your pre-pregnancy size. In addition, your weight may have shifted so you have more around your middle and your hips. It is okay! You will get your body back if you take simple, easy steps each day to care for yourself:

- Continue eating a healthy diet rich in vegetables, whole grains, fruits, and lean meats.

- Avoid sugary and processed foods, sugary drinks (including juice), and boxed meals that are high in fat and sodium.

- To get optimal nutrition from each meal, make soups, stews, casseroles, and sandwiches from scratch. Even better, have your partner cook these healthy meals.

- Remember that frozen vegetables and fruits are just as good as fresh ones, especially when certain fresh fruits and vegetables are not in season. Keeping vegetables and fruits on hand in the freezer makes it more likely you will eat them.

- Drink lots of water. Keep your own water bottle or cup nearby while you are feeding your baby.

- Exercise as much as you can. One of the easiest things to do is take a walk with your baby in a baby carrier or stroller.

- Try to get in 30 minutes of exercise daily. Remember, it is just as effective to walk twice a day for 15 minutes or three times a day for 10 minutes as it is to do 30 minutes all at once.

- In order to trim your midsection, try Pilates or yoga. You can do sit-ups, which can strengthen muscles that have been stretched out of shape while you were pregnant. Get your doctor's okay if you have had a C-section.

- Buy exercise DVDs you can do at home while your baby sleeps or find an exercise program on television, online, or in the "on demand" section of your cable programming.
- Congratulate yourself for any effort (big or small) that you take each day to stay healthy and care for yourself! Focus on the great job you are doing.

Be aware that the images in the media of celebrities who are back in pre-baby shape within three weeks of birth are just so much hype. If you had three nannies, a personal chef, a full-time trainer, a make-up artist, and someone to airbrush your photographs, you'd look pretty good yourself!

The most important thing to do when getting back in shape is to enlist your PMA (positive mental attitude) again. Your body took 10 months to get where it is, and it deserves time to get back to where it was. Be loving and positive toward your body, and it will respond in kind!

Postpartum Depression or Just the Baby Blues?

It is extremely common to feel overwhelmed and a bit down after the birth of your baby. It can happen as early as 24 hours after the delivery of the baby or within a few weeks of delivery. Your hormone levels of estrogen, progesterone, and hCG will drop dramatically after birth, causing feelings of sadness, depression, and low energy. These feelings are common and usually transient, lasting just a day or a few days. When these feelings persist for more than two weeks or become more intense, it is likely you have a

more serious condition called postpartum depression. Let's look at both.

Baby Blues

The emotional phenomenon called the "baby blues" happens to some degree in almost all women who have a new baby. About half of all women experience full-blown "blues," so don't panic and assume you are sliding into depression if you find yourself sobbing in the shower. You can often improve your mood by taking a long, hot bath or by relaxing with some soothing music. Exercise, taking naps, talking to a supportive friend or family member, and eating a healthy diet will all help improve your mood as well.

Mood changes following the birth of your child can also occur for reasons other than hormones. These can include the following life changes and worries:

- Worry about taking care of your baby and your parenting skills
- Changes in your body due to pregnancy, delivery, and possibly breast-feeding
- Having less time to yourself and less personal freedom
- Being sleep deprived
- Dealing with changes in your relationships
- Having concerns about your work status

It is completely normal to have feelings of tearfulness, restlessness, and anxiety after your baby is born. The baby blues often pass within two weeks of the baby's birth and require no specific treatment. Often, the most reassuring thing to do is to talk to another mother who has been through this emotional turmoil and can empathize with you. It is also important to let your partner know how you feel. Partners may think it is helpful to say,

Don't be embarrassed or ashamed if you are having symptoms of postpartum depression. Know that it is fairly common and it is treatable. Don't waste time suffering with it—seek help immediately if you think you have an issue. You and your baby deserve for you to feel your best!

—Becca, 36, mother of two

"It's just the hormones," but this can feel invalidating and make you angry as well as sad! Partners can help by giving practical support and by acknowledging that your feelings are intense and real to you. Sometimes a hug and a few kind words make a huge difference.

Postpartum Psychosis

Postpartum psychosis is a relatively rare condition (one or two instances in a thousand births), but it is serious and needs immediate treatment. It usually develops within two weeks of birth. In this condition, the new mother may become disoriented and find her thinking is irrational. She may see or hear things that are not really there (hallucinations) or believe things that could not possibly be true (delusions). She may have irrational thoughts that someone or something is trying to harm her or her baby or hear voices. She may actually attempt to harm herself or her baby. Once again, this is a rare condition, but if you have any concerns that your thinking is becoming seriously disordered, tell a loved one, and contact your healthcare provider or the emergency department of a hospital immediately. This is a treatable condition, but it is a medical emergency.

Postpartum Depression

Postpartum depression is a much more severe condition than the baby blues, but it is not uncommon. In fact, 15 percent of women experience some symptoms of depression after the birth of a baby. Symptoms can begin as early as immediately after delivery or sometime in the first year of your baby's life. Most cases, however, begin within three months of birth.

Symptoms of postpartum depression can be similar to those of the baby blues, but in postpartum depression the symptoms do not go away after two weeks and often intensify.

Increased risk of postpartum depression: There are some risk factors that make it more likely a woman will have postpartum depression, such as

• being a teen mother

• having a stressful pregnancy or delivery, including the death of a family member, an emergency delivery, or a preterm birth

• having a baby who has a birth defect or a significant medical problem

• being in an intimate relationship characterized by a lack of support, conflict, physical or sexual violence, or sexual coercion

• having a history of premenstrual dysphoric disorder (PDD) or severe premenstrual syndrome (PMS)

• having had an unplanned pregnancy or having mixed feelings about parenthood

• having a history of anxiety, depression, or bipolar disorder before becoming pregnant or associated with a previous pregnancy; having been depressed during pregnancy

- having a close family member who has had depression or anxiety
- living in poverty or experiencing serious financial stress
- being single
- having poor family support
- abusing alcohol or taking illicit drugs
- smoking

Symptoms of postpartum depression: The major symptoms of postpartum depression include

- feeling withdrawn or disconnected from others
- feeling more irritable
- having a change in appetite
- showing little pleasure in normal activities
- having a lack of energy and concentration
- experiencing negative feelings toward your new baby or excessive worry about your baby
- exhibiting significant anxiety
- having thoughts of death, suicide, or homicide

In severe cases of postpartum depression, a new mother may find herself unable to care for her baby or herself. She also may be frightened when facing the possibility of being alone with her baby or may exhibit a lack of interest in her baby, intense worry about her baby, or have thoughts of harming her baby.

Women with postpartum depression rarely act on their thoughts. But if you do experience thoughts of harming your baby, you should talk to your healthcare provider or a therapist right away about possible causes and treatment or go to the emergency department of a nearby hospital. It is also important to confide in your partner, a friend, or a family member who is supportive and can help you to get through this difficult time.

Edinburgh Postnatal Depression Scale: There is a simple test, the Edinburgh Postnatal Depression Scale, which can assess your risk for postpartum depression. We have reproduced the test for you on the next page as a handy resource.

Basic information on postpartum depression: New mothers who are struggling with low mood can benefit from learning about postpartum depression. Even if you are not severely depressed, you may need additional emotional support during this time, and some of the suggestions below can be helpful.

- Anyone can get postpartum depression, even without a history of depression in the past. Postpartum depression is not your fault, so there should be no shame about seeking help.
- If you have had postpartum depression in the past and begin taking medications for depression right after delivery, your chances of getting postpartum depression drop significantly.
- There can be a medical reason for depression after having a baby, including postpartum hypothyroidism (when your thyroid is underfunctioning), which is not uncommon. All postpartum women with depression should have blood tests to make sure they don't have postpartum hypothyroidism.
- If you think you have postpartum depression, check with your healthcare provider so he or she can evaluate whether or not you would benefit from medication.

Edinburgh Postnatal Depression Scale

Fill in the answer that comes closest to how you have felt in the past seven days, not just how you feel today. Here is an example, already completed.

I have felt happy:
- Yes, all the time
- Yes, most of the time (This would mean: "I have felt happy most of the time" during the past week.)
- No, not very often
- No, not at all

In the past <u>seven</u> days:

1. I have been able to laugh and see the funny side of things
   - As much as I always could
   - Not quite so much now to cope at all
   - Definitely not so much now
   - Not at all

2. I have looked forward with enjoyment to things
   - As much as I ever did
   - Rather less than I used to
   - Definitely less than I used to
   - Hardly at all

3. *I have blamed myself unnecessarily when things went wrong
   - Yes, most of the time
   - Yes, some of the time
   - Not very often
   - No, never

4. I have been anxious or worried for no good reason
   - No, not at all
   - Hardly ever
   - Yes, sometimes
   - Yes, very often

5. *I have felt scared or panicky for no good reason
   - Yes, quite a lot
   - Yes, sometimes
   - No, not much
   - Hardly ever

6. *Things have been getting on top of me
   - Yes, most of the time I have been unable to cope
   - Yes, sometimes I have been unable to cope
   - No, most of the time I have been able to cope well
   - No, I have been able to cope as well as ever

7. *I have been so unhappy that I have had difficulty sleeping
   - Yes, most of the time
   - Yes, sometimes
   - Not very often
   - No, not at all

8. *I have felt sad or miserable
   - Yes, most of the time
   - Yes, quite often
   - Not very often
   - Not at all

9. *I have been so unhappy that I have been crying
   - Yes, most of the time
   - Yes, quite often
   - Only occasionally
   - Never

10. *The thought of harming myself has occurred to me
    - Yes, quite often
    - Sometimes
    - Hardly ever
    - Never

SCORING

QUESTIONS 1, 2, & 4 are scored 0, 1, 2 or 3 with top box scored as 0 and the bottom box scored as 3.

QUESTIONS 3, 5-10 (marked with an *) are reverse scored, with the top box scored as a 3 and the bottom box scored as 0.

A maximum score of 30 indicates the most severe depression and any score of 10 or above indicates possible postpartum depression. The authors ask that special attention be paid to item 10 for evidence of suicidal thoughts.

If your score is 10 or above, call your healthcare provider right away! Bring a copy of your completed questionnaire with you.

(Reproduced by permission of the authors.)

Cox, J.L., Holden, J.M., and Sagovsky, R. 1987. Detection of postnatal depression: Development of the 10-item Edinburgh Postnatal Depression Scale. *British Journal of Psychiatry 150*:782-786.)

- See a therapist for help. If you have health insurance, call your insurance company for a referral. If you are uninsured, there are community mental health centers that often work on a sliding-fee scale. Ask your healthcare provider to help you find a therapist. Be sure to ask if the therapist has training and experience in treating postpartum depression. Both cognitive behavioral therapy and interpersonal therapy have been shown to be effective in treating this condition, so ask what kind of treatment the therapist provides.
- Enlist help from your partner, family members, and friends to care for you and help you care for your baby. This is hard to do when you are feeling sad and inadequate, but it is crucial. Often those who care about you want to help, but they don't know what you need or want. Your healthcare provider or therapist can also talk directly to your loved ones to let them know how they can support you.
- If you are in a relationship where you are afraid or where there is physical or sexual violence or coercion, or if you have a history of past abuse, you may find it helpful to talk to an advocate at a domestic violence or sexual abuse program in your community. These services are confidential and generally free. They are not a substitute for therapy if you are severely depressed, but they can provide additional support. See Chapter 1 for information about advocacy services.
- Talk about your feelings with supportive loved ones.
- Do not make major life decisions while you are suffering from depression.
- Set small goals (such as making a pediatri-

cian appointment or washing one load of laundry), and celebrate your successes.
- Stay active and engage in activities you find pleasurable.
- Exercise and eat well; sleep when the baby is sleeping. Take time to get out of the house and visit with friends or relatives.
- If you are diagnosed with postpartum depression, you can use medications to control your symptoms that are safe for breast-feeding, including nortriptyline, paroxetine, and sertraline.
- Support groups are also very effective. Your healthcare provider should be able to help you find a support group.

You need to call your doctor if you feel you have the baby blues, but the symptoms change in the following ways:

- They do not go away after two weeks.
- Your symptoms intensify.
- You cannot perform activities of daily living.
- You cannot care for yourself or your infant.
- You develop thoughts that are not rational.
- You have thoughts of harming yourself or the baby.

Don't hesitate to seek help because of embarrassment or worry about what others may think. Untreated depression can interfere with your ability to care for your baby and can have lasting effects on your child.

Postpartum Anxiety Disorders

In addition to postpartum depression, new mothers are at risk for anxiety disorders, including generalized anxiety, posttraumatic stress disorder, and obsessive compulsive disorder. If you find yourself troubled by constant worry and are unable to relax or enjoy your time with your new baby, seek help from your healthcare provider or a therapist. These conditions can be treated successfully with talk therapy, medication, or a combination. Don't hesitate to reach out for assistance, since anxiety can drain your life of joy and make it difficult for you to effectively care for your baby.

Navigating the Emotional Challenges of New Parenthood

Most new mothers do not experience postpartum depression, but many find the adjustment to parenthood to be something of a challenge. This challenge may be intensified by the relentless expectation of others that you must be exceptionally happy at this time in your life. The media depicts smiling young parents with perfect babies, while the reality is often messier and less positive. You will, in fact, probably feel intense happiness and joy about your baby. You may also feel somewhat disoriented about all the changes that have happened in your life, resentful about the demands on your time, and confused about your identity as a new mother. These are normal, transitory feelings, and they don't make you a bad mother. As long as you can put your baby's needs first and you are mostly in a positive frame of mind, you are doing okay.

Talk to your partner and to other mothers, and keep your positive mental attitude (PMA) at the forefront. Don't forget your sense of humor—it can be your best ally. Psychological research has shown that being mindful of those things for which you are

grateful can improve mood, so take the time each day to be grateful for your baby and the other things and people that improve your life. Be kind to yourself and appreciate the importance of the job you are doing as a parent.

Fun and Frolic: Postpartum Sex and Contraception

Life is a whirlwind after your new baby arrives. You and your partner are adjusting to a completely new way of life. You are both focused on the needs of your baby, you are healing from 10 months of pregnancy and from giving birth, and both of you are likely exhausted. So, if the thought of having sex right after having a baby seems overwhelming or impossible, it is understandable! As with everything else in your life, you need to be patient and give yourself time to transition into a "new normal" routine, and that includes sexual intimacy with your partner.

Most doctors recommend you wait six weeks after birth to resume sexual intercourse with your partner. This is the time it takes for a C-section incision, an episiotomy, or a tear to heal; any bleeding to stop; and your cervix to close properly.

Resuming Sexual Activity

- Resume sex on your own timeline. If you do not feel ready by the time your baby is six weeks old, wait until you are ready. Exhaustion and postpartum depression may keep you from having sex right away.

- Keep the lines of communication with your partner open and active. Talk to each other about how you are feeling about everything, including your sex life. Listen compassionately to each other and respond to each other's needs.

- If you are experiencing pressure from your partner to have sex before you are ready, or if you are afraid to say "no," seek help from a confidential sexual violence advocacy program. (Call 1-800-656-HOPE for a referral to a local program.)

- For the first few months after the baby is born, sex may feel different due to soreness in the vaginal area and from being exhausted after caring for a newborn baby all day and night. Again, give yourself time to adjust.

- If you are breast-feeding or experiencing hormonal changes, your vagina may be sore and dry. Use a lubricating jelly to aid intercourse and try positions that hurt less and are more pleasurable.

- If sex is painful after the first few times, see your doctor and ask about the use of an estrogen cream that can build the tissues of your vagina so that you can restore natural lubrication. (Note: Estrogen cream can decrease your milk supply if you are breast-feeding.)

- Low vaginal tone may also cause sex to feel different. There will be a decrease in friction between the penis and the vaginal wall. This is a temporary phenomenon, and the vagina will become less relaxed over time.

- Try Kegel exercises for five seconds at a time, building up to 10-second intervals. Repeat a pelvic floor contraction every 10 seconds or so for about 10 times total. Do three sets of these exercises per day and your pelvic muscles will soon be back in the shape they were in before you got pregnant.

- Do not set high expectations on sexual activity, especially right after birth. Understand that the changes in your body are to be accepted—even appreciated. Relax as a couple and know that with a little extra understanding, effort, and patience your sex life will get back to normal as you both adjust to your new life as parents!

If you are too tired or not interested in sex, be sure to convey your feelings to your partner. Having a baby and caring for him or her all day long and into the night can be exhausting. So, by necessity, sex must take a backseat to the other aspects of your life. Try to replace or augment sex with other types of intimacy and be close to your partner as much as you can. You may want to remind your partner that there is nothing sexier than consideration and practical help. Keep your sense of humor and take time to talk and laugh together. There are ways to be intimate without having sex!

Contraception: Something to Think About Now!

You can become pregnant again as early as even one month after having a baby if you have sex without contraception. This can happen even if you are breast-feeding! Although breast-feeding can delay your period, it is not a reliable method of birth control.

As you know from the days before you were trying to become pregnant, the options for birth control are numerous and varied. If you are breast-feeding, you can still use barrier methods or spermicides in order to reduce your chances of pregnancy. Barrier methods include condoms and the diaphragm. If you are breast-feeding and still want a birth control pill, choose the "mini-pill," which

> We had to adjust our sex life to our new situation, just like we had to adjust everything else. Give yourselves time, keep communicating about it, and find the humor in your situation. No need to get angry when you plan to have sex and fall asleep before your partner makes it to bed—laugh about it instead and know that, like everything else, it will get better!
>
> —*Suzanna, 40, mother of three*

contains only progesterone. The mini-pill does not reduce milk supply, which can occur with the regular combination (estrogen plus progesterone) pills.

Whether or not you are breast-feeding, talk about birth control options with your obstetrician/gynecologist or with your primary care doctor at your six-week checkup, or sooner if you plan to resume intercourse earlier. He or she will be able to go over your options in detail and advise you on what method of birth control will provide you the best protection with the fewest side effects.

Women who are sexually active but not in a stable or supportive relationship may need to talk to their healthcare providers about methods of birth control that cannot be detected by their partner. If you are in this situation, you probably want to avoid a rapid repeat pregnancy.

Bonding with Baby

Bonding with your baby happens differently for every new parent. Some women feel a strong bond with their baby even during pregnancy, and this bond strengthens after the baby's birth. Other women may feel more overwhelmed by the birth of their child and will warm up more slowly to their baby's presence in their lives. The important thing is not to put undue pressure on yourself or your baby in terms of bonding. In general, the bond between parents and babies is intense and natural and will in fact happen, whether immediately or more slowly over time.

It is instinctual for parents to want to nurture and protect their children. The powerful love you feel for your newborn is likely beyond anything you could have imagined. Bonding is a natural product of so much love. As you connect, bonding will help your baby feel secure and help develop a sense of positive self-esteem. It can also affect your infant's sociability as well as his or her cognitive development.

Bonding Tips

The following are some simple ways that you and your baby can bond:

- Babies bond through touch. They love skin-on-skin contact and eye contact with their parents. Babies can follow objects that move in front of them and will attempt to mimic your gestures and facial expressions—even as newborns. They love when you talk to them and they will listen to conversations—the topic is not important, just the talking itself.

- Interacting with your baby through physical contact like cradling him or her in your arms, breast-feeding, or carrying the baby on your body in a front carrier rather than a stroller are simple, natural ways to promote bonding. You can also try going skin-on-skin with your diapered child or take a bath with your baby. Your infant will learn to recognize your smell and the feel of your touch.

• Gentle baby massage is an excellent way to bond with preterm babies or babies with health concerns. If your baby has been in the neonatal intensive care unit (NICU) or special-care nursery, ask your nurses about the art of infant massage. Some hospitals and community education centers offer classes in infant massage.

• Use your baby's wakeful periods to spend time talking or singing to him or her, making silly faces, and expressing your love verbally. Babies love to hear the voices of their parents, and there is no need to sound like Frank Sinatra or Mariah Carey when belting out the ABC's! It is simply an effective, fun way to connect with your baby.

• Partners can bond with baby using the same techniques as Mom, particularly if they spend a lot of time with the child. While your partner cannot breast-feed your baby, he or she can give the baby pumped breast milk and can still sing or rock the baby to sleep. Bonding might not occur as rapidly with your partner as it will for you, but it will still happen over time.

• Partners can increase the pace of bonding with newborns by participating in the labor and delivery process as a couple, by feeding the baby on occasion, by singing or reading to the baby, and by giving the baby a bath. Partners can spend time mimicking the baby's sounds and copying the baby's movements. They can use a front carrier to cradle the baby during routine chores or shopping. Let the baby touch the partner's face so that the difference between Mom and partner can be recognized and appreciated.

• Bonding with baby can be enhanced by joining a mother-and-baby support group. Not only will you feel supported by other moms and bond with your baby, you will likely find an instant playgroup for your baby as he or she grows up. If you are breast-feeding, a local La Leche League meeting can serve as a support group.

Dads and partners sometimes feel awkward handling a fragile new baby. Here are some simple tips:
• Start by placing one hand under the baby's head and one under the bottom.
• Look at your baby's face and talk to him or her as you pick the child up.
• Be careful to keep your movements slow and controlled so you don't startle the baby.
• Continue to support the baby's head.
• Bring the baby close to your body and enjoy the cuddle!

Situations That Can Make Bonding More Difficult or Delayed

While bonding is a natural occurrence between parent and child, sometimes there are factors that pose challenges and can cause delays.

• Bonding can be delayed in situations of adoption or when the baby is preterm.

• The hormonal changes going on in your body can temporarily affect the way you bond with your infant.

- Postpartum depression can impair bonding.
- You may be too exhausted to fully enjoy your newborn.
- Having a difficult labor and delivery may leave you physically and emotionally spent.
- Your child may have medical or developmental problems that interfere with bonding or the opportunity to spend time together.

If you are having trouble bonding with your baby, try to relax and remember that bonding will happen but it may take a little more time than you expected. Know that bonding happens eventually in even the most difficult of circumstances. If you feel you are having problems bonding with your baby, talk to your healthcare provider or to a therapist. There may be something else going on that is interfering with your ability to bond. Also, you can share your bonding issues

My son would cry hysterically when I tried to put him in the stroller, so I ended up carrying him in a front carrier until he was nine months old. It was a blessing in disguise because I believe it made our bond that much stronger. Go with the flow. Everything has a silver lining!
—*Johanna, 39, mother of two*

with a mother-and-baby support group. Other new parents often have a lot of insight about this issue.

During the first few weeks, you may benefit from the support of a doula, an individual who is specially trained to support women through the childbirth and postpartum process. Some doulas even have additional training in supporting women who have a history of trauma or abuse that may make mothering more of a challenge. Doulas will come to your home and can give you the extra information and care you may need to feel secure in your parenting abilities.

Special Needs Babies

Even with the best medical care and the best self-care, you baby may be born with problems. Special needs babies may have Down syndrome, another genetic abnormality, a cleft palate, autism, other physical illness, or developmental disabilities. One out of every 28 mothers will find themselves with an infant who has a chronic illness, a physical handicap, or a developmental delay. Even if you had genetic testing and expected your baby to have special needs, few parents feel as if they are prepared for the realities of having a special needs child. And that is normal! The wonderful news is that no matter what issues special needs children may have, you will still bond with them, love them, and understand their needs just as you would a typical child, if not more so.

Parents with special needs children need to give themselves time to grieve over the reality that their child is not the typical, healthy baby they wanted and expected. There is often an emotional upheaval that occurs due to the suddenness of the situation and the reality that their child is different from what they had hoped for. Feelings of anger, resentment, fear, sadness, and even tentative optimism are all normal responses to having a special needs child. Grief is a highly individual thing and how you experience it depends on you and your support system. You can grieve alone or grieve together with your partner. Your grief will come and go, depending on the circumstances. It is normal to feel sadness and grief, even when the baby seems to be heading in the right direction and making strides at his or her own pace.

If you have a partner, pay special attention to your relationship as you begin your parenting journey with a special needs baby. Often one parent (usually the mother) becomes the "expert" on the child's problems, and the other parent feels excluded and uncertain. Include your partner in your child's care and in learning how to respond to your baby's condition so you can be true partners in the raising of your special needs child and you can preserve your bond as a couple.

Over time, you will experience the joy and individual strengths and beauty of your new baby. Even if your baby is sick or disabled, you can trust that soon you will be an expert regarding the child's particular condition and be your baby's advocate and cheerleader. You may not have the baby you expected, but he or she is the baby you received, and you will learn to love your baby and care for him or her in the best way you know how.

It is also normal for parents to look for reasons for their baby's disability and wonder if they are to blame by having done something wrong during pregnancy. Do not waste precious time and energy blaming yourself or your partner or either of your genetic backgrounds! Embrace your situation as best you can; find a positive mental attitude (PMA again!) and know that every child blossoms when he or she is deeply loved.

Make sure you ask for help from doctors, therapists, and support groups for families with special needs children. Many communities have early intervention programs that offer support for parents in their homes. Focus on your priority, which is to love, protect, and support your newborn infant. Some things you thought you would be doing with your child may not now be possible, so you need to redirect your actions and energy toward everything that is in the best interest of your child.

Common Questions

Here are some typical questions and answers you might have during this postpartum period:

Question: My partner is avoiding having sex with me. He stopped when I was pregnant and his drive for sex hasn't returned even now that the baby is two months old. What should I do?

Answer: Sex between partners is often disrupted with pregnancy and after the birth of a new child. The first step to take is to try to talk openly and compassionately with your partner about his feelings as well as yours. Be patient and focus on having fun and talking together. If he still is reluctant to have sex with you or you are finding it difficult to communicate about the issue, consider seeing a marriage and family therapist who can support you both around this issue and help you find ways to move forward.

I believe that the baby you receive is the baby you are meant to have because you possess everything they need from you as a parent. Like every parent, you will grow with your child and learn how to best help him or her become who they are meant to be. Allow your feelings of grief, or anger, or sadness, but remind yourself that you are the perfect parent for your special needs child! —*Lola, 42, mother of two*

Question: I don't feel comfortable in my own skin since I delivered my baby just four months ago. My partner has no objections with the way I look, but every time I look at my stretch marks, I feel awful about myself. What should I do?

Answer: Your feelings about your body image are perfectly normal. It is important to remember that your body has just gone through an amazing and miraculous process and needs time to adjust back to its pre-pregnancy state. Besides getting exercise when you can and eating a healthy diet, you need to talk to yourself in a loving way about your body. Use positive affirmations and focus on your positive features and things you love about your body. If your partner loves and cares about you, follow his or her lead and learn to love who you are now—the mother of a beautiful child.

Question: My husband and I just found out that we're pregnant again after having a son just two months ago. How do we tell our friends and family?

Answer: If you have joy and jubilance over the upcoming birth of your next child, your family and friends will likely share that. If you are upset about it, do not hide it. Use this time to bond with the baby you already have and talk with those you love and trust about your feelings surrounding having another baby so soon after your first. They will likely understand and support you.

Question: I feel like I'm overly bonded with my six-month-old daughter. It's not getting better as she gets older. Work is becoming intolerable because I miss her so much, and when I have time with her I don't want to let her go.

Answer: It is wonderful you have bonded deeply with your child! Your feelings are completely normal. Even moms who have all the time in the world with their baby feel as if time is passing them quickly and they don't want to miss a minute of their baby's life. You can have a tight emotional bond with your baby without having to be with her every minute of the day. If you leave work to be with your baby, it may not change these intense feelings you have regarding your infant. Talk with your spouse or partner about your feelings and any possibility or desire you have to leave work to be home with your daughter. If you must work, focus on the quality of the time you have together.

Question: I don't feel as bonded with my second infant, who is now two months old, as I did with my first child. Is there something wrong with me?

Answer: It is normal to feel an instant natural bond with your first child. Now that you have to divide your time between your personal life, your first child, and your infant, it can take longer and be more challenging to feel the same intensity in bonding with your second child. Make one-on-one time for you and your new baby. If you are feeling low energy and low mood, you could have postpartum depression, which is completely treatable. Ask your healthcare provider for advice.

Question: My baby is nine months old and doesn't even want to crawl. How do I get her to develop normally?

Answer: All babies develop at their own pace. You cannot force a child to crawl or walk if he or she is not ready developmentally. If she is otherwise reaching her landmarks for speech and cognition, it is likely that she is simply not ready to crawl. Give her as much "tummy time" as she will tolerate. Tummy time is simply time when your baby is able to play and explore while lying on her tummy (see Chapter 16 for more on this topic). Trust that she will begin to crawl when her legs are strong enough and she becomes motivated. If you have serious concerns, contact your pediatrician.

Question: My baby hates his tummy time. I was told by my pediatrician that he needs 15 to 20 minutes per day on his tummy, but he cries after 2 to 3 minutes. What should I do?

Answer: Your baby will eventually learn to like being on his tummy. If he only tolerates a few minutes, wait an hour or two and try

One night I came to bed and my husband had left a note on my pillow: "Roses are red, Violets are blue, I want another baby, How about you?" I was exhausted from lack of sleep, had been spit up on four times that day, hadn't gotten my hair done in two months, and forgot to eat dinner. I wrote back, "Roses are red, Violets are blue, If you try to touch me tonight, I might hit you!" We both laughed over it, then actually talked about when we might try for another child. That night, my husband kissed me and just held me close while I fell asleep. The next night, however, was a different story! And we have a little girl to prove it! —*Lisette, 41, mother of three*

again. You can also get right down on your tummy with him so he has someone to talk to while on his tummy, or start by lying down on the floor and laying him on your tummy. Babies are easily distractible with toys, so interest him with those as well. You can also purchase a special mat designed to enhance tummy time. Try one out if your baby is having problems being on his tummy. (See Chapter 16 for tummy time information.)

I remember one afternoon when my husband and I had finally gotten our four-week-old to sleep for a nap. The baby had been up most of the night, and we were both exhausted and slumped on the couch. We looked around at the messy family room, the pile of dishes in the sink, and the spit-up on our clothes. My husband turned to me and said, "Who have we become?" And I answered, "Face it, Babe—we've become parents!" —*Heidi, 37, mother of two*

Chapter 16

Beginning Your Journey as New Parents—Embracing Change

No doubt you have heard the saying that everything in life changes. But there are few changes greater than the switch from being a couple to being a couple of parents! Everything in your life is different. Your priorities have been rearranged, and your focus has shifted from yourself and your partner to your baby and his or her needs. And if it feels like this happened overnight, it is because it did!

After your 10-month-long pregnancy journey, you are now in a new role as mother. In addition, you may have decided to be a mom full-time (at least during maternity leave), leaving the routine and regular adult contact of your previous job behind. Your days (and nights) are no longer your own and revolve around the care of your infant. Your finances may be in flux as well as you adjust to your new circumstances and the additional costs of having a new little person in the household.

I've kept a journal since I was in third grade. One night when I couldn't get to sleep after nursing the baby I found the journal I'd kept during my pregnancy. I flipped to a page and found something I'd written when I was about eight months pregnant:

I already know that my job as mother is to do everything in my power to help my child become who he is meant to be on this earth. We all have a purpose here and a parent's job is really to teach their children to become themselves, even if that means becoming something that we might not choose for them. My child is not mine to possess, but mine to nurture and support his own journey. My child is not mine to shape, but mine to teach and then allow to shape himself. My child is not mine to hold on to, but rather to let go of so he can soar like a kite while I hold the string until he is ready to fly on his own....

I took a look at the tiny little life sleeping so peacefully in his crib and I knew that for me, what I had written was true. I would do everything in my power to help my son become the best version of himself that he could possibly be. And I am proud to say, 22 years down the road, he has!

—Betty Ann, 58, mother of two

Having a new baby is one of life's most stressful events, even if most of the stress is positive! Between sleepless nights and hectic days, your body will be more susceptible to illness—and the very last thing you can afford now is to be sick. At least for now, keeping a perfect house is no longer possible or a priority, and for some women this is a tough place to let go of perfection. In addition, your partner may be feeling a bit like a third wheel as your focus switches to your new baby—especially if you are breast-feeding. The demands on your time may feel as if they are coming from everywhere all at once, and the first thing you let go of is time for yourself.

As you adjust to your new life, it is important to keep things in perspective and give everything time and patience. You will need to find a way to keep meeting your own needs as well as your partner's as you both adjust to your new world. Communication, love, compassion, and patience will help you and your partner manage through this extremely wonderful, joyful, crazy period of new parenthood!

In this chapter, we will talk about ways to adjust and adapt to your new life with baby:

- What are some "survival tips" to help me through this time?
- How can my partner and I parent as a team?
- How can we make time for each other, and how can I have a little time for myself?
- Are we stuck at home now that we have a baby?
- What if I am a single mom?
- What are normal developmental milestones for my baby?

- What is "tummy time," and how can it help my baby's development?
- Now what?

Early Survival Tips

The number one tip for new parents is to relax and go with the flow. You are in the midst of perhaps the greatest change of your life, and tackling your newfound role as parent can only be made easier with patience and a positive outlook! Here are some other tips for making those first few weeks and months with your baby more pleasurable:

Be Aware of the "Baby Blues" and Help Your Partner to Understand Them as Well

Be sure that your needs are being met and be active in combating those low feelings. Engaging in activities you enjoy and participating in things you did before you were pregnant can help you feel grounded again. It can be something as simple as a solo trip to your favorite store, beginning your running routine again (with the baby in the jogging stroller?), or taking a long bubble bath. Remember: You have just been through 10 rigorous months emotionally and physically, and you need and deserve some time to transition back to normal. If the baby blues do not go away after about two weeks, talk to your healthcare provider. See Chapter 15 for more about mood problems.

Try to Get Enough Sleep

Ask someone you trust to watch the baby while you take a nap, or try to nap when your infant does. It is easy to use your baby's naptime to get things done—like the dishes, cooking dinner, checking emails, or catch-

I hate to admit it, but I had no idea what to do with our baby. I felt awkward holding her and couldn't change a diaper properly. Quite frankly, I was scared of her! I started to avoid helping out and my wife was getting angry. But I didn't know how to admit my ignorance and fears or to ask for help. Finally, one day she brought it up. Once I finally told her how I was feeling, she was completely supportive and understanding. She taught me what to do and made me feel supported, not criticized. After a while, I got the hang of it. Guys, don't be afraid to let your partner know you have no idea what you are doing! As hard as it might be, ask for help! —*Michael, 34, dad of two*

ing up with texts and phone calls. Since your newborn will sleep up to 16 hours per day, force yourself to use some of that time to catch up on sleep and rest yourself. And if you are not breast-feeding, let your partner take some of the nighttime feedings. If you need additional rest, your partner can give the baby a bottle of formula or breast milk at night.

Create a Bedtime Routine for Your Newborn

Even newborn babies will respond to a nighttime schedule. You can try a schedule that starts with a bath, then changing into nighttime clothes, feeding your baby, singing or reading to your baby while he or she is in the crib or bassinette, and then lights out. Consistency is key. If you keep up your schedule for a few days, your baby may learn the cues for falling asleep, and certainly over the months to come a bedtime routine will help your baby to sleep with some regularity.

Ask for Help

Your first weeks and months with a new baby can be overwhelming. Learning to ask for help will make your life so much easier. Even if you are the type of person who likes to do everything herself, this is a great time to become flexible. So many of your friends and family are likely dying to spend time with your baby and help you as well. Taking small increments of time away from your baby, when you feel ready, is healthy for you. Allow your best friend to come over to clean or let your mom watch the baby while you go for a walk. Remind yourself it is okay to have help!

Expect and Allow Imperfection

There is no such thing as a supermom or superdad or a perfectly clean house! You will make mistakes, dishes will get left in the sink, and some days you many not even get out of your pajamas! It is all okay and normal. Learn to embrace imperfection. Talk to other parents who are going through the same thing and you will realize no one in the history of parenting is ever 100 percent perfect. And thank goodness! How boring would that be?

Know That You Are the Expert When It Comes to Your Baby

You are (or are becoming) your baby's expert. Learn his or her likes and dislikes as well as his or her habits and routines. Ask questions of the doctor or nurse, but do not expect that they know more than you do about your own baby.

Remember Your Baby Is a Stranger in a Strange Land

Your little one just showed up here and doesn't know the rules and customs yet.

What's more, he or she doesn't speak the language. Be patient and educate yourself about what to expect at different developmental stages. Don't expect to have instant understanding, and don't expect your baby to instantly understand what you want. Both of you will be frustrated from time to time, and it's your job to overcome that frustration with kindness and love.

Feed Yourself!

Try to squeeze in three meals daily, and eat the foods you really like. Make sure that, especially if you are breast-feeding, you get plenty of dairy products, eggs, meat and fish, fruits, vegetables, and whole grains. Drink as much milk, water, and juice as you can. Avoid caffeine if you are breast-feeding and take only Tylenol for pain or fever.

Exercise

Take your baby for a walk, shop in a large mall with plenty of walking space, join a gym that has babysitting, or find a trusted caretaker to watch your baby while you exercise. You can even find a friend with a baby and switch off time watching each other's children while you get back in shape.

You can find exercise classes and videos that will show you how to exercise in a safe and fun manner with your baby!

Partners Can Do Everything Moms Can—Except Breast-feed!

Parenting, in most cases, is a partnership, and both partners need to fully participate in the experience. If your partner is unsure or nervous about what to do for your baby, teach him or her what to do and be encouraging! Do not complain if your partner does not do things exactly as you do. Your child needs to become as comfortable with your partner's care as he or she is with yours. Let your inner Control Queen take a break.

Take Care of Each Other's Needs

As you likely know, intimacy is more than just sex. While you cannot have intercourse for about six weeks after the baby is born, you can still connect with your partner physically by cuddling, kissing, and hugging, as well as other creative sexual acts. Take time every day to talk to one another about the changes in your lives and how you feel about them. (If your partner is not the kind of person who generally enjoys talking about feelings, however, that is unlikely to change right now.) Ask each other what needs you have and try to meet them. Be kind, supportive, and find the humor in your new situation! Both of you are experiencing a major life change and can grow closer if you make a conscious effort to share the experience with each other. Know that your life will get to a new normal in short order and you can grow closer as that happens.

Connect with Your Mother or Another Older Woman

Don't forget your own mother, grandmother, or other older woman as a source of support. Your mother-in-law might even be

Task List

Here is a list of things that need to be done when you have a new baby:

- Picking up baby items and putting them away
- Cleaning the house, including the kitchen, living areas, bedrooms, and bathrooms
- Doing the dishes
- Doing the laundry and folding clothes
- Purchasing food items and baby items (diapers, wipes, etc.)
- Cooking breakfast, lunch, and dinner
- Entertaining other kids in the house (This is an issue for parents with older children, especially when their little friends come to play.)
- Paying bills
- Feeding the baby
- Holding the baby while the other caregiver is taking a shower or getting dressed
- Rocking the baby to sleep
- Changing the baby's diaper
- Bathing the baby and washing his or her hair
- Dressing the baby
- Maintaining the household vehicles
- Taking out the garbage
- Miscellaneous chores and duties

the one you turn to! Be realistic about the quality of your relationship, and don't expect a loving response now from someone who has not supported you in the past. Use your own good judgment to distinguish helpful relatives from those who are toxic to you. You don't have to take every piece of advice, but don't perceive all advice-giving as criticism. To some degree, we have lost the continuity of mothering skills that traditional societies enjoy, but older women still have important wisdom to share from their life experiences.

Meet Other Moms

Try to meet other moms with newborn babies. This will provide a chance to compare notes and talk about common concerns. Just don't get into a competitive spirit about your parenting skills or your baby's development, and avoid people who can't stop comparing. Parenting is not a race. Connecting with other mothers can be a great way to get support.

Parenting Is a Team Sport!

Yes, it is true. Parenting is a team sport! You and your partner have to follow the same game plan, know what the plays are, run them together, and have each other's backs when the game gets tough! There are a host of new responsibilities in your life, and getting organized around who is going to take care of what will keep stress and arguments to a minimum—especially during those weeks of sleep deprivation when your nerves will be frayed.

Dads and partners need to participate in a baby's care.

Make up a list of tasks that you and your partner need to do now that you have a baby. Decide together what you will do and what your partner will do. You can always trade off if one person gets overwhelmed with his or her task. Appeal to your partner's sense of fairness if you believe you are carrying more than your share. Looking over the list together may help your partner realize that you aren't lying around doing nothing all day! Be kind and loving, and do not expect perfection from yourself or your partner.

Remember that your partner cannot read your mind. Sometimes a simple, clear request can make all the difference. For example, you might ask your partner to get up 20 minutes earlier so that he or she can watch the baby while you take a quick shower to feel more prepared to face the day. Don't wait until you are completely exhausted and resentful to ask for what you need, and encourage your partner to speak up as well.

Keep in mind that, even with two people, your house will not always be clean, your refrigerator will not always be full, and you may not have as much time for conversation or sex as you would like. And it is all okay! Do the best you can, be loving toward each other, and eventually everything will fall into place.

Finding Time for Yourself and for Each Other

Yes, the dynamic duo (you and your partner) has now become a trio—or more, if you have other children. But this does not mean you no longer have a relationship separate from your role as parents. For parents, the key to a happy, healthy family life is making time for each other and time for yourselves, individually—away from your baby and children.

This is no easy task! With the demands of a newborn, sleep deprivation, and financial concerns, it may seem like a monumental task to coordinate an evening out together or even find time for a leisurely shower. But even if you spend two hours together, it is essential that you and your partner continue to be a couple even after your baby arrives.

Ensuring Balance

Here are some ideas to help overcome concerns you might have when it comes to making time for each other and for yourselves as individuals:

Planning is key: Whatever your personal needs are—be it taking a regular shower or bath, reading a book each day, working at a satisfying job, or taking a walk solo—if you plan, you can find time to meet those needs. With your partner or a sitter, schedule personal time each week. Decide what you want to do each day and strive to get those things accomplished with help, but be flexible around your baby's needs and wants.

Hire help: Compared to the negative effects that failing to meet your needs can have, hiring a sitter for a few hours a week is cheap (or often priceless!). If you have financial constraints, swap babysitting with a friend, enlist your partner, or have a family member help out. If you are breast-feeding, you will need to master the art of pumping breast milk and freezing it so a caregiver can feed your child while you are out. Even if you can only pump an ounce at a time, you can combine the expressed milk you've pumped in a single day into a three- to four-ounce container. This is plenty for a single feeding, which will give you two to four hours of freedom to do whatever you need.

The nurse who conducted our birthing class made us all promise the following: "No matter what, one month after your baby is born, you must leave your baby with a family member, sitter, friend, or trusted neighbor and go out of the house with your partner for two hours. No excuses. No exceptions. Just do it!" She made us sign a pact with ourselves, too. Well, when our baby was one month old, my husband made arrangements for my mom to come over for two hours, and, when I protested, he pulled out the paper that I'd signed. I didn't want to leave my baby, but after much prompting we went out. I cried most of the two hours and called home three times, but I know now that if I hadn't done it, I may have never felt comfortable leaving my baby at home. And that was exactly why the nurse had us promise to do it! —Fanny, 36, mother of two

Get into the habit of leaving your new baby in someone else's care:
For a variety of reasons, many new mothers do not want to leave their babies with anyone but their partner, and even that can be a challenge at first. Consider having an infant-savvy close relative or trusted friend babysit for you. It really is healthy for you and your baby if you give yourself the breaks you need. Even if you only go out for an hour, give yourself that gift at least once a week. Trust your own judgment about this. Initially, having someone watch the baby while you stay home and take a nap or a bubble bath may be sufficient.

Have a "date night" once weekly: You and your partner will also need time to spend together as a couple. Whether you go out or you stay at home while someone else cares for your child, it does not really matter. As long as you are spending time together without your baby, you can focus on each other. Some couples have a sitter come in, and they stay at home and make a meal together and watch a movie while the sitter cares for the baby. This may be a great way to start if Mom or Dad is uncomfortable leaving their baby in someone else's care. Work your way up to leaving the house for entire night out. And eventually, you can even schedule a glorious weekend away together if you have a trusted caregiver. The important thing is not what you do, but that you have uninterrupted time together.

Having a baby does not increase the risk of divorce: Good news! But remember that all relationships need attention, caring, and love. Remain partners, keep communication, and make time for each other. The healthier and happier you are as a couple, the healthier and happier your baby will be!

Share your day-to-day challenges as well as hopes and dreams: Remember to pay attention and ask about any challenges your partner is facing on a daily basis (work tasks, personal goals, or relationship conflicts). In addition, talk together about how you want your family to develop, the goals you have as parents and for your child, and your dreams for the future. These talks will ensure emotional closeness despite everything else that is going on.

Sleep with your partner in the same bed:
It may sound silly, but many couples have their infant sleep in bed with them or make a practice of falling asleep in the baby's room. Having the baby in your bed is generally considered unsafe, but more practically, it keeps you from contact with your spouse or partner. Because your relationship is essential to the healthy functioning of your family, try to have your baby close by but not in the bed with you.

Doing Things as a Family

Generally speaking, you can take a baby anywhere! Here are some things to consider:

- Remember that other restaurant customers and moviegoers deserve their time out as well. Be prepared to remove your baby immediately if he or she begins to cry or fuss.

- Feed your baby before going out, in the hope of promoting sleep. Be sure to bring along formula or pumped breast milk. Alternatively, you can learn to breast-feed in public in a way that is comfortable for you, possibly using a blanket or a nursing cover.

- Taking baby on errands and for walks is also fun family time. You will enjoy the attention your little one will receive from strangers and other parents and you can get things accomplished while the baby sleeps. Making use of a front carrier is a great way to free your hands while shopping and keep baby close and happy at the same time. When you use a stroller instead, it should be sturdy and have a roomy area beneath it for your baby bag or purse.

- Instead of having family and friends come

to you all the time for a visit, take your growing family out to visit. (As an added bonus: You don't have to clean up the house!)

- Plan outings such as picnics in the park or have a backyard barbecue with friends. To lighten your load, ask guests to bring a dish and help with cleanup. Good friends will be more than willing to pitch in!

- Try to work your activities around your baby's routine. Showing up at

> I used to hate the way people cringed when we walked into a restaurant with our sleeping infant! But we had no family in the area and little money for sitters, so we were careful to be sure to spend time out when our baby was asleep. Ignore the nasty looks and just be sure to leave the establishment immediately if your baby fusses—everyone deserves their time out! —*Krista, 38, mother of three*

Grandma's in the middle of naptime will probably result in a fussy baby.

- Babies travel well, so do not avoid vacations or long trips. Careful planning will ensure you have everything you need when you arrive at your destination.

Single Parenthood

Whether you have chosen single parenthood or have accepted an unplanned baby into your life, you will face all of the same challenges as other parents and some that are unique to raising a child on your own. What is important for single parents is to find support systems and trusted help along the parenting path.

It may help to know you are certainly not alone. More than 40 percent of babies are born to unmarried women; nearly 50 percent of women will spend some time as a single parent while their children are growing up. The stigma associated with being a single mother has largely dissipated, but you may still feel some disapproval from others, especially if you are young. Hold your head high and seek role models who are successfully handling single parenthood.

Nearly all the information in this book applies to your situation, including things like

- napping when your infant naps
- using additional naptime to get chores and tasks completed
- enlisting friends and family in babysitting, preparing meals, housecleaning, and moral support in those first weeks and months of motherhood
- finding affordable daycare
- adjusting your budget and finances to accommodate baby
- socializing with other new mothers for support
- being sure to take care of your own needs and make time for yourself
- taking baby along when shopping, exercising, and socializing
- watching for signs of the baby blues and postpartum depression

Some of your needs are unique to your status as a single mom. Here are some suggestions:

- Find a support group for single parents or a therapist to help you process any anger or resentment you may feel about your situation—especially if it was not planned.
- Let go of perfection and become comfortable letting unimportant tasks wait.
- Remain positive and compliment yourself often on the amazing job you are doing.
- Choose the people in your life carefully. You may be vulnerable emotionally after having a baby, and you want to surround yourself with positive, considerate individuals.
- Find the right balance between receiving help and being independent if your mother is your support person. This can be a tricky road to navigate, since you need her help but you want to retain your status as an adult and a mom.
- Remember you and your baby are a family. Be intentional about how you set up your routines and manage your household, since this is the setting in which your baby will develop.
- Take advantage of any community or state programs you qualify for that may provide food, health insurance, daycare, or financial support.

Adjusting to single parenthood, though filled with joy and amazement, can still be stressful. Being organized and sticking with a solid routine will be one of the most important things you can do to keep yourself relaxed and happy as a new parent. Laying out clothes the night before, keeping your diaper bag packed with essentials, making lists for groceries and other chores, and scheduling time for yourself and time for bonding with your baby are ways you can minimize stress.

Most importantly, embrace your situation and remember that quality time with your child is what counts. Providing your child with love, affection, and a sense of security is something every mother can do, whether she has a partner or not.

A Look to the Future with Your Baby

You will not have a newborn baby forever. You will be amazed at how quickly he or she grows and develops! By about six to eight weeks, your child will smile at you for the first time, and those smiles will continue to melt your heart for years to come. Your baby will not just lie in your arms forever but soon will be moving around and rolling over.

The following are general guidelines for your baby's developmental milestones. Remember, these are just guidelines; every baby is different and will develop at his or her own pace.

Physical Developmental Milestones

A baby needs time to develop the balance, coordination, and muscle strength for a variety of activities, and they do not develop in a linear fashion.

Smiling: Your baby will offer a genuine smile for the first time at around six to eight weeks of age. This is called a social smile. Your baby smiles best and most often when you are smiling back at him or her. Babies are born with the propensity to smile at a smiling face,

I chose to be a single parent. One of the first things I made sure of was that I would have support. I moved closer to where my parents live, researched daycare near my workplace, found a support group for single parents, and met with a financial planner to adjust my budget and plan for the future. So once I had my baby, I was ready and life was easier. Even if you find yourself unexpectedly pregnant, you can do the same things to plan before your baby is born. Being prepared really reduces stress! —Ann, 42, mother of one

but they are not developmentally prepared to do so until six to eight weeks of age. Before that, most smiles occur during REM (rapid eye movement) sleep, the phase of sleep in which the baby is dreaming.

Rolling over: Your baby can begin to roll over as early as two months or as late as six months. You should give your baby tummy time (see below) and watch him or her carefully. If your baby's arms and legs are strong enough, he or she will soon roll over, first from tummy to back and then from back to tummy. For this reason, never leave your baby unattended on a diaper changing table or a bed. He or she can suddenly roll over at any time!

Tummy time: Tummy time is a great way to help your baby increase strength and mobility. Because babies should sleep on their backs, they need time when they are awake to lie on their tummy and play. The tummy position will help your baby strengthen upper

Making the Most of Tummy Time

- Start by letting your little one lie across your lap (also a good burping position) or lie on your chest while you are reclining. This is a nice opportunity for skin-to-skin contact with your newborn, who should wear only a diaper for this version of tummy time.

- Use a blanket or soft towel on the floor. Be sure your baby likes the texture of the blanket or towel and that it is not too warm or too cold in the area you choose.

- Don't try tummy time when your baby has just eaten (to prevent spitting up) or is hungry (to prevent fussiness).

- You can also use a nursing pillow or a rolled-up towel to support the baby's upper body. Be sure to stay right by the baby's side to ensure safety.

- Play and have fun with your baby during tummy time! Get down on the floor (use an exercise mat if that is more comfortable for you) and smile, sing, laugh, tickle, and talk to your baby.

- As your baby gets older, introduce age-appropriate toys such as a rattle, a toy that crinkles or makes a musical sound, a ball, an unbreakable mirror, or a vinyl book. Eventually, your baby will reach out for these toys, which encourages motor development.

- Play music that you both like!

- Encourage older siblings or your nieces and nephews to get down on the floor and play (gently) with baby, under your supervision.

- Try to give your baby the opportunity for tummy play at least once a day.

- Let your baby's enjoyment guide the amount of tummy time. There is no set amount of time you should aim for. If your baby gets a little fussy, you can try to distract him or her, but don't prolong tummy time if your baby is clearly ready to stop.

- If someone else cares for your baby during the day, ask the caregiver to be sure to include tummy time in your baby's routine. Share these tips with the caregiver and demonstrate tummy time if he or she is unfamiliar with the activity.

back and neck muscles and may help the head develop a nice round shape, instead of being flattened from lying on the back. You can start tummy time even with a newborn, as long as the umbilical cord doesn't create discomfort. Remember never to leave your baby unattended, even momentarily. "Making the Most of Tummy Time" offers some suggestions for terrific tummy times!

Grabbing: By age three to four months, your baby will begin grabbing a bottle, his or her

pacifier, or a rattle. Your baby is learning that items can be manipulated, and he or she will soon learn exactly how to manipulate them to meet his or her needs. In the beginning, your baby will drop things quite a bit, but he or she will soon pick things up and set them down with ease.

Hugging: A baby will learn to hug you, your partner, or a favorite toy. Your baby will learn hugging best by seeing others hug and by being hugged, even if he or she does not seem too interested in it at first. Find times when the baby is more affectionate, such as before a nap or before bedtime, and use that time for hugging. This usually begins around five months of age. Because each baby is a little individual, each varies in his or her enjoyment of physical contact such as hugging. Encourage, but don't insist. It is never too early to show respect for your child's legitimate wishes.

Playing peek-a-boo: Your baby will find peek-a-boo hilarious at around six months of age. Use a baby blanket or your hands, get close enough to your baby to be able to gain his or her attention, and watch your little one's delight when you uncover your eyes and say "peek-a-boo!" After a few months, your baby will actively play peek-a-boo with you and

> The one thing no one can explain or describe to you when you are pregnant is the intense love you are going to feel for your child. It is unlike any love you have ever felt—including the love of your partner. Everyone says things like "get sleep now" or "get in a lot of movies" when they find out you are pregnant. But what I tell newly pregnant women is this: "Get ready to experience the biggest, grandest love of your life!" —Eleanor, 44, mother of four

hide his or her own eyes. Make the game different and interesting each time and you will be able to play for months.

Developmental Concerns

You know your baby best. If you have any reason to suspect that your baby is not developing at an appropriate pace, be sure to contact your pediatrician or clinic. Developmental screening should be included in well-baby visits, but don't wait until the next appointment if you are worried or you see a marked change in your child's development. It is scary to think that your baby may have a problem, but if that is the case, the earlier it is addressed, the better. Many developmental problems can be helped by appropriate medical or therapeutic treatment, and early intervention is often the key.

Sitting up: Your baby will most likely be able to sit unassisted at about six to eight months. In addition to balance, it takes control of trunk muscles, the lower body, and the head and neck to be able to sit up without assistance. Try putting a favorite toy in front of your baby and help the child get into the sitting position. The baby will often use his or her hands to balance in the "tripod sit," but soon your baby will sit without using hands.

Crawling: Babies usually start to crawl between six and ten months. Your baby will likely begin this process by repositioning his or her body from a sitting position, or will get up on all fours and rock back and forth. Some babies scoot with their elbows or hands and drag their legs behind them. Others crawl backwards at first before they get the hang of forward crawling. Before your child begins to crawl, be sure to baby-proof your house!

Pulling up to stand: At around eight months, your baby will be able to pull up onto furniture and stand from a seated position. Try standing your baby up next to a soft but sturdy piece of furniture and let him or her hang on in a standing position with your careful observation and guidance. Soon the baby will reach up and pull himself or herself to stand. Make sure all corners and sharp edges are protected so baby does not fall against objects that can hurt him or her, because falls are inevitable.

Walking: Walking happens between 10 to 18 months and is a gigantic developmental jump forward! This means that balance, strength, and coordination are all joined in the interests of forward locomotion. The baby's center of gravity goes from being only a few inches from the ground to being more than a foot off the ground. Your baby is well on the way to running, climbing, and doing all sorts of wonderful things!

Speech and Communication Developmental Milestones

Although your baby's senses are working at birth, he or she must learn how to be in and relate to the world.

Birth to three months: At this point, your infant will respond with a startle to sounds and will be quiet when he or she is spoken to. The baby will learn to recognize your voice and will eventually make cooing sounds. He or she will have different types of cries that mean different things. It's up to you to learn your baby's language! Your baby will smile back at you or smile in order to engage you in smiling back.

If you are at all concerned that your child is lagging behind in development, contact your pediatrician immediately. It has been proven that the earlier your child gets help, the better the outcome will be! Don't ignore a problem or pretend it doesn't really exist. This will only be a disservice to your child. Put any fears or embarrassment aside and get the help your baby needs. —*Kimmie, 37, mother of two*

Four to six months: Your baby will move in the direction of specific sounds and recognize different tones in your voice. The baby will also pay attention to music and will babble with different sounds, including making vowel sounds and consonants like the g, p, b, and m sounds. He or she will get excited by some things or voice displeasure with other things. Your infant will babble to himself or herself when left alone to play. A fascinating fact: Babies babble differently depending on the language of their parents. For example, babies whose parents speak French or Hebrew will have distinctive sounds in their babbling that are different from babies raised in an English-speaking environment.

Seven months to one year: Your baby will play peek-a-boo and will play pat-a-cake. He or she will recognize simple words like "shoe," "cup," "juice," or "ball." The baby will hold his or her arms up in order to be picked up and will respond to simple requests. Eventually, your baby will learn to imitate speech sounds and will say simple words like "hi," "dog," "dada," and "mama." He or she will say at least a couple of simple words by the time he or she reaches the age of one year.

Some parents find that teaching babies simple sign language signs helps to improve communication and reduce frustration in the period before speech is fully developed. For example, babies can learn the signs for "more," "eat," or "drink." This is enjoyable for many parents and their babies. You can find books and online information to help you learn and teach simple signs.

The most important thing you can do to encourage your baby's language development is to talk to your baby! Describe what is happening, tell your baby what things are called, and just chat away. Research has shown that the more verbal interaction a parent has with a child, the greater the child's verbal skills will be. Don't forget to read to your baby every day. Choose books that you enjoy, and of course, keep them very simple and geared to your baby's developmental stage. While an infant will not understand the plot of a storybook, he or she will enjoy the closeness and the sound of your voice and will soon demonstrate an interest in looking at sturdy books with simple, bright-colored pictures. Reading a book is a good transitional activity before naptime or bedtime, helping your child to settle down. It is a great habit to start early and maintain throughout childhood.

If your baby seems to be lagging behind in speech or physical development, and you have given your baby plenty of practice time to learn the skill, see your doctor for your baby to have a developmental screen. Early childhood intervention with physical or speech therapy can make the difference between a child who is always behind or a child who catches up

and thrives after learning new skills. Early intervention can also help children with more serious developmental problems function at their top potential.

Enjoy Your Journey!

You will be amazed at how quickly the crazy, wonderful days of your pregnancy and the intense emotional and physical experience of giving birth give way to a passionate focus on simply caring for your baby. Through exhaustion, sleepless nights, and rearranging the world you used to live in, you will find yourself facing new challenges each day. Your priorities have changed, and your purpose from morning to night is to raise a healthy, happy, well-adjusted child.

Happy and healthy families come in a variety of forms, but they are all based on love and consideration.

As with all of life, you will have ups and downs as a parent. The best advice is to be patient, seek support and help when you need it, and go with the flow. Each day will bring new joys and new challenges as your little one grows and develops. Cherish each day and spend as much quality time with your child as possible so he or she can benefit from your loving guidance.

Perhaps the greatest gift of parenthood is the inexplicable love and joy you experience with your new baby, no matter if your child has special needs, was born premature, or is a typically developing infant. There is a natural and instinctual bond with children that is truly beyond words, and, as you move along on your journey as parents, this bond and love will only grow. Stay strong and positive through the tough times and embrace the little joys that your developing child will bring you each day. You have accepted the role of a lifetime, and now you will have a lifetime of being your child's support, guide, teacher, and mentor. Congratulations and good luck! You can be proud of all you have accomplished so far!

Recommended Web Resources

For ease of use, this resource list is also available on the Lesson Ladder website (*http://www.lessonladder.com*). Some links were shortened for convenience.

Preparing for Pregnancy
From Bellies to Babies and Beyond
http://www.birth.com.au
The "Getting Pregnant" section of this website includes information on emotional readiness, fertility, and preparing your body for pregnancy.

The Fertility Authority
www.fertilityauthority.com
This site provides comprehensive information on topics related to fertility and a directory of fertility doctors.

Before You Get Pregnant
www.womenshealth.gov/pregnancy
WomensHealth.gov has some excellent resources. Check the section called "Before You Get Pregnant – Information for All Women" to learn about preconception health, knowing if you are pregnant, and unplanned pregnancy.

Ensuring a Healthy Pregnancy
MedlinePlus—Pregnancy and Nutrition
http://www.nlm.nih.gov/medlineplus/pregnancyandnutrition.html
This is a guide to healthy eating during pregnancy, including healthy weight gain.

Checklist of Foods to Avoid During Pregnancy
http://www.foodsafety.gov/poisoning/risk/pregnant/chklist_pregnancy.html
This government website offers up-to-date information about potentially dangerous foods.

Nutritional Needs During Pregnancy
http://www.choosemyplate.gov/pregnancy-breastfeeding/pregnancy-nutritional-needs.html
Create your own profile and develop a customized daily food plan for healthy eating during pregnancy on this site. There is also information about food safety and healthy weight gain.

Health Information from the American Congress of Obstetricians and Gynecologists
www.acog.org
Under "For Patients," the Pregnancy section has short, informative articles about Exercise During Pregnancy, High Blood Pressure During Pregnancy, Morning Sickness, and a variety of other health-related topics.

Gestational Diabetes—American Diabetes Association
http://www.diabetes.org/diabetes-basics/gestational
This site contains extensive information about gestational (pregnancy-related) diabetes. You can also enter "pregnancy" as a search topic on the home page to discover resources on prenatal care and diabetes as well as a free online tool to help you manage the factors that affect blood sugar.

SmokeFree Women—Pregnancy
http://women.smokefree.gov/topic-pregnancy.aspx
This site explains how quitting smoking helps both you and your baby and identifies resources to help you become a nonsmoker.

Hazards During Pregnancy and Breast-feeding
http://www.otispregnancy.org
The Organization of Teratology Information Specialists (OTIS) offers clear, scientifically based information about environmental hazards during pregnancy and breast-feeding. Click on "Resources" to access fact sheets on medication safety, maternal chronic illness, illicit substances, herbal products, infections and vaccines, and other exposures. There is also an interesting 3D video on fetal development and a toll-free number to obtain advice about exposures during pregnancy and breast-feeding.

Managing the Emotional Rollercoaster of Pregnancy and the Postpartum Period

Stress and Pregnancy
http://www.marchofdimes.com/pregnancy/lifechanges_indepth.html
The March of Dimes explains common stressors during pregnancy, how stress affects you and may affect your baby, and practical steps you can take to manage or reduce stress. This page includes a three-minute video on managing stress during pregnancy.

Fatigue and Mood Swings During Pregnancy
http://www.pregnancyandchildren.com/pregnancy/pregnancy_fatigue_and_moods.htm
This article explains the normal ups and downs of pregnancy in terms of mood and energy.

Not Just the Pregnancy Blues
http://is.gd/PrenatalDepression
This three-part series by Jessica Grose in Slate.com tells how depression in pregnancy is often overlooked or dismissed. It is "must reading" for anyone whose sadness or lethargy goes beyond "the blues." The author shares her story and those of other women along with resources and the results of an informal survey.

Psychiatric Disorders of Pregnancy
http://www.womensmentalhealth.org/specialty-clinics/
psychiatric-disorders-during-pregnancy
The Massachusetts General Hospital Center for Women's Health describes the mental health concerns related to pregnancy and gives a thorough review of the safety of psychiatric medications for pregnant women.

Anxiety (and Depression) During Pregnancy and Postpartum
http://www.postpartum.net/Get-the-Facts/Anxiety-During-Pregnancy-and-Postpartum.aspx
Postpartum Support International has developed a comprehensive website for emotional and mental health concerns during pregnancy and postpartum. This webpage contains an article about managing overwhelming anxiety, and there are links to prenatal and postpartum depression and posttraumatic stress disorder articles. There is a link to find local help and information about crisis hotlines. Bookmark this site if you are struggling with your moods!

Keeping Your Relationship Happy and Healthy

Relationships and Sex During Pregnancy
http://www.healthtalkonline.org/pregnancy_children/pregnancy/Topic/2019/
In addition to information based on actual research, this site offers informative short videos based on real-life experiences of parents. There are also links to articles on other physical and emotional aspects of pregnancy.

The Rainbow Babies
www.therainbowbabies.com
The Rainbow Babies site offers lesbian, gay, bisexual, and transgender parents information about pregnancy and parenting, including relationship issues.

New Dads Survival Guide
http://www.newdadssurvivalguide.com
This website is British, so you may have to do little translating (nappies are diapers, for example), but the information is excellent and engaging. New dads learn about what pregnancy entails, have access to a dad's diary, and get answers to questions about everything from supporting a distraught partner to caring for a new baby.

Relationships During Pregnancy
http://parenthelp123.org/pregnancy/during-pregnancy/relationships
This information, from Washington State's ParentHelp123 site, will help you understand if your relationship is safe and healthy or not.

Partners and Pregnancy
http://www.babies.sutterhealth.org/during/preg_partners.html
This article suggests ways in which a partner can support the mother-to-be and includes some frank talk about sex and sexuality during pregnancy (did you know that orgasms may last longer during pregnancy?).

First Trimester Concerns

First Trimester—Questions to Discuss With Your Doctor (Harvard Medical School)
http://www.health.harvard.edu/fhg/doctor/preg1.shtml
This is a list of questions your doctor (or midwife) is likely to ask you at your first prenatal appointment. The article also describes what your first appointment will be like.

About Midwives

www.midwife.org

The American College of Nurse-Midwives is the professional organization for certified nurse-midwives and certified midwives in the United States. To learn about midwives' philosophy of care, credentials, history, and scope of practice, click the "About Midwives" tab. The site also includes a midwife locator.

Pregnancy Due Dates Calculator

http://www.medcalc.com/pregnancy.html

Using the date of your last menstrual period (LMP), you can calculate your due date. With either your LMP or your projected due date, you can calculate the end of your first and second trimesters, and by entering today's date, you can see exactly how many weeks pregnant you are (easier than counting on your fingers!).

Ectopic Pregnancy

http://www.ncbi.nlm.nih.gov/pubmedhealth/PMH0001897/

This article describes ectopic (tubal) pregnancy, including risk factors, symptoms, treatment, prognosis, and prevention.

Managing Morning Sickness

http://www.webmd.com/baby/guide/managing-morning-sickness

Morning sickness can make you miserable. Learn about practical, medically sound action steps for home management of morning sickness.

Ultrasound Imaging of the Pelvis

http://www.radiologyinfo.org/en/info.cfm?pg=pelvus

Despite the medical-sounding title, this article by the Radiological Society of North America and the American College of Radiologists provides descriptions in clear language. It explains both abdominal and vaginal ultrasounds—how to prepare, what they will feel like, and why they are performed.

Pregnancy Loss

http://womenshealth.gov/pregnancy/you-are-pregnant/pregnancy-loss.cfm

Many women worry about miscarriage during the first trimester. This article explains why it happens and how to cope and offers links to many other resources.

National Organization of Mothers of Twins Clubs, Inc.

http://www.nomotc.org

If you have just found out you are pregnant with twins, triplets, or more, you will appreciate the range of information on pregnancy and raising multiples. The site also offers help in locating a local Mothers of Twins club, where you can get moral support face to face.

Second Trimester Concerns

Amniocentesis (Beyond the Basics)

http://www.uptodate.com/contents/amniocentesis-beyond-the-basics

For those who want to delve into the pros and cons of amniocentesis and learn more about the procedure itself, this is a good article that does not "talk down" to the reader.

Pelvic Girdle Pain and Symphysis Pubis Instability
http://www.wellmother.org/resources-support/articles-research
Women who experience pelvic pain will benefit from tips about exercise and birth positions.

Melasma (Skin Darkening)
http://www.aad.org
The American Academy of Dermatology offers several articles on preventing and treating melasma. Simply enter "melasma" as a search topic on the home page.

12 Tips for Traveling While Pregnant
http://www.parentsconnect.com/pregnancy/12_tips_for_traveling_pregnant.html
Here are some very practical bits of advice for the pregnant mom who is on the go.

Childbirth Education Class Comparison
http://is.gd/ChildbirthClassComparison
Overwhelmed by the choices in childbirth preparation classes? This one-page chart prepared by a doula service displays six types of childbirth classes with brief descriptions of their principles and format. The contact information is local to New York only, but there are links to the national websites of each type of childbirth class, where you can explore more information.

Commission for the Accreditation of Birth Centers
http://www.birthcenteraccreditation.org
If you are considering the possibility of using a birthing center to have your baby, you may wish to explore the accreditation process and find an accredited birth center on this website.

Third Trimester Concerns
How Much Does a Baby *Really* Cost?
http://www.redbookmag.com/money-career/tips-advice/money-baby-cost
Now that you are close to giving birth, you may decide you don't want to know the financial cost of having a child! If you are curious or worried, however, this Redbook article gives the results of their parent survey along with practical tips on saving money and handling financial stress.

Donate Cord Blood
http://marrow.org/Get_Involved/Donate_Cord_Blood/Donate_Cord_Blood.aspx
Learn the whys and hows of cord blood donation and banking so you can decide if you wish to save or donate umbilical cord blood when your baby is born.

Pregnancy and Sleep
http://www.sleepfoundation.org/article/sleep-topics/pregnancy-and-sleep
The National Sleep Foundation explores the impact of pregnancy on sleep and some possible complicating factors. The article includes suggestions for better sleep.

Braxton Hicks or True Labor Contractions?

http://www.medicinenet.com/braxton_hicks_contractions/article.htm

This article offers detailed information on the difference between Braxton Hicks contractions and true labor.

The Win-Win Birth Plan

https://www.pennysimkin.com/download/Articles-Handouts/The_WinWin_Birth_Plan.pdf

Penny Simkin, childbirth educator extraordinaire, says "A Win-Win birth plan states the parents' personal preferences but does not compromise quality of care. Its tone is respectful and flexible." This article gives concrete advice for achieving this goal.

What Is Premature Birth?

http://www.cdc.gov/features/prematurebirth

This Centers for Disease Control article provides definitions, risk factors, warning signs, and an extensive resource list on preterm labor and birth.

If Your Baby Is Breech

http://is.gd/IfYourBabyIsBreech

The American Congress of Obstetricians and Gynecologists answer frequently asked questions about babies in the breech (bottom-down) position, including information about trying to turn the baby before birth (external cephalic version) and the risks of vaginal delivery of breech babies.

Labor and Delivery

10 Labor Tips

http://www.lamaze.org/10LaborTips

These tips will help you to have a more relaxed and comfortable labor.

Position Statement—The Pros and Cons of 11 Common Labor Positions

http://www.lamaze.org/LaborPositions

Expand your options by reading this detailed description, with photos, of a variety of labor positions.

Your Guide to a Healthy Birth

http://www.health.ny.gov/publications/2935.pdf

This free online booklet from the New York Department of Health contains a wealth of information about labor and delivery.

Dads/Birth Partners and Doulas

http://www.getbabied.com/about-doulas/dads-and-doulas

Dads and other birth partners may have concerns that they won't be needed if the mom chooses to have a doula involved in childbirth. This article allays those fears and explains how doulas can support both the woman giving birth and her partner.

The Best Cesarean Possible

https://www.pennysimkin.com/download/Articles-Handouts/Best%20Cesarean%20
Possible.pdf

*In the "Articles and Handouts" section of Penny Simkin's website, you will find this article with loads
of suggestions for having a fulfilling childbirth experience even if you must have a C-section. It would
be smart to read this even if you don't plan to have a surgical birth, since things don't always happen
the way you plan them.*

I Will Survive (Thoughts on Survivors Giving Birth)

http://www.pandys.org/articles/survivorsgivingbirth.html

*Katie Wise is a doula, childbirth educator, and birth advocate, and she is also a survivor of sexual
assault. She offers wisdom for other survivors on transforming childbirth from an additional trauma
to a healing experience.*

Childbirth: Health Information from Other Trustworthy Sources

www.WomensHealth.gov

*The easiest way to find this great list of online resources from a wide variety of sources is to use the "A–Z
Health Topics" tab, choose "C," and then "Childbirth." You will find links to articles on everything from
water births to having a vaginal birth after a cesarean.*

Postpartum Issues

Survival Tips for Parents of a New Baby

http://www.health.ny.gov/community/infants_children/child_health/parents.htm

*This article offers tips for sleeping (the parents, that is!), eating, and feeling good after you've had a
baby. There is some advice for new dads as well as moms.*

Nutritional Needs While Breast-feeding

http://www.choosemyplate.gov/pregnancy-breastfeeding/breastfeeding-nurtitional-needs.html

*This government-sponsored site offers information on healthy eating for breast-feeding moms. You can
create a confidential, customized profile and develop a personalized daily food plan.*

Plugged Milk Ducts

http://www.askdrsears.com/topics/breastfeeding/common-problems/plugged-milk-ducts

*Breast-feeding moms sometimes develop painful plugged milk ducts, and this article explains how to
deal with the problem.*

New Rules About Breast Pumps at Work

http://parenting.blogs.nytimes.com/2010/04/09/new-rules-about-breast-pumps-at-work

*If you are a breast-feeding mom who is returning to work, you will probably need to pump milk during
the workday. This article from* The New York Times *explains your legal rights.*

Breast-feeding as a Rape or Sexual Abuse Survivor

http://www.pandys.org/articles/breastfeeding.html

One in four women is a survivor of sexual abuse, and many women have experienced sexual assault as adults. If you are a survivor who wants to breast-feed but are worried that it may trigger unwelcome feelings, this article will give you reassuring, highly practical advice. You may want to share it with your healthcare providers.

Dads Get Blue Too

http://www.slate.com/articles/double_x/doublex/2010/11/dads_get_blue_too.html

While postpartum depression in women is gaining more attention, you may be surprised to learn that as many as 10 percent of fathers may become depressed after the birth of their baby as well.

Baby Care

Proper Positioning and Latch-On Skills

http://www.askdrsears.com/topics/breastfeeding/rightstart-techniques/
proper-positioning-and-latch-skills

Learning how to position your baby correctly and help with effective latch-on to the breast can make a big difference in your breast-feeding success. Dr. Sears explains and troubleshoots these issues.

International Lactation Consultant Organization

www.ilca.org

Lactation consultants are healthcare professionals who specialize in supporting successful breast-feeding. This site is mostly designed for professionals themselves, but it does include a "lactation consultant finder" that allows parents to find a nearby consultant by zip code.

La Leche League

http://www.lllusa.org

La Leche League supports and advocates for breast-feeding mothers. The site offers breast-feeding information, a breast-feeding helpline, and contact information for local La Leche League groups throughout the United States.

Kangaroo Care

http://www.med.umich.edu/nicu/pdf/C.3KangarooCare.pdf

This practice (with the fun name!) involves skin-to-skin contact with the newborn to encourage bonding and health. This article explains the rationale and how to do it.

Circumcision

http://www.nlm.nih.gov/medlineplus/circumcision.html

The National Institutes of Health offer a brief overview of circumcision and links to several articles to help parents make up their minds about this procedure. Recommendations have recently changed, and the site offers up-to-date information.

Newborn Sleep Patterns

http://www.lpch.org/DiseaseHealthInfo/HealthLibrary/newborn/behrslep.html

What is normal sleep for a new baby? How can you help your baby to sleep well? This article from Lucille Packard Children's Hospital at Stanford, California, gives authoritative information.

General Baby Health and Safety
www.healthychildren.org
The American Academy of Pediatrics provides a wealth of information for new parents on this site. Click on "Ages and Stages" and select "Baby: 0–12 months" for advice on feeding, diapers and clothing, crying, tooth care, and much more. The "Sleep" topic is especially valuable, with information and a video about sleep safety for babies. You can also find a pediatrician through this site and sign up for a parenting newsletter.

Five Essential Tummy Time Moves
http://is.gd/TummyTime
This video (less than five minutes) is a terrific demonstration of how to introduce "tummy time" to your baby. Parents, grandparents, and caregivers will benefit from learning how to incorporate this developmental booster strategy into the baby's everyday routines.

Communication: Birth to One Year
http://www.asha.org/public/speech/development/01.htm
The American Speech-Language-Hearing Association explains what your baby's communication skills should be at various points in development, how to promote good speech and language skills, and what to do if you have a concern.

Baby Milestones
http://www.parenting.com/article/parenting-guide-baby-milestones
The editors of Parenting *magazine describe this article as identifying "the 9 major physical baby milestones, signs of developmental delays, and what you can expect along the way."*

Overview of Early Intervention
http://nichcy.org/babies/overview
If you have any concerns about your baby's development, or if you know that your baby has a disability, this article from the National Dissemination Center for Children with Disabilities explains how early intervention works and points you to appropriate resources.

When the New Baby Has Special Needs
http://psychcentral.com/lib/2006/when-the-new-baby-has-special-needs
Parents of special needs babies often feel isolated and overwhelmed. This article describes parents' experiences and offers support.

Baby Gear: Smart and Economical Choices
Checklist: Baby Basics Shopping List
http://www.parents.com/baby/gear/registries-buying-guides/checklist-baby-basics-shopping

Parents *magazine suggests the absolute basic supplies you will need to care for a newborn, with links to suggestions for "nice to have" items.*

Buying Baby Gear

http://www.cbsnews.com/moneywatch

CBS News MoneyWatch has a variety of informative articles about buying baby gear. Just enter "baby gear" into the search to see everything from "Super High-End Baby Gear" to "Baby Gear: The Only Five Items You Need."

The New Crib Standard: Questions and Answers

http://www.cpsc.gov/onsafety/2011/06/the-new-crib-standard-questions-and-answers

As you set up your nursery, this information from the Consumer Product Safety Commission will answer your questions about crib safety.

Juvenile Products Manufacturing Association

http://www.jpma.org/content/parents/the-parenthood

This website contains safety tips, information on product recalls, safety videos (including one about setting up a safe nursery), and updates on innovative products for babies.

Child Car Seat Inspection Station Locator

http://www.nhtsa.gov/cps/cpsfitting/index.cfm

This site allows you to search by state or zip code to find a local inspection station that will teach you how to install your baby's car seat safely, usually without cost. You can even find stations with Spanish-speaking technicians and learn where to find local child seat safety events.

General Pregnancy/Postpartum Information

Text4Baby

https://text4baby.org

This noncommercial site offers texted tips "4 Mom & Mom 2B." Sign up at any point during pregnancy or your baby's first year, and you will receive free text messages with useful information customized to your stage of pregnancy or your baby's age.

Prenatal Information from the American Academy of Pediatrics

www.healthychildren.org

This user-friendly site offers updated information on health topics related to pregnancy and childbirth. Click on "Ages and Stages" and select "Prenatal."

March of Dimes

www.marchofdimes.com

The March of Dimes is a nonprofit dedicated to the health of babies, with a special emphasis on preventing premature births. Their site offers numerous articles on healthy pregnancy and baby care.

Childbirth Connection

http://www.childbirthconnection.org

"Childbirth Connection promotes safe, effective and satisfying evidence-based maternity care and is a voice for the needs and interests of childbearing families." Their website helps pregnant women and their partners decide on an appropriate birth venue and offers checklists of questions to ask when touring the hospital or birth center. They provide extensive information to help parents participate in all the necessary decisions about induction of labor, pain control in childbirth, cesarean sections, and other elements of the pregnancy and birth process.

Women, Infants, and Children (WIC)
http://www.fns.usda.gov/wic
Good nutrition is especially critical for pregnant women and young children. The government offers free resources for families that have limited income. In addition to supplying supplementary food and formula, WIC supports breast-feeding moms with information and supplies such as breast pumps.

Pregnancy, Childbirth, and Parenting as a Rape or Sexual Abuse Survivor
http://www.pandys.org/articles/childbirthafterrape.html
Because sexual abuse and assault are so common, many new mothers are survivors and can benefit from information to support them on their journey to parenthood.

Plus-Size Pregnancy Website
http://www.plus-size-pregnancy.org
This site bills itself as offering "empowering information for women of size (and women of all sizes)." The information represents the personal views of a childbirth educator and so should be examined critically, but larger women may find comfort and practical advice geared to their situation that seems lacking on other sites.

Notes:

Index

effacement in, 283
cesarean section
    gestational diabetes and, 181
    healthcare providers and, 62
    information on, 271–276
    placenta previa and, 16–17
    questions regarding, 96
changing tables, nursery essentials, 165
charting
    pregnancy experience, 66–67
    weight, 31–33
checklist, birth plan, 204–205
cheeses, healthy eating and, 29
chemical peels, melasma and, 207
chemical pregnancies, 100–101
chemicals, safety concerns, 47
chemotherapy drugs, safety risks of, 42
chicken, healthy eating and, 28
chicken pox vaccine, 316
Child Care Seat Inspection Stations, 167
child care while away, 202
childbirth classes, 184–185
chlamydia infections, 46
Chlorpheniramine, safety risks of, 44
chorionic villus sampling (CVS), 115–116
chronic high blood pressure, 249
chronic illnesses, 13–14
chronicling thoughts, 156
Cimetidine, safety risks of, 45
circulatory system development, 75
circumcision, care of, 318
circumcision, pros and cons, 317
Claritin, safety risks of, 44
cleaning products, 47
cleft lip or palette, 157
Clindamycin, safety risks of, 45
Clomiphene (Clomid), 22
clothing items and accessories, 163–168
co-sleepers, nursery essentials, 165
cocaine
    placental abruption and, 248
    safety risks of, 41, 48–49
cocoa butter moisturizer, 159–160
cod, healthy eating, 29
Colace, safety risks of, 45
cold cuts, healthy eating and, 29
colostrum, 133, 240, 282
combined epidural and spinal anesthesia (CSE), 289
comfrey, foods to avoid, 31

communication
    developmental milestones, 371–372
    stress reduction and, 51–52, 54
community advocacy services, 7
compazine, safety risks of, 42
complete placenta previa, 182
compression stockings, 161
conceiving
    enhancing fertility, 22–23
    how it happens, 18
    ovulation, 18–21
    problems with, 21–22
    when it occurs, 59
concentration, troubles with, 134, 138, 155
conditions, prior medical, 87
conehead look, 309
confirmatory amniocentesis, 142
consignment stores, baby items at, 163
constipation
    medications for, 45
    nutrition and, 35
contact sports, 164
contraception
    oral, 44
    postpartum, 351–352
contraction stress tests, 245
controlling partners, 7
convertible cribs, 211
cookies, healthy eating and, 28
cooking smells, morning sickness and, 80–81
cord blood banking, 45, 230–233
corticosteroids
    preterm labor and, 228
    safety risks of, 40
corticotrophin-releasing hormone (CRH), 285
cost and coverage of healthcare, 63
cough medications, 45
coumadin, safety risks of, 41
counseling
    See therapy
counseling and genetic testing, 12–13
cow's milk formulas, 326
cradle cap treatment, 333
cradle hold, 342
crafting, product hazards, 47
Craigslist, baby items on, 163
cramping, pregnancy health and, 99–100
cravings, 176–177
crawling, milestones, 370

early days and, 362
early pregnancy and, 33–36
eighth month, 228
gestational diabetes and, 181
as a mood booster, 137
morning sickness and, 81
prenatal visit questions, 93–94
regimes of, 33
rewards and, 146
sex as, 125
smaller increments of, 251
walking, 19, 34
ExerSaucers, playtime essentials, 167
exhaustion, postpartum feelings, 336–337
expected date of confinement (EDC), 86
external cephalic version (ECV), 242–243

F

facial pigment changes, 155
fallopian tube blockage, 22
false labor, 224–226
family balancing, readiness and, 8
family practice doctors, 64, 229
fathers
    See dads
fatigue
    exercise and, 33
    on the job, 49–50
    second month, 77–78
    sex and, 53
    third month, 109
fears
    emotional readiness and, 6, 83
    labor and delivery, 199, 222–223
feelings
    See emotional changes
fencing position, 312
fern test, 289
fertility specialists, 21–22
fertilization process, 17–19, 59
feta cheese, foods to avoid, 29
fetal alcohol syndrome, 31
fetal distress, breech and, 242–243
fetal monitoring, 138
fetal nonstress test, 245
fetal position, 298
fetal tests, 244–245
fevers, 92
fifth month
    bodily changes, 152–155

buying baby gear, 162–168
emotions, 155–156
feeling movement, 157–158
growth and development, 150–152
highlights, 149–150
Kegel exercises, 162
stretch marks, 159–160
traveling, 160–161
finances
    financial counseling for, 178
    multiples and, 119
    preconception considerations, 9
    worries about, 200
first month
    body changes, 61
    charting, 66–67
    common questions, 67–70
    finding healthcare provider, 62–66
    hormonal changes, 62
    ovulation to pregnancy, 57–59
    pregnancy, 59–61
first trimester
    first month, 58–73
    second month, 74–105
    third month, 106–129
fish, healthy eating and, 28–29
Flagyl, safety risks of, 45
flounder, healthy eating and, 29
flu shot, 316
fluid retention, exercise and, 36
Foley catheter treatment, ripening cervix and, 292
folic acid, 10
follicle stimulating hormones, 21
Food and Drug Administration (FDA), 42
foods to avoid, 28–31
foot care, 196–197
football hold, breast-feeding and, 304, 342
formula, selecting, 325, 327
four to six month milestones, 371
fourth month
    bodily changes, 132–136
    depression and, 138–141
    emotions during, 136–137
    genetic testing options, 141–145
    growth and development, 130–132
    highlights about, 129–130
    maternity clothes, 145–147
    prenatal visit, 137–138
fraternal twins, 59
freckles, increased numbers in, 155

fresh vegetables, healthy eating and, 31
friends and family, 123–124
fruits and vegetables, 27–28
fun, taking time for, 156

G

Galant reflex, 312
garage sales, baby items at, 163
gardening, safety precautions, 46
gas and bloating medications, 45
Gas-X, safety risks of, 45
gastroesophageal reflux disease (GERD), 78–79
gender of baby, 120–121, 157
genetic testing
    Chorionic villus sampling, 141–145
    fifth month, 157–158
    information regarding, 114–118
    preconception counseling, 12–13
genetics
    family diseases and, 9
    inheritance and, 90
    mutations and miscarriage, 101
    special needs babies and, 354–355
German measles, 46, 89
gestational diabetes
    glucose tolerance testing and, 178–180, 201
    high-risk pregnancies and, 36
    information regarding, 180–182
    preeclampsia and, 250
    see also diabetes
gestational hypertension, 249
gestational *vs.* embryonic age, 61
ginger, safety risks of, 44–45, 49, 82
Glucophage, safety risks of, 45
glucose levels, monitoring, 37–38
glucose tolerance test (GTT), 95, 178–182
glycolic acid, stretch marks and, 343
gonorrhea infections, 46
grabbing, milestones, 369
grieving, special needs and, 354–355
grooming tools, bath essentials, 166
group B streptococcus, 244
grouper, foods to avoid, 29
growth and development
    first month, 58–61
    second month, 74–76
    third month, 107–109
    fourth month, 130–132
    fifth month, 150–152
    sixth month, 172–173

    seventh month, 194–196
    eighth month, 216–218
    ninth month, 236–237
    tenth month, 258–260
guilt, feelings of, 139
gynecological issues
    cervical cancer/dysplasia, 14–15
    double uterus, 15
    history, 87–88
    polycystic ovarian syndrome, 14

H

habits, lifestyle changes and, 48–49, 95
haddock, healthy eating, 29
hair perms and dyes, 47
hand washing, 29, 46
hats, baby accessories, 165
hay fever, medications and, 44
hazards
    bath time and, 332
    crib bumpers and, 211
    questions regarding, 92–93
    toxins to avoid, 46–48
headaches
    medicines for, 44
    posture and, 134
    preeclampsia and, 250
health issues
    avoiding teratogens, 40–41
    diabetes, 36–38
    high blood pressure, 38–39
    medications and, 41–46
    rheumatic and autoimmune diseases, 39–40
    at work, 49–52
healthcare providers
    choosing, 62–66, 229–230
    fifth month, 156–158
    first visit, 85–92
    ninth month visit, 241
    preconception appointment, 9–10
    seventh month visit, 201–202
    sixth month visit, 177–178
    talking to, 4
    tenth month visit, 265
    when to call, 101, 110
healthy eating
    See nutrition
The Healthy Woman (WomensHealth), 10
hearing loss
    preterm birth and, 226

state of mind and, 6–7
treatment for, 43
mercury, safety risks of, 30, 41, 47
metabolic diseases, jaundice and, 319
Metamucil, safety risks of, 45
metformin, safety risks of, 45
methotrexate, safety risks of, 40–41
methydopa, safety risks of, 44
Metoclopramide, safety risks of, 45
Micronase, safety risks of, 45
midway monitor, 166
midwives, 64–65, 94
milk, unpasteurized, 28
milk ducts, plugged, 340
milk of magnesia, safety risks of, 44
mindset, natural childbirth and, 286–287
minerals, foods containing, 29
MiraLAX, safety risks of, 44–45
miscarriages
    amniocentesis and, 144
    bed rest and, 246
    bleeding and, 68, 99, 110
    blood clots, 39
    caffeine and, 30
    causes of, 101
    chorionic villus sampling and, 116
    dilation and curettage, 189
    early pregnancy and, 68–69
    emergency room and, 101–102
    herbal teas and, 31
    high-risk pregnancies and, 36
    history of, 87
    hormone levels and, 97–98
    intercourse and, 53, 125
    Listeria and, 29
    multiple pregnancies and, 122–123
    multiples and, 118
    preconception testing and, 12–15
    questions regarding, 68–69, 93, 95
    recreational drugs and, 49
    Rh sensitization and, 206
    second trimester, 111
    symptoms of, 100
    teratogens and, 40–42
    third month, 111
    understanding, 101
MMR vaccine, 316
mobiles, nursery essentials, 165
modified bed rest, 246

moisturizer, stretch marks and, 159
molar pregnancy, 98
Monistat cream, safety risks of, 44, 46
monitors, nursery essentials, 165
mood swings
    See emotional changes
morning sickness, 79–82
Moro reflex, 311
morphine, labor medication, 287
morula, 59
Motrin, safety risks of, 43
movement, feeling, 70, 158–159, 195
mucus plug, labor and, 283
multiples
    babies weight gain, 217–218
    bed rest and, 194, 246
    breech babies and, 241–242
    care at home, 119
    cesarean section, 272
    fraternal or identical, 117
    high-risk pregnancy, 116–119
    placental abruption and, 248
    progesterone supplements and, 228
    uterine measurements, 137–138
muscle ache medicines, 44
muscles, joints and, 135
music, playing for baby, 151
musical toys, playtime essentials, 166
mycophenolate, safety risks of, 40
Mylanta, safety risks of, 45, 78–79

N

naproxen, safety risks of, 43
Narcan, labor medication, 287
narcotic pain relief, 96
nasal congestion medication, 44
National Blood Marrow Donor Programs, 233
National Cord Blood Program, 233
National Domestic Violence Hotline, 7, 179
National Highway Traffic Safety Administration, 167
National Sexual Assault Hotline, 7
natural childbirth, 184–185, 285–287
natural foods, 27
natural labor *vs.* medically aided, 96
natural remedies, depression and, 140
nausea
    calling healthcare provider for, 101
    category X medications and, 42
    ginger and, 44
    HELLP syndrome and, 251

information regarding, 160–161

tristomy syndrome, 143

true labor, 224–226

tubal ligations, 122

tuberculosis, 91

tubs, bath essentials, 166

TUCKS, safety risks of, 45

tummy time, milestones, 357, 368–369

TUMS, safety risks of, 44–45, 78, 136

tuna, foods to avoid, 29

turkey, healthy eating and, 28

Turner syndrome, 143

twelve-month clothing, 164

twins

    See multiples

two-cell stage, 59

Tylenol, safety risks of, 43–44

type 2 diabetes, 36–38

U

ultrasound

    determining gender, 120

    first prenatal, 91–92

    how to read, 156

    nuchal translucency screening, 115

    seeing ultrasonographer, 156–158

    vaginal, 102

umbilical cord development, 75

unintended pregnancies, handling, 8–9

Unisom, safety risks of, 46

unpasteurized cheeses, 29

unplanned pregnancies, emotions and, 82–83

unsafe medications, 40

unwashed fresh vegetables, 31

urinalysis testing, 223

urinary tract infections

    circumcision and, 317

    information about, 177–178

    medications for, 45

    sex and, 54

urination frequency, 82, 110, 133

urine and glucose tolerance testing, 201

urine flow, Kegels and, 162

uterus

    changes in, 154, 176, 196

    contractions and, 237

    growth of, 113

    measurements of, 137–138

    structure problems, 101

V

vaginal birth after cesarean section (VBAC), 276–277

vaginal bleeding

    exercise and, 33

    placental abruption and, 249

vaginal delivery, twins and, 119

vaginal infections, sex and, 54

vaginal secretions, 54

vaginal ultrasounds, 102

valproic acid, safety risks of, 41

varicella screen, 89–90

vegetables, healthy eating and, 27–28, 31

vernix caseosa, 151, 237, 302

viral infections, 46

vision loss, preterm birth and, 226

Vistaril, labor medication, 287

visual changes, preeclampsia and, 250

vitamin K shot, 312–313

vitamins, 27, 41, 69, 160

vomiting, extreme case of, 98–99, 109

W

walking

    exercise and, 19, 34–35

    milestones, 371

warfarin, safety risks of, 40–41

washcloths, bath essentials, 166

water births, 285

water retention, 135, 218

web resources, 374–384

weight gain

    calculator, 33

    how much, 31–33

    preeclampsia and, 250

    staying on target, 152–153

    stretch marks and, 159

    third month, 109

weight lifting, exercise and, 35

wheat germ oil, stretch marks and, 160

whole grains, healthy eating and, 28

wipes, nursery essentials, 166

Women, Infants, and Children (WIC), 200, 253, 322

WomensHealth (website), 10

work

    balancing life and, 8

    demands of, 136–137

    safety at, 49

    sharing baby news at, 124–125

    stress reduction at, 51

    toxins at, 51

More great books from the *What Now?* Series!

Lesson Ladder is dedicated to helping you prepare for life's most fundamental challenges. We provide practical tools and well-rounded advice that help you achieve your goals while climbing the personal or professional ladder—whether it is preparing to start a family of your own, getting your child potty trained, or learning a new kind of financial management.

I Had My Baby! A Pediatrician's Essential Guide to the First 6 Months

Gain confidence to experience the true joy of parenthood! From learning what to expect during those first minutes in the hospital through your baby's first 6 months, this concise, reader-friendly, and reassuring guide covers core topics you'll need to know as a new parent. $16.99

Making Kid Time Count for Ages 0–3: The Attentive Parent Advantage

Whether you're a working or stay-at-home parent, this book shows you how to maximize your time with your baby or toddler to strengthen the parent-child relationship and ensure your child's strong cognitive, social, and emotional development. $16.99

I'm Potty Training My Child: Proven Methods That Work

Respecting that children and parenting styles differ, we created this guide to offer a variety of effective training solutions to help today's busy parents with easy, fast reading, and even faster results! $12.99

Better Behavior for Ages 2–10: Small Miracles That Work Like Magic

For the harried parent, this book offers the compassion, help, and proven solutions you need to manage—and prevent—difficult child behavior. $16.99

Call toll-free to order! **1-800-301-4647**
Or order online: **www.LessonLadder.com**

CPSIA information can be obtained at www.ICGtesting.com
Printed in the USA
LVOW01s1902131013

356717LV00013B/16/P

9 780984 865734